Skip·Beat!

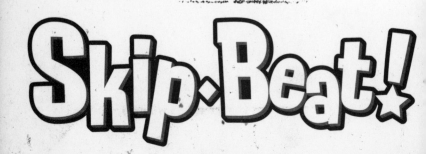

Shojo Beat

Skip·Beat!

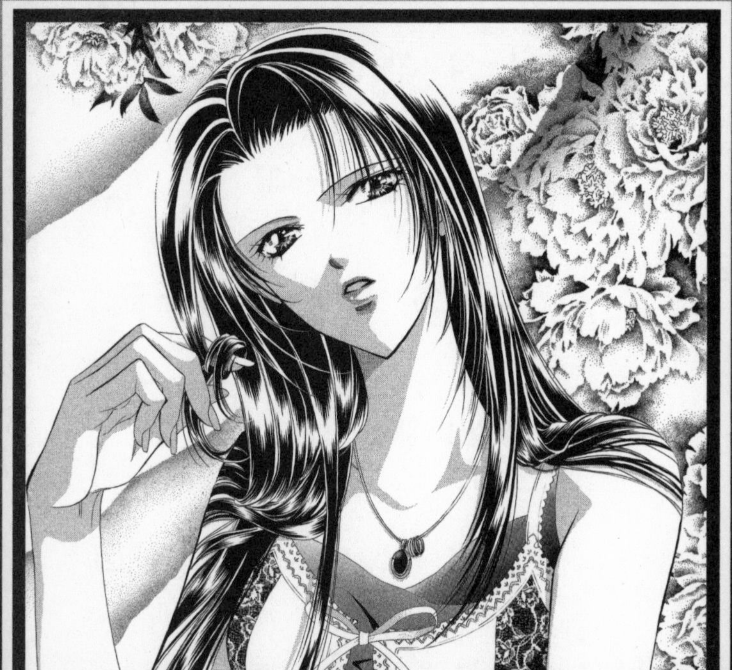

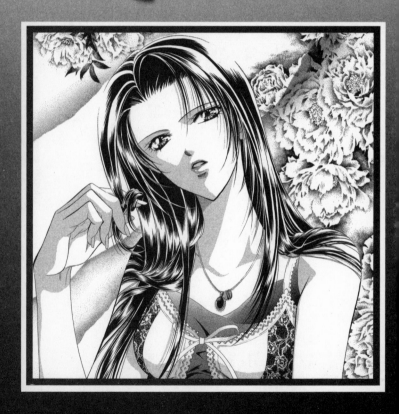

5

Story & Art by Yoshiki Nakamura

Skip·Beat!

Volume 5

CONTENTS

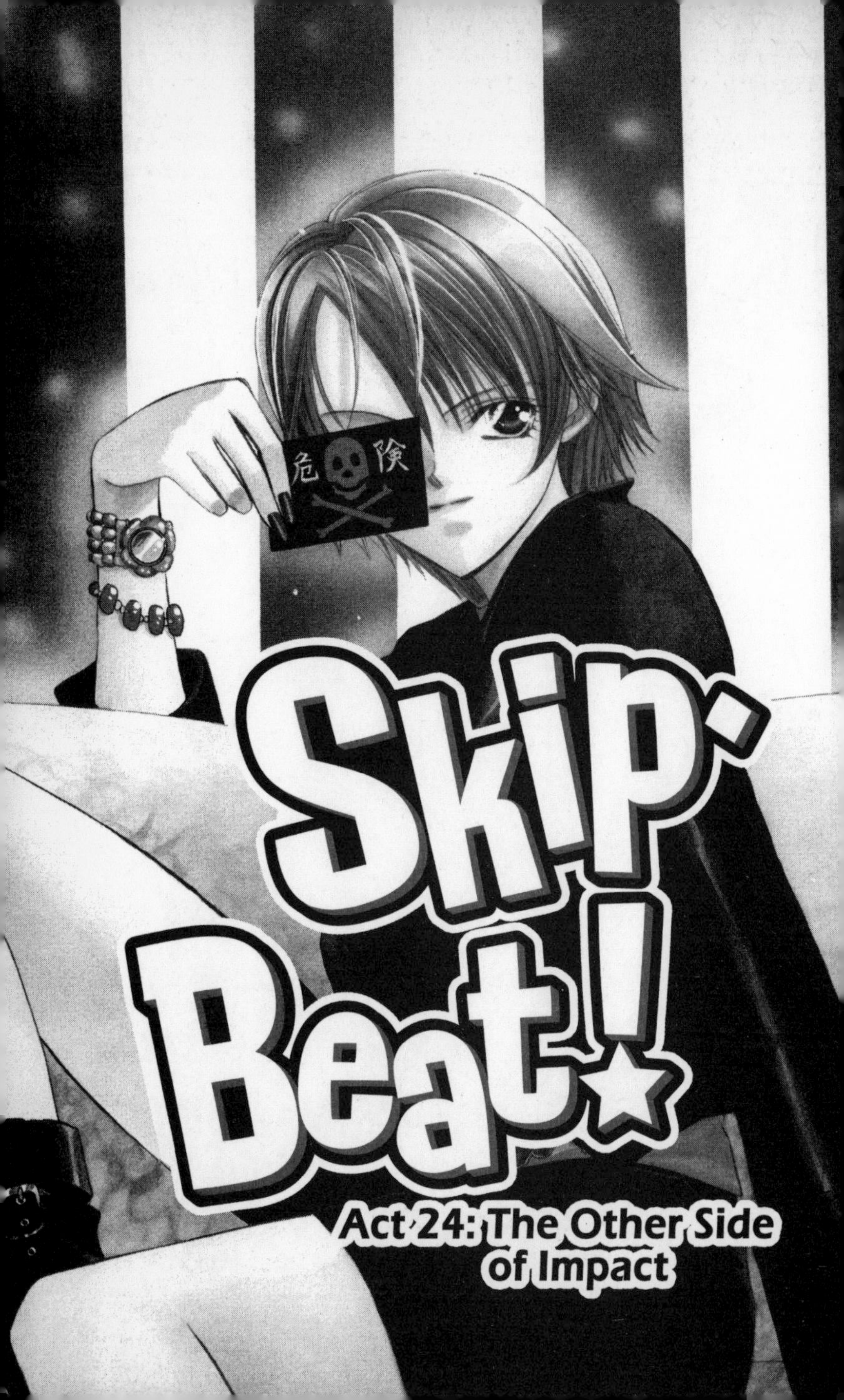
危険
Skip Beat!
Act 24: The Other Side of Impact

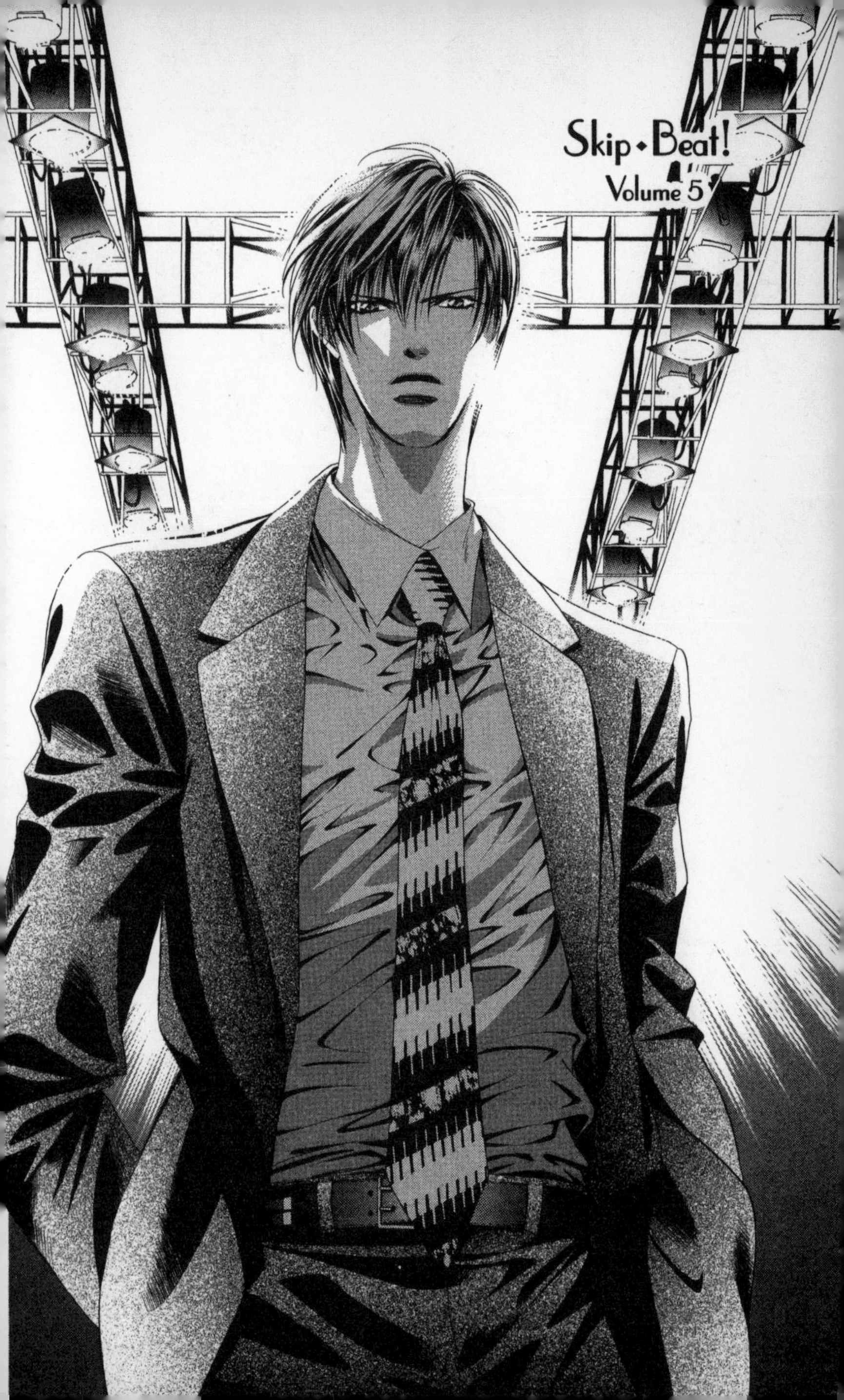
Skip • Beat!
Volume 5

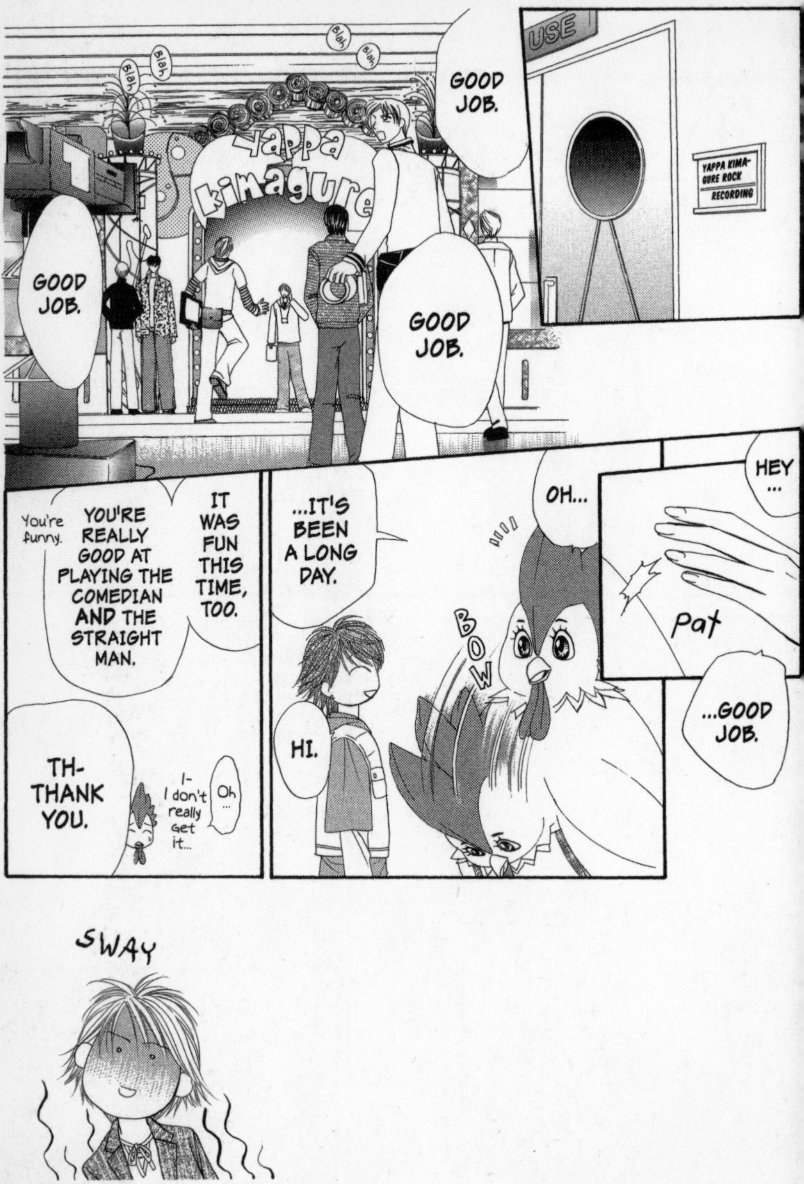
USE
YAPPA KIMAGURE ROCK
RECORDING
GOOD JOB.
Blah
Blah
Blah
Blah
Yappa Kimagure
GOOD JOB.
GOOD JOB.
HEY...
Pat
...GOOD JOB.
OH...
BOW
...IT'S BEEN A LONG DAY.
HI.
IT WAS FUN THIS TIME, TOO.
YOU'RE REALLY GOOD AT PLAYING THE COMEDIAN AND THE STRAIGHT MAN.
You're funny.
TH-THANK YOU.
Oh...
I- I don't really get it...
SWAY

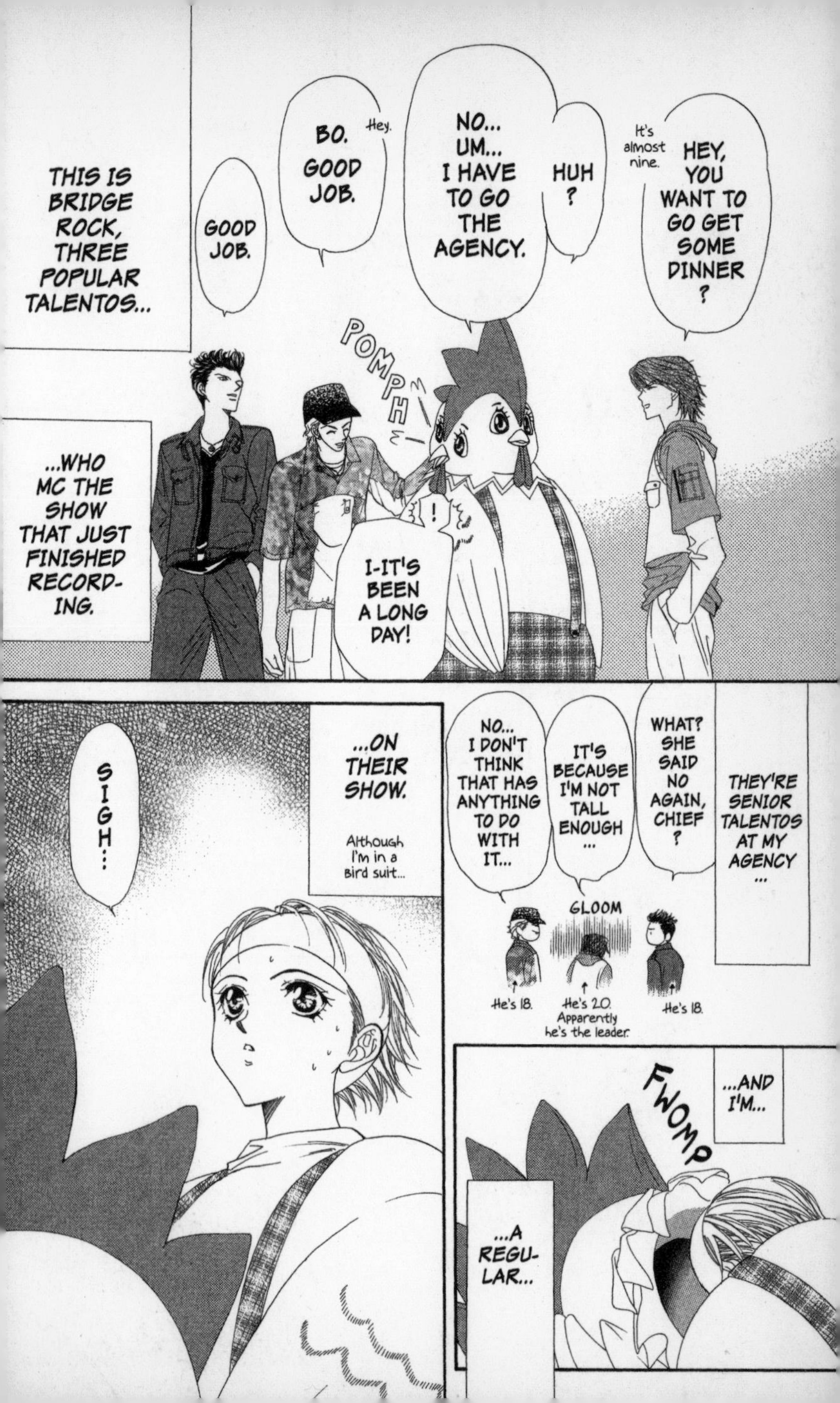
HEY, YOU WANT TO GO GET SOME DINNER?
It's almost nine.
HUH?
NO... UM... I HAVE TO GO THE AGENCY.
BO. GOOD JOB.
Hey.
GOOD JOB.
THIS IS BRIDGE ROCK, THREE POPULAR TALENTOS...
POMPH
!
I-IT'S BEEN A LONG DAY!
...WHO MC THE SHOW THAT JUST FINISHED RECORD-ING.
THEY'RE SENIOR TALENTOS AT MY AGENCY...
WHAT? SHE SAID NO AGAIN, CHIEF?
IT'S BECAUSE I'M NOT TALL ENOUGH...
NO... I DON'T THINK THAT HAS ANYTHING TO DO WITH IT...
GLOOM
He's 18.
He's 20. Apparently he's the leader.
He's 18.
...AND I'M...
FWOMP
...A REGU-LAR...
...ON THEIR SHOW.
Although I'm in a Bird suit...
SIGH...

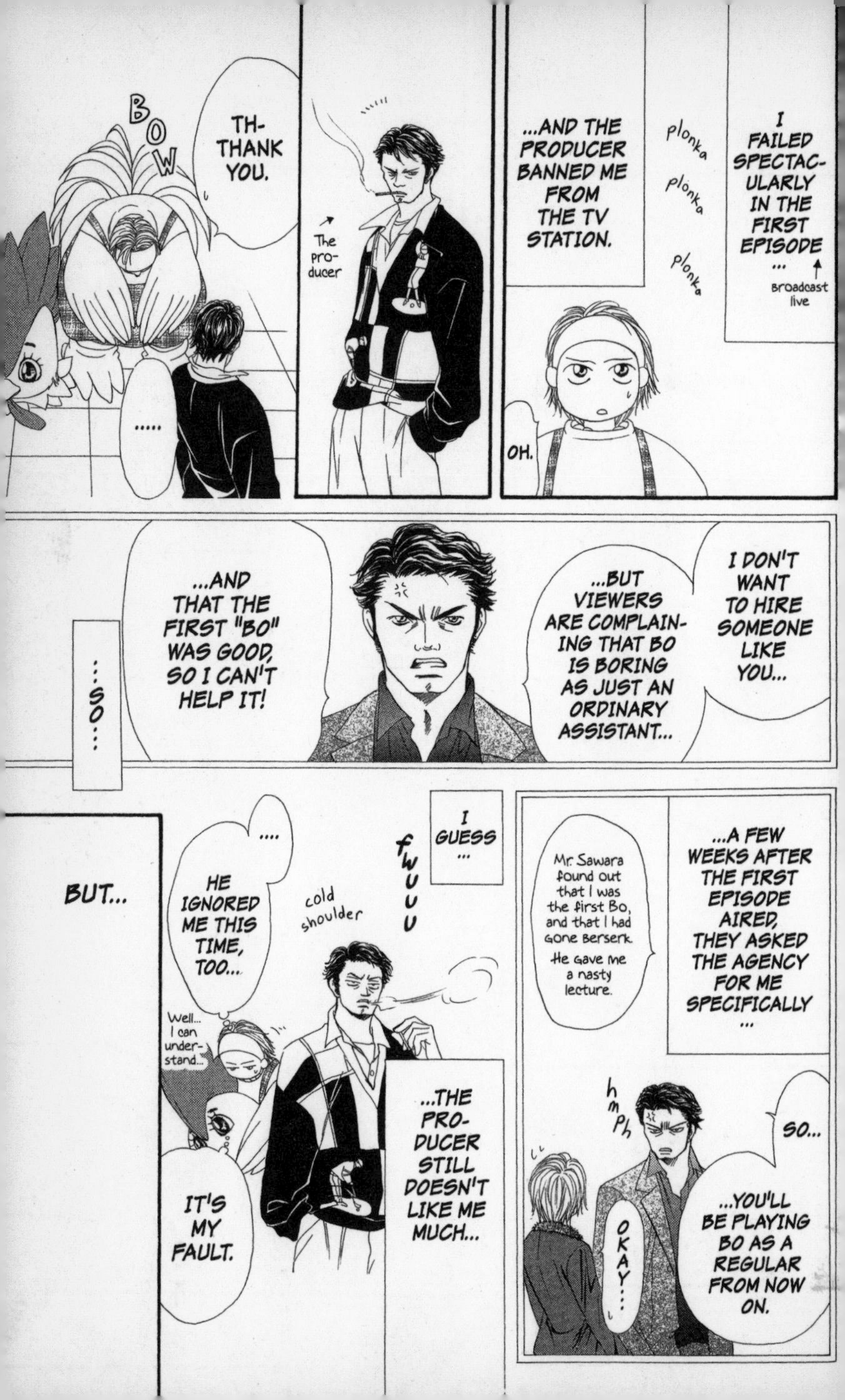
I FAILED SPECTACULARLY IN THE FIRST EPISODE...
Broadcast live
...AND THE PRODUCER BANNED ME FROM THE TV STATION.
plonka
plonka
plonka
OH.
The producer
BOW
TH-THANK YOU.
.....
I DON'T WANT TO HIRE SOMEONE LIKE YOU...
...BUT VIEWERS ARE COMPLAINING THAT BO IS BORING AS JUST AN ORDINARY ASSISTANT...
...AND THAT THE FIRST "BO" WAS GOOD, SO I CAN'T HELP IT!
...SO...
...A FEW WEEKS AFTER THE FIRST EPISODE AIRED, THEY ASKED THE AGENCY FOR ME SPECIFICALLY...
Mr. Sawara found out that I was the first Bo, and that I had gone berserk. He gave me a nasty lecture.
SO...
...YOU'LL BE PLAYING BO AS A REGULAR FROM NOW ON.
hmph
OKAY...
I GUESS...
fwuuu
....
HE IGNORED ME THIS TIME, TOO...
cold shoulder
Well... I can understand...
...THE PRODUCER STILL DOESN'T LIKE ME MUCH...
IT'S MY FAULT.
BUT...

BE-CAUSE...

...TOMORROW...

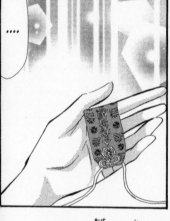

....

Do your best. ...But here. It may only help you to relax...

...I...

HEE...

...I'M GOING TO BECOME A STAR THAT HE CAN'T IGNORE!

I FEEL BAD, SINCE THEY SPECIFICALLY REQUESTED ME FOR THE PART...

...BUT I NEED TO FIND SOMEONE ELSE TO PLAY BO.

shup shup

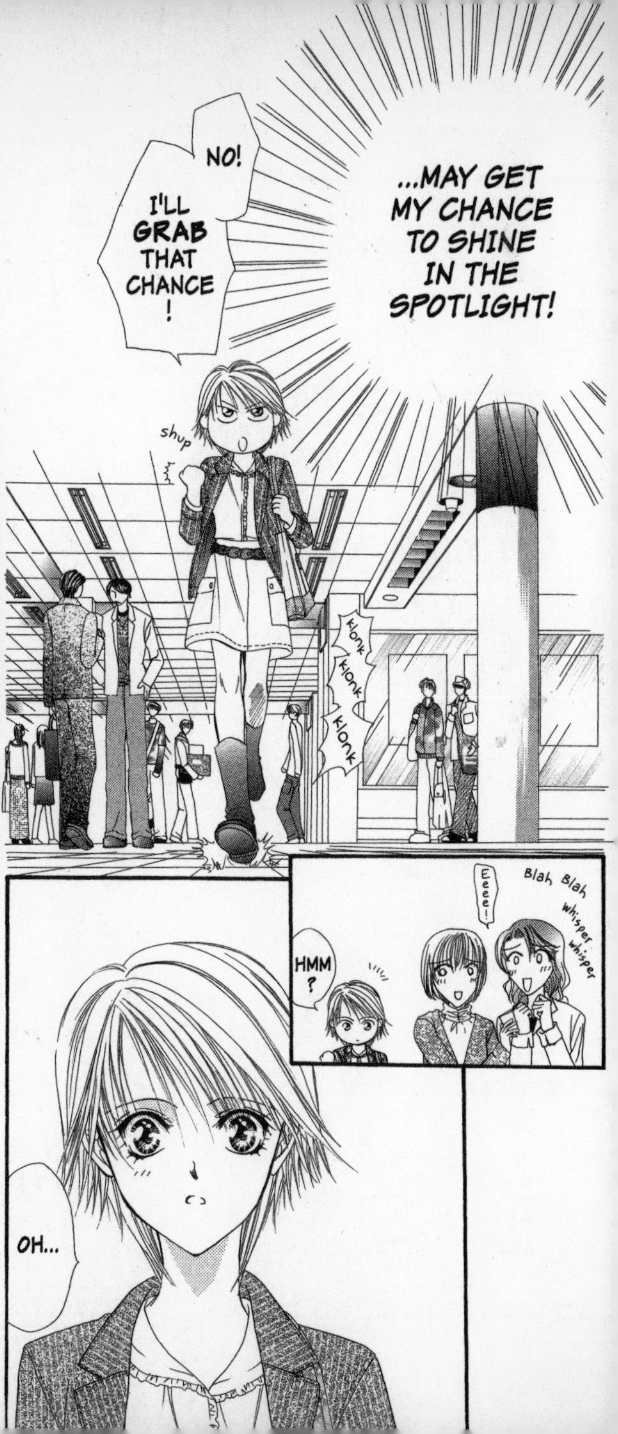
...MAY GET MY CHANCE TO SHINE IN THE SPOTLIGHT!
NO!
I'LL GRAB THAT CHANCE!
shup
klonk klonk klonk
Blah Blah
whisper whisper
Eeee!
HMM?
OH...

Nao and Kazumi

These two were created solely to make Kyoko think "Best friends are nice..." ♡ Therefore in the beginning, they were supposed to be really lovey-dovey girls who make you want to say "You girls, there's something a little wrong with you"...

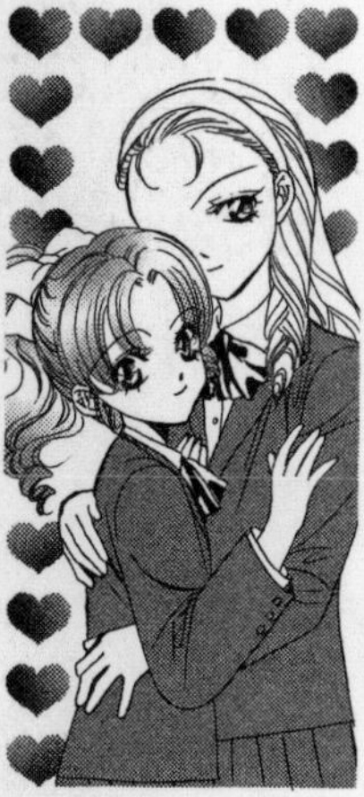

But somehow, when the audition began, they split wonderfully. I was thinking as I was drawing that in reality, people like them could exist. It became fun drawing these two, who only appeared occasionally. However, I was really surprised that Nao became important enough to get long shots in some panels (as Erika's partner)... ...an amazing promotion... they were just supporting players...

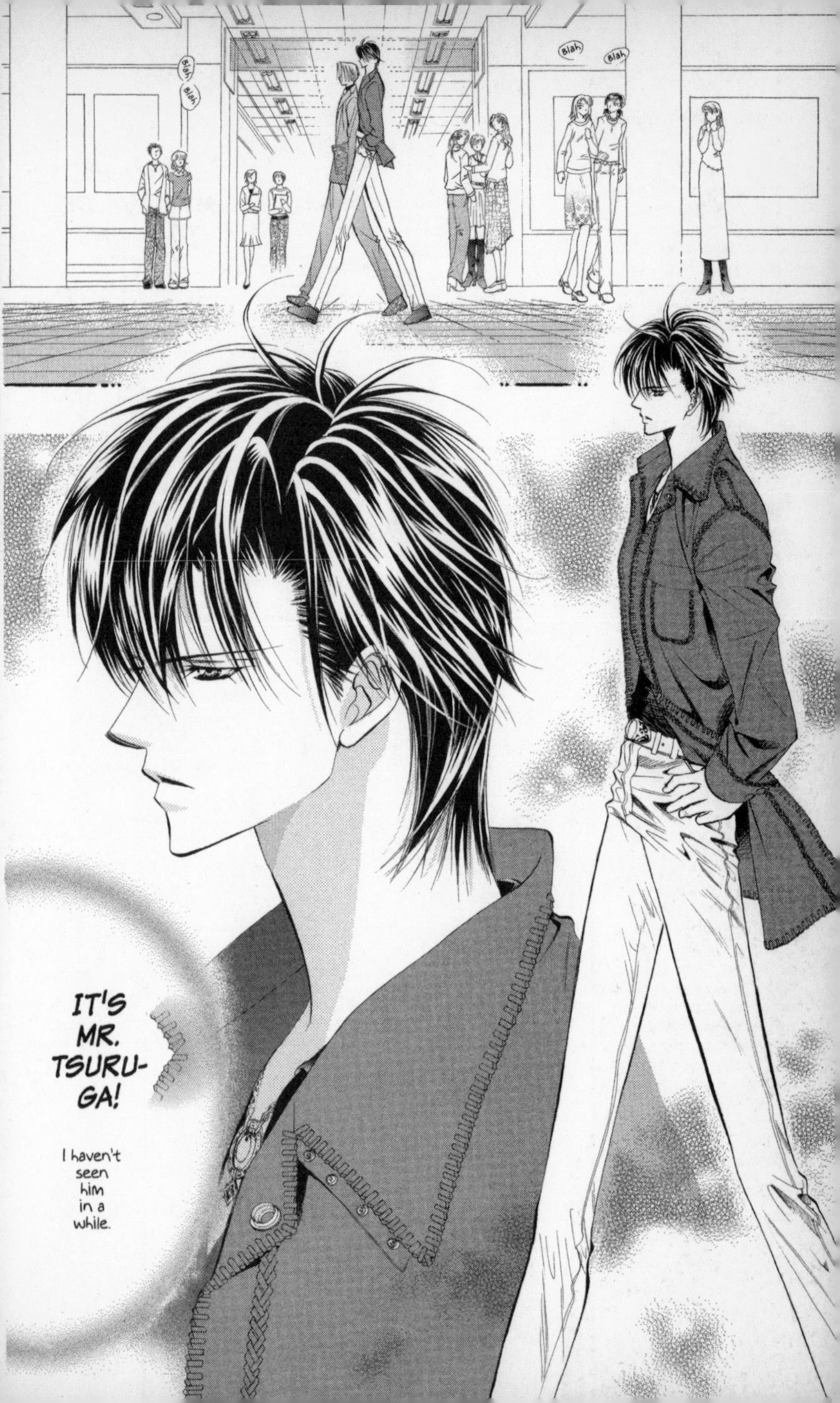
Blah
Blah
Blah
Blah
Blah
IT'S MR. TSURU-GA!
I haven't seen him in a while.

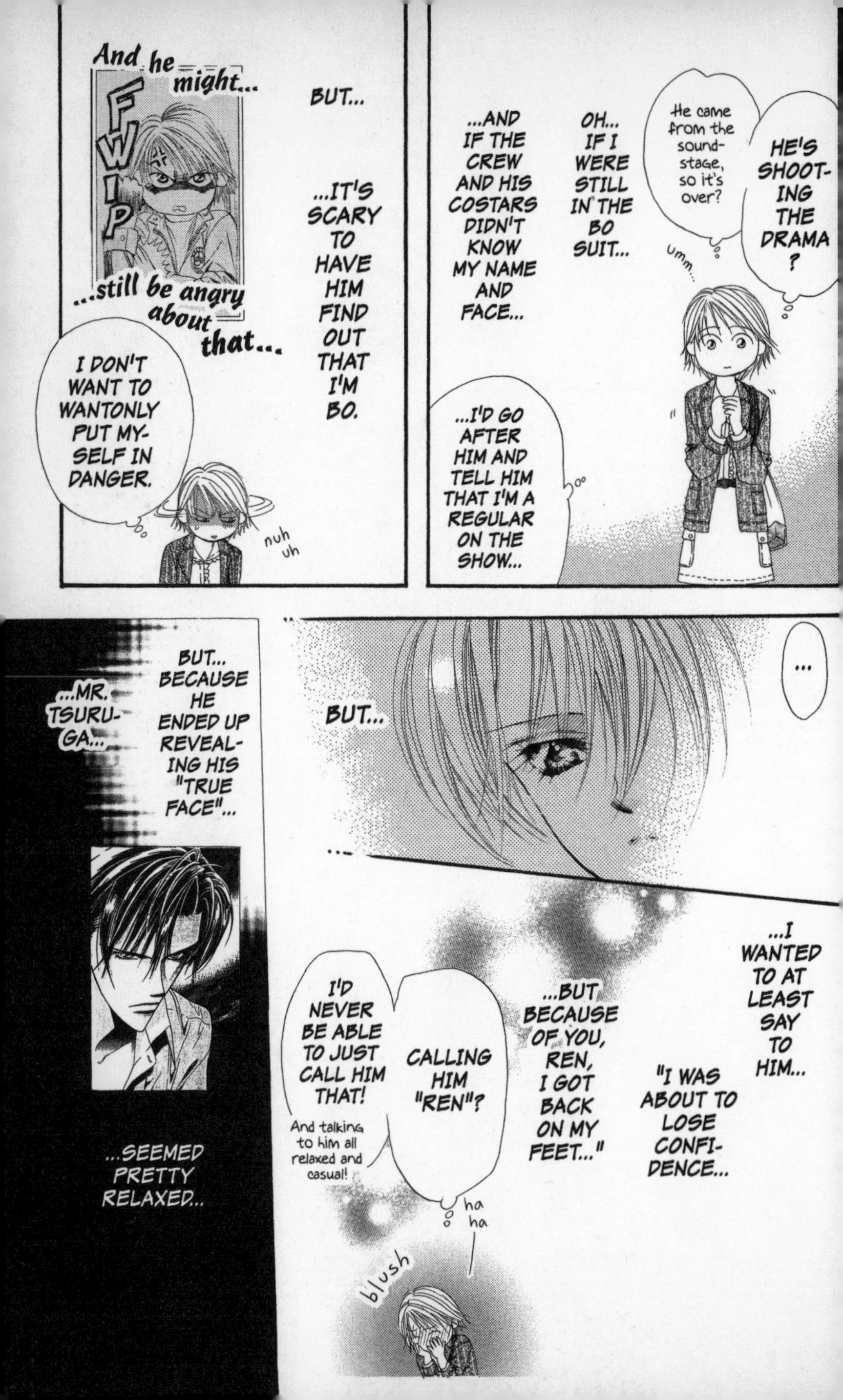
HE'S SHOOTING THE DRAMA?
He came from the soundstage, so it's over?
umm...
OH... IF I WERE STILL IN THE BO SUIT...
...AND IF THE CREW AND HIS COSTARS DIDN'T KNOW MY NAME AND FACE...
...I'D GO AFTER HIM AND TELL HIM THAT I'M A REGULAR ON THE SHOW...
BUT...
...IT'S SCARY TO HAVE HIM FIND OUT THAT I'M BO.
And he might...
FWIP
...still be angry about that...
I DON'T WANT TO WANTONLY PUT MYSELF IN DANGER.
nuh uh
...
BUT...
...I WANTED TO AT LEAST SAY TO HIM...
"I WAS ABOUT TO LOSE CONFIDENCE...
...BUT BECAUSE OF YOU, REN, I GOT BACK ON MY FEET..."
CALLING HIM "REN"?
I'D NEVER BE ABLE TO JUST CALL HIM THAT!
And talking to him all relaxed and casual!
ha ha
blush
BUT... BECAUSE HE ENDED UP REVEALING HIS "TRUE FACE"...
...MR. TSURUGA...
...SEEMED PRETTY RELAXED...

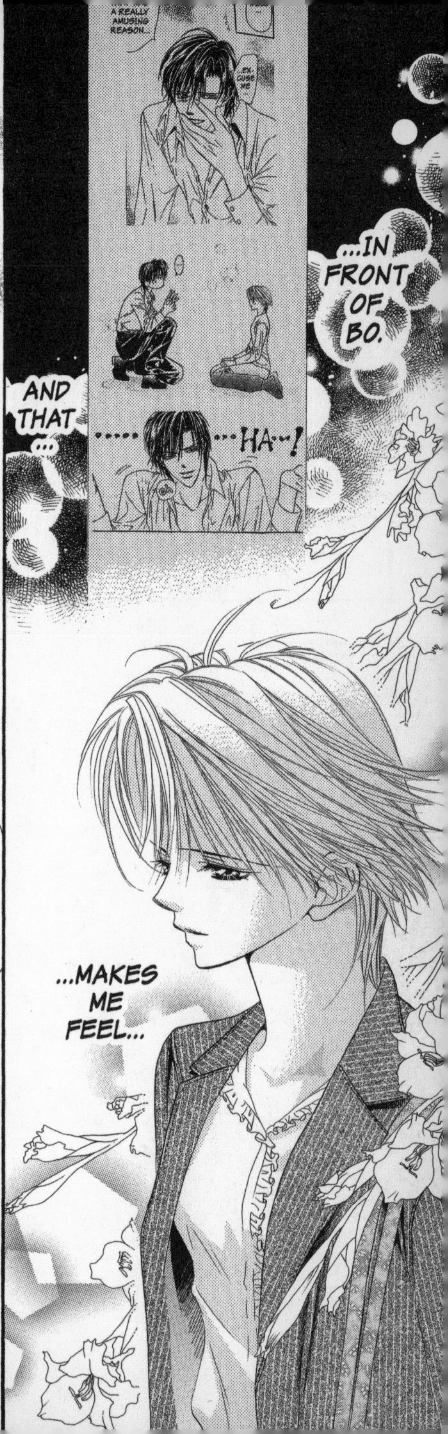
A REALLY AMUSING REASON...
EX-CUSE ME
...IN FRONT OF BO.
AND THAT...
......HA--!
...MAKES ME FEEL...
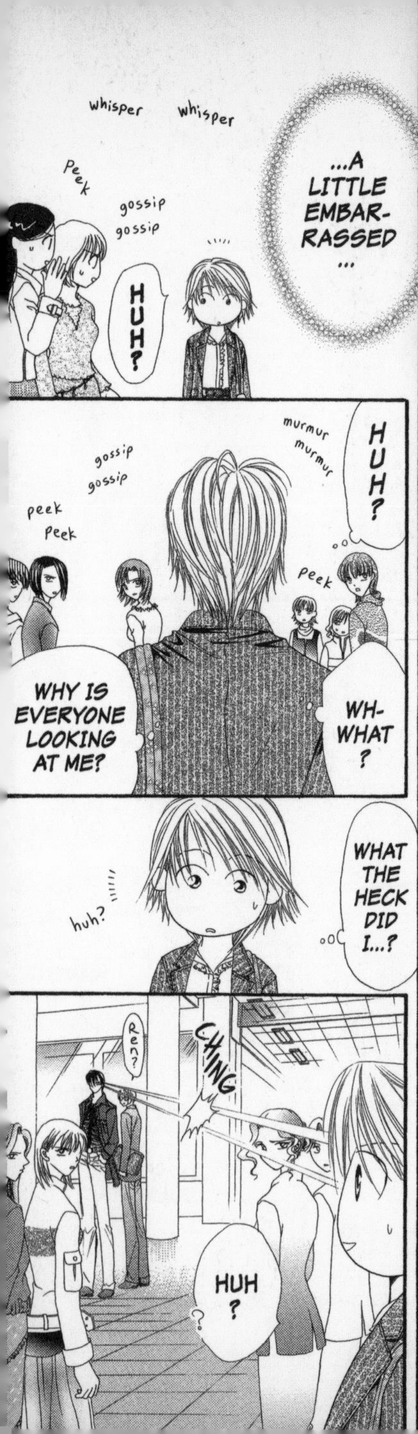
...A LITTLE EMBARRASSED...
whisper whisper
peek
gossip gossip
HUH?
HUH?
murmur murmur
gossip gossip
peek peek
peek
WH-WHAT?
WHY IS EVERYONE LOOKING AT ME?
WHAT THE HECK DID I...?
huh?
CHING
Ren?
HUH?

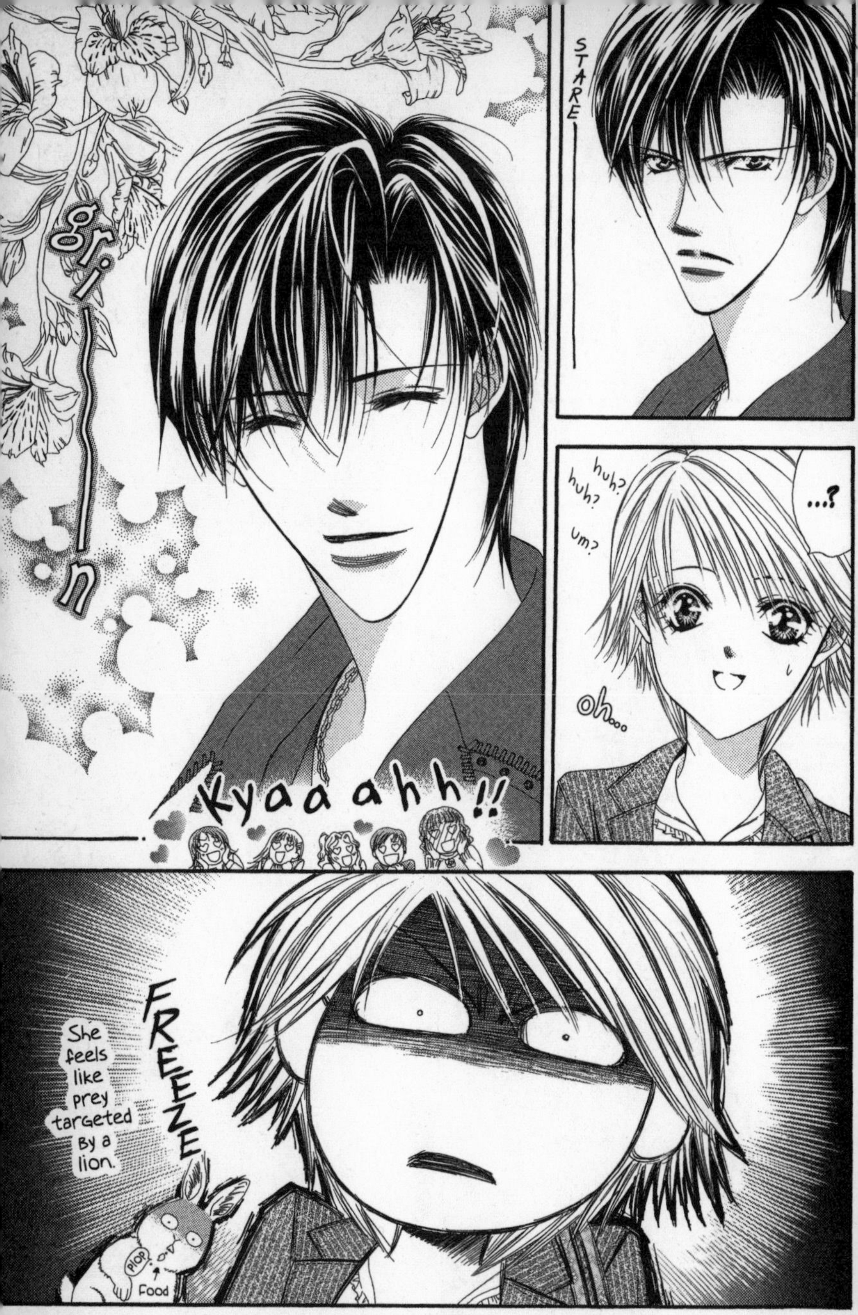
STARE
...?
huh?
huh?
um?
oh...
gri—n
Kyaaahh!!
FREEZE
She feels like prey targeted by a lion.
PLOP
Food

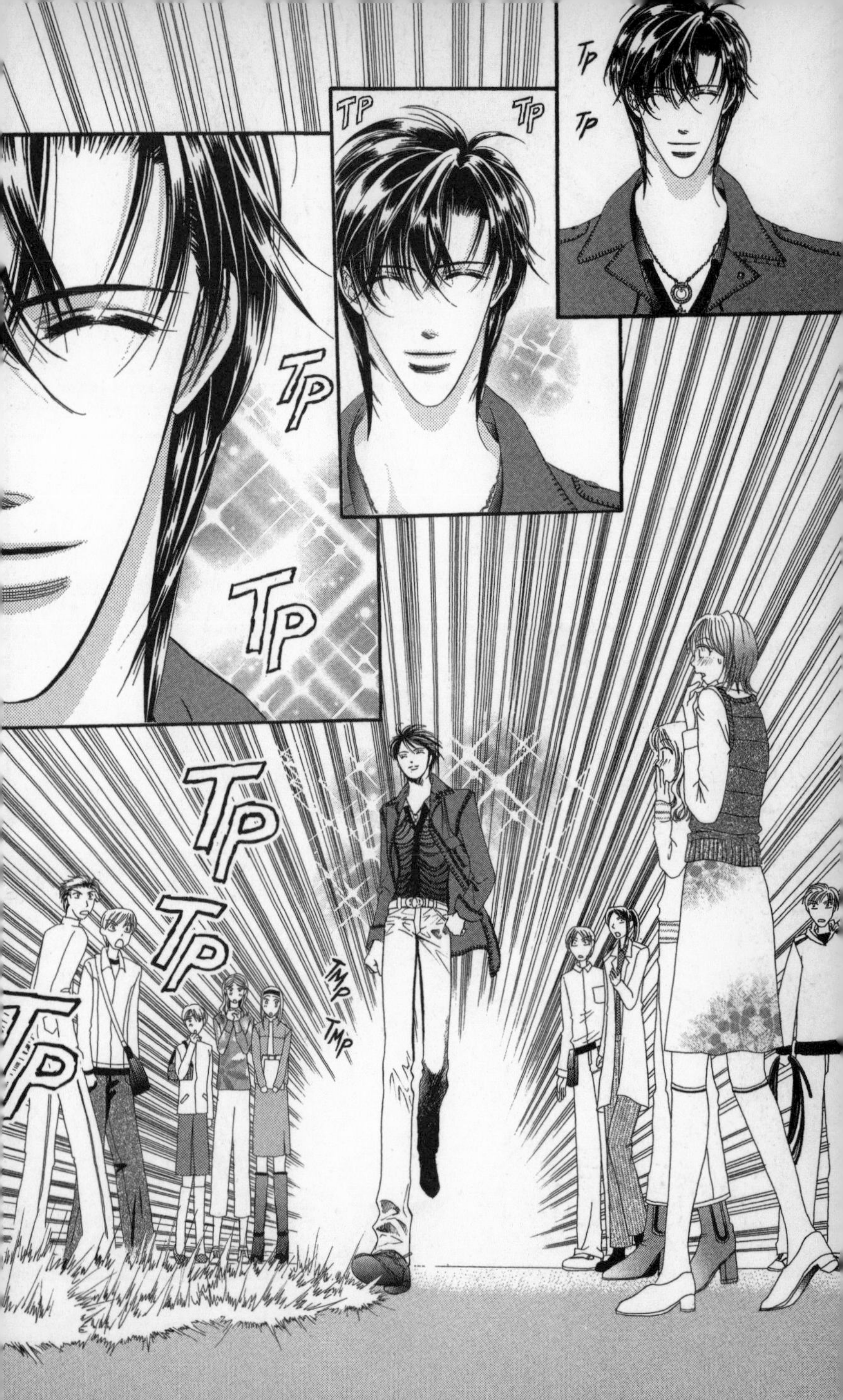
TP
TP
TP
TP
TP
TP
TP
TP
TP
TMP
TMP

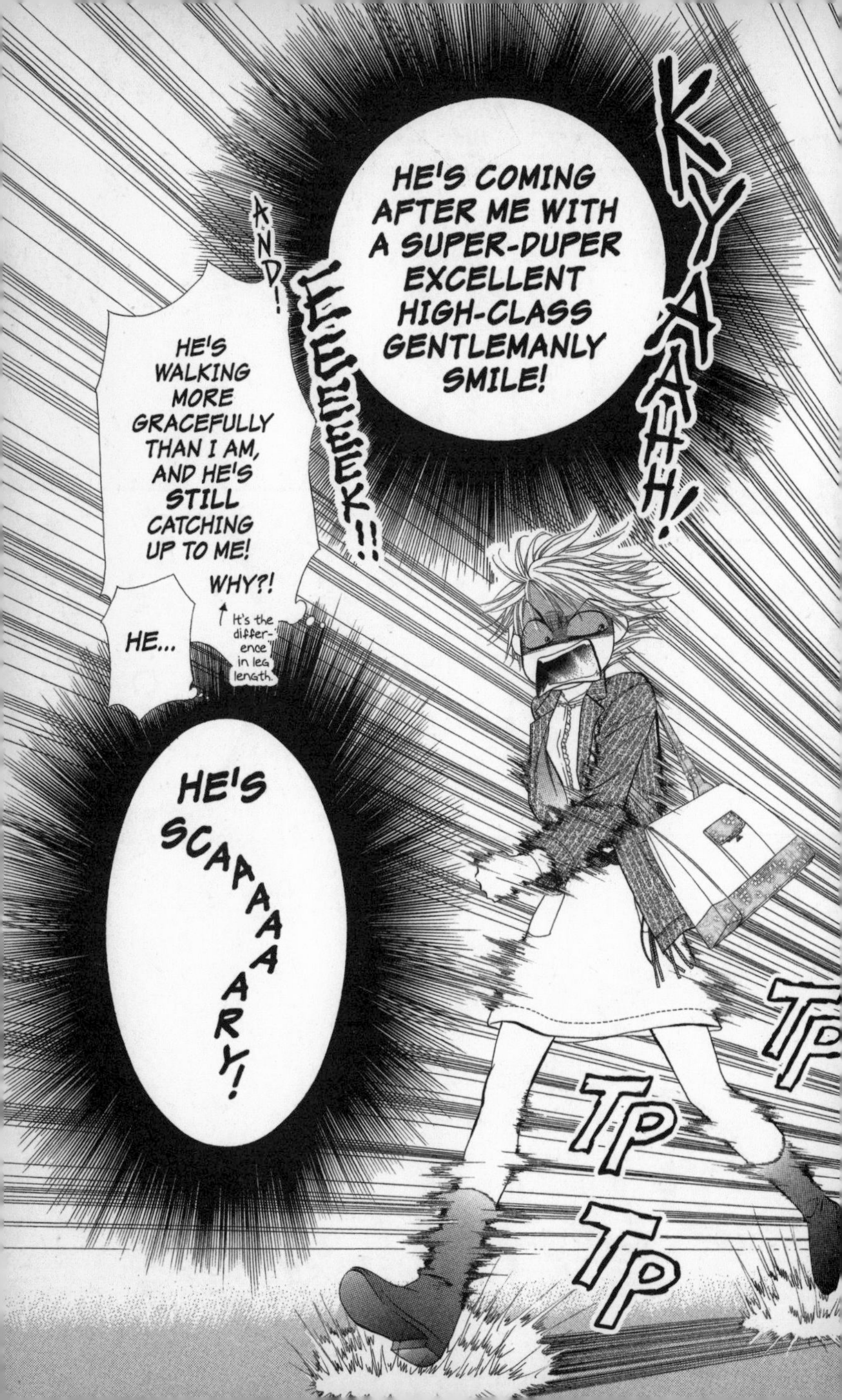
KYAAAH!
HE'S COMING AFTER ME WITH A SUPER-DUPER EXCELLENT HIGH-CLASS GENTLEMANLY SMILE!
EEEEEEK!!
AND!
HE'S WALKING MORE GRACEFULLY THAN I AM, AND HE'S STILL CATCHING UP TO ME!
WHY?!
It's the difference in leg length.
HE...
HE'S SCAAAAAARY!
TP
TP
TP

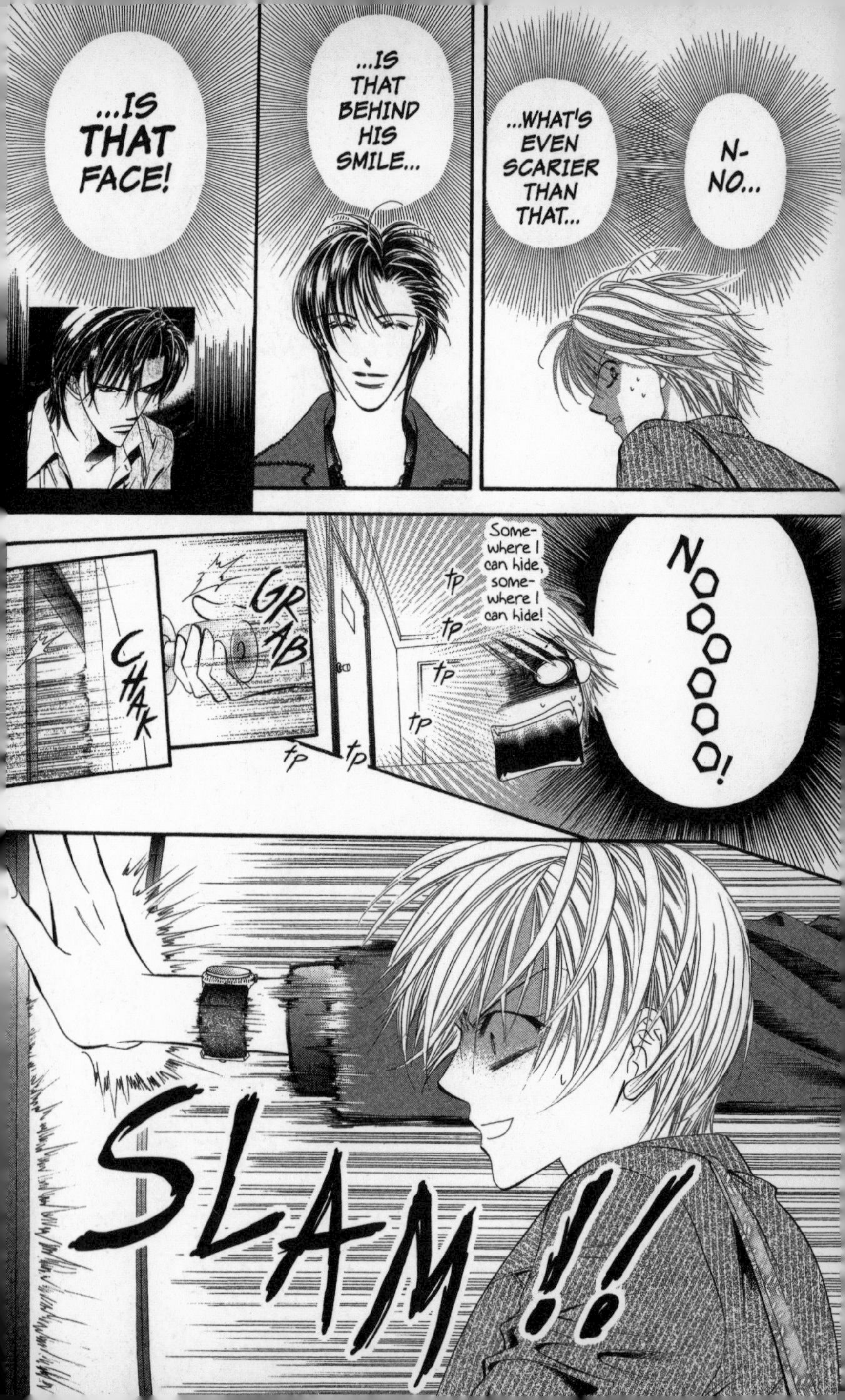
N-NO...
...WHAT'S EVEN SCARIER THAN THAT...
...IS THAT BEHIND HIS SMILE...
...IS THAT FACE!
NOOOOOO!
Some-where I can hide, some-where I can hide!
tp tp tp tp tp tp
GRAB
CHAK
SLAM!!

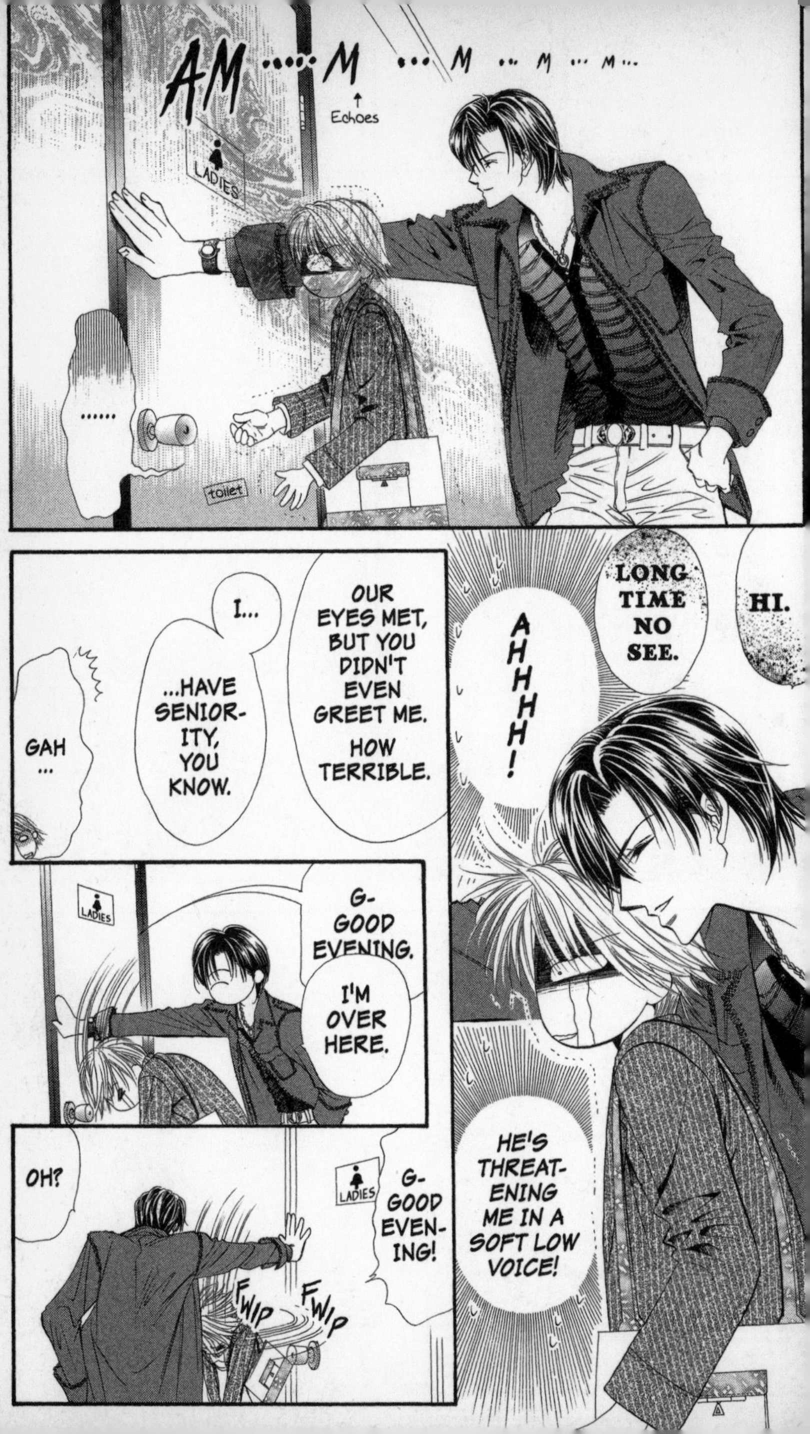
AM.....M ... M .. M .. M...
Echoes
LADIES
......
toilet
HI.
LONG TIME NO SEE.
AHHHH!
HE'S THREATENING ME IN A SOFT LOW VOICE!
OUR EYES MET, BUT YOU DIDN'T EVEN GREET ME.
HOW TERRIBLE.
I...
...HAVE SENIORITY, YOU KNOW.
GAH...
LADIES
G-GOOD EVENING.
I'M OVER HERE.
LADIES
G-GOOD EVENING!
OH?
FWIP
FWIP

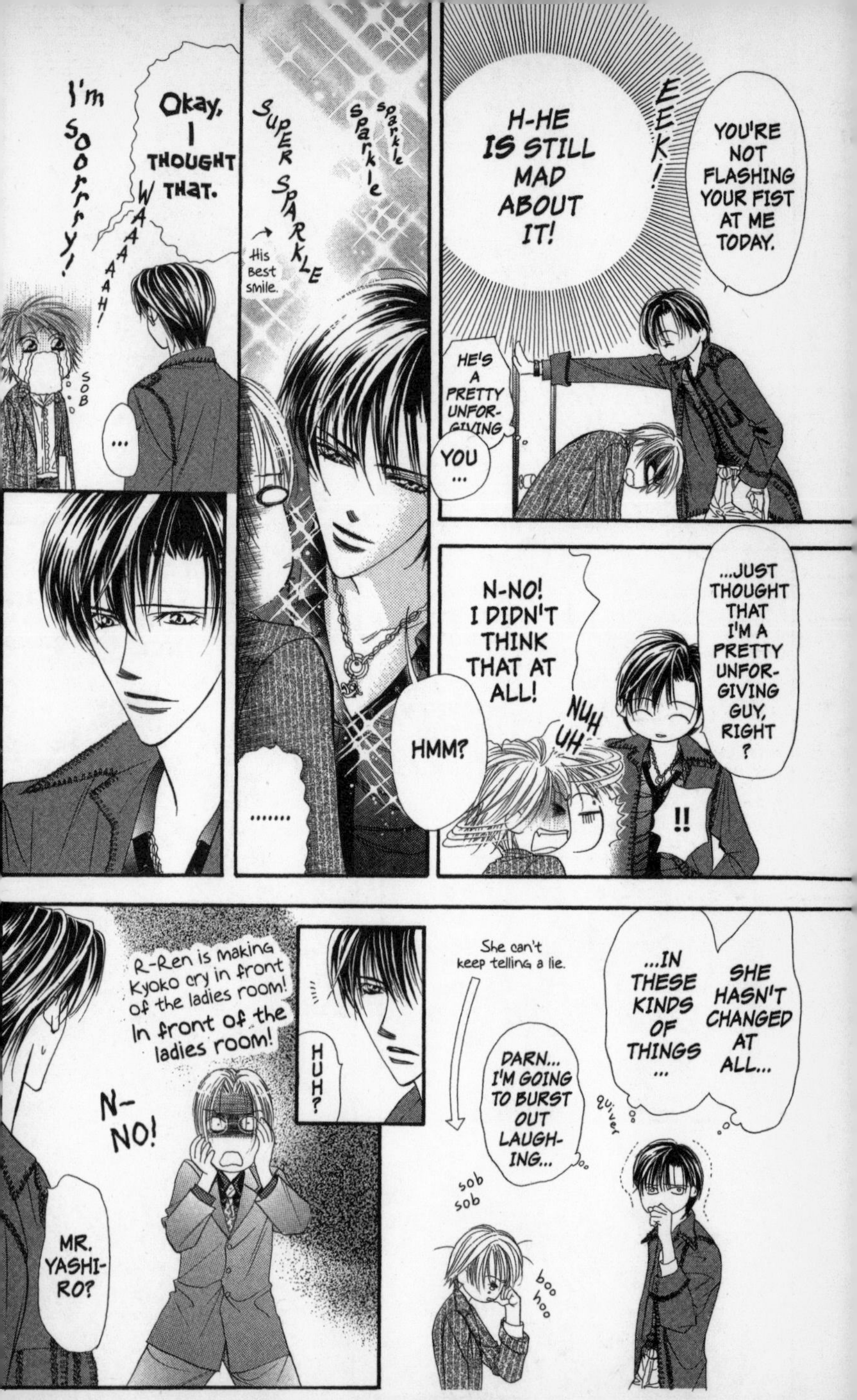

YOU'RE NOT FLASHING YOUR FIST AT ME TODAY.
EEK!
H-HE IS STILL MAD ABOUT IT!
HE'S A PRETTY UNFORGIVING
YOU...
...JUST THOUGHT THAT I'M A PRETTY UNFORGIVING GUY, RIGHT?
N-NO! I DIDN'T THINK THAT AT ALL!
NUH UH
!!
sparkle sparkle
SUPER SPARKLE
His best smile.
HMM?
....
Okay, I thought that.
I'm soorrry!
WAAAAAH!
SOB
...
SHE HASN'T CHANGED AT ALL...
...IN THESE KINDS OF THINGS...
quiver
DARN... I'M GOING TO BURST OUT LAUGHING...
She can't keep telling a lie.
sob sob
boo hoo
HUH?
R-Ren is making Kyoko cry in front of the ladies room! In front of the ladies room!
N-NO!
MR. YASHIRO?

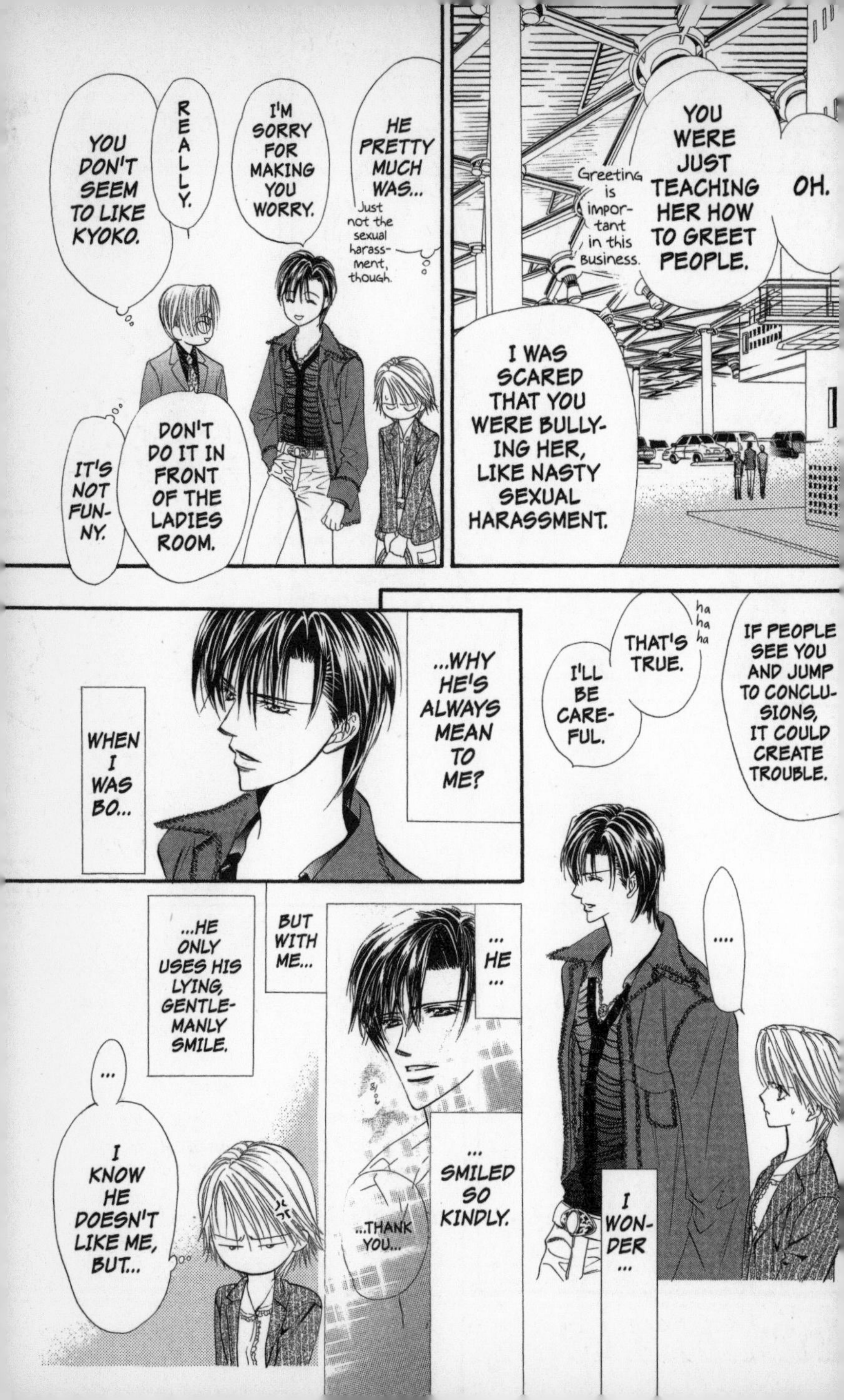
OH.
YOU WERE JUST TEACHING HER HOW TO GREET PEOPLE.
Greeting is impor-tant in this business.
I WAS SCARED THAT YOU WERE BULLY-ING HER, LIKE NASTY SEXUAL HARASSMENT.
HE PRETTY MUCH WAS...
Just not the sexual harass-ment, though.
I'M SORRY FOR MAKING YOU WORRY.
REALLY.
YOU DON'T SEEM TO LIKE KYOKO.
DON'T DO IT IN FRONT OF THE LADIES ROOM.
IT'S NOT FUN-NY.
IF PEOPLE SEE YOU AND JUMP TO CONCLU-SIONS, IT COULD CREATE TROUBLE.
ha ha ha
THAT'S TRUE.
I'LL BE CARE-FUL.
...WHY HE'S ALWAYS MEAN TO ME?
WHEN I WAS BO...
....
I WON-DER ...
... HE ...
... SMILED SO KINDLY.
...THANK YOU...
BUT WITH ME...
...HE ONLY USES HIS LYING, GENTLE-MANLY SMILE.
...
I KNOW HE DOESN'T LIKE ME, BUT...

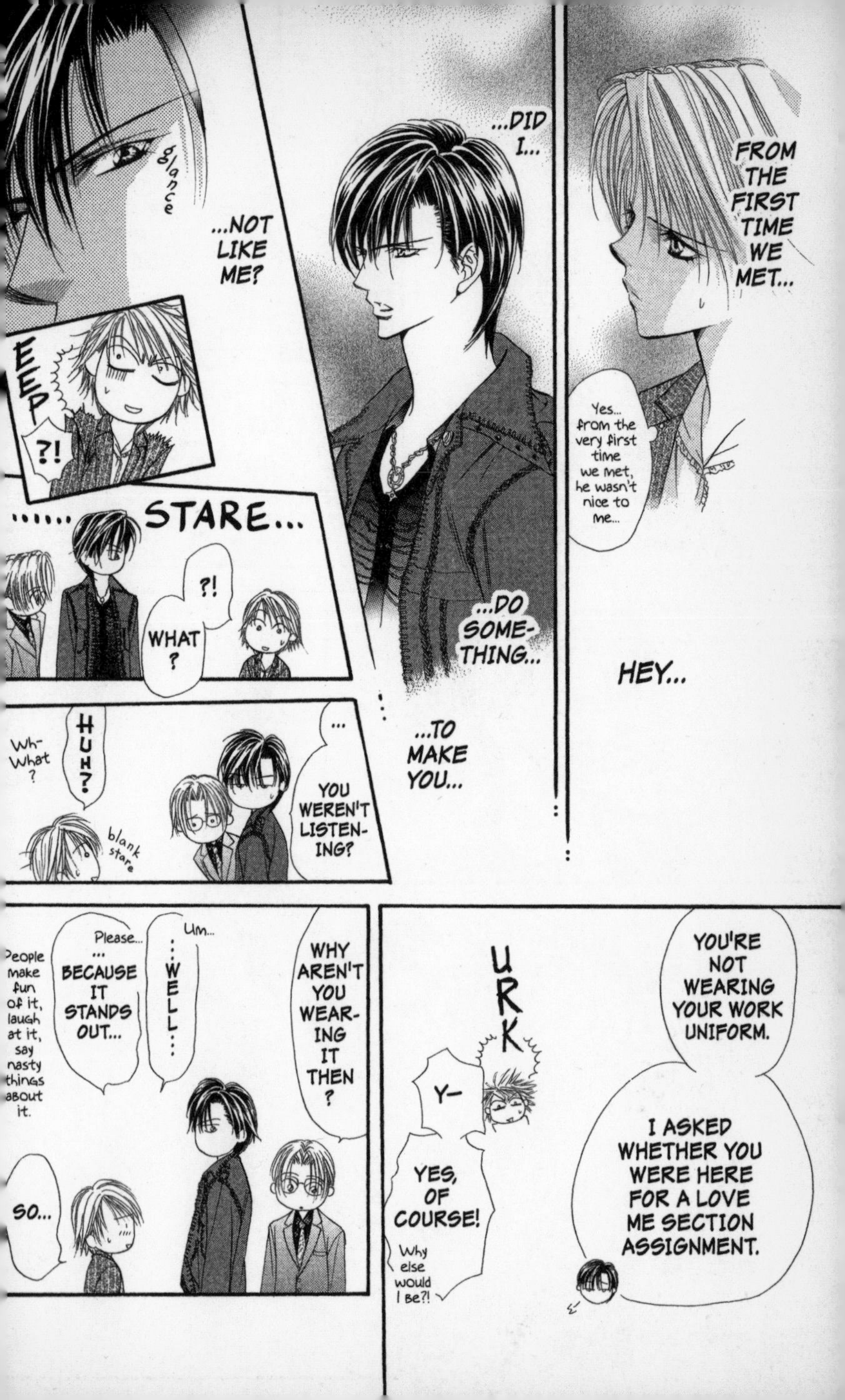
FROM THE FIRST TIME WE MET...
Yes... from the very first time we met, he wasn't nice to me...
HEY...
...DID I...
...DO SOMETHING...
...TO MAKE YOU...
glance
...NOT LIKE ME?
EEP
?!
......STARE...
?!
WHAT?
...
YOU WEREN'T LISTENING?
HUH?
Wh- What?
blank stare
YOU'RE NOT WEARING YOUR WORK UNIFORM.
I ASKED WHETHER YOU WERE HERE FOR A LOVE ME SECTION ASSIGNMENT.
URK
Y—
YES, OF COURSE!
Why else would I be?!
WHY AREN'T YOU WEARING IT THEN?
Um...
...WELL...
Please... ...BECAUSE IT STANDS OUT...
People make fun of it, laugh at it, say nasty things about it.
SO...

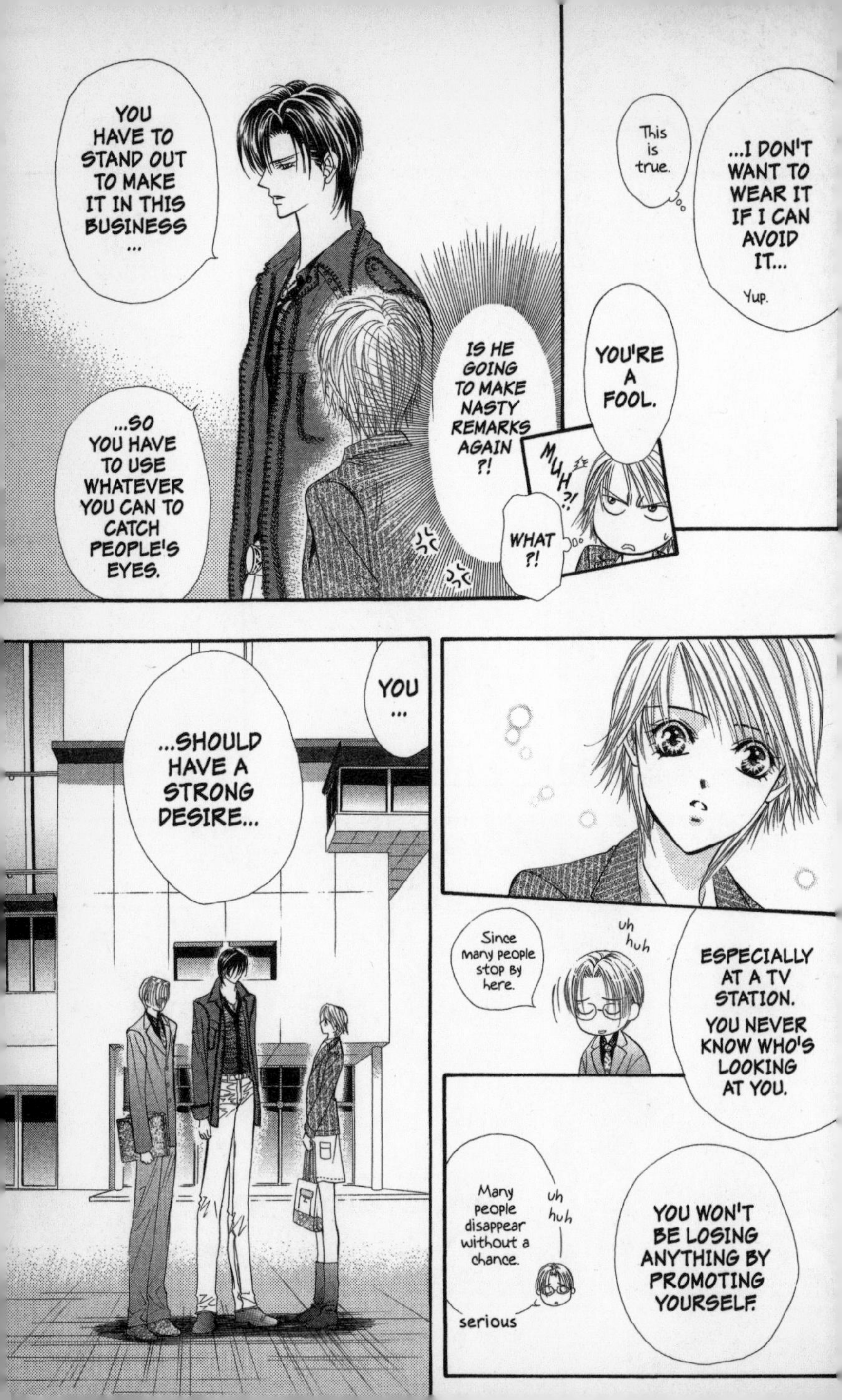
...I DON'T WANT TO WEAR IT IF I CAN AVOID IT...
This is true.
Yup.
YOU'RE A FOOL.
MUH ?!
WHAT ?!
YOU HAVE TO STAND OUT TO MAKE IT IN THIS BUSINESS ...
IS HE GOING TO MAKE NASTY REMARKS AGAIN ?!
...SO YOU HAVE TO USE WHATEVER YOU CAN TO CATCH PEOPLE'S EYES.
ESPECIALLY AT A TV STATION. YOU NEVER KNOW WHO'S LOOKING AT YOU.
uh huh
Since many people stop by here.
YOU WON'T BE LOSING ANYTHING BY PROMOTING YOURSELF.
uh huh
Many people disappear without a chance.
serious
YOU ...
...SHOULD HAVE A STRONG DESIRE...

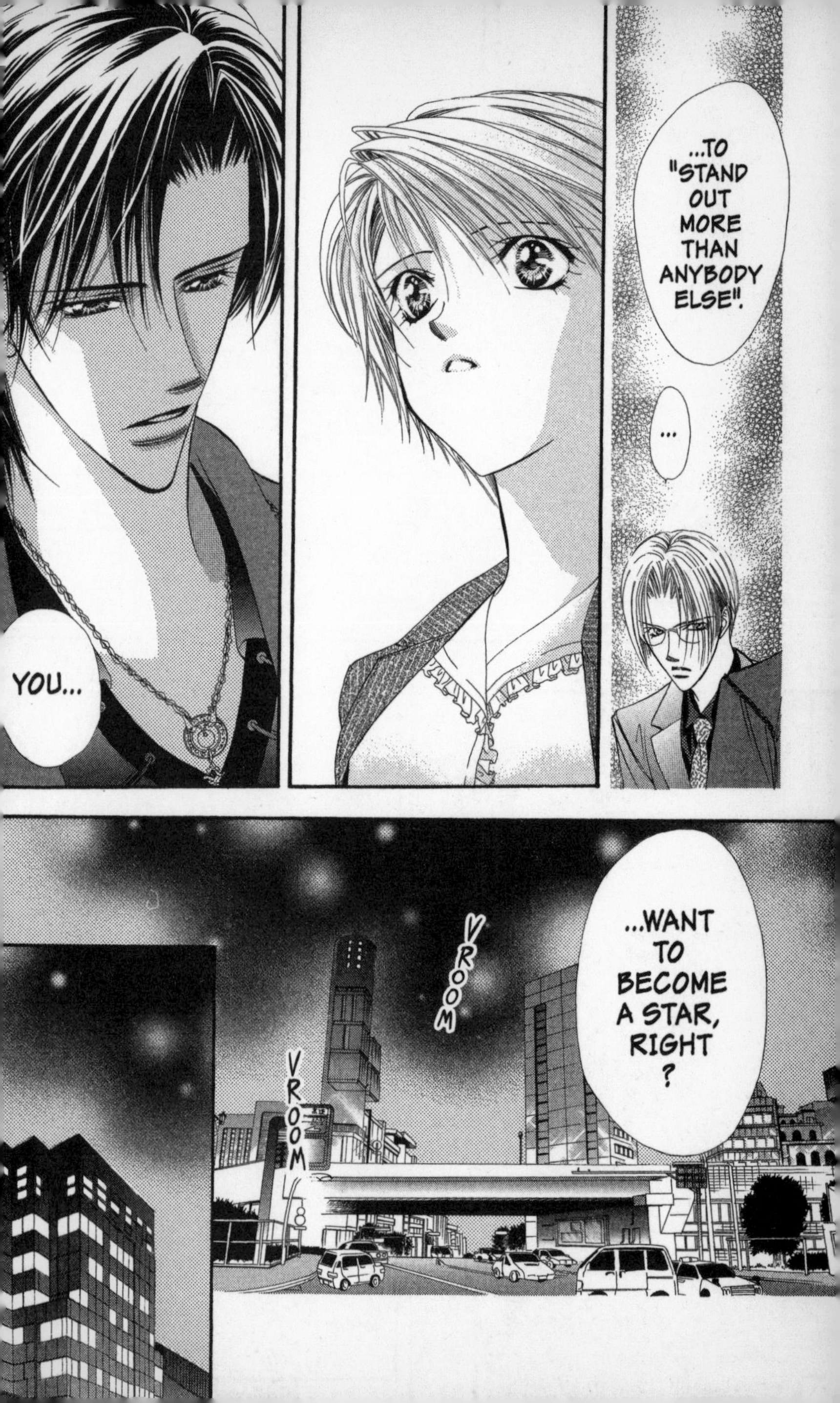
...TO "STAND OUT MORE THAN ANYBODY ELSE".
...
YOU...
...WANT TO BECOME A STAR, RIGHT?
VROOM
VROOM

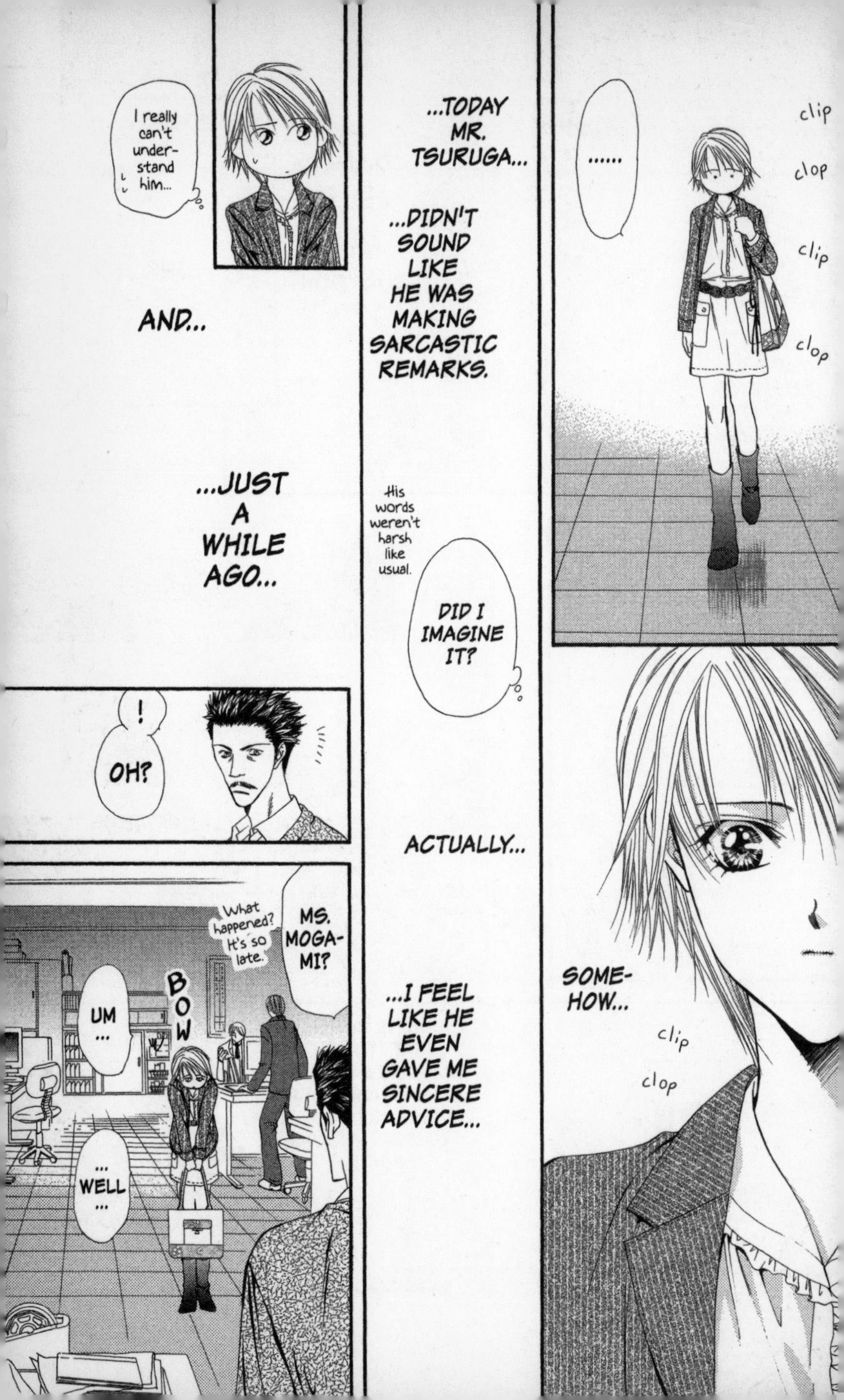

......
clip
clop
clip
clop
SOME-HOW...
clip
clop
...TODAY MR. TSURUGA...
...DIDN'T SOUND LIKE HE WAS MAKING SARCASTIC REMARKS.
His words weren't harsh like usual.
DID I IMAGINE IT?
ACTUALLY...
...I FEEL LIKE HE EVEN GAVE ME SINCERE ADVICE...
I really can't under-stand him...
AND...
...JUST A WHILE AGO...
!
OH?
MS. MOGA-MI?
What happened? It's so late.
BOW
UM...
...WELL...

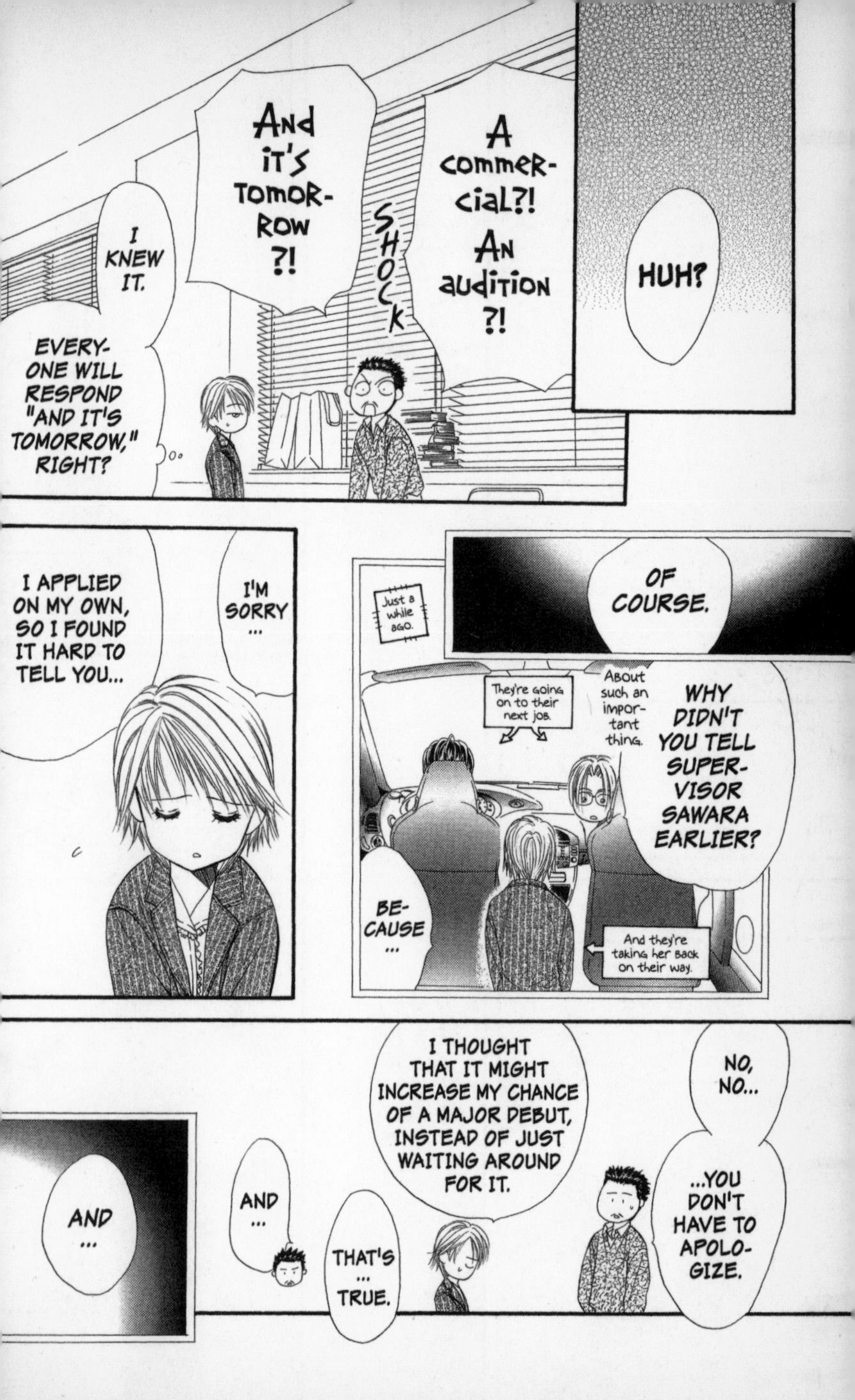
HUH?
A commercial?! An audition?!
SHOCK
And it's tomorrow?!
I KNEW IT.
EVERYONE WILL RESPOND "AND IT'S TOMORROW," RIGHT?
OF COURSE.
Just a while ago.
WHY DIDN'T YOU TELL SUPERVISOR SAWARA EARLIER?
About such an important thing.
They're going on to their next job.
BECAUSE...
And they're taking her back on their way.
I'M SORRY...
I APPLIED ON MY OWN, SO I FOUND IT HARD TO TELL YOU...
NO, NO...
...YOU DON'T HAVE TO APOLOGIZE.
I THOUGHT THAT IT MIGHT INCREASE MY CHANCE OF A MAJOR DEBUT, INSTEAD OF JUST WAITING AROUND FOR IT.
THAT'S... TRUE.
AND...
AND...

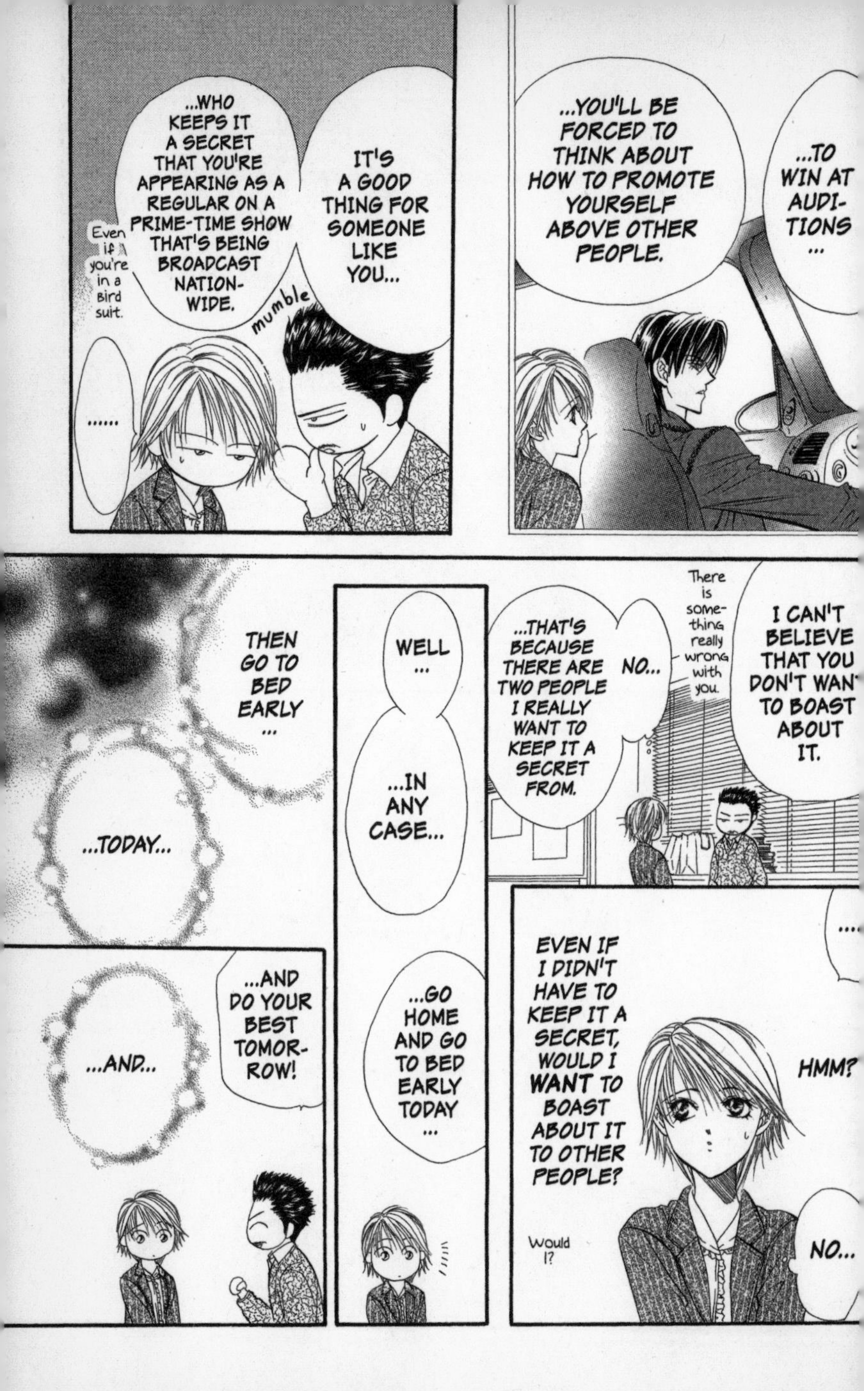

...TO WIN AT AUDITIONS...
...YOU'LL BE FORCED TO THINK ABOUT HOW TO PROMOTE YOURSELF ABOVE OTHER PEOPLE.
IT'S A GOOD THING FOR SOMEONE LIKE YOU...
...WHO KEEPS IT A SECRET THAT YOU'RE APPEARING AS A REGULAR ON A PRIME-TIME SHOW THAT'S BEING BROADCAST NATION-WIDE.
Even if you're in a Bird suit.
mumble
......
I CAN'T BELIEVE THAT YOU DON'T WAN' TO BOAST ABOUT IT.
There is some-thing really wrong with you.
NO...
...THAT'S BECAUSE THERE ARE TWO PEOPLE I REALLY WANT TO KEEP IT A SECRET FROM.
...
HMM?
EVEN IF I DIDN'T HAVE TO KEEP IT A SECRET, WOULD I **WANT** TO BOAST ABOUT IT TO OTHER PEOPLE?
NO...
Would I?
WELL...
...IN ANY CASE...
...GO HOME AND GO TO BED EARLY TODAY...
THEN GO TO BED EARLY...
...TODAY...
...AND DO YOUR BEST TOMOR-ROW!
...AND...

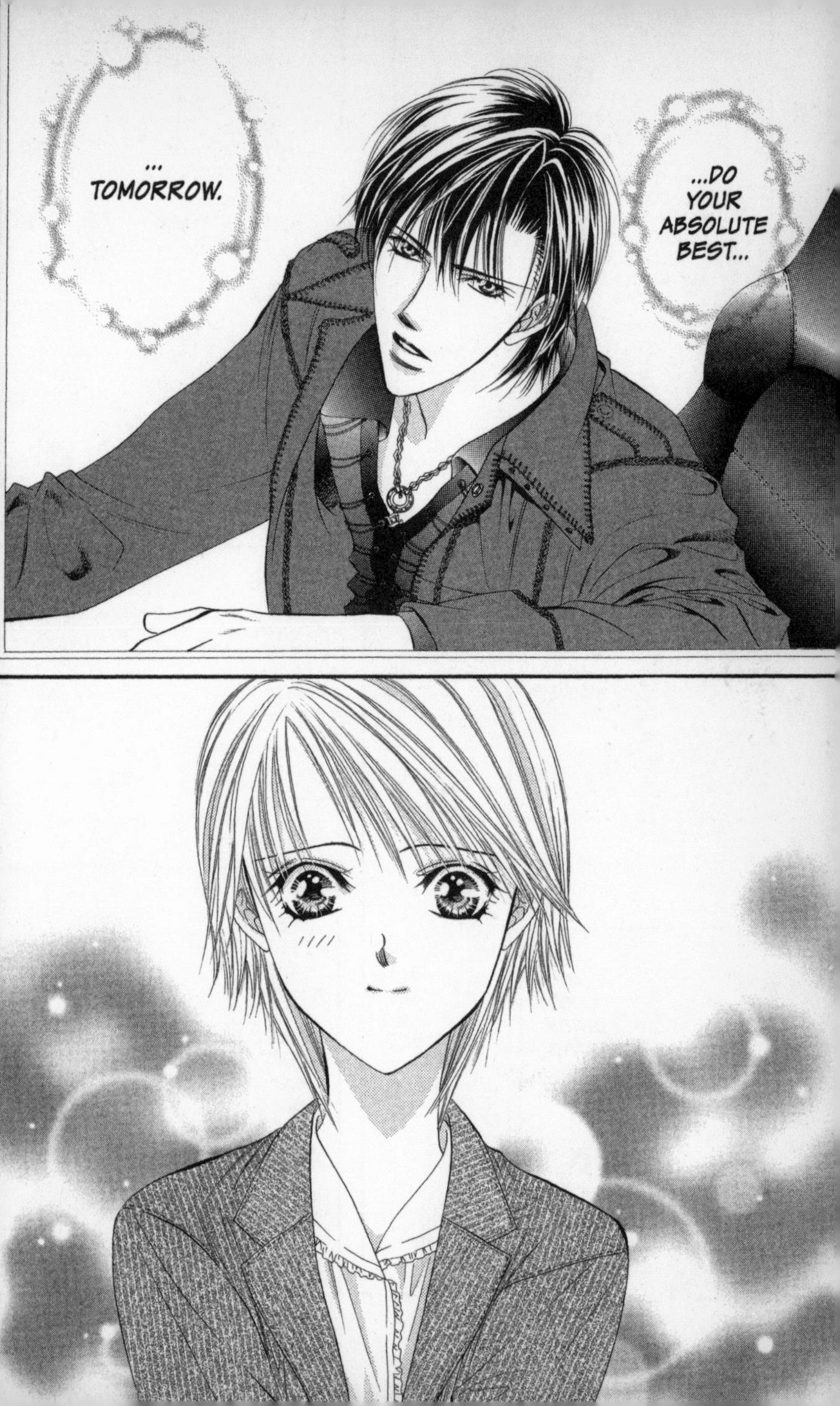
...DO YOUR ABSOLUTE BEST...
... TOMORROW.

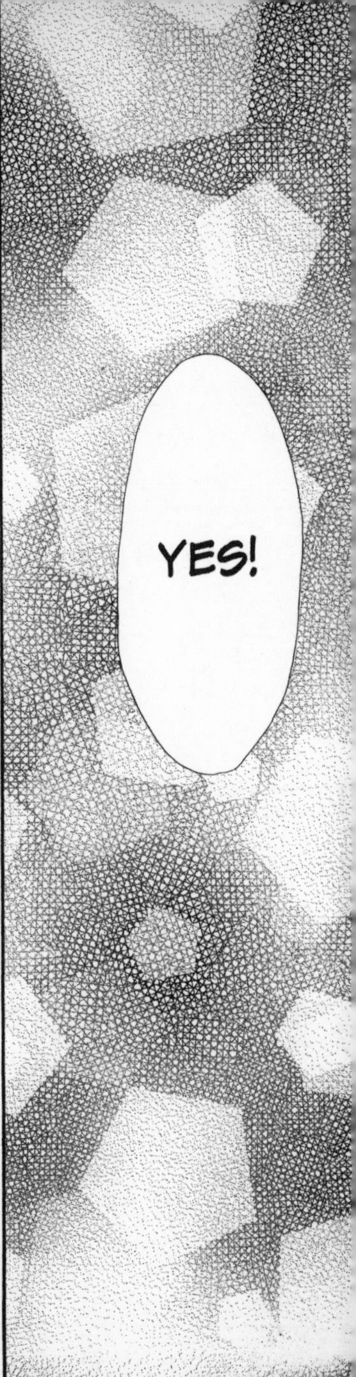
YES!
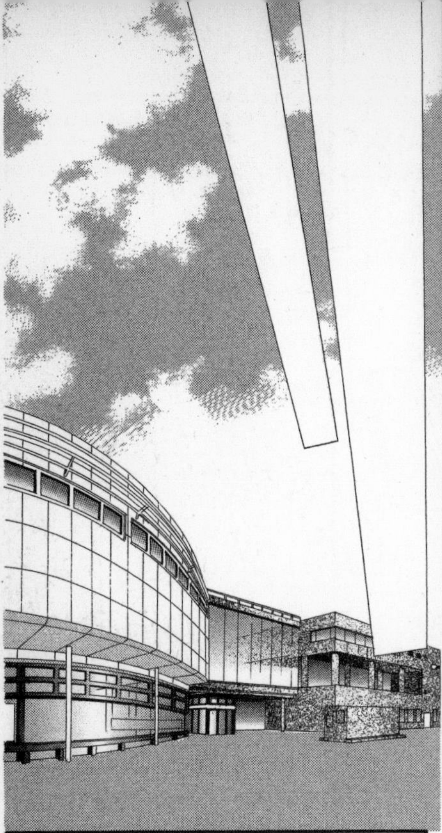
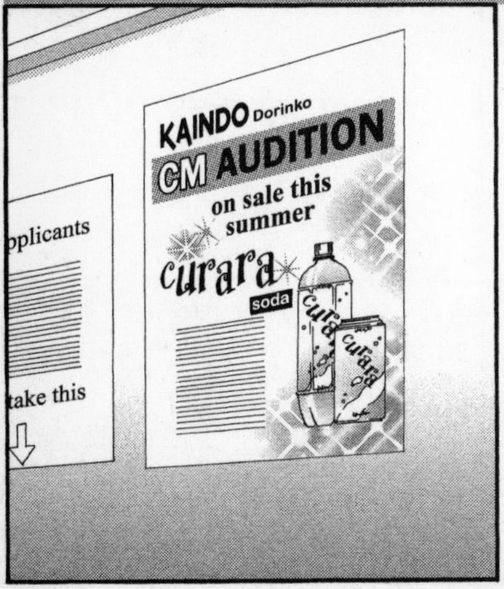
KAINDO Dorinko
CM AUDITION
on sale this summer
curara
soda
pplicants
take this

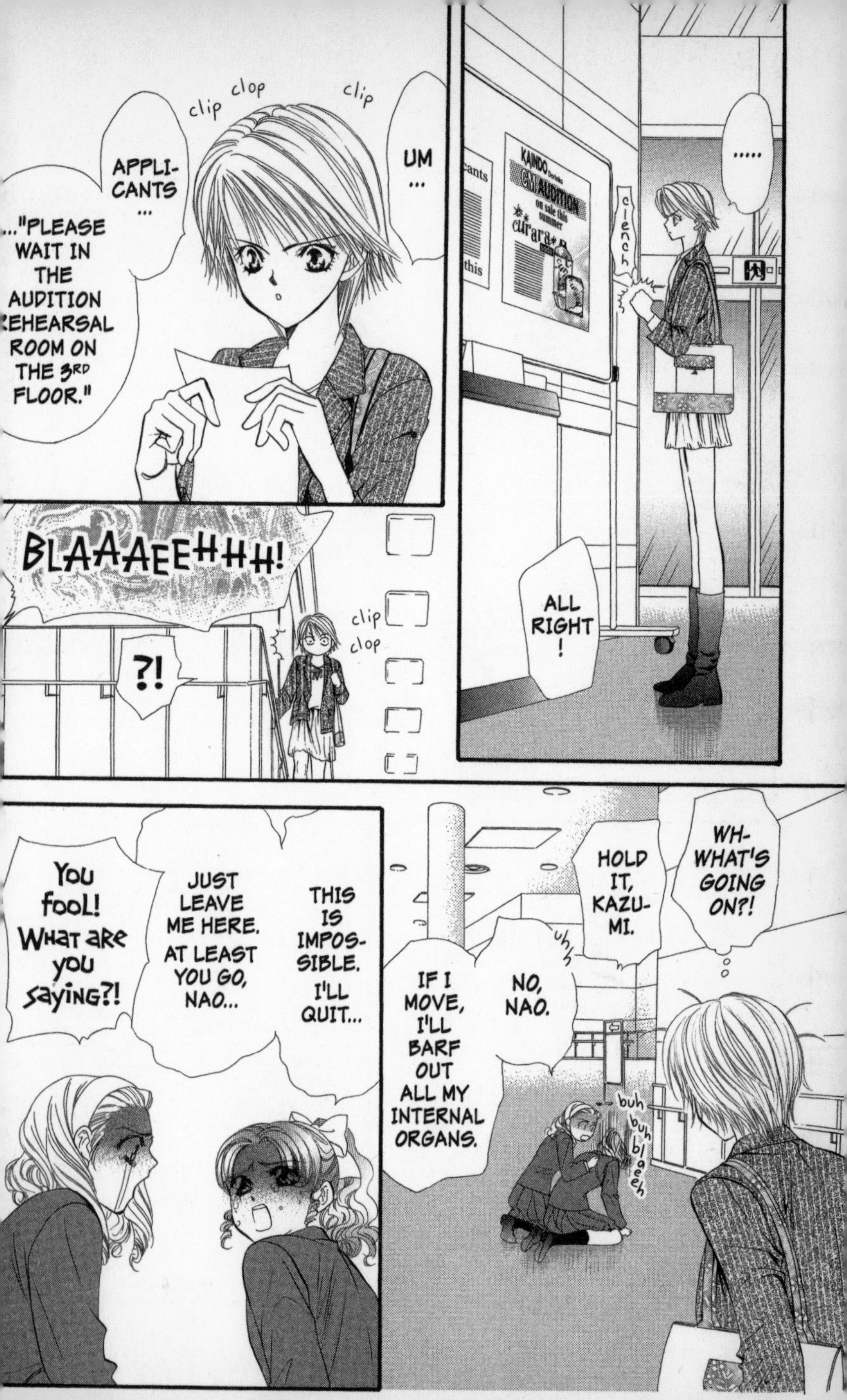
.....
clench
ALL RIGHT!
clip
clop
clip
UM ...
APPLICANTS ...
..."PLEASE WAIT IN THE AUDITION REHEARSAL ROOM ON THE 3RD FLOOR."
BLAAAEEHHHH!
?!
clip
clop
WH-WHAT'S GOING ON?!
HOLD IT, KAZUMI.
uh
NO, NAO.
IF I MOVE, I'LL BARF OUT ALL MY INTERNAL ORGANS.
buh
buh
blaeeh
THIS IS IMPOSSIBLE. I'LL QUIT...
JUST LEAVE ME HERE. AT LEAST YOU GO, NAO...
You fool! What are you saying?!

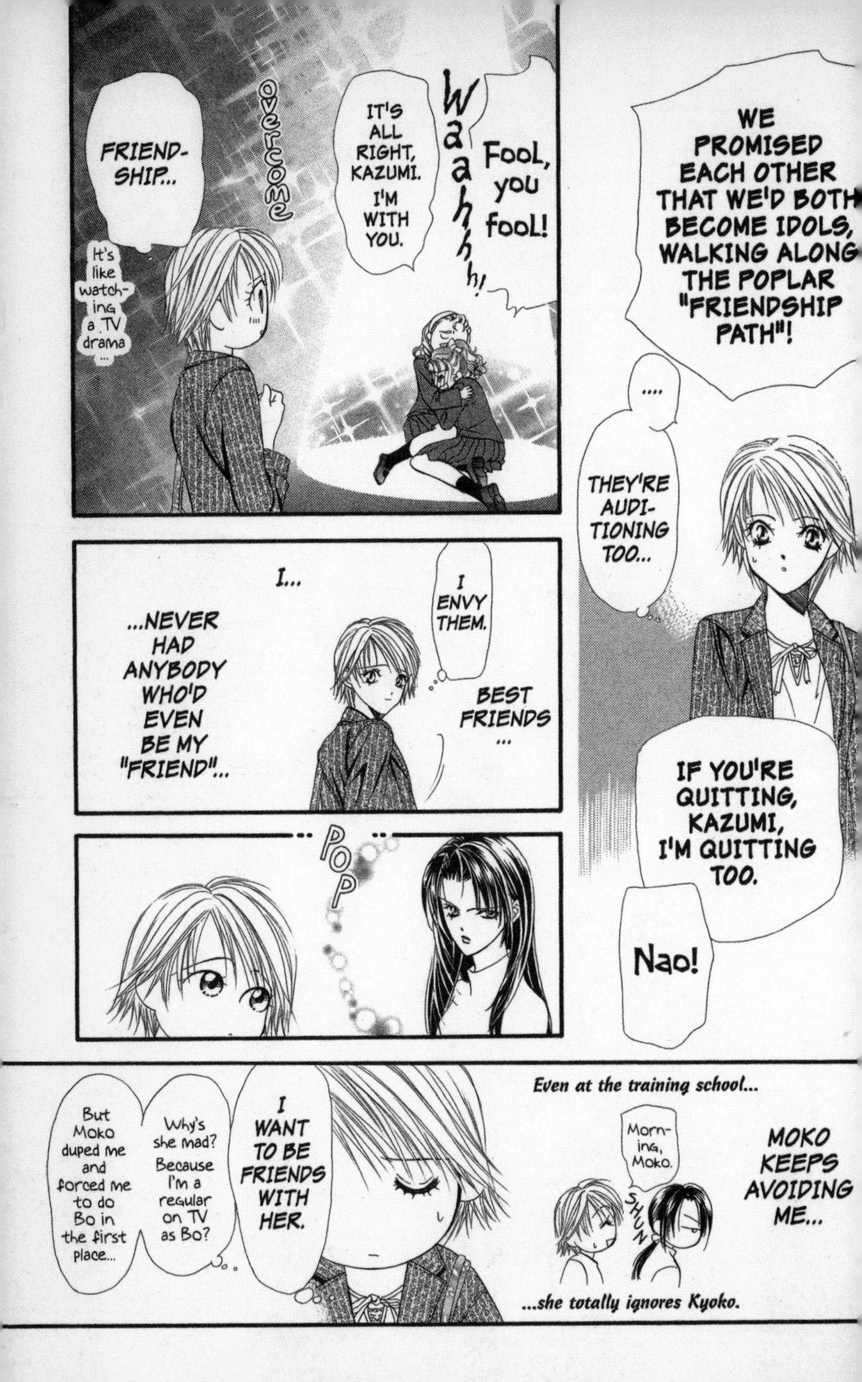
WE PROMISED EACH OTHER THAT WE'D BOTH BECOME IDOLS, WALKING ALONG THE POPLAR "FRIENDSHIP PATH"!
....
THEY'RE AUDITIONING TOO...
IF YOU'RE QUITTING, KAZUMI, I'M QUITTING TOO.
Nao!
Fool, you fool!
Waahhhh!
IT'S ALL RIGHT, KAZUMI. I'M WITH YOU.
overcome
FRIENDSHIP...
It's like watching a TV drama...
I ENVY THEM.
BEST FRIENDS...
I...
...NEVER HAD ANYBODY WHO'D EVEN BE MY "FRIEND"...
POP
Even at the training school...
MOKO KEEPS AVOIDING ME...
Morning, Moko.
SHUN
...she totally ignores Kyoko.
I WANT TO BE FRIENDS WITH HER.
Why's she mad? Because I'm a regular on TV as Bo?
But Moko duped me and forced me to do Bo in the first place...

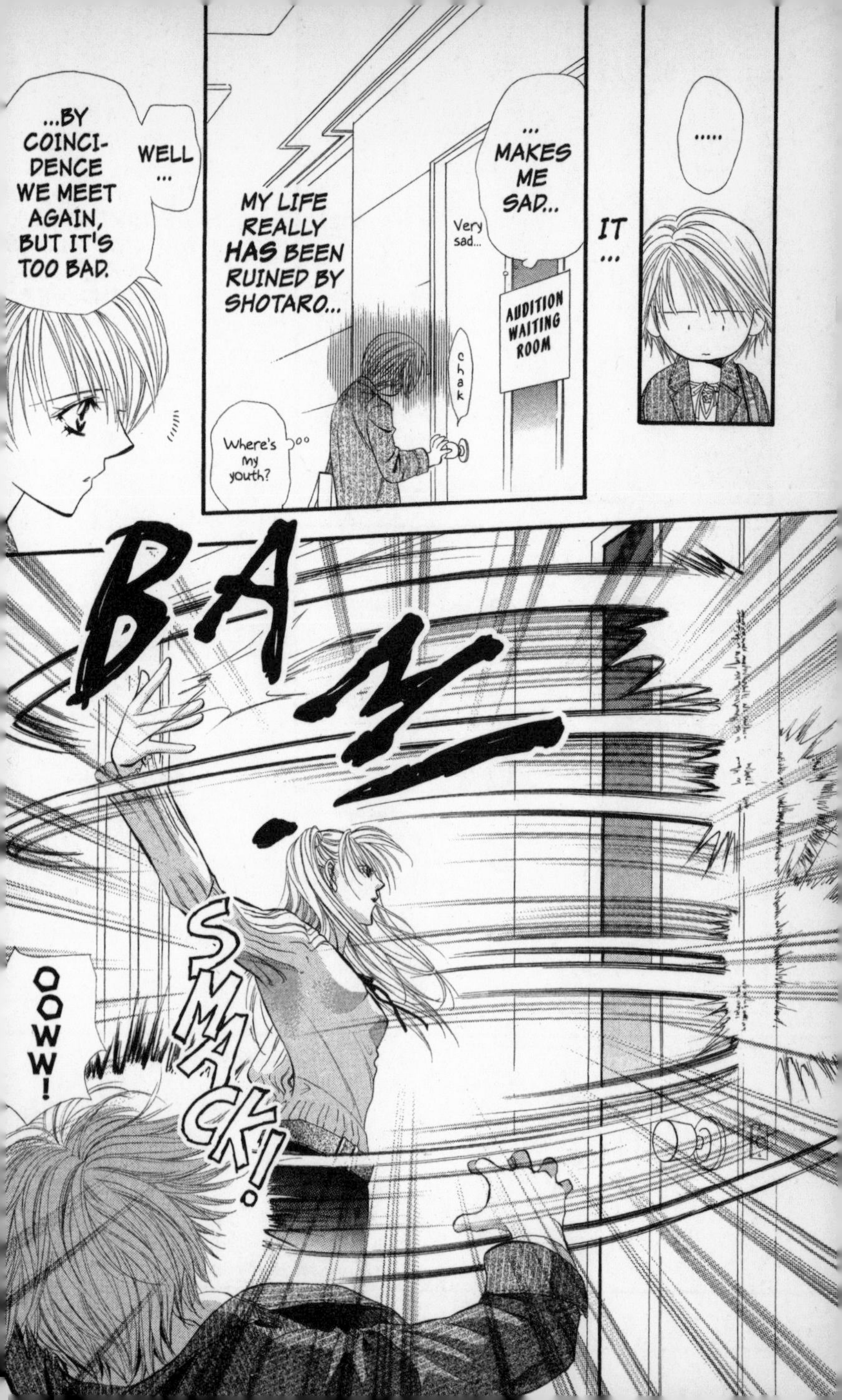
.....
IT ...
... MAKES ME SAD...
Very sad...
AUDITION WAITING ROOM
MY LIFE REALLY HAS BEEN RUINED BY SHOTARO...
chak
Where's my youth?
WELL ...
...BY COINCI-DENCE WE MEET AGAIN, BUT IT'S TOO BAD.
BAM
SMACK!
OOWW!

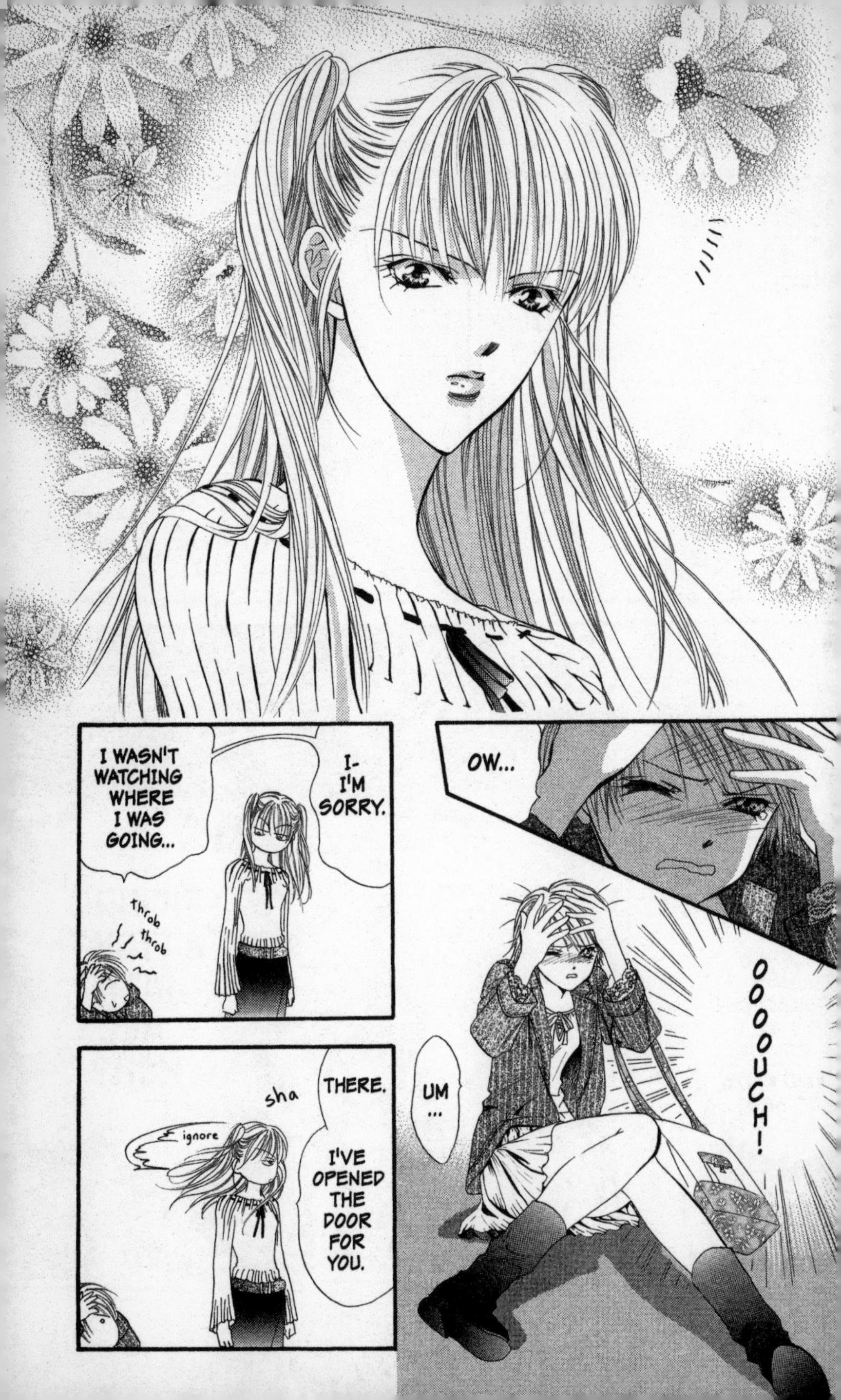
OW...
OOOOUCH!
UM...
I- I'M SORRY.
I WASN'T WATCHING WHERE I WAS GOING...
throb throb
THERE.
I'VE OPENED THE DOOR FOR YOU.
sha
ignore

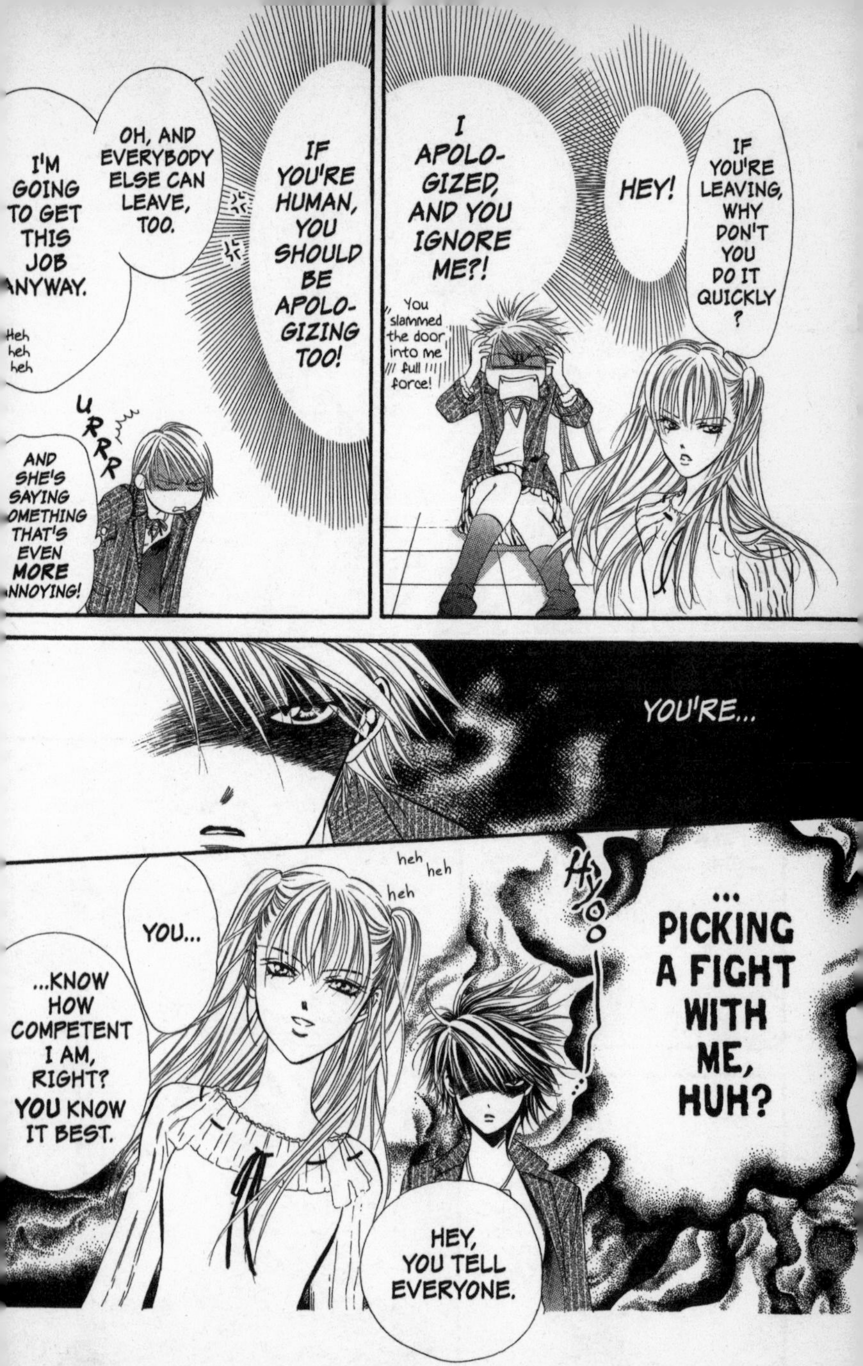

IF YOU'RE LEAVING, WHY DON'T YOU DO IT QUICKLY?
HEY!
I APOLOGIZED, AND YOU IGNORE ME?!
You slammed the door into me full force!
IF YOU'RE HUMAN, YOU SHOULD BE APOLOGIZING TOO!
OH, AND EVERYBODY ELSE CAN LEAVE, TOO.
I'M GOING TO GET THIS JOB NYWAY.
Heh heh heh
URRR
AND SHE'S SAYING OMETHING THAT'S EVEN MORE NNOYING!
YOU'RE...
...PICKING A FIGHT WITH ME, HUH?
Hyoo
heh heh heh
YOU...
...KNOW HOW COMPETENT I AM, RIGHT? YOU KNOW IT BEST.
HEY, YOU TELL EVERYONE.

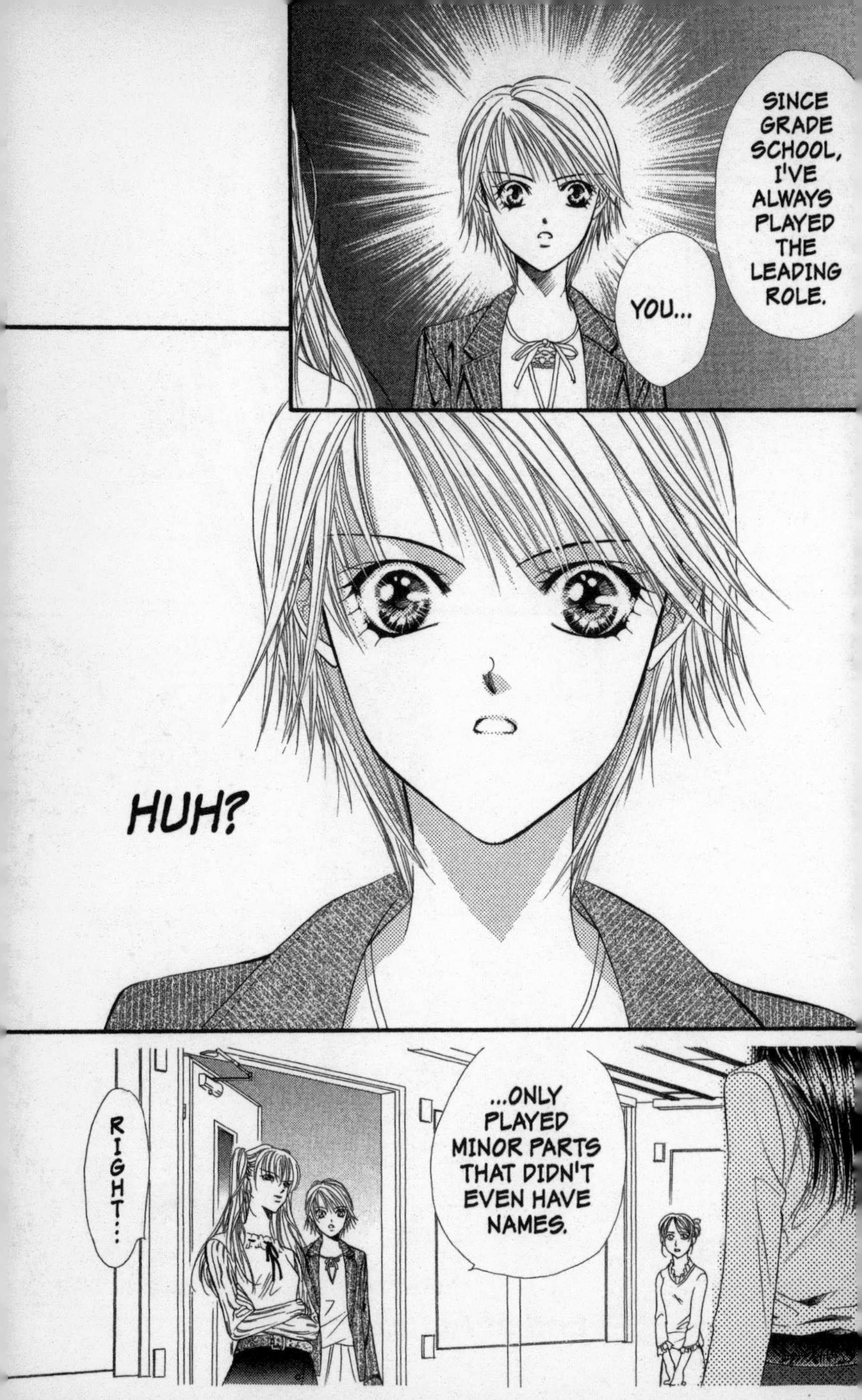
SINCE GRADE SCHOOL, I'VE ALWAYS PLAYED THE LEADING ROLE.
YOU...
HUH?
...ONLY PLAYED MINOR PARTS THAT DIDN'T EVEN HAVE NAMES.
RIGHT...

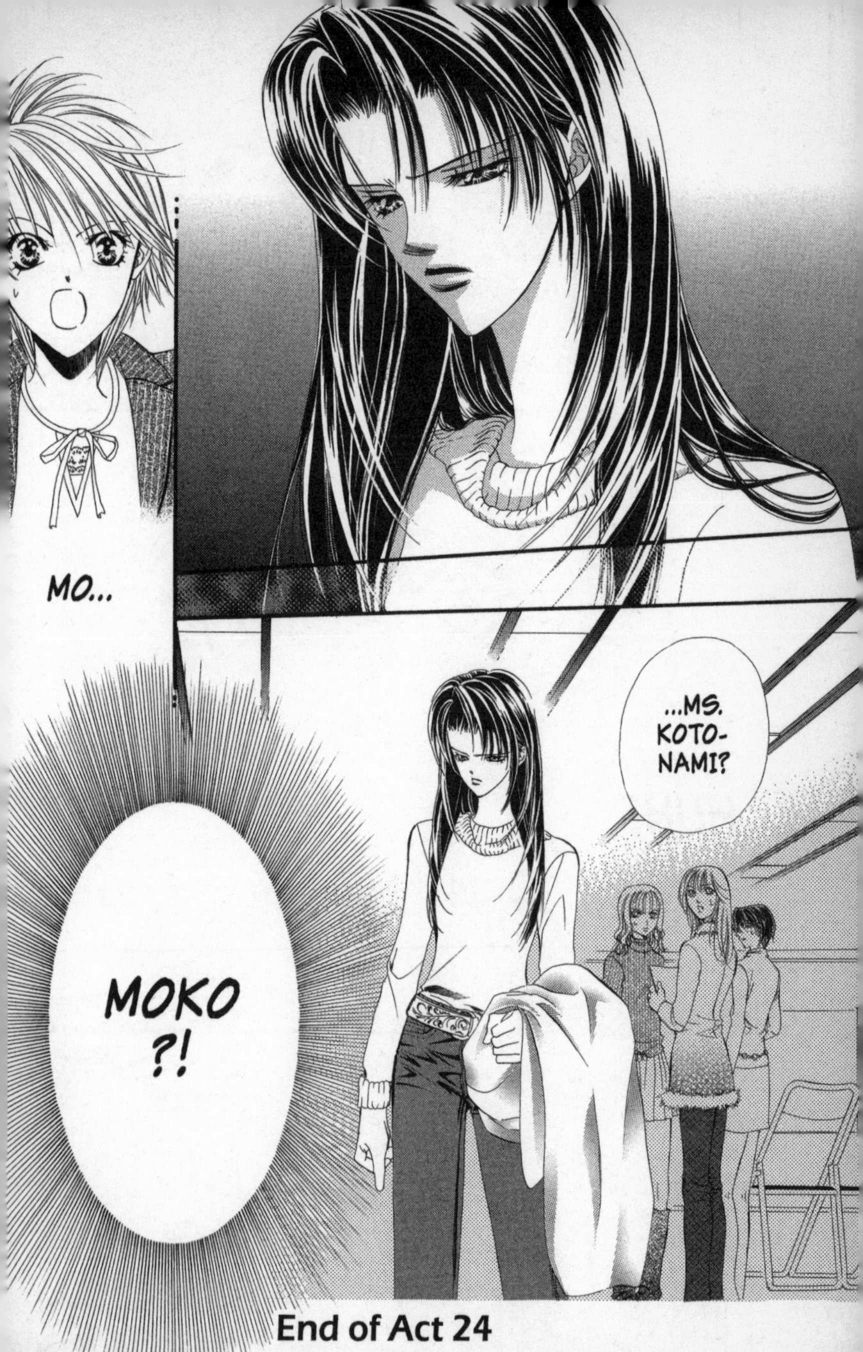
MO...
...MS. KOTO-NAMI?
MOKO ?!

End of Act 24

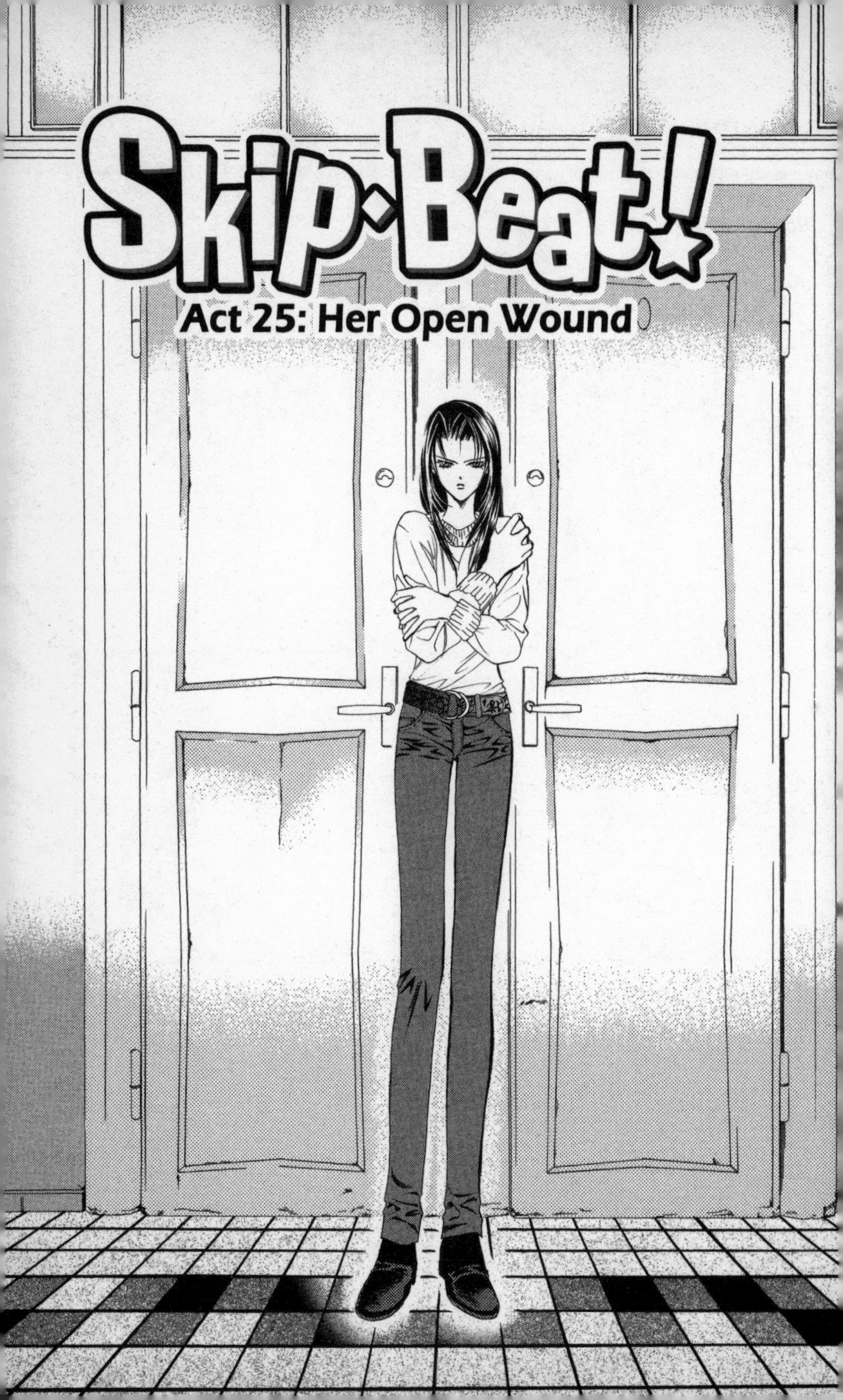
Skip·Beat!
Act 25: Her Open Wound

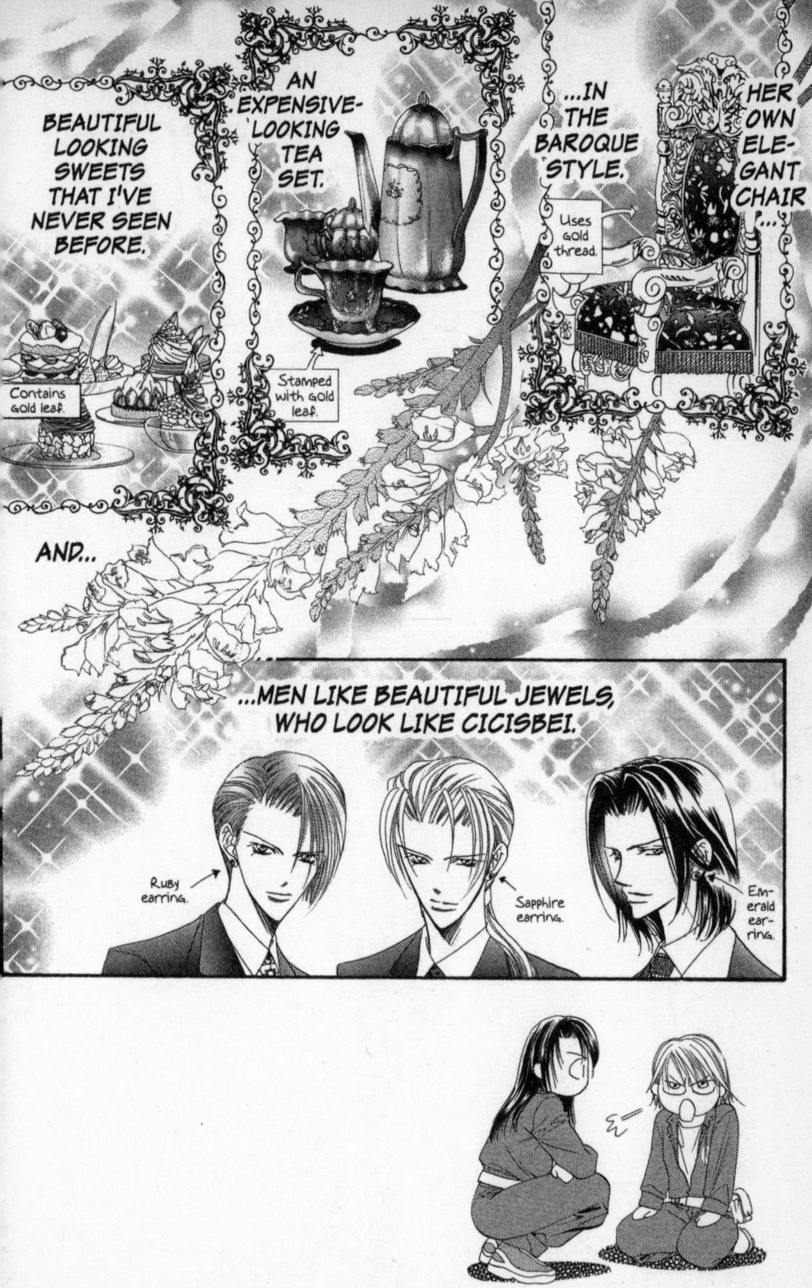
HER OWN ELE-GANT CHAIR...
...IN THE BAROQUE STYLE.
Uses gold thread.
AN EXPENSIVE-LOOKING TEA SET.
Stamped with gold leaf.
BEAUTIFUL LOOKING SWEETS THAT I'VE NEVER SEEN BEFORE.
Contains gold leaf.
AND...
...MEN LIKE BEAUTIFUL JEWELS, WHO LOOK LIKE CICISBEI.
Em-erald ear-ring.
Sapphire earring.
Ruby earring.

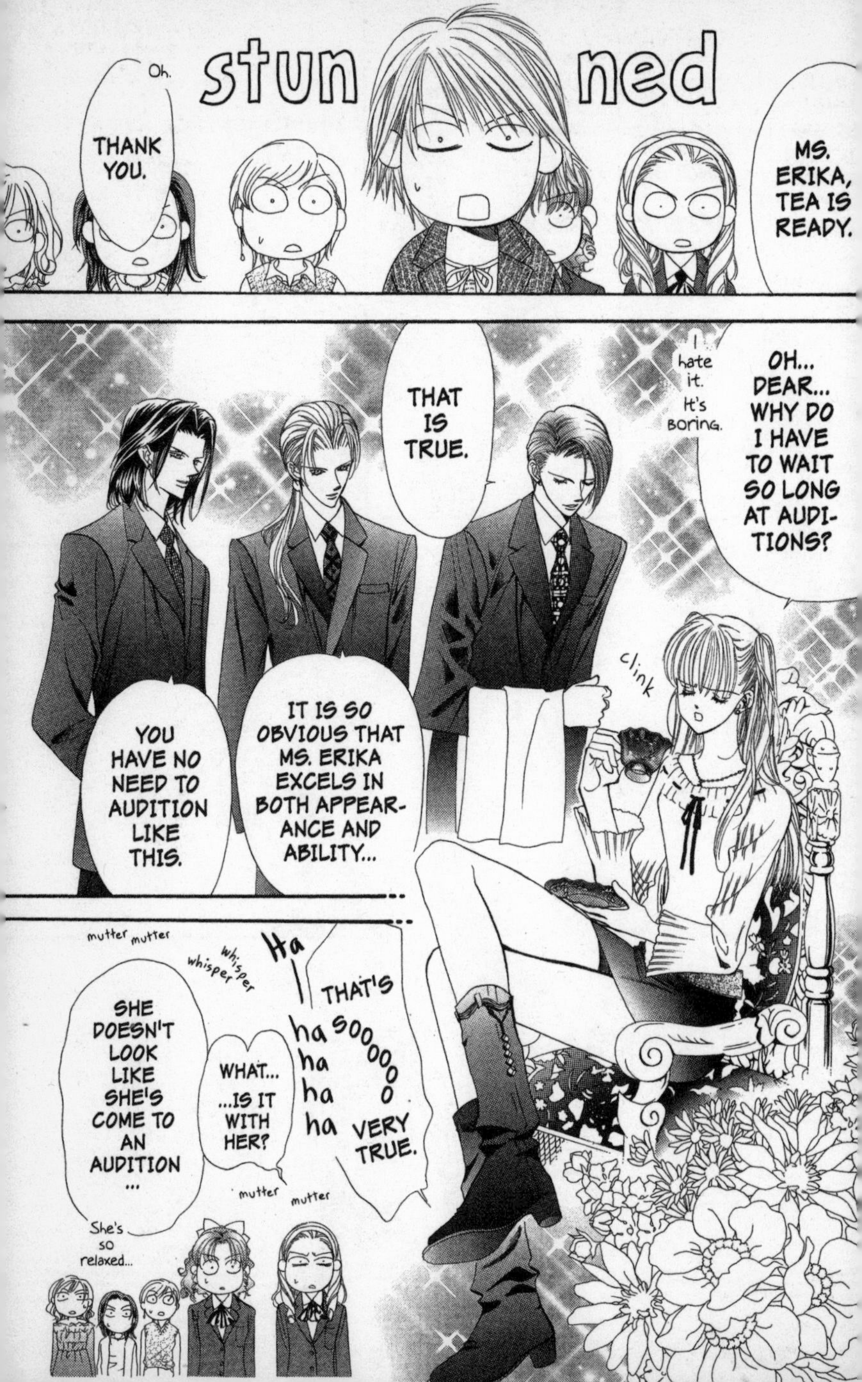
MS. ERIKA, TEA IS READY.
stunned
Oh.
THANK YOU.
OH... DEAR... WHY DO I HAVE TO WAIT SO LONG AT AUDITIONS?
I hate it. It's boring.
THAT IS TRUE.
clink
IT IS SO OBVIOUS THAT MS. ERIKA EXCELS IN BOTH APPEARANCE AND ABILITY...
YOU HAVE NO NEED TO AUDITION LIKE THIS.
THAT'S SOOOOOOO VERY TRUE.
Ha ha ha ha ha
whisper whisper
WHAT... ...IS IT WITH HER?
mutter mutter
SHE DOESN'T LOOK LIKE SHE'S COME TO AN AUDITION ...
mutter mutter
She's so relaxed...

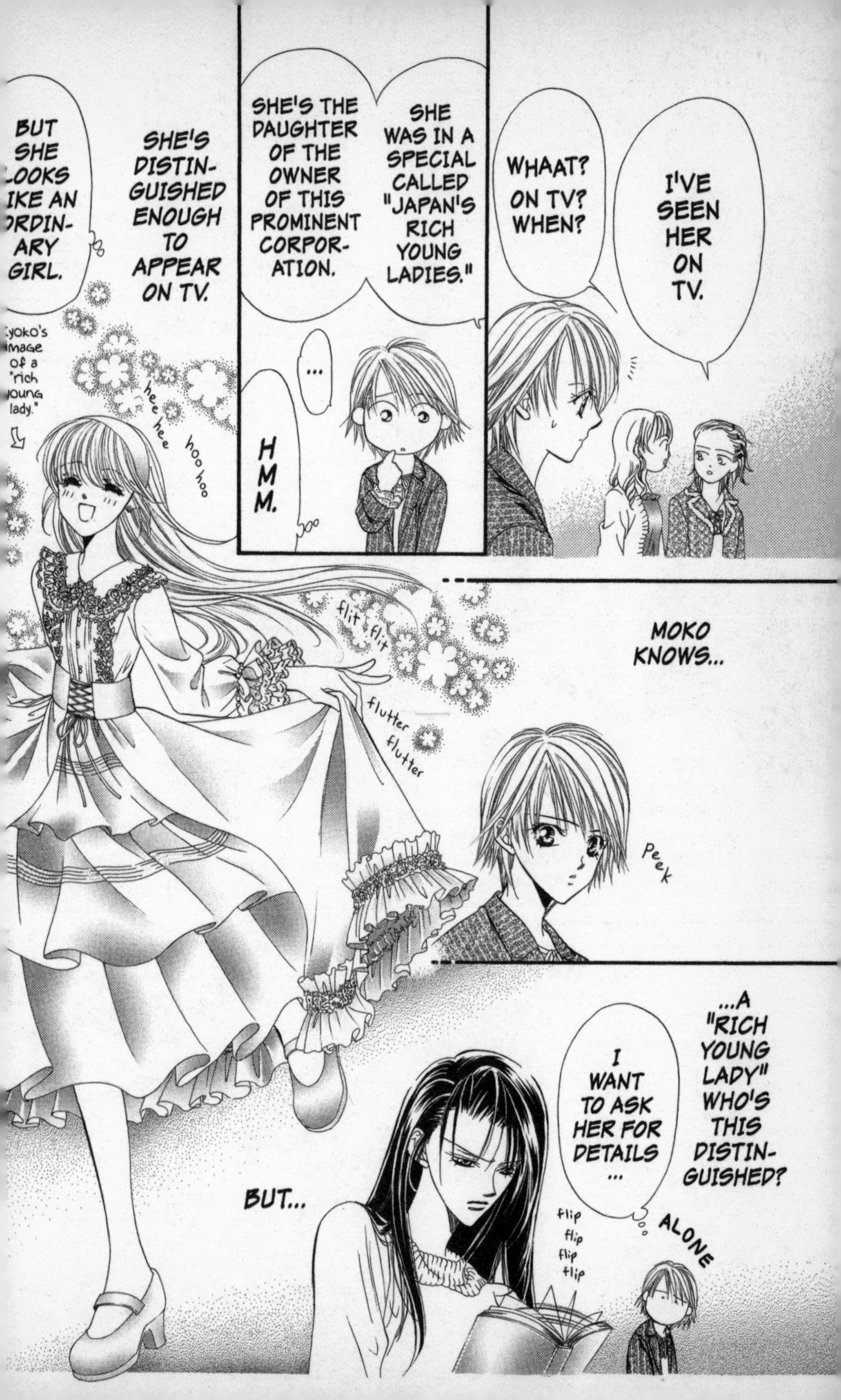
I'VE SEEN HER ON TV.
WHAAT? ON TV? WHEN?
SHE WAS IN A SPECIAL CALLED "JAPAN'S RICH YOUNG LADIES."
SHE'S THE DAUGHTER OF THE OWNER OF THIS PROMINENT CORPORATION.
...
HMM.
SHE'S DISTINGUISHED ENOUGH TO APPEAR ON TV.
BUT SHE LOOKS LIKE AN ORDINARY GIRL.
Kyoko's image of a "rich young lady."
hee hee
hoo hoo
flit flit
flutter flutter
MOKO KNOWS...
Peek
...A "RICH YOUNG LADY" WHO'S THIS DISTINGUISHED?
I WANT TO ASK HER FOR DETAILS...
BUT...
ALONE
flip flip flip flip

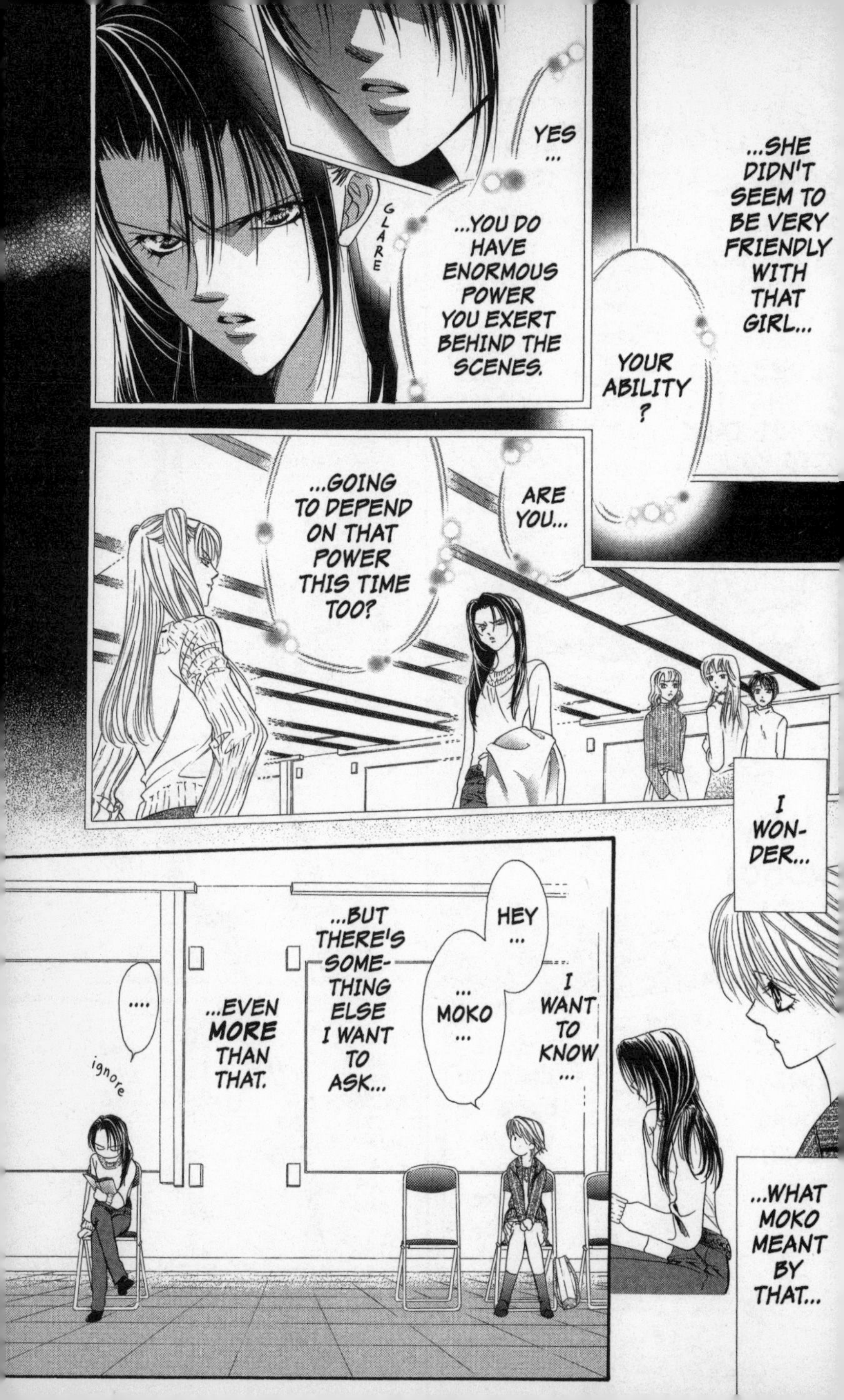
...SHE DIDN'T SEEM TO BE VERY FRIENDLY WITH THAT GIRL...
YOUR ABILITY?
YES...
...YOU DO HAVE ENORMOUS POWER YOU EXERT BEHIND THE SCENES.
GLARE
ARE YOU...
...GOING TO DEPEND ON THAT POWER THIS TIME TOO?
I WONDER...
...WHAT MOKO MEANT BY THAT...
HEY...
...MOKO...
I WANT TO KNOW...
...BUT THERE'S SOMETHING ELSE I WANT TO ASK...
...EVEN MORE THAN THAT.
....
ignore

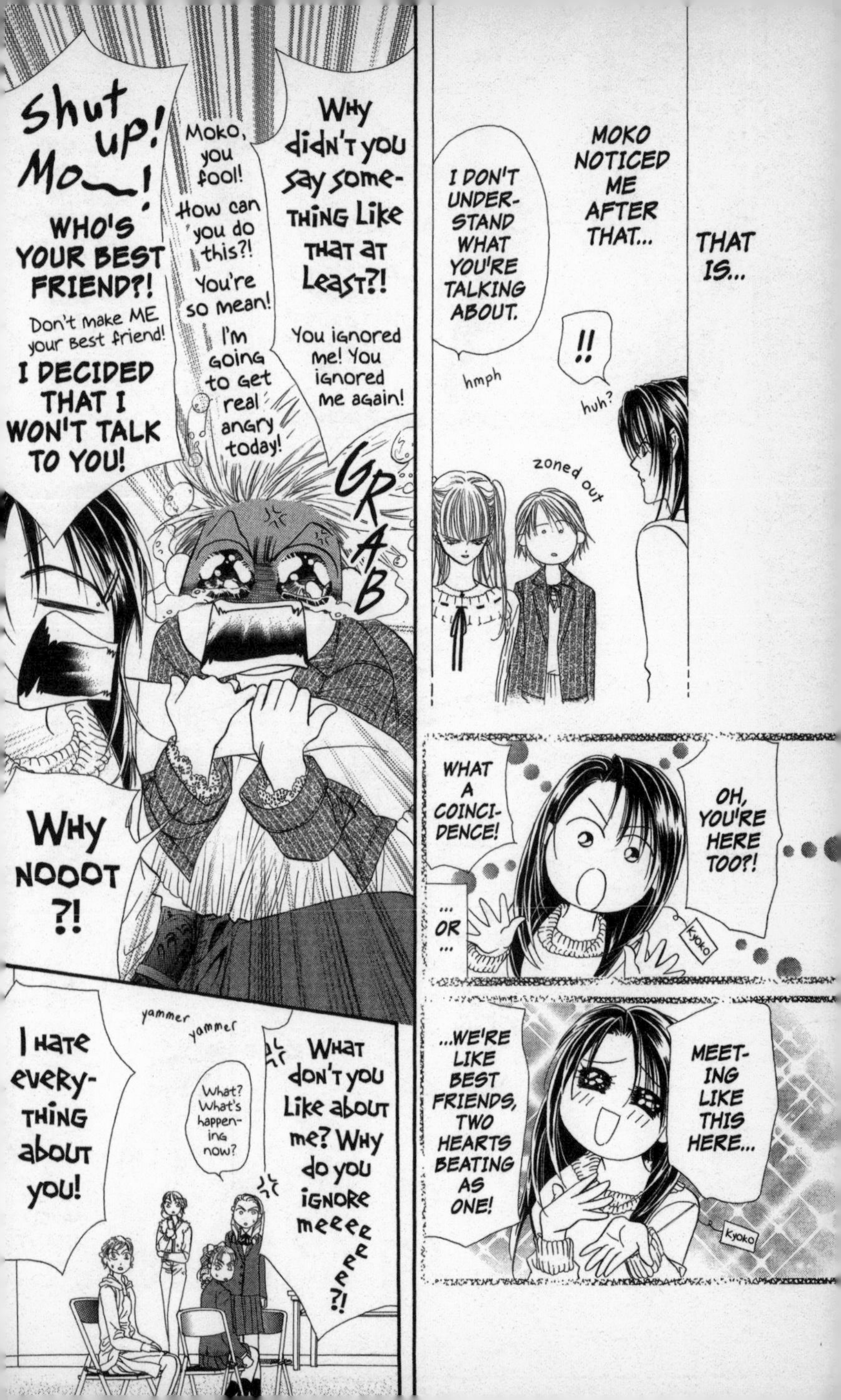
THAT IS...
MOKO NOTICED ME AFTER THAT...
!!
huh?
I DON'T UNDERSTAND WHAT YOU'RE TALKING ABOUT.
hmph
zoned out
OH, YOU'RE HERE TOO?!
Kyoko
WHAT A COINCIDENCE!
...OR...
MEETING LIKE THIS HERE...
...WE'RE LIKE BEST FRIENDS, TWO HEARTS BEATING AS ONE!
Kyoko
Why didn't you say something like that at least?!
You ignored me! You ignored me again!
Moko, you fool! How can you do this?! You're so mean! I'm going to get real angry today!
GRAB
Shut up! Mo~! WHO'S YOUR BEST FRIEND?!
Don't make ME your best friend!
I DECIDED THAT I WON'T TALK TO YOU!
Why NOOOT?!
What don't you like about me? Why do you ignore meeeeeee?!
What? What's happening now?
yammer yammer
I hate everything about you!

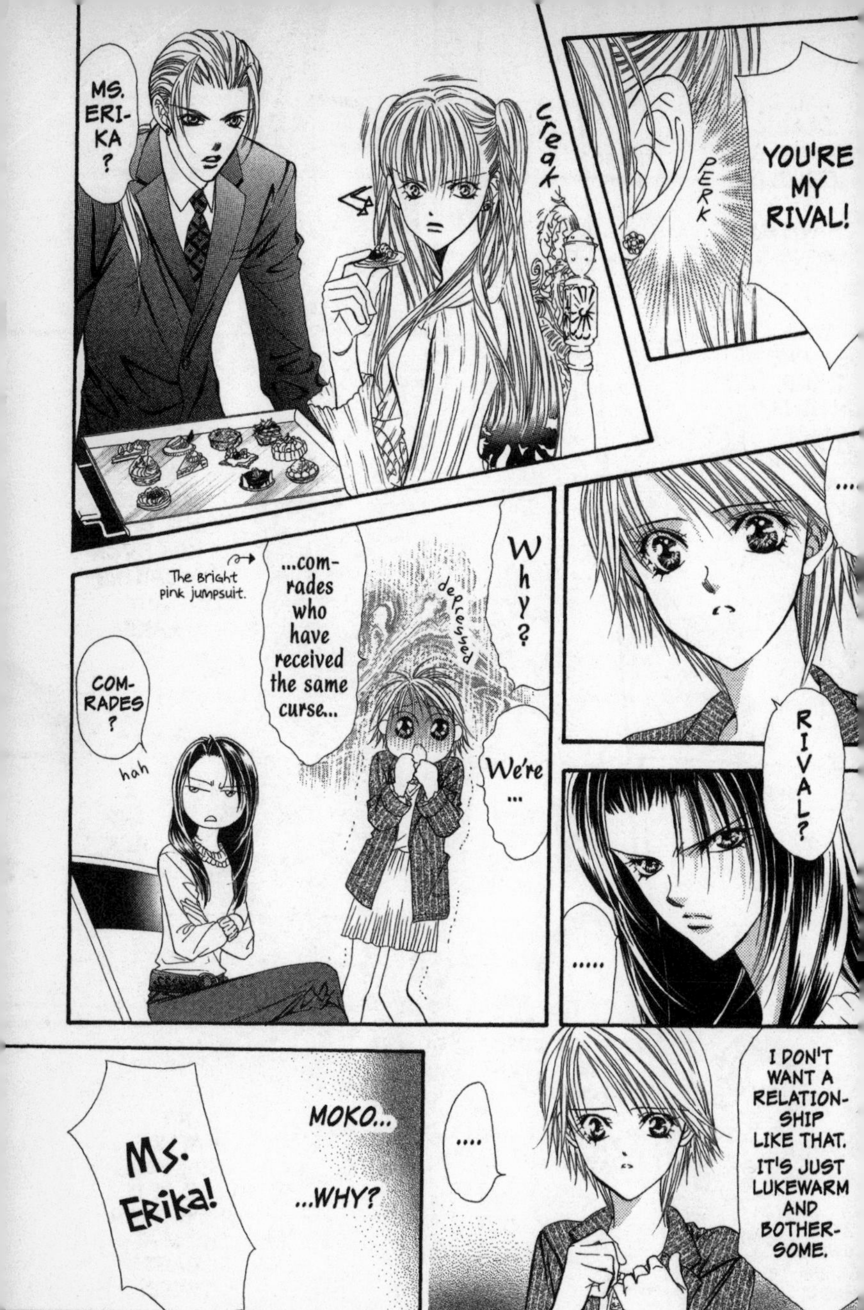
YOU'RE MY RIVAL!
PERK
creak
MS. ERI-KA?
....
RIVAL?
.....
Why?
We're ...
depressed
...com-rades who have received the same curse...
The Bright pink jumpsuit.
COM-RADES?
hah
I DON'T WANT A RELATION-SHIP LIKE THAT.
IT'S JUST LUKEWARM AND BOTHER-SOME.
....
MOKO...
...WHY?
Ms. Erika!

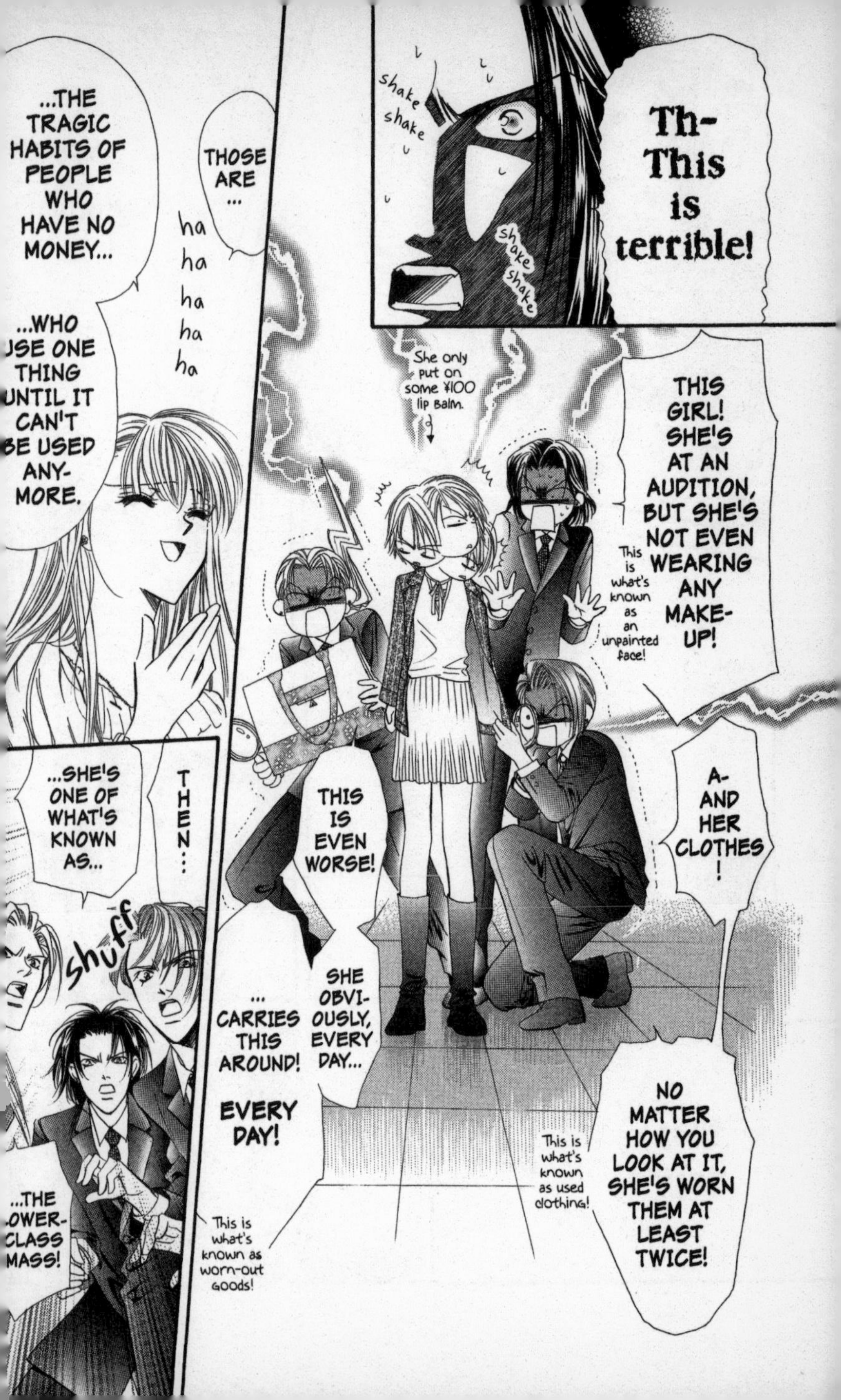
shake shake
shake shake
Th-This is terrible!
THIS GIRL! SHE'S AT AN AUDITION, BUT SHE'S NOT EVEN WEARING ANY MAKE-UP!
This is what's known as an unpainted face!
She only put on some ¥100 lip balm.
A-AND HER CLOTHES!
THIS IS EVEN WORSE!
NO MATTER HOW YOU LOOK AT IT, SHE'S WORN THEM AT LEAST TWICE!
This is what's known as used clothing!
SHE OBVIOUSLY, EVERY DAY...
...CARRIES THIS AROUND!
EVERY DAY!
This is what's known as worn-out goods!
THOSE ARE...
ha ha ha ha ha
...THE TRAGIC HABITS OF PEOPLE WHO HAVE NO MONEY...
...WHO USE ONE THING UNTIL IT CAN'T BE USED ANYMORE.
THEN...
...SHE'S ONE OF WHAT'S KNOWN AS...
Shuff
...THE LOWER-CLASS MASS!

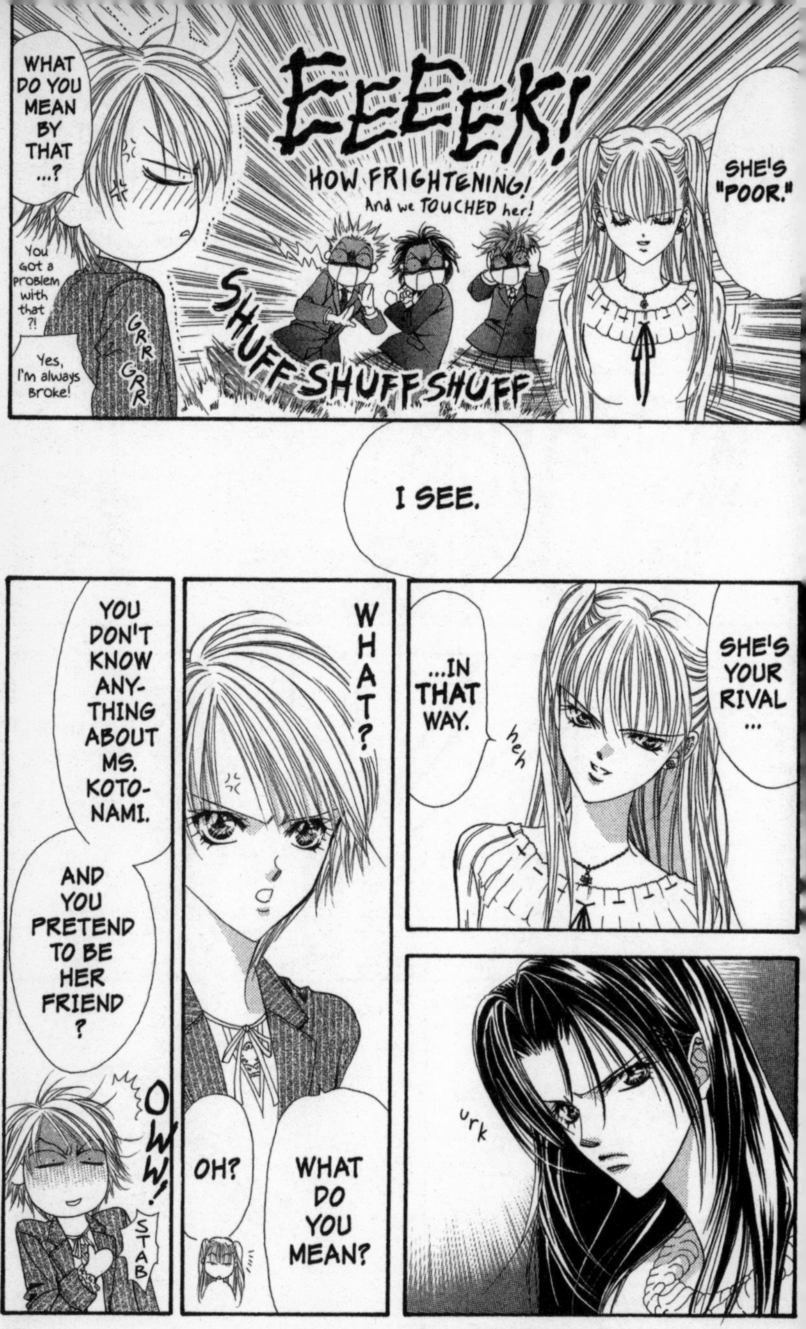
SHE'S "POOR."
EEEEK!
HOW FRIGHTENING!
And we TOUCHED her!
SHUFF SHUFF SHUFF
WHAT DO YOU MEAN BY THAT ...?
You got a problem with that?!
Yes, I'm always broke!
GRR GRR
I SEE.
SHE'S YOUR RIVAL ...
...IN THAT WAY.
heh
urk
WHAT?
OH?
WHAT DO YOU MEAN?
YOU DON'T KNOW ANYTHING ABOUT MS. KOTONAMI.
AND YOU PRETEND TO BE HER FRIEND?
OWW!
STAB

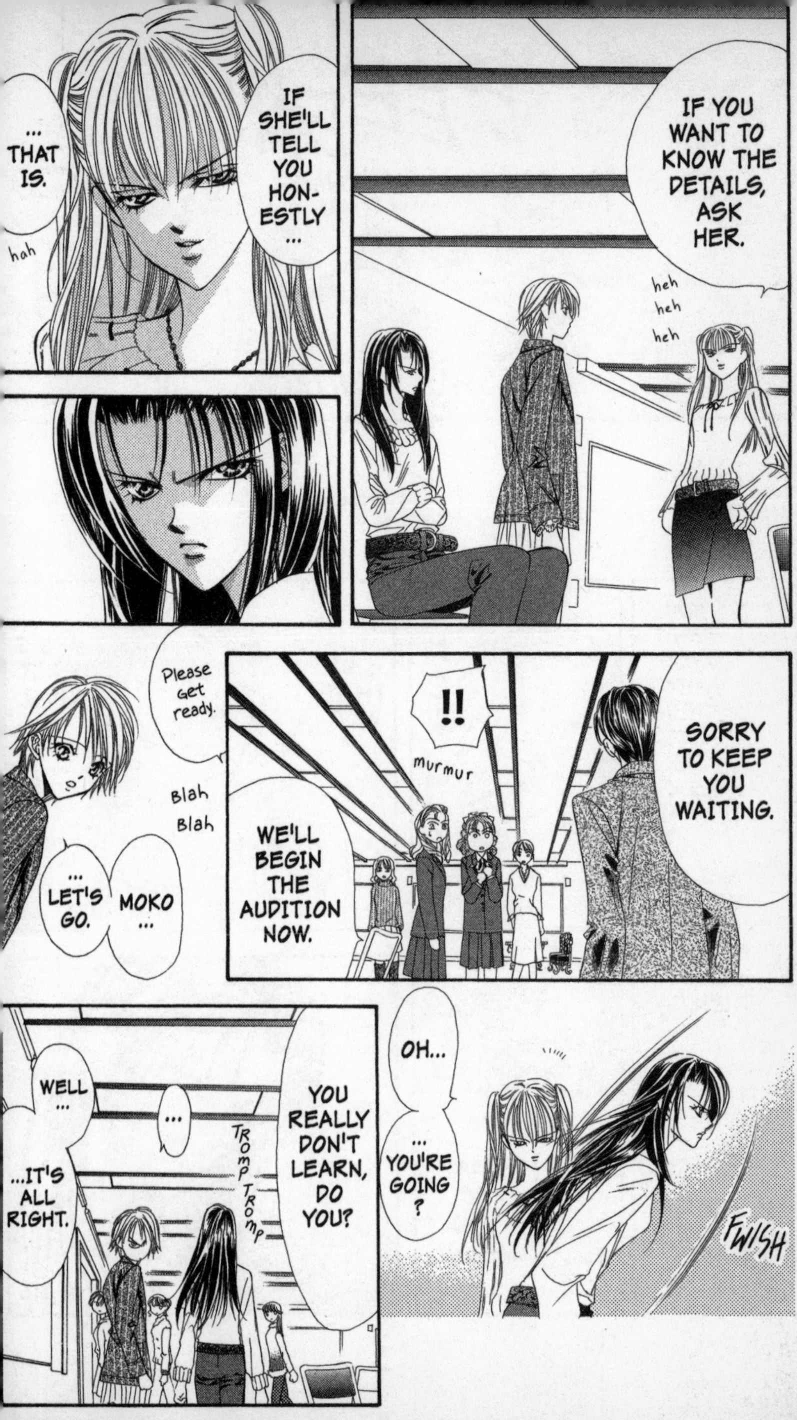
IF YOU WANT TO KNOW THE DETAILS, ASK HER.
heh heh heh
IF SHE'LL TELL YOU HON-ESTLY ...
... THAT IS.
hah
SORRY TO KEEP YOU WAITING.
!!
murmur
WE'LL BEGIN THE AUDITION NOW.
Please get ready.
Blah Blah
MOKO ...
... LET'S GO.
OH...
... YOU'RE GOING ?
FWISH
YOU REALLY DON'T LEARN, DO YOU?
TROMP TROMP TROMP
...
WELL ...
...IT'S ALL RIGHT.

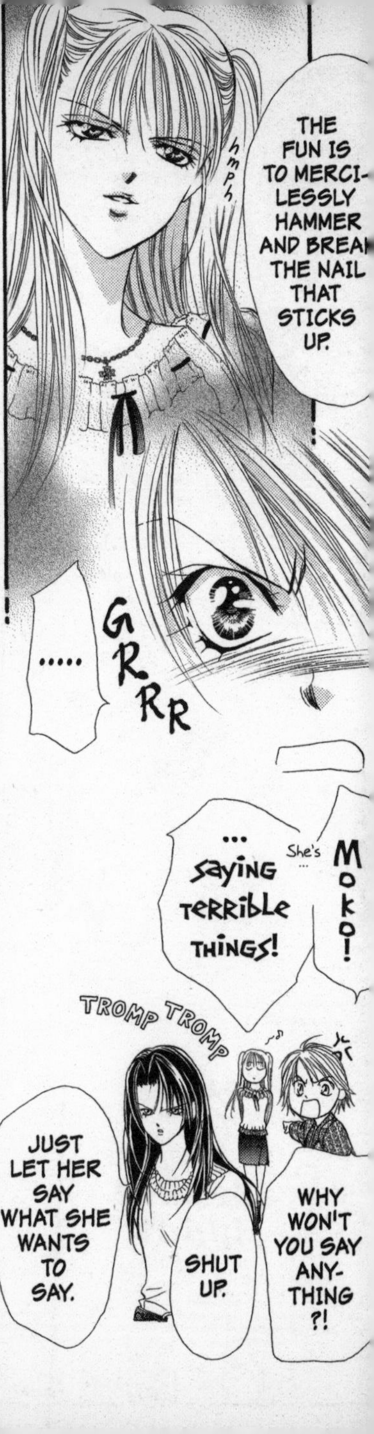
hmph
THE FUN IS TO MERCILESSLY HAMMER AND BREA THE NAIL THAT STICKS UP.
.....
GRRR
MOKO!
She's ...
... saying terrible things!
TROMP TROMP
WHY WON'T YOU SAY ANYTHING?!
SHUT UP.
JUST LET HER SAY WHAT SHE WANTS TO SAY.
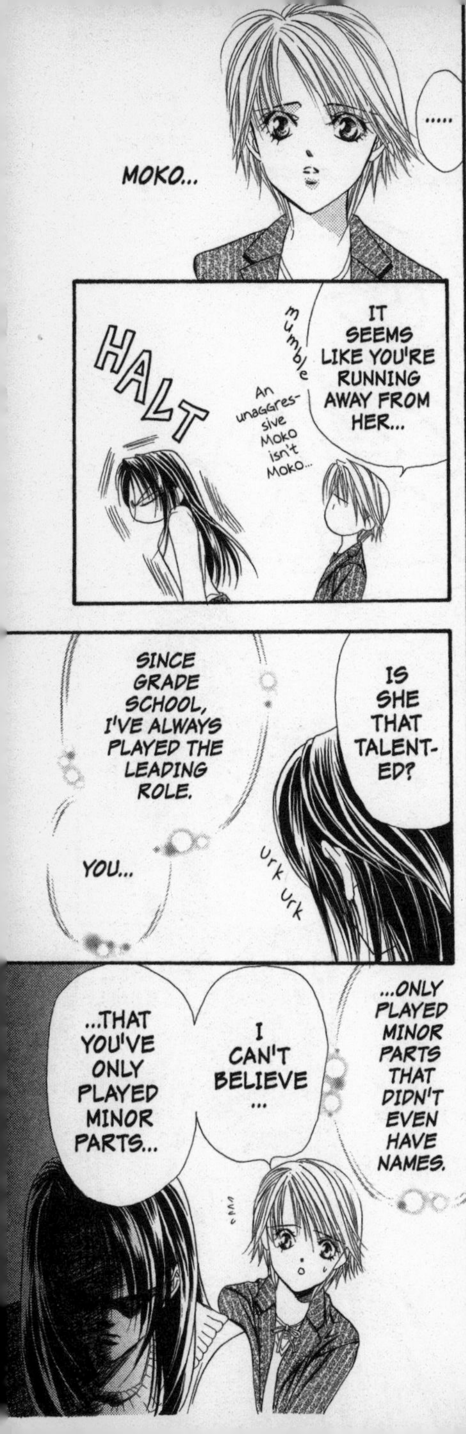
.....
MOKO...
IT SEEMS LIKE YOU'RE RUNNING AWAY FROM HER...
mumble
An unaggressive Moko isn't Moko...
HALT
IS SHE THAT TALENTED?
Urk Urk
SINCE GRADE SCHOOL, I'VE ALWAYS PLAYED THE LEADING ROLE.
YOU...
...ONLY PLAYED MINOR PARTS THAT DIDN'T EVEN HAVE NAMES.
I CAN'T BELIEVE ...
...THAT YOU'VE ONLY PLAYED MINOR PARTS...

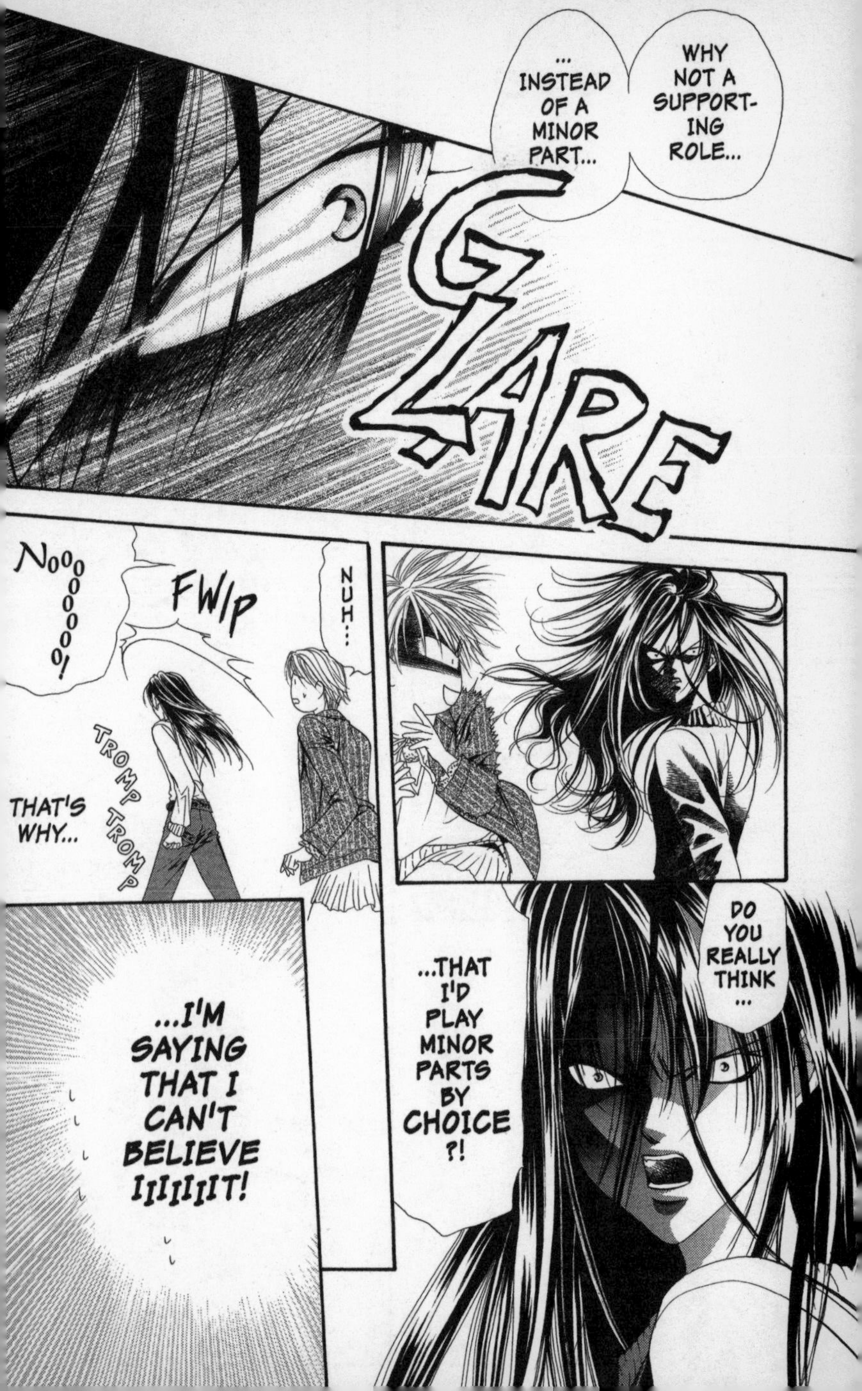
WHY NOT A SUPPORT-ING ROLE...
...INSTEAD OF A MINOR PART...
GLARE
NUH...
FWIP
Nooooooooooo!
TROMP TROMP
THAT'S WHY...
DO YOU REALLY THINK...
...THAT I'D PLAY MINOR PARTS BY CHOICE?!
...I'M SAYING THAT I CAN'T BELIEVE IIIIIIIT!

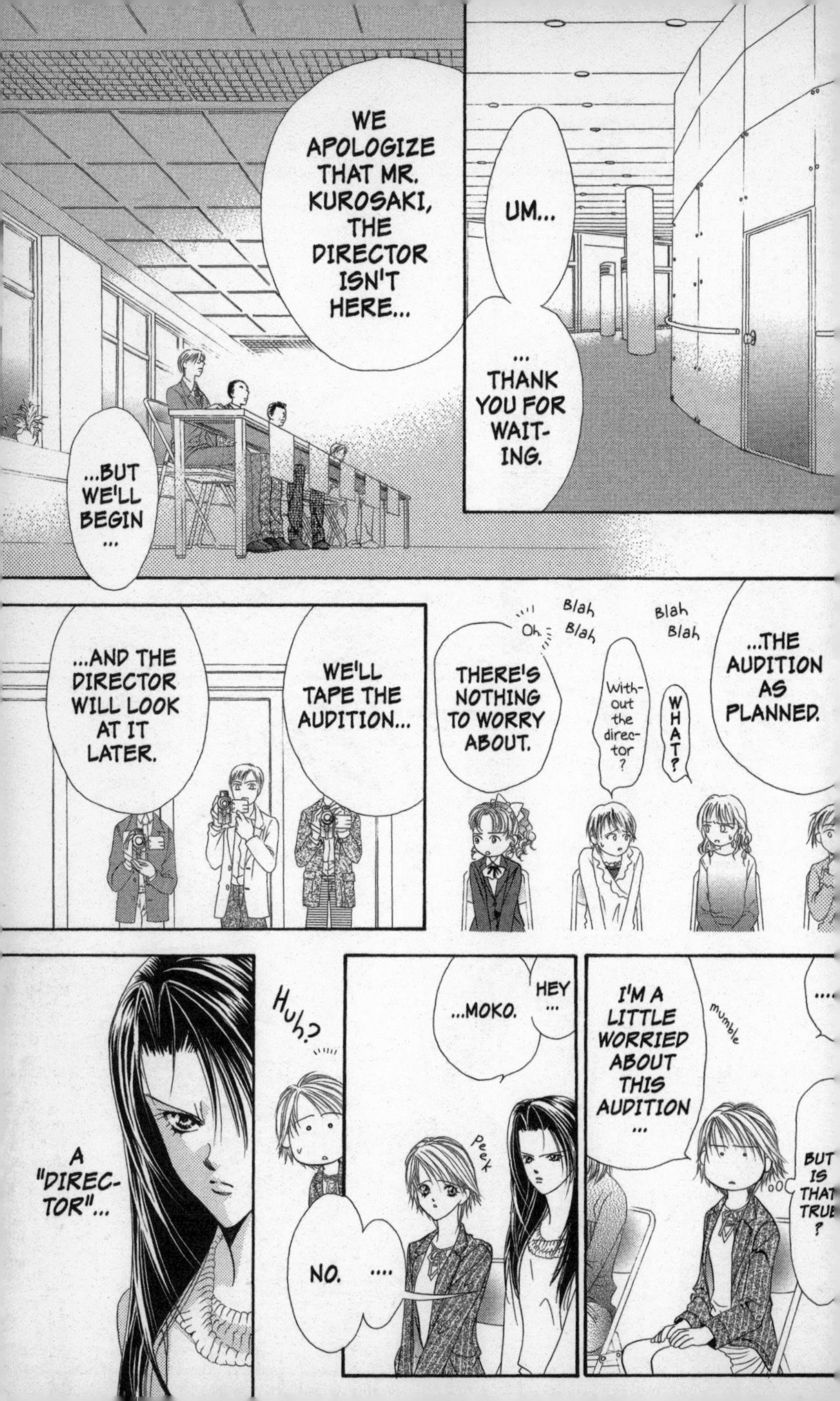
UM...
...THANK YOU FOR WAIT-ING.
WE APOLOGIZE THAT MR. KUROSAKI, THE DIRECTOR ISN'T HERE...
...BUT WE'LL BEGIN...
...THE AUDITION AS PLANNED.
Blah Blah
WHAT?
Blah Blah
Without the director?
Oh.
THERE'S NOTHING TO WORRY ABOUT.
WE'LL TAPE THE AUDITION...
...AND THE DIRECTOR WILL LOOK AT IT LATER.
....
BUT IS THAT TRUE?
mumble
I'M A LITTLE WORRIED ABOUT THIS AUDITION...
HEY...
...MOKO.
Peek
NO. ....
Huh?
A "DIREC-TOR"...

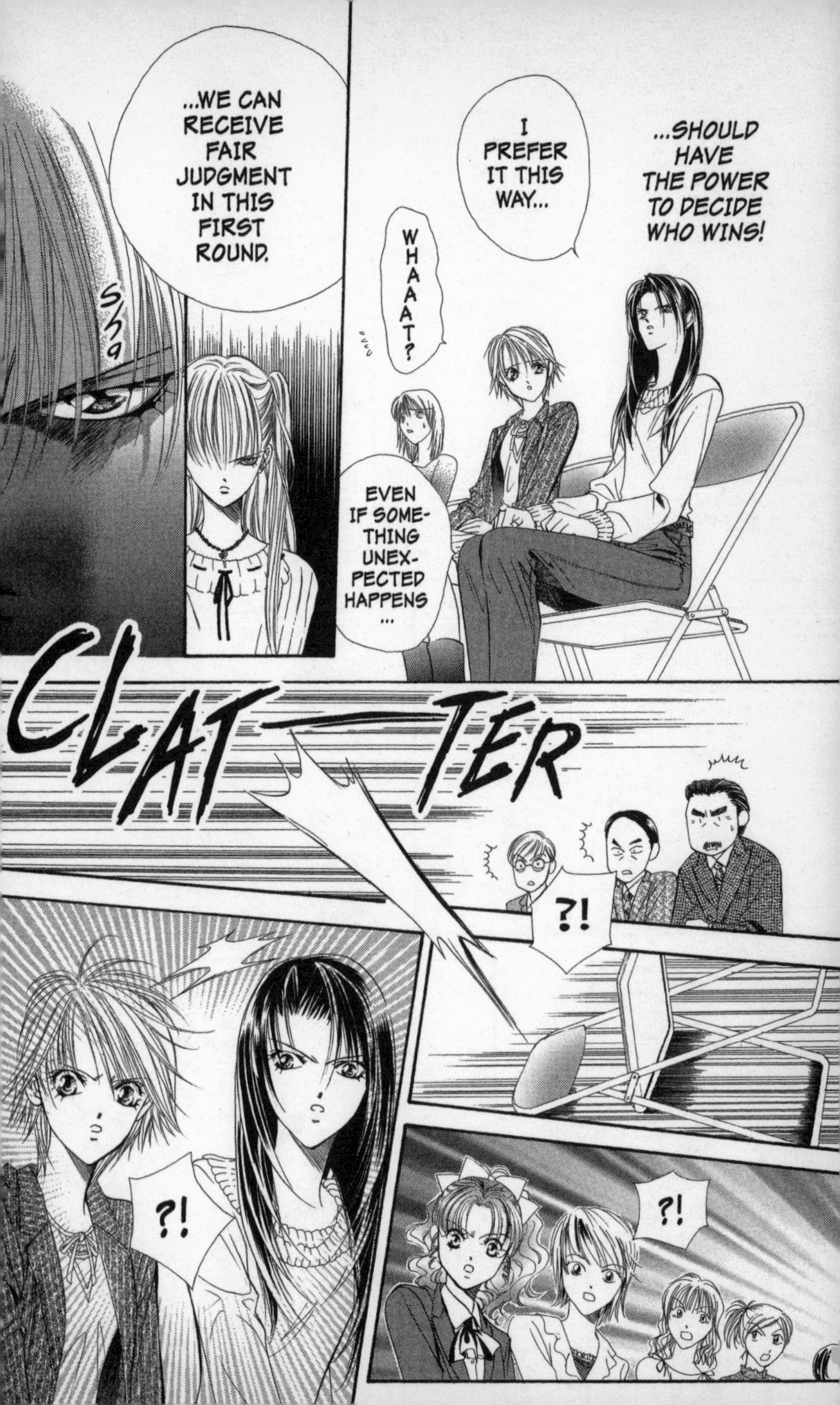

...SHOULD HAVE THE POWER TO DECIDE WHO WINS!
I PREFER IT THIS WAY...
WHAAAT?
EVEN IF SOMETHING UNEXPECTED HAPPENS...
...WE CAN RECEIVE FAIR JUDGMENT IN THIS FIRST ROUND.
CLAT—TER
?!
?!
?!

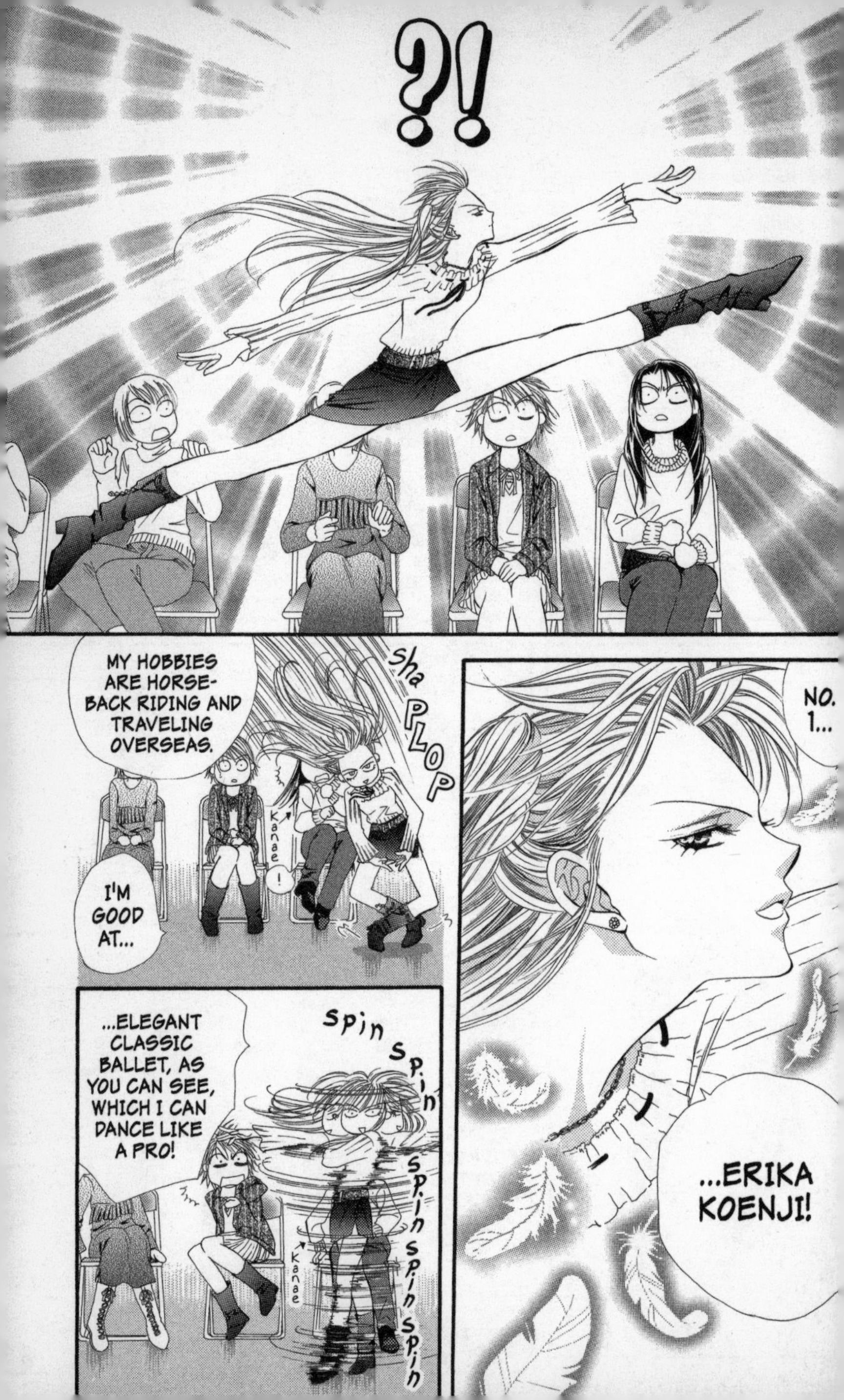
?!
NO. 1...
...ERIKA KOENJI!
Sha PLOP
MY HOBBIES ARE HORSE-BACK RIDING AND TRAVELING OVERSEAS.
Kanae
!
I'M GOOD AT...
spin spin
...ELEGANT CLASSIC BALLET, AS YOU CAN SEE, WHICH I CAN DANCE LIKE A PRO!
spin spin spin spin
Kanae

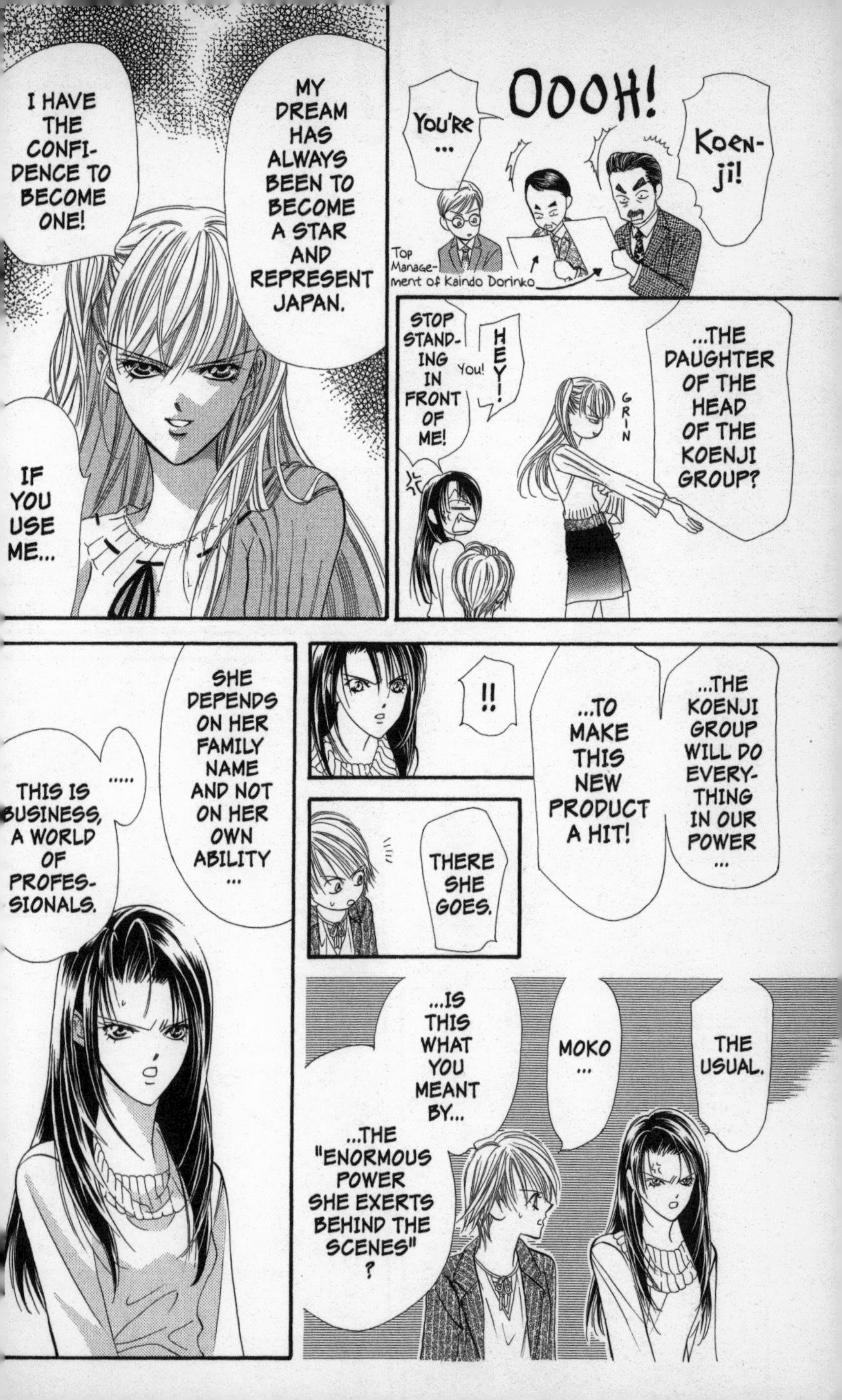

Koen-ji!
OOOH!
You're ...
Top Manage-ment of Kaindo Dorinko
...THE DAUGHTER OF THE HEAD OF THE KOENJI GROUP?
GRIN
HEY!
You!
STOP STAND-ING IN FRONT OF ME!
MY DREAM HAS ALWAYS BEEN TO BECOME A STAR AND REPRESENT JAPAN.
I HAVE THE CONFI-DENCE TO BECOME ONE!
IF YOU USE ME...
...THE KOENJI GROUP WILL DO EVERY-THING IN OUR POWER ...
...TO MAKE THIS NEW PRODUCT A HIT!
!!
THERE SHE GOES.
THE USUAL.
MOKO ...
...IS THIS WHAT YOU MEANT BY...
...THE "ENORMOUS POWER SHE EXERTS BEHIND THE SCENES"?
SHE DEPENDS ON HER FAMILY NAME AND NOT ON HER OWN ABILITY ...
.....
THIS IS BUSINESS, A WORLD OF PROFES-SIONALS.

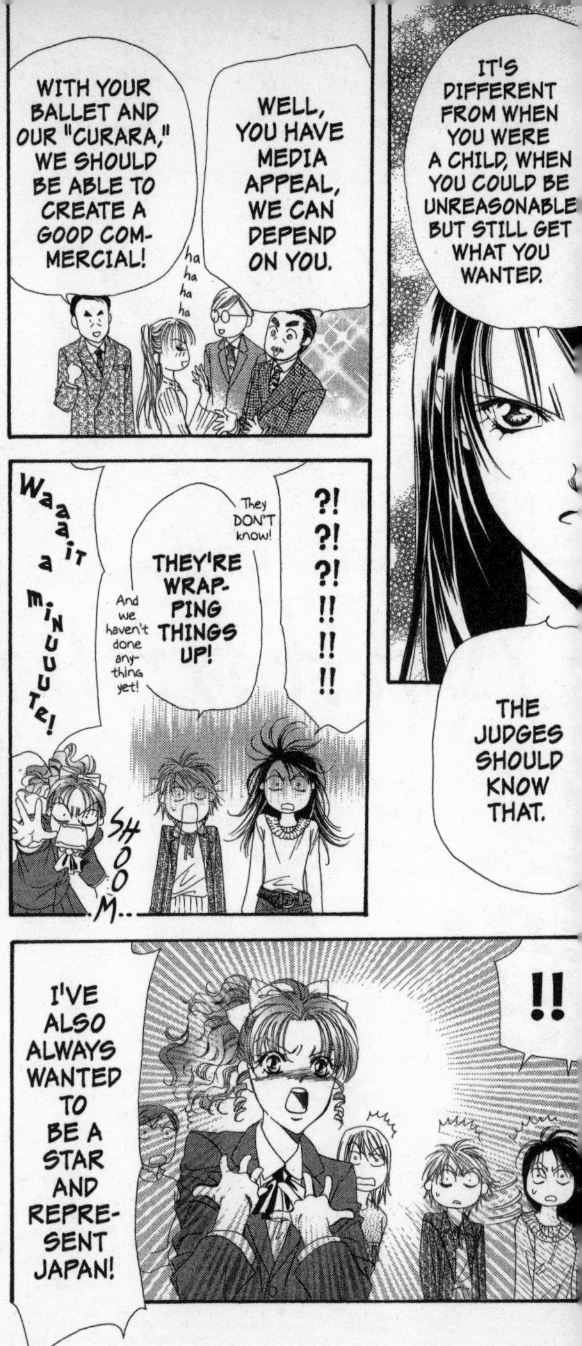
IT'S DIFFERENT FROM WHEN YOU WERE A CHILD, WHEN YOU COULD BE UNREASONABLE BUT STILL GET WHAT YOU WANTED.
THE JUDGES SHOULD KNOW THAT.
WELL, YOU HAVE MEDIA APPEAL, WE CAN DEPEND ON YOU.
ha ha ha ha
WITH YOUR BALLET AND OUR "CURARA," WE SHOULD BE ABLE TO CREATE A GOOD COM-MERCIAL!
?! ?! ?! !! !! !!
They DON'T know!
THEY'RE WRAP-PING THINGS UP!
And we haven't done any-thing yet!
Waaait a minuuuute!
SHOOOM..
!!
I'VE ALSO ALWAYS WANTED TO BE A STAR AND REPRESENT JAPAN!

Erika Koenji

Stubborn middle-age guys and rich young ladies are a must in Nakamura's manga now...I myself think "What is this...?" But they are easy to handle, so I can't help it... A rich young lady for a rival is really easy to deal with... sigh...

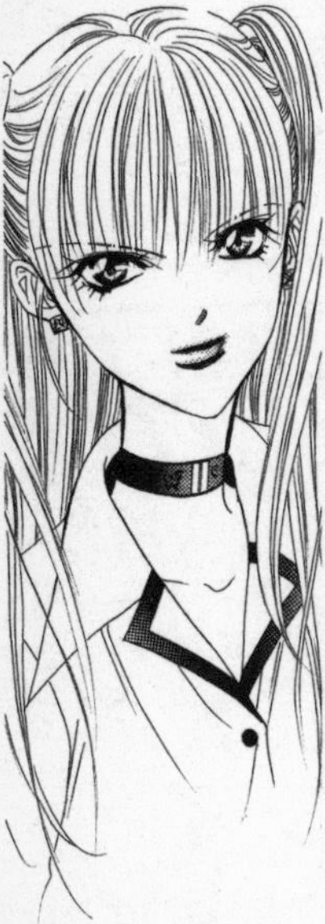

This girl's obsession with Kanae is kind of like love... ...well...you know...in this world, the line between love and hate is a fine one... Kyoko is just like that. She hates Shotaro more than anybody or anything, but that is why she can't get him out of her head... Um... *Skip•Beat!* is a really negative manga... All of the characters...

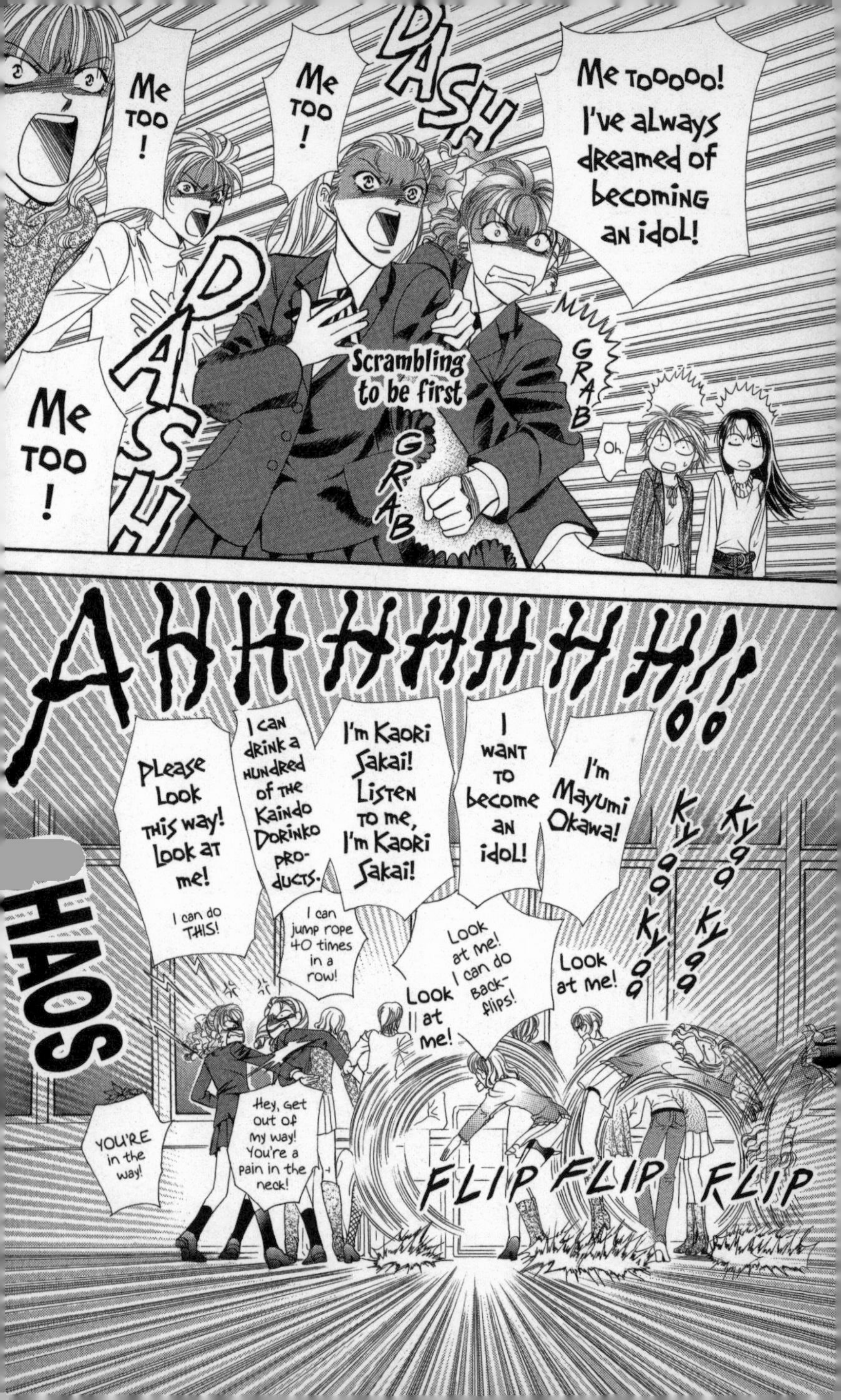

Me TOOOOO! I've always dreamed of becoming an idol!
DASH
Me TOO!
Me TOO!
GRAB
Oh.
Scrambling to be first
GRAB
DASH
Me TOO!
AHHHHHHHH!!
Kyaa kyaa
Kyaa kyaa kyaa
I'm Mayumi Okawa!
I want to become an idol!
I'm Kaori Sakai! Listen to me, I'm Kaori Sakai!
I can drink a hundred of the Kaindo Dorinko pro-ducts.
Please look this way! Look at me!
Look at me!
Look at me! I can do back-flips!
Look at me!
I can jump rope 40 times in a row!
I can do THIS!
HAOS
FLIP FLIP FLIP
Hey, get out of my way! You're a pain in the neck!
YOU'RE in the way!

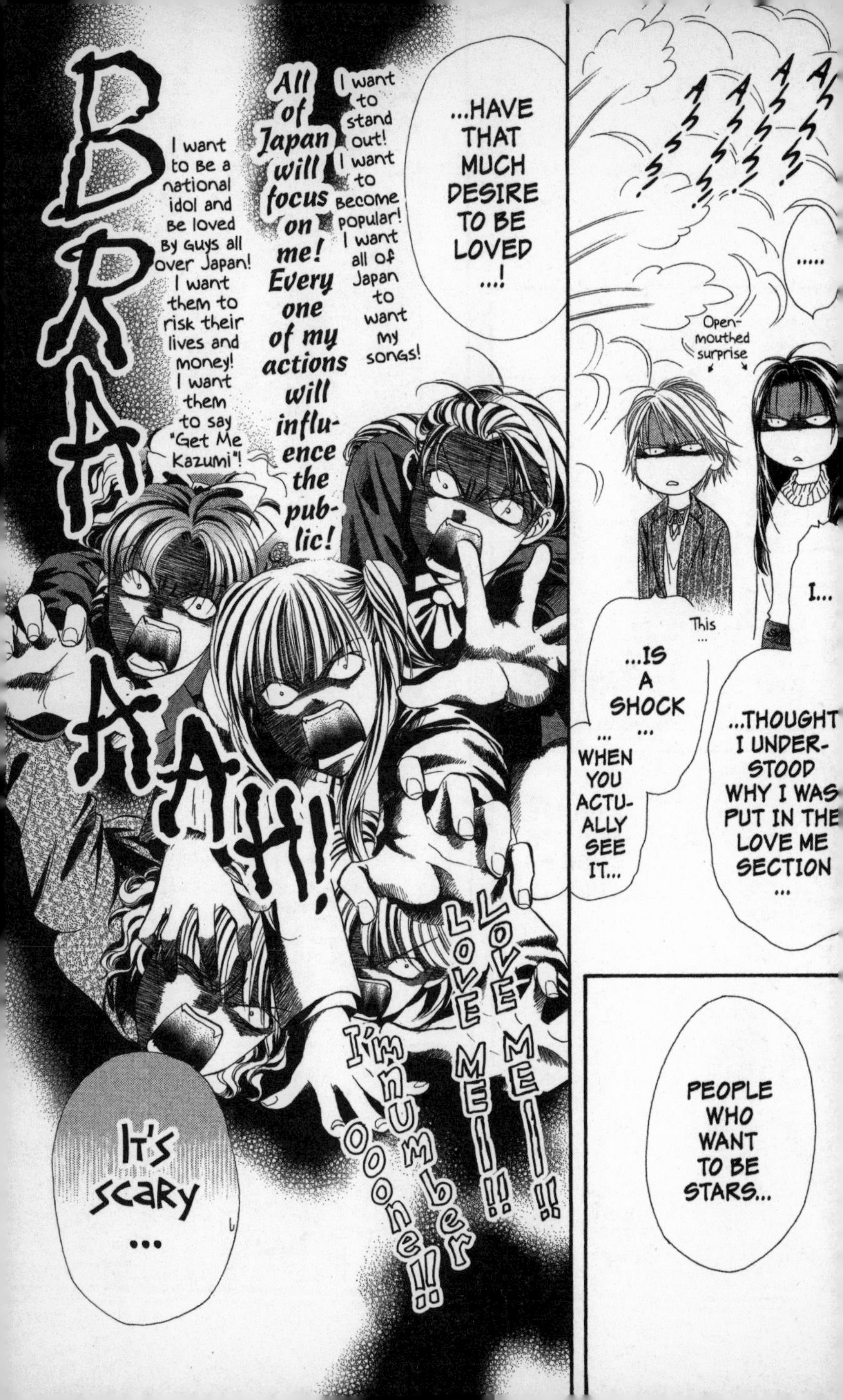
Ahhhh...!
Ahhhh...!
Ahhhh...!
Ahhhh...!
.....
Open-mouthed surprise
I...
...THOUGHT I UNDERSTOOD WHY I WAS PUT IN THE LOVE ME SECTION ...
This ...
...IS A SHOCK ...
... WHEN YOU ACTUALLY SEE IT...
PEOPLE WHO WANT TO BE STARS...
...HAVE THAT MUCH DESIRE TO BE LOVED ...!
I want to stand out! I want to become popular! I want all of Japan to want my songs!
All of Japan will focus on me! Every one of my actions will influence the public!
I want to be a national idol and be loved by guys all over Japan! I want them to risk their lives and money! I want them to say "Get Me Kazumi"!
BRAAAAH!
LOVE ME!!
LOVE ME!!
I'm number ooone!!
It's scary ...

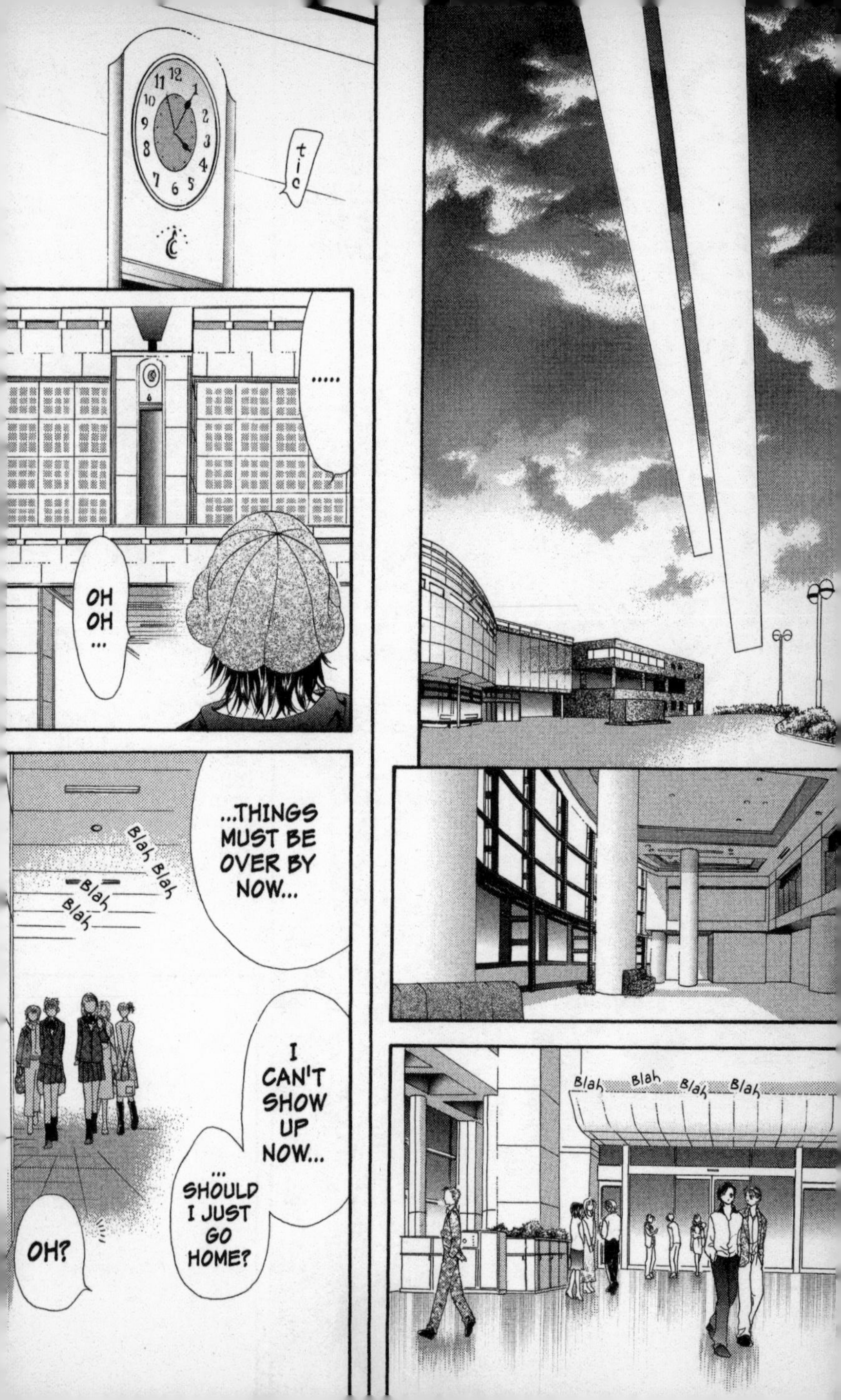
Blah Blah Blah Blah
tic
......
OH OH ...
...THINGS MUST BE OVER BY NOW...
Blah Blah Blah Blah
I CAN'T SHOW UP NOW...
... SHOULD I JUST GO HOME?
OH?

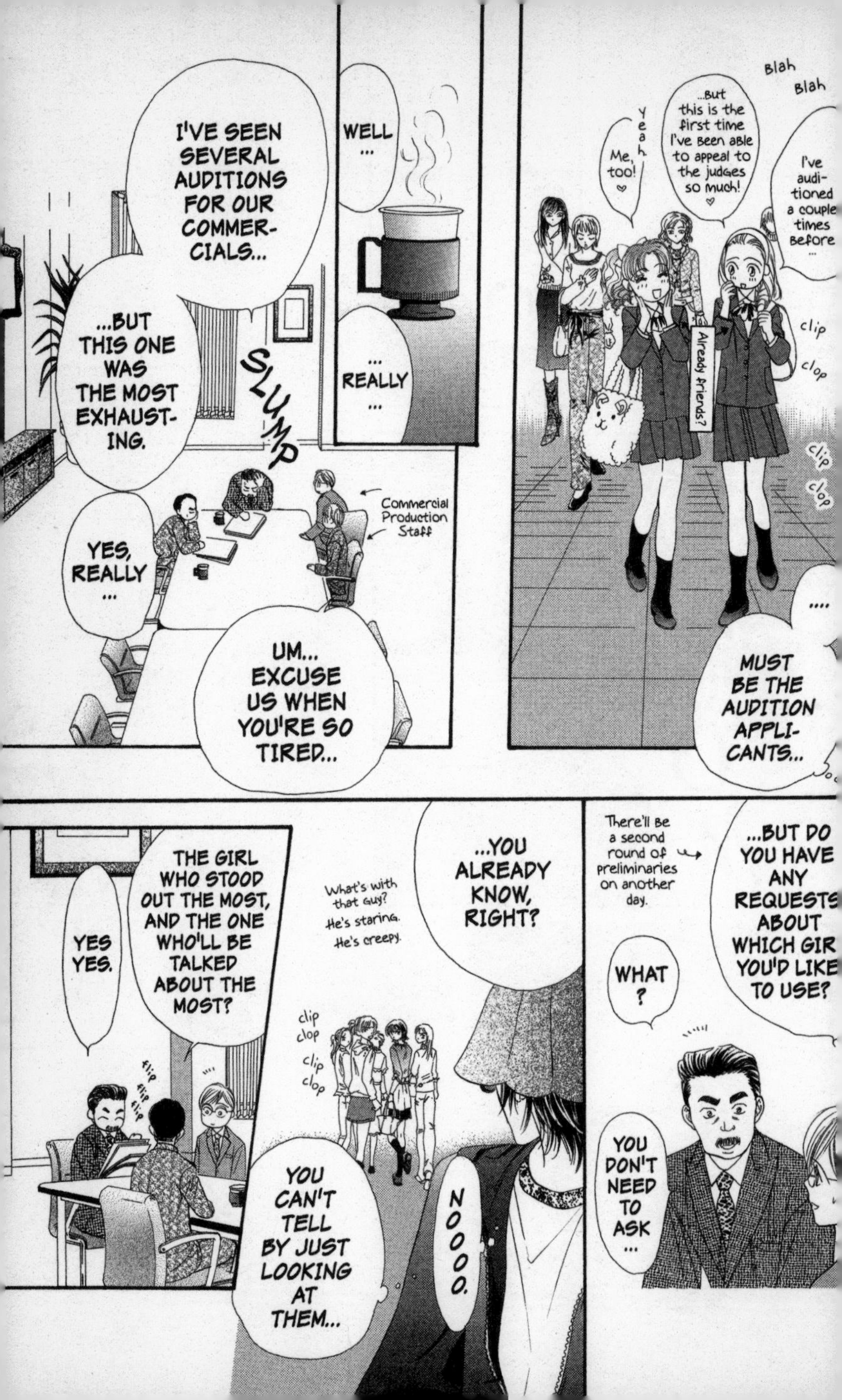

Blah
Blah
I've auditioned a couple times before ...
...But this is the first time I've been able to appeal to the judges so much! ♡
Yeah
Me, too! ♡
Already friends?
clip clop
clip clop
....
MUST BE THE AUDITION APPLICANTS...
WELL ...
... REALLY ...
I'VE SEEN SEVERAL AUDITIONS FOR OUR COMMERCIALS...
...BUT THIS ONE WAS THE MOST EXHAUSTING.
SLUMP
Commercial Production Staff
YES, REALLY ...
UM... EXCUSE US WHEN YOU'RE SO TIRED...
...BUT DO YOU HAVE ANY REQUESTS ABOUT WHICH GIR YOU'D LIKE TO USE?
There'll be a second round of preliminaries on another day.
WHAT ?
YOU DON'T NEED TO ASK ...
...YOU ALREADY KNOW, RIGHT?
What's with that guy? He's staring. He's creepy.
clip clop
clip clop
NOOOOO.
YOU CAN'T TELL BY JUST LOOKING AT THEM...
THE GIRL WHO STOOD OUT THE MOST, AND THE ONE WHO'LL BE TALKED ABOUT THE MOST?
YES YES.
flip flip flip
...

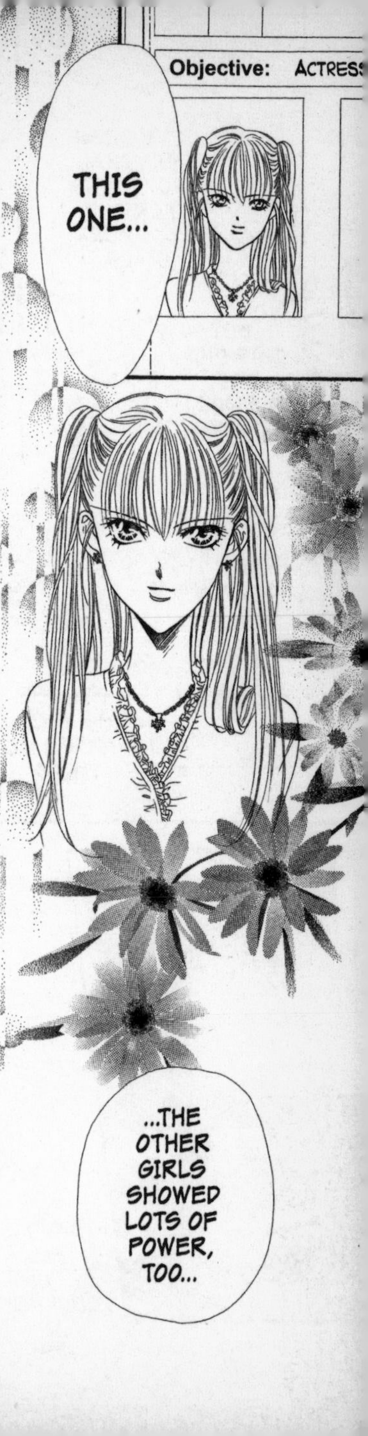
Objective: ACTRESS
THIS ONE...
...THE OTHER GIRLS SHOWED LOTS OF POWER, TOO...

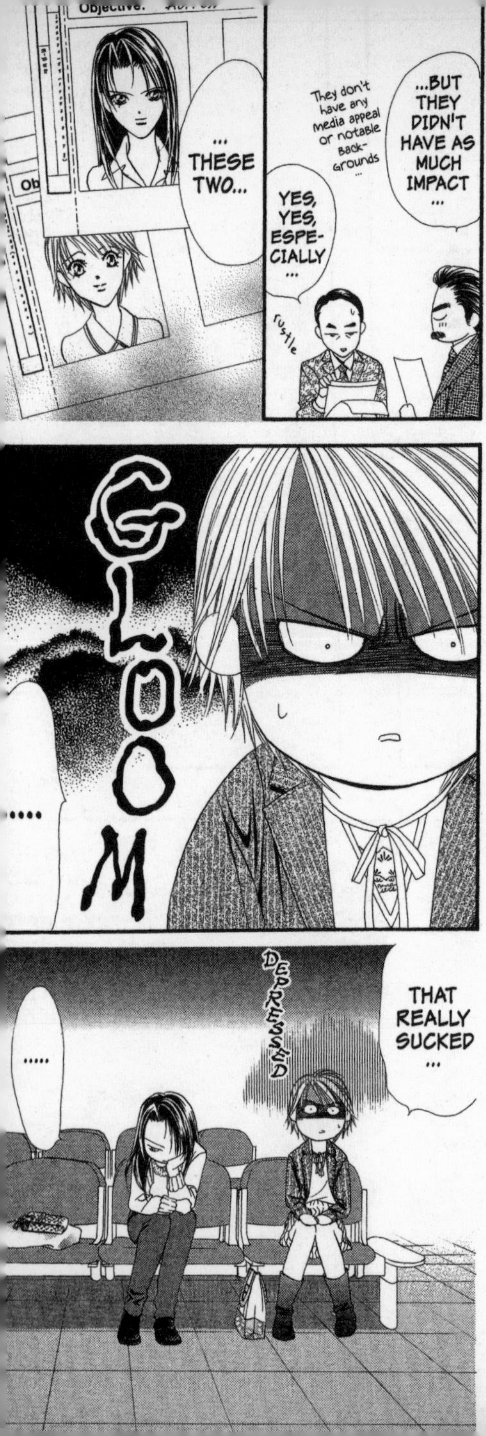
...BUT THEY DIDN'T HAVE AS MUCH IMPACT ...
They don't have any media appeal or notable back-grounds ...
YES, YES, ESPE-CIALLY ...
rustle
... THESE TWO...
GLOOM
....
THAT REALLY SUCKED ...
DEPRESSED
.....

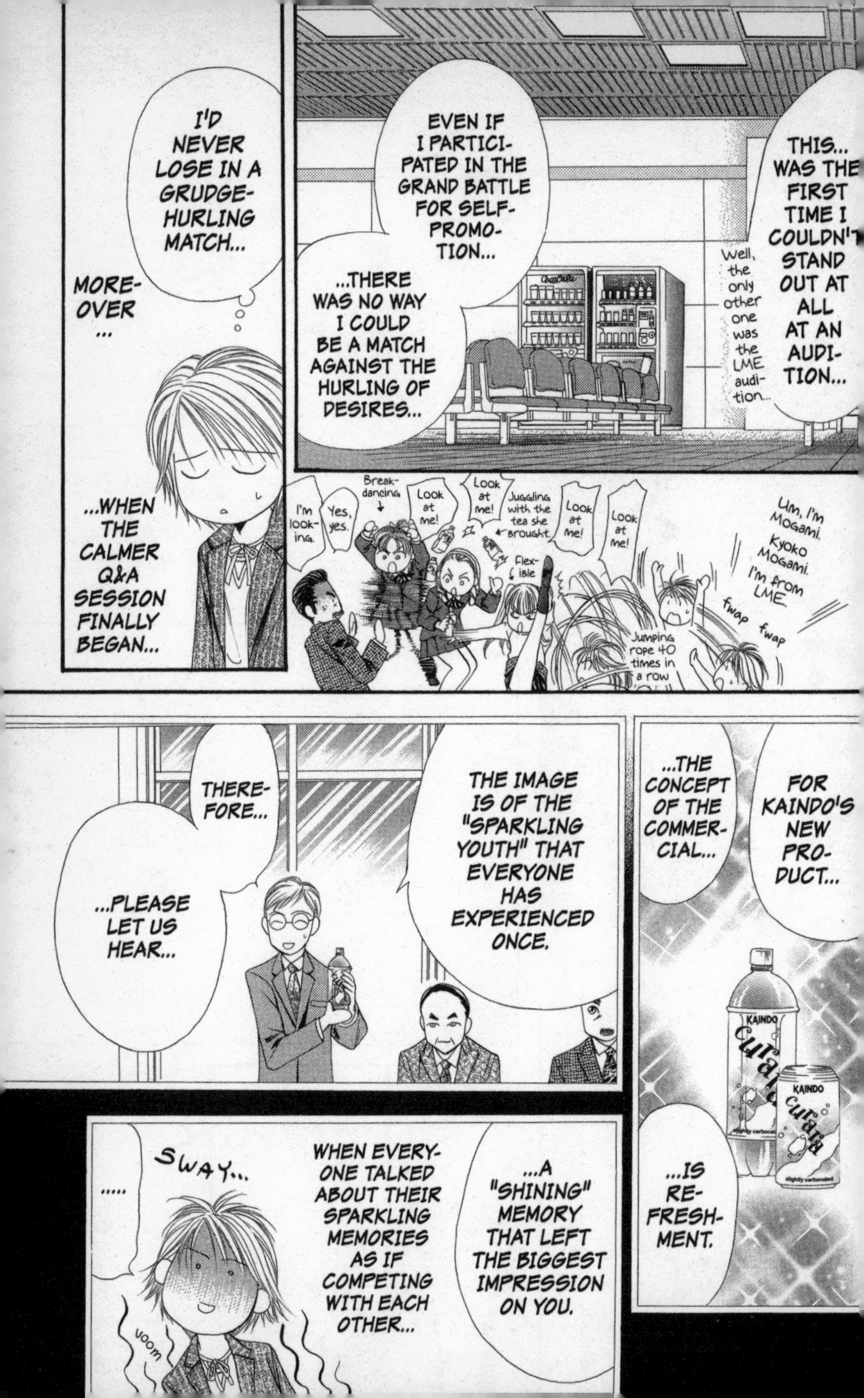
THIS... WAS THE FIRST TIME I COULDN'T STAND OUT AT ALL AT AN AUDITION...
Well, the only other one was the LME audition...
EVEN IF I PARTICIPATED IN THE GRAND BATTLE FOR SELF-PROMOTION...
...THERE WAS NO WAY I COULD BE A MATCH AGAINST THE HURLING OF DESIRES...
Um, I'm Mogami. Kyoko Mogami. I'm from LME.
fwap fwap
Jumping rope 40 times in a row
Look at me!
Look at me!
Flexible
Juggling with the tea she brought.
Look at me!
Look at me!
Break-dancing
Yes, yes.
I'm looking.
I'D NEVER LOSE IN A GRUDGE-HURLING MATCH...
MOREOVER...
...WHEN THE CALMER Q&A SESSION FINALLY BEGAN...
FOR KAINDO'S NEW PRODUCT...
...THE CONCEPT OF THE COMMERCIAL...
...IS REFRESHMENT.
KAINDO curara
KAINDO curara
THE IMAGE IS OF THE "SPARKLING YOUTH" THAT EVERYONE HAS EXPERIENCED ONCE.
THEREFORE...
...PLEASE LET US HEAR...
...A "SHINING" MEMORY THAT LEFT THE BIGGEST IMPRESSION ON YOU.
WHEN EVERYONE TALKED ABOUT THEIR SPARKLING MEMORIES AS IF COMPETING WITH EACH OTHER...
SWAY...
.....
voom

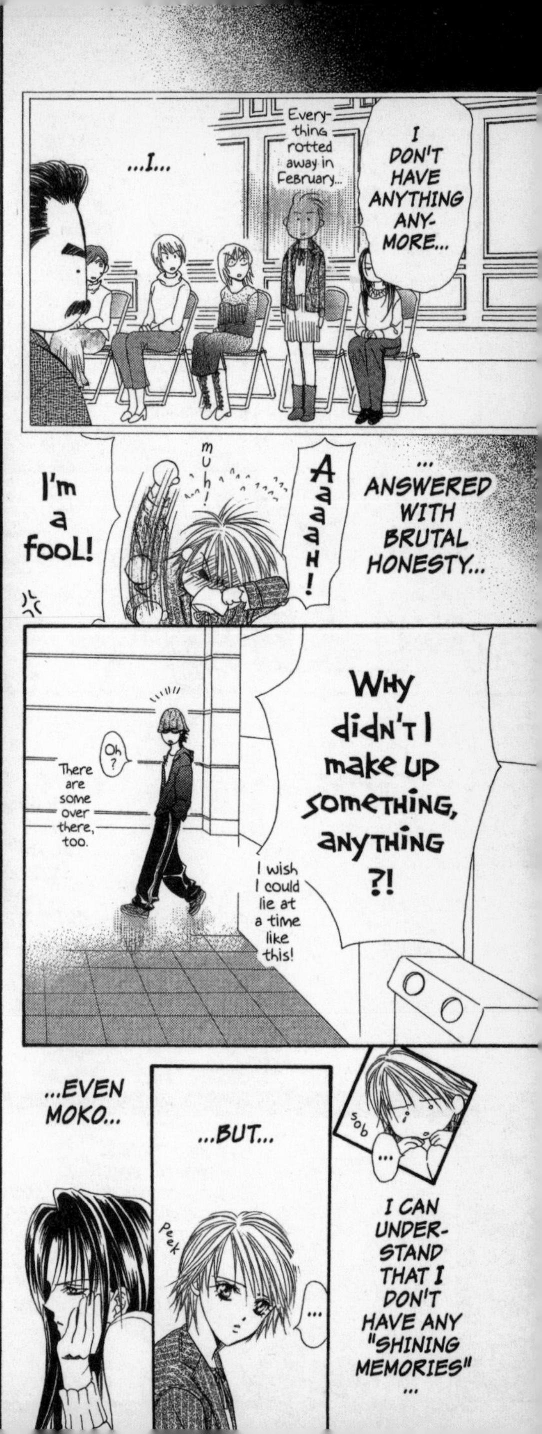
I DON'T HAVE ANYTHING ANYMORE...
Everything rotted away in February...
...I...
...ANSWERED WITH BRUTAL HONESTY...
Aaaaah!
muh!
I'm a fool!
Why didn't I make up something, anything?!
I wish I could lie at a time like this!
Oh?
There are some over there, too.
...
sob
I CAN UNDERSTAND THAT I DON'T HAVE ANY "SHINING MEMORIES"...
...BUT...
...
Peek
...EVEN MOKO...
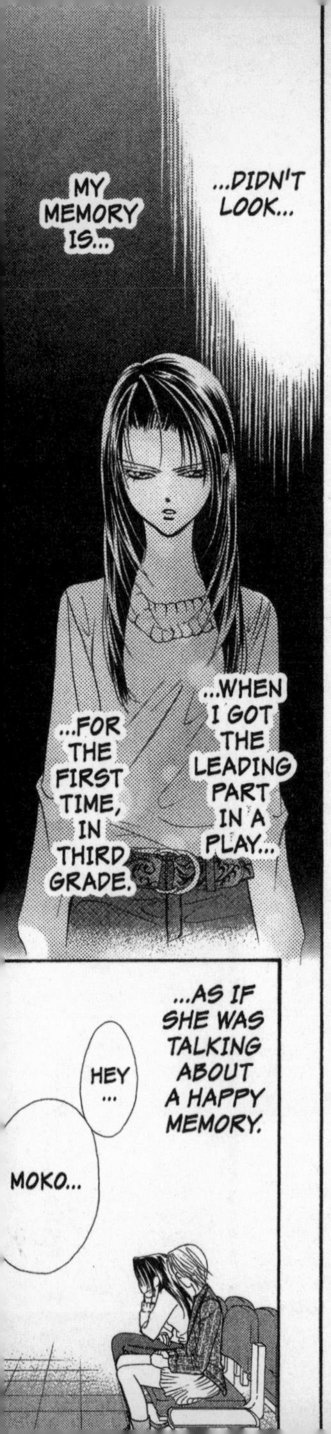
...DIDN'T LOOK...
MY MEMORY IS...
...WHEN I GOT THE LEADING PART IN A PLAY...
...FOR THE FIRST TIME, IN THIRD GRADE.
...AS IF SHE WAS TALKING ABOUT A HAPPY MEMORY.
HEY...
MOKO...

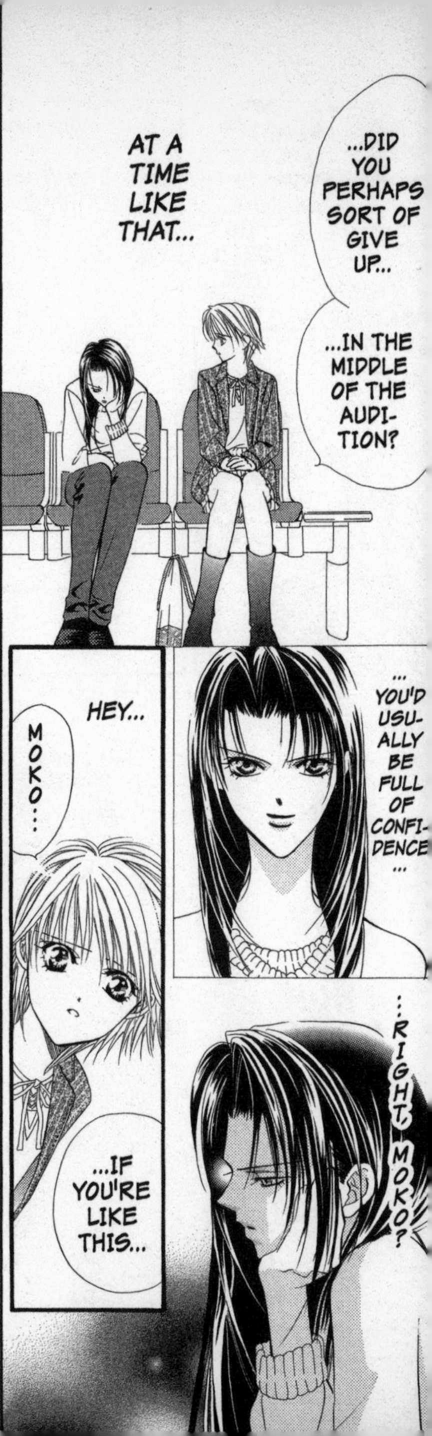
...DID YOU PERHAPS SORT OF GIVE UP...
...IN THE MIDDLE OF THE AUDITION?
AT A TIME LIKE THAT...
... YOU'D USUALLY BE FULL OF CONFIDENCE ...
...RIGHT, MOKO?
HEY...
MOKO...
...IF YOU'RE LIKE THIS...
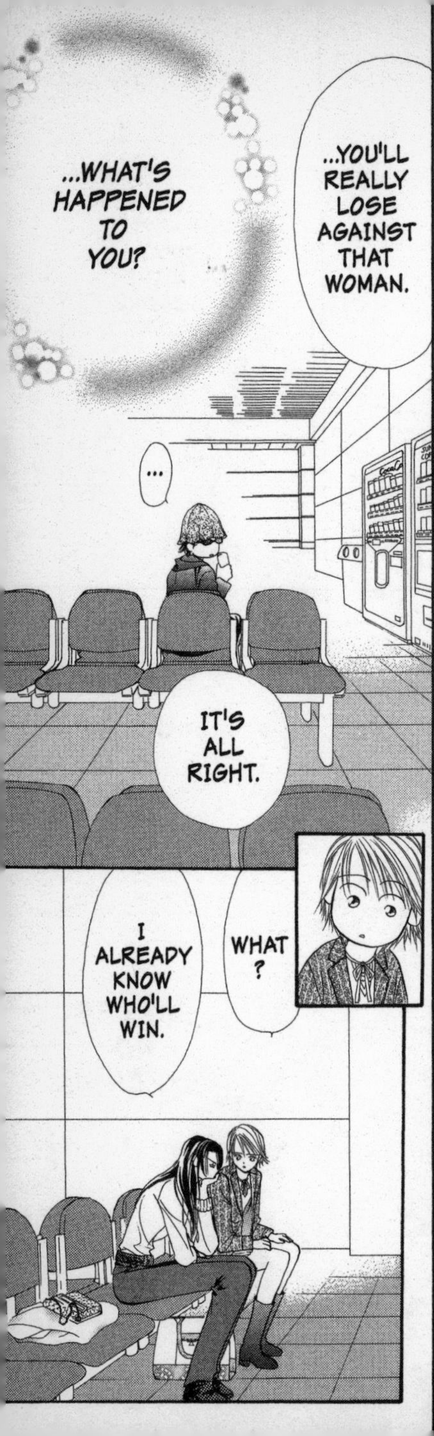
...YOU'LL REALLY LOSE AGAINST THAT WOMAN.
...WHAT'S HAPPENED TO YOU?
...
IT'S ALL RIGHT.
WHAT?
I ALREADY KNOW WHO'LL WIN.

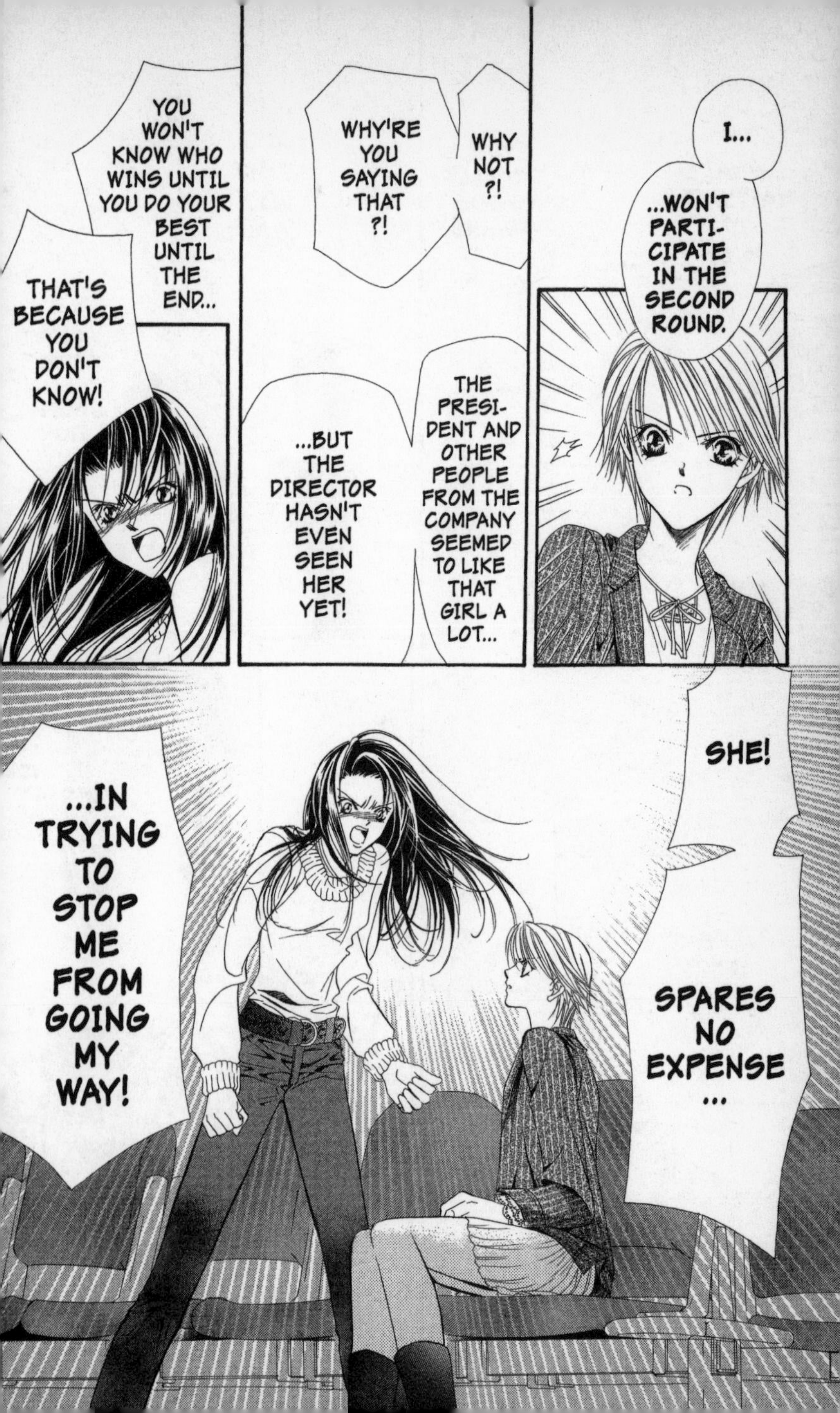
I...
...WON'T PARTI-CIPATE IN THE SECOND ROUND.
WHY NOT ?!
WHY'RE YOU SAYING THAT ?!
THE PRESI-DENT AND OTHER PEOPLE FROM THE COMPANY SEEMED TO LIKE THAT GIRL A LOT...
...BUT THE DIRECTOR HASN'T EVEN SEEN HER YET!
YOU WON'T KNOW WHO WINS UNTIL YOU DO YOUR BEST UNTIL THE END...
THAT'S BECAUSE YOU DON'T KNOW!
SHE!
SPARES NO EXPENSE ...
...IN TRYING TO STOP ME FROM GOING MY WAY!

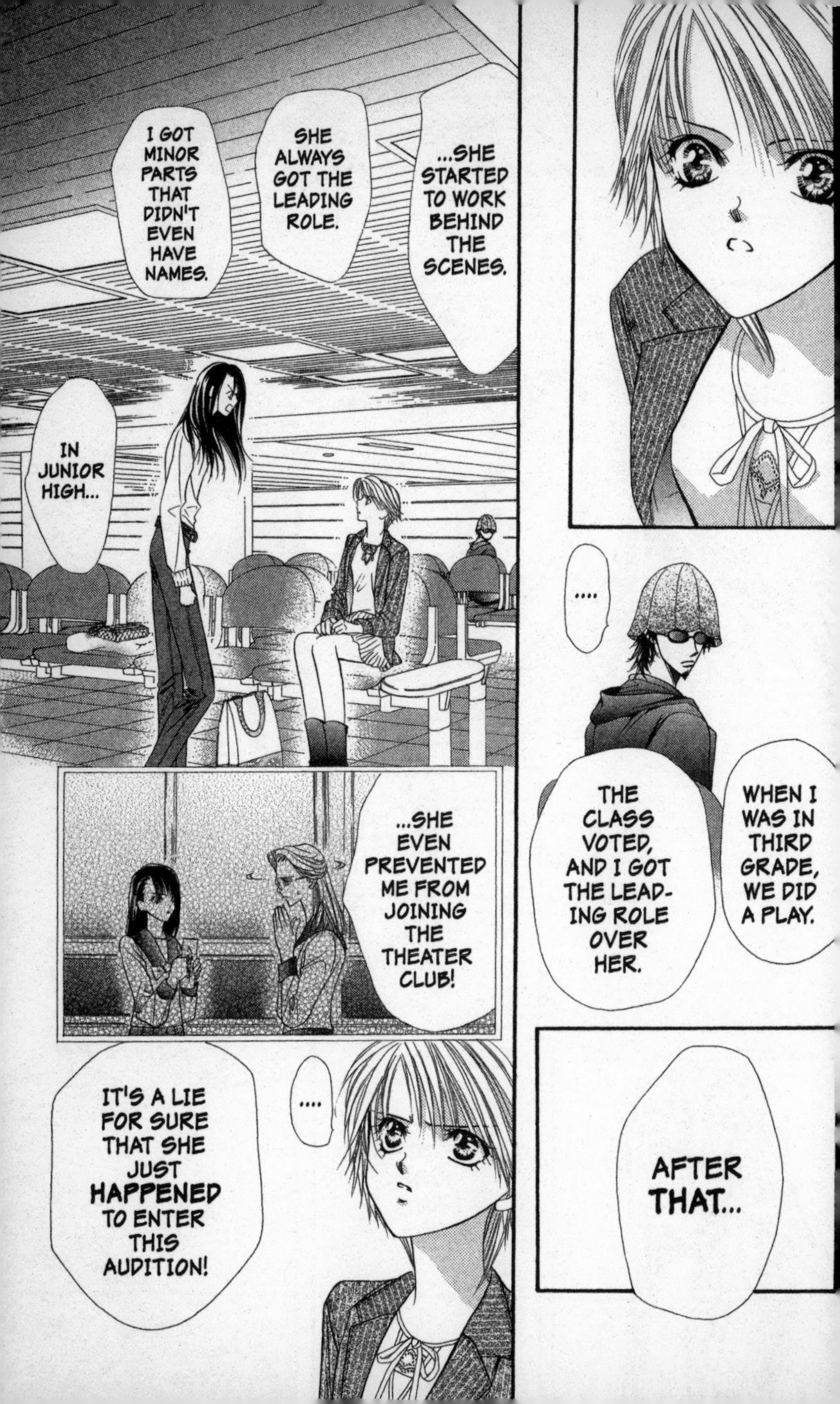
....
WHEN I WAS IN THIRD GRADE, WE DID A PLAY.
THE CLASS VOTED, AND I GOT THE LEADING ROLE OVER HER.
AFTER THAT...
...SHE STARTED TO WORK BEHIND THE SCENES.
SHE ALWAYS GOT THE LEADING ROLE.
I GOT MINOR PARTS THAT DIDN'T EVEN HAVE NAMES.
IN JUNIOR HIGH...
...SHE EVEN PREVENTED ME FROM JOINING THE THEATER CLUB!
....
IT'S A LIE FOR SURE THAT SHE JUST HAPPENED TO ENTER THIS AUDITION!

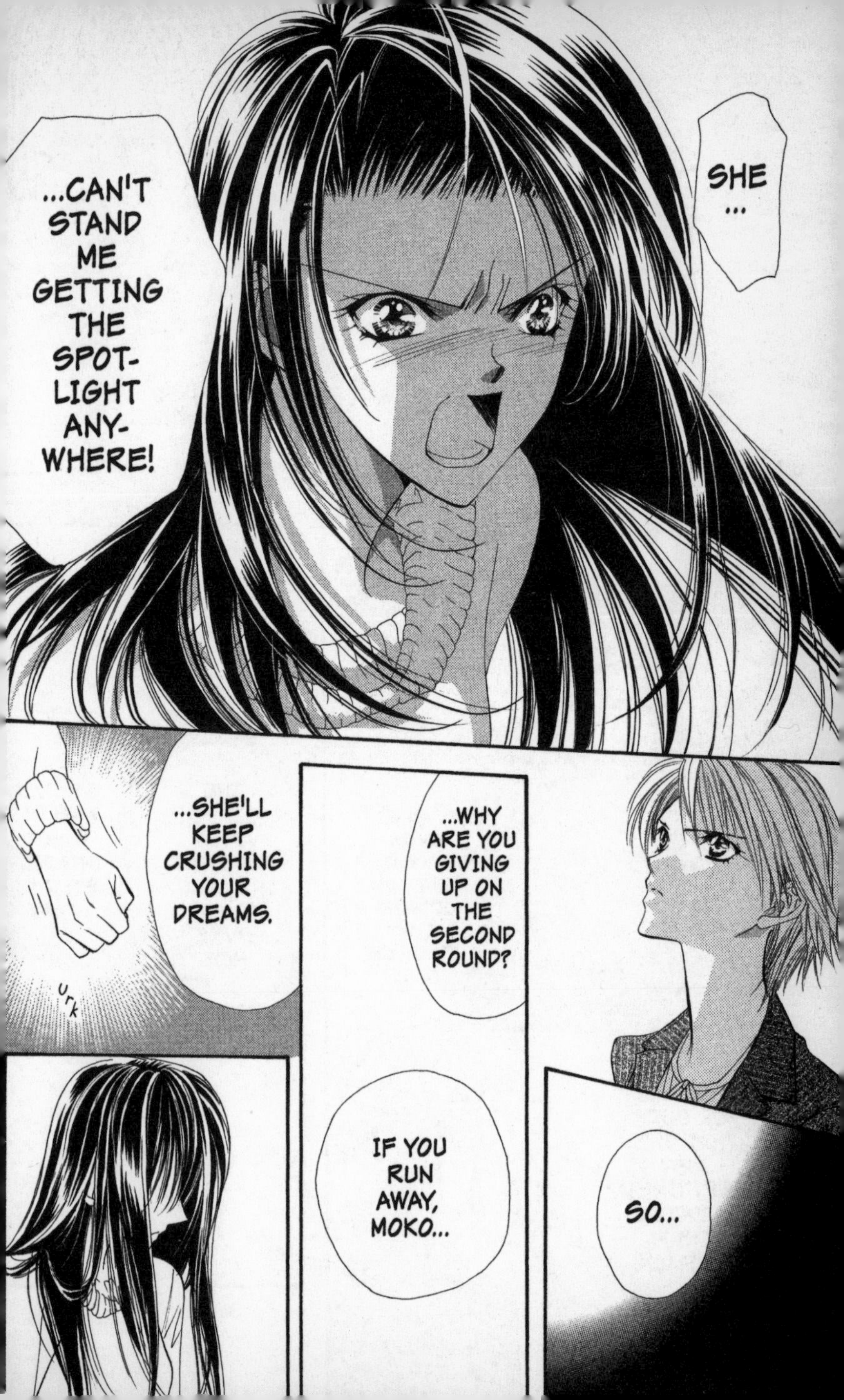
SHE ...
...CAN'T STAND ME GETTING THE SPOT-LIGHT ANY-WHERE!
...WHY ARE YOU GIVING UP ON THE SECOND ROUND?
SO...
IF YOU RUN AWAY, MOKO...
...SHE'LL KEEP CRUSHING YOUR DREAMS.
Urk

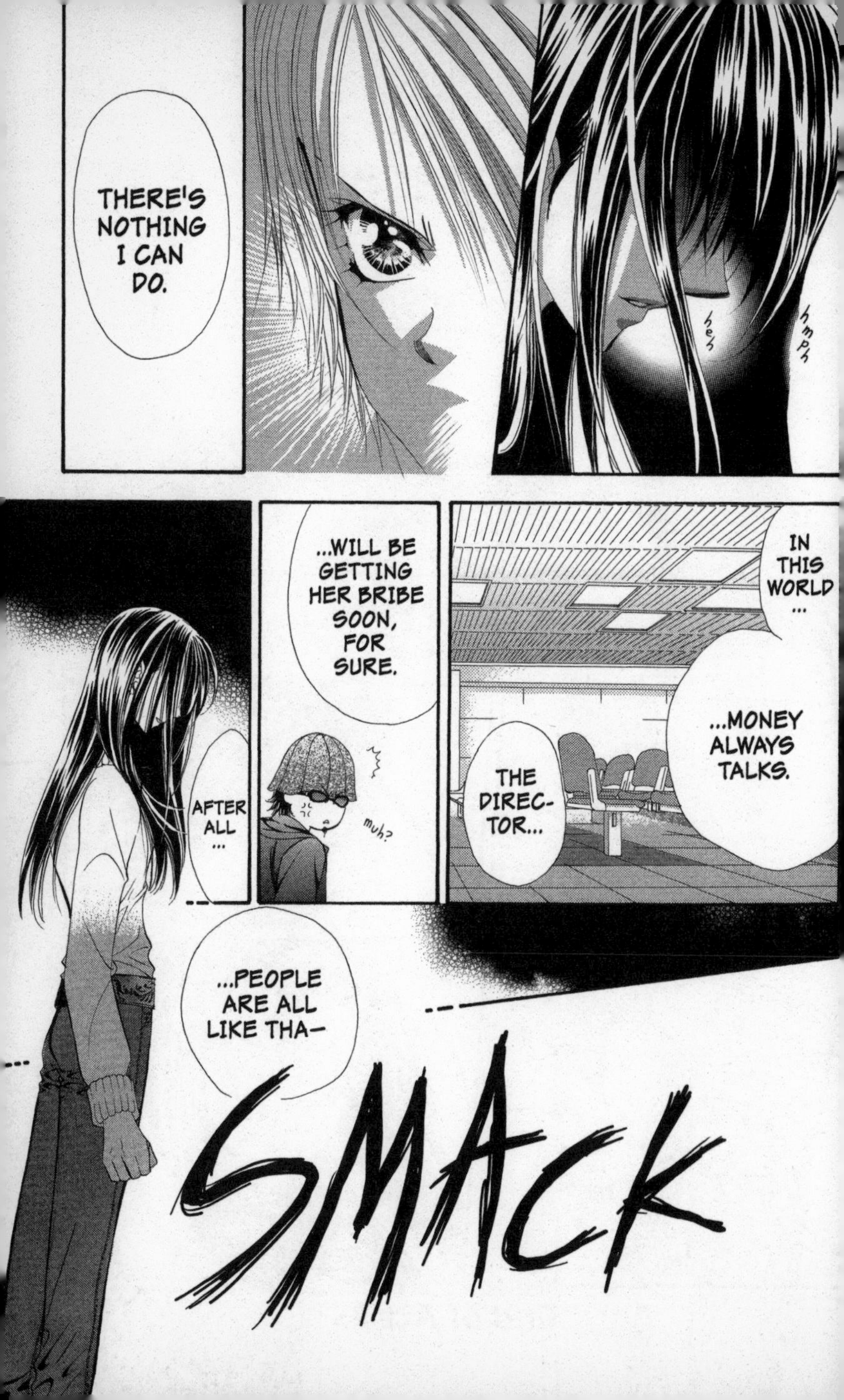
hmph
heh
THERE'S NOTHING I CAN DO.
IN THIS WORLD...
...MONEY ALWAYS TALKS.
THE DIRECTOR...
...WILL BE GETTING HER BRIBE SOON, FOR SURE.
muh?
AFTER ALL...
...PEOPLE ARE ALL LIKE THA—
SMACK

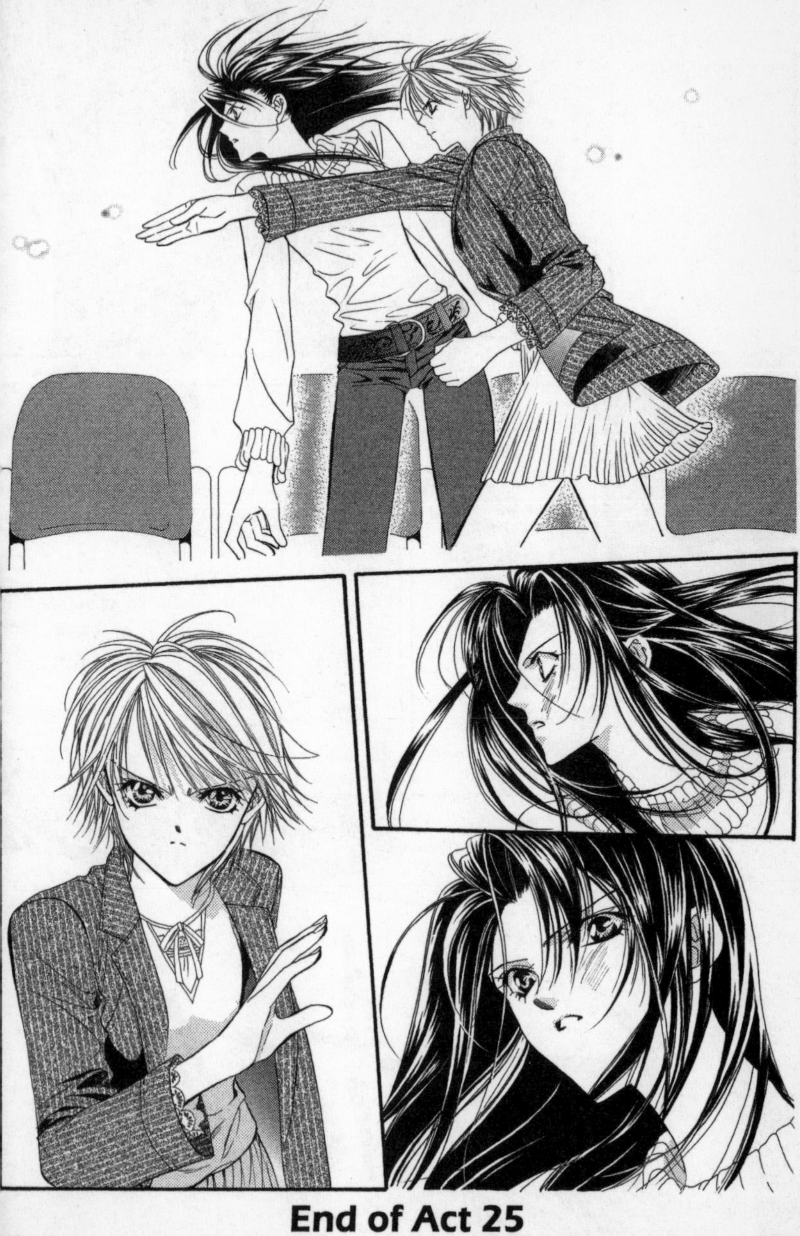

End of Act 25

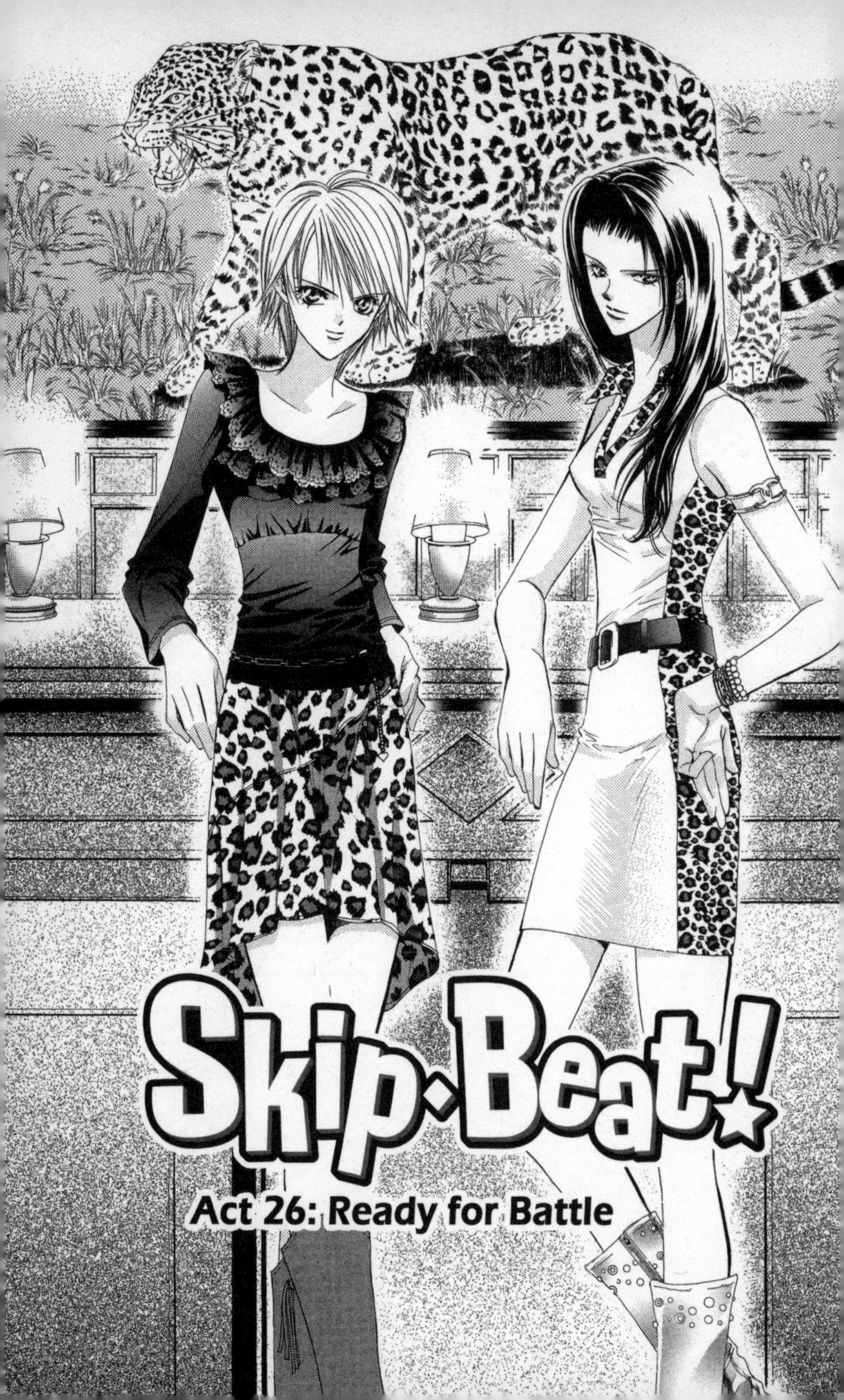
Skip·Beat!
Act 26: Ready for Battle

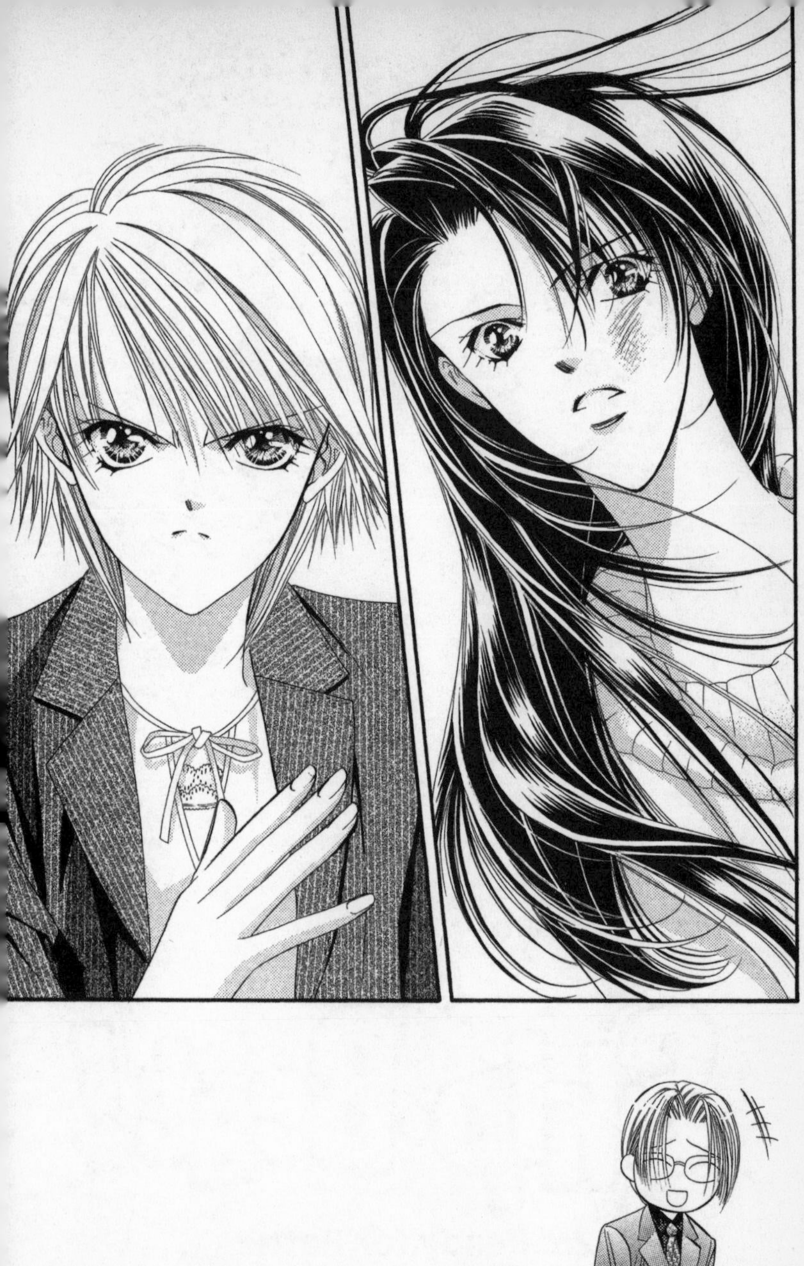

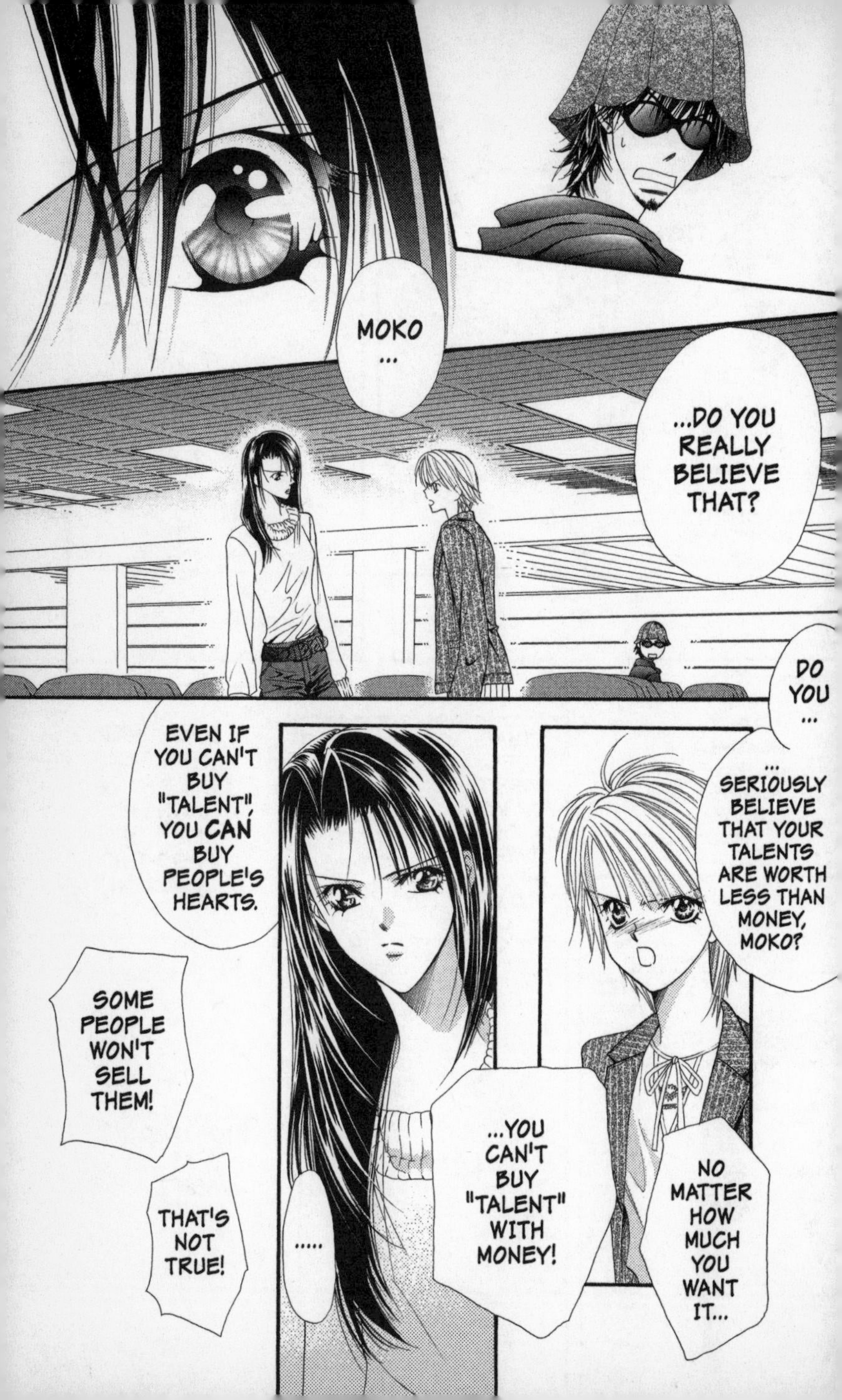
MOKO ...
...DO YOU REALLY BELIEVE THAT?
DO YOU ...
... SERIOUSLY BELIEVE THAT YOUR TALENTS ARE WORTH LESS THAN MONEY, MOKO?
NO MATTER HOW MUCH YOU WANT IT...
...YOU CAN'T BUY "TALENT" WITH MONEY!
.....
EVEN IF YOU CAN'T BUY "TALENT", YOU CAN BUY PEOPLE'S HEARTS.
THAT'S NOT TRUE!
SOME PEOPLE WON'T SELL THEM!

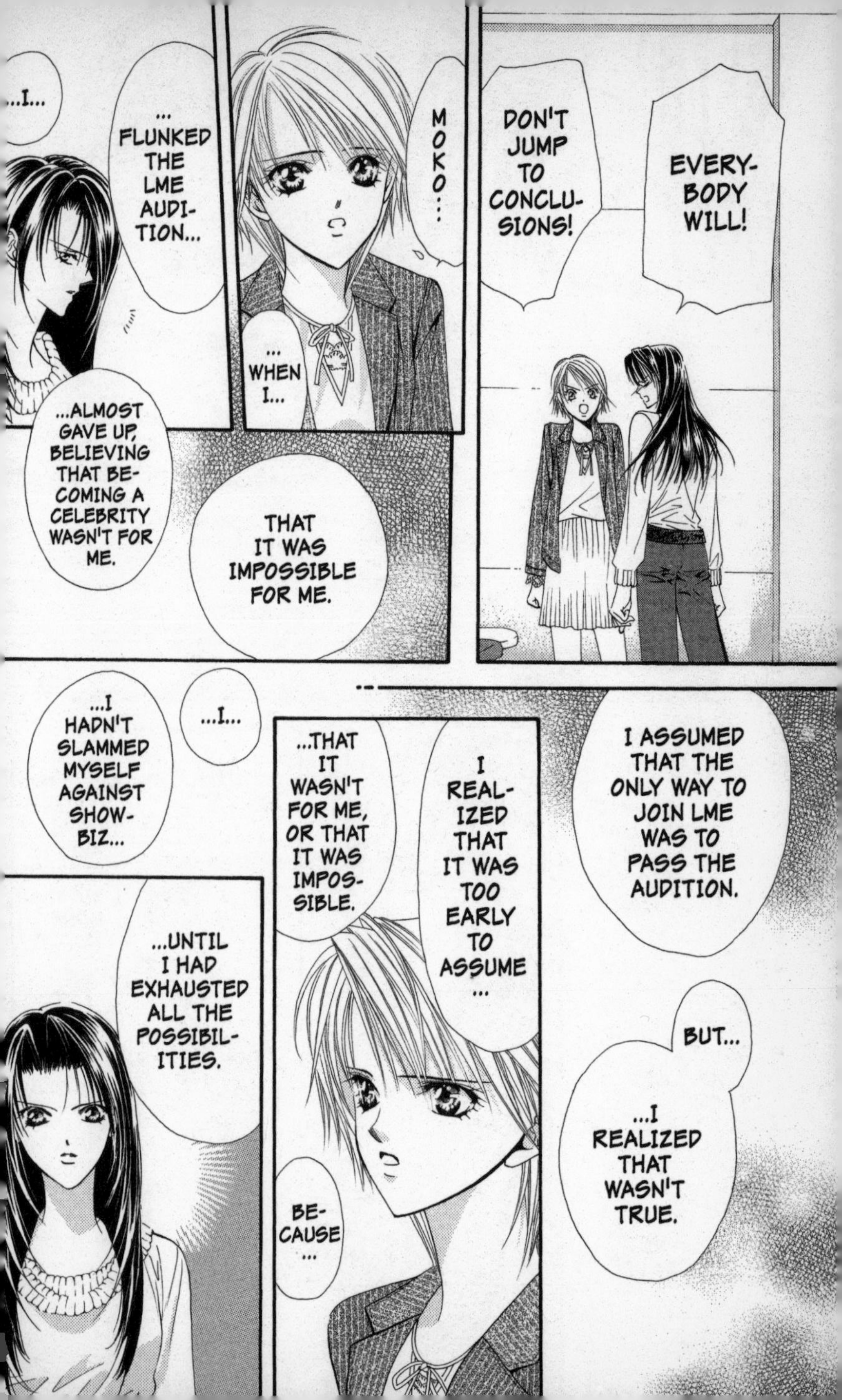
EVERY-BODY WILL!
DON'T JUMP TO CONCLU-SIONS!
MOKO...
...WHEN I...
...I...
...FLUNKED THE LME AUDI-TION...
...ALMOST GAVE UP, BELIEVING THAT BE-COMING A CELEBRITY WASN'T FOR ME.
THAT IT WAS IMPOSSIBLE FOR ME.
I ASSUMED THAT THE ONLY WAY TO JOIN LME WAS TO PASS THE AUDITION.
BUT...
...I REALIZED THAT WASN'T TRUE.
I REAL-IZED THAT IT WAS TOO EARLY TO ASSUME...
...THAT IT WASN'T FOR ME, OR THAT IT WAS IMPOS-SIBLE.
BE-CAUSE...
...I...
...I HADN'T SLAMMED MYSELF AGAINST SHOW-BIZ...
...UNTIL I HAD EXHAUSTED ALL THE POSSIBIL-ITIES.

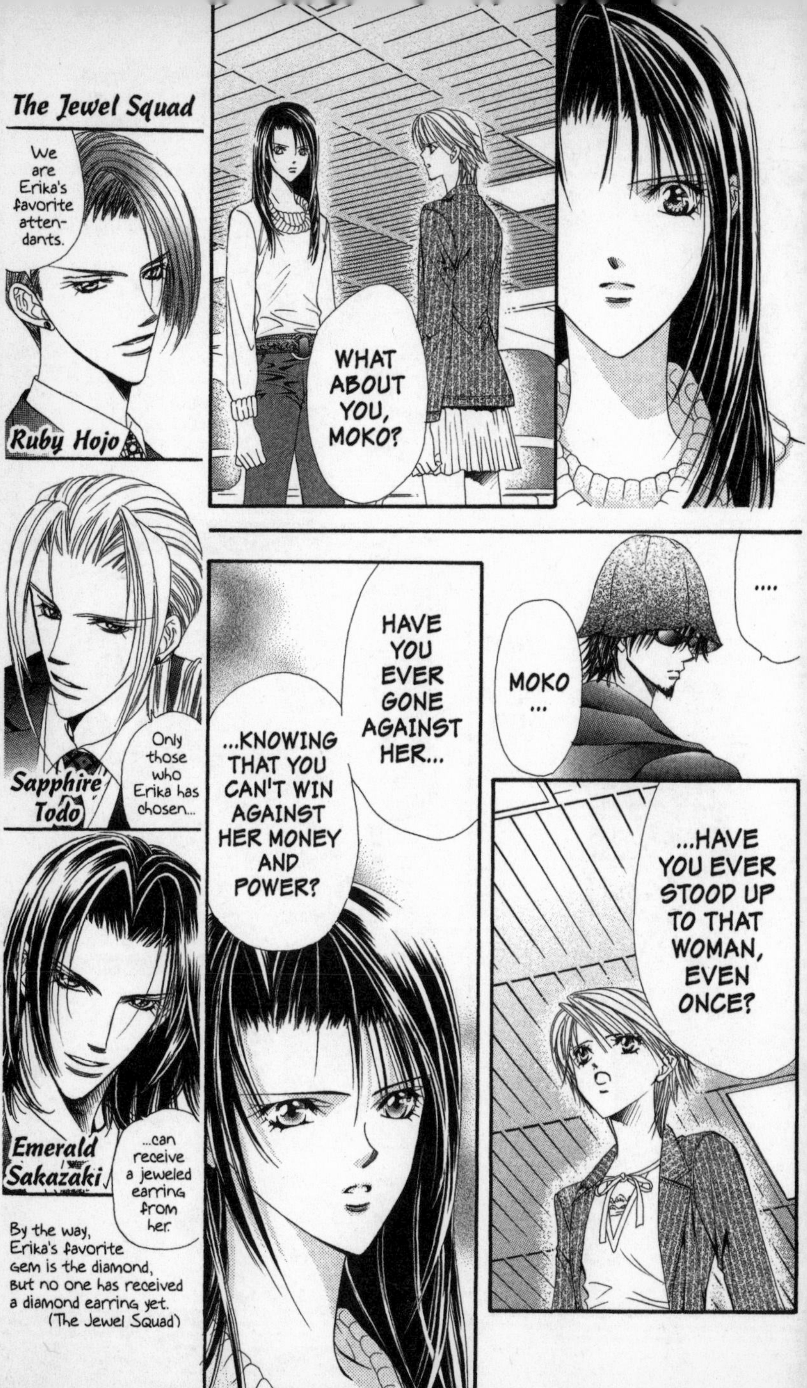
WHAT ABOUT YOU, MOKO?
....
MOKO ...
...HAVE YOU EVER STOOD UP TO THAT WOMAN, EVEN ONCE?
HAVE YOU EVER GONE AGAINST HER...
...KNOWING THAT YOU CAN'T WIN AGAINST HER MONEY AND POWER?
The Jewel Squad
We are Erika's favorite attendants.
Ruby Hojo
Only those who Erika has chosen...
Sapphire Todo
...can receive a jeweled earring from her.
Emerald Sakazaki
By the way, Erika's favorite gem is the diamond, but no one has received a diamond earring yet. (The Jewel Squad)

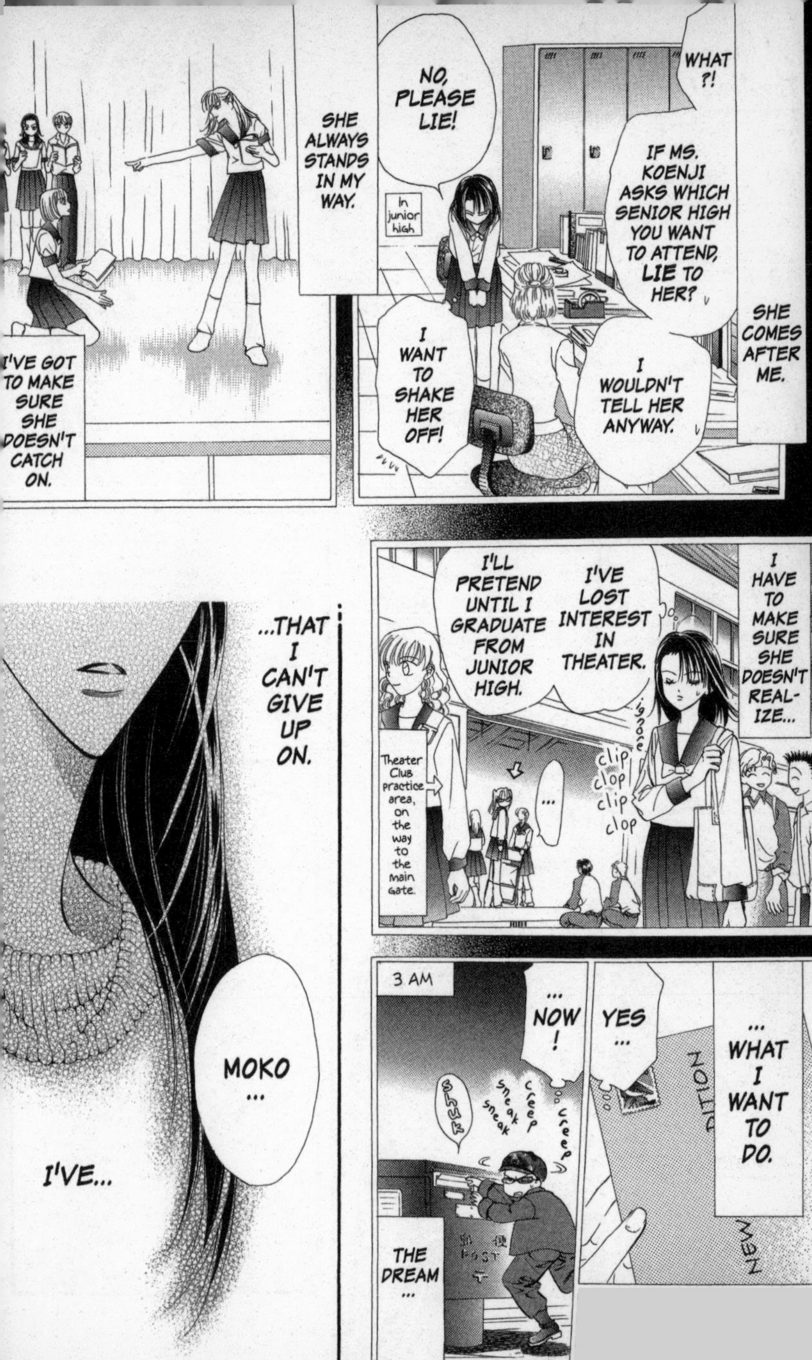
WHAT ?!
IF MS. KOENJI ASKS WHICH SENIOR HIGH YOU WANT TO ATTEND, LIE TO HER?
SHE COMES AFTER ME.
NO, PLEASE LIE!
In junior high
I WOULDN'T TELL HER ANYWAY.
I WANT TO SHAKE HER OFF!
SHE ALWAYS STANDS IN MY WAY.
I'VE GOT TO MAKE SURE SHE DOESN'T CATCH ON.
I HAVE TO MAKE SURE SHE DOESN'T REAL-IZE...
I'VE LOST INTEREST IN THEATER.
I'LL PRETEND UNTIL I GRADUATE FROM JUNIOR HIGH.
ignore
clip clop clip clop
...
Theater Club practice area, on the way to the main Gate.
... WHAT I WANT TO DO.
YES ...
... NOW !
3 AM
creep creep
sneak sneak
shuk
THE DREAM ...
...THAT I CAN'T GIVE UP ON.
MOKO ...
I'VE...

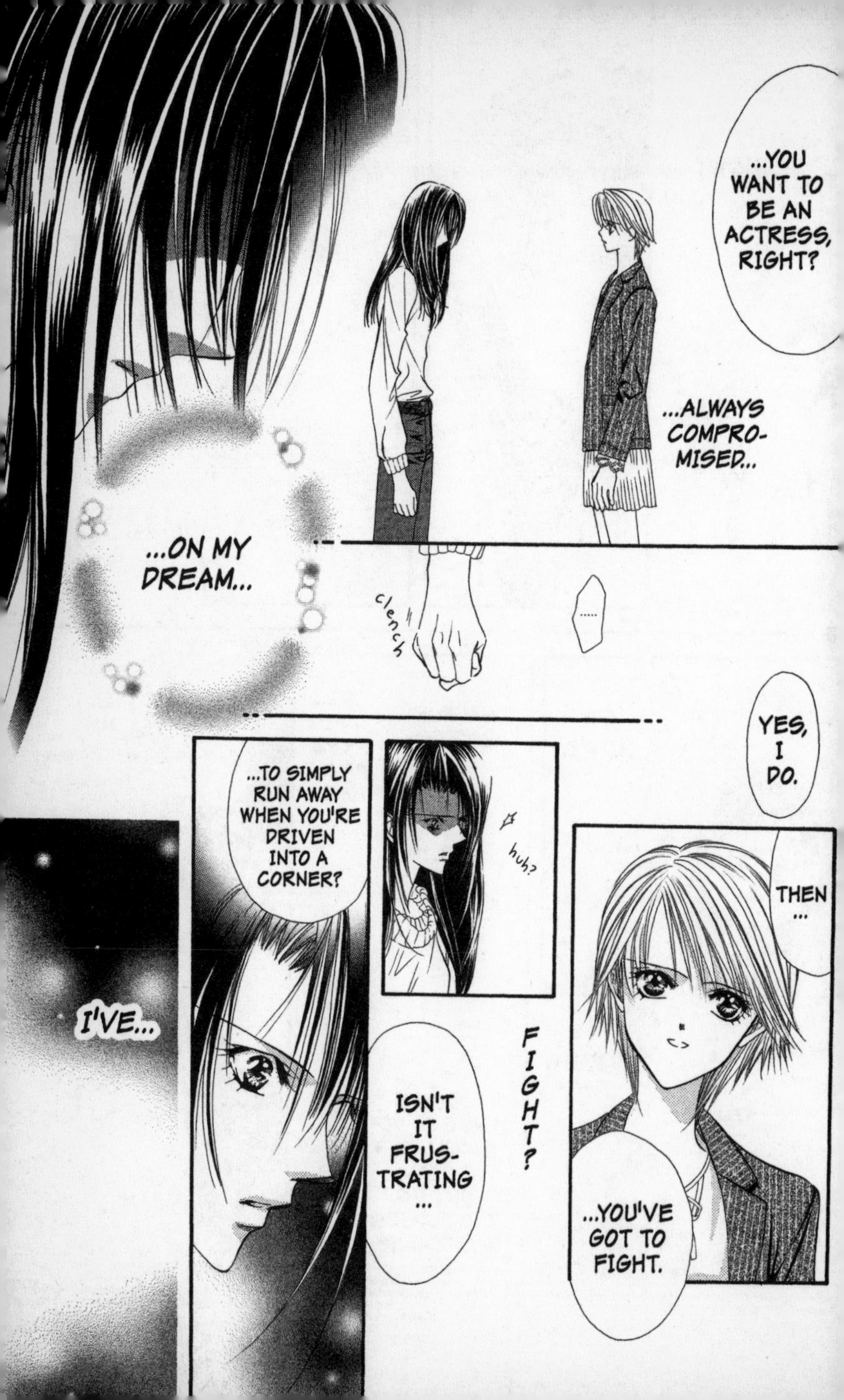
...YOU WANT TO BE AN ACTRESS, RIGHT?
...ALWAYS COMPROMISED...
......
clench
...ON MY DREAM...
YES, I DO.
THEN ...
...YOU'VE GOT TO FIGHT.
FIGHT?
huh?
...TO SIMPLY RUN AWAY WHEN YOU'RE DRIVEN INTO A CORNER?
ISN'T IT FRUSTRATING ...
I'VE...

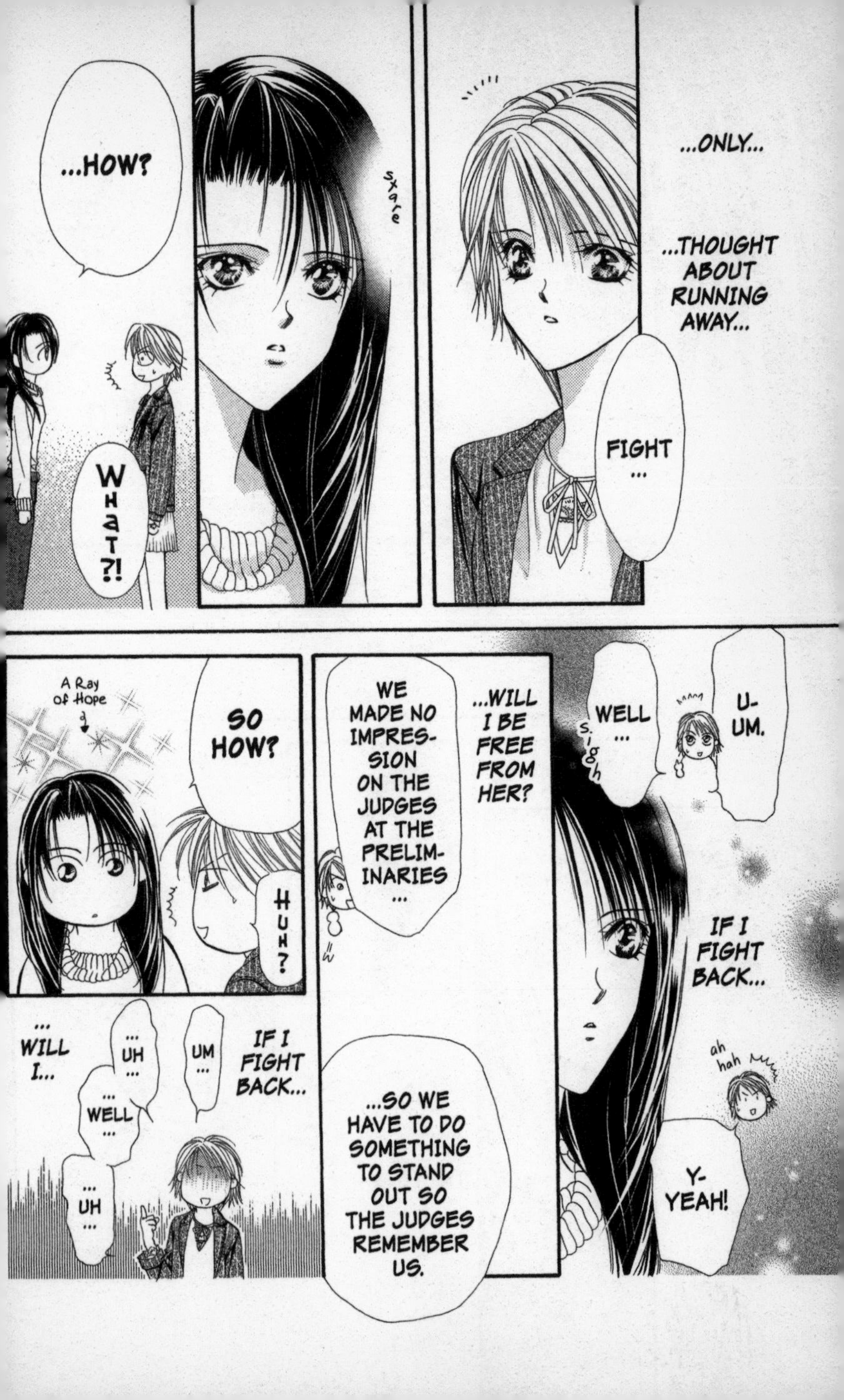
...ONLY...
...THOUGHT ABOUT RUNNING AWAY...
FIGHT ...
stare
...HOW?
WHAT?!
U-UM.
WELL ...
sigh
IF I FIGHT BACK...
ah hah
Y-YEAH!
...WILL I BE FREE FROM HER?
WE MADE NO IMPRESSION ON THE JUDGES AT THE PRELIMINARIES ...
...SO WE HAVE TO DO SOMETHING TO STAND OUT SO THE JUDGES REMEMBER US.
SO HOW?
A Ray of Hope
HUH?
IF I FIGHT BACK...
UM ...
... UH ...
... WILL I...
... WELL ...
... UH ...

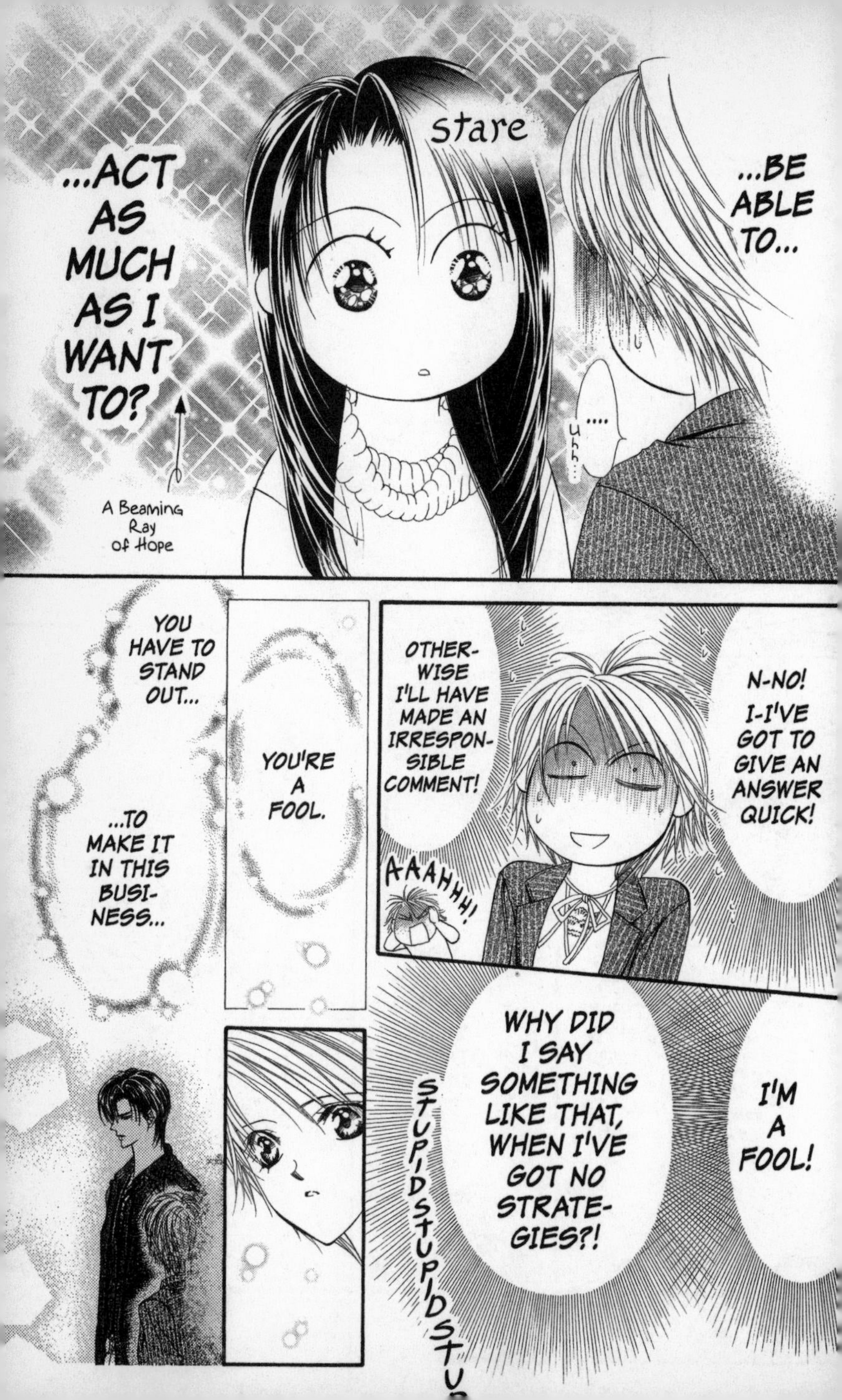
...BE ABLE TO...
Stare
....
Uhh...
...ACT AS MUCH AS I WANT TO?
A Beaming Ray of Hope
N-NO! I-I'VE GOT TO GIVE AN ANSWER QUICK!
OTHER-WISE I'LL HAVE MADE AN IRRESPON-SIBLE COMMENT!
AAAHHH!
I'M A FOOL!
WHY DID I SAY SOMETHING LIKE THAT, WHEN I'VE GOT NO STRATE-GIES?!
STUPIDSTUPIDSTU
YOU'RE A FOOL.
YOU HAVE TO STAND OUT...
...TO MAKE IT IN THIS BUSI-NESS...

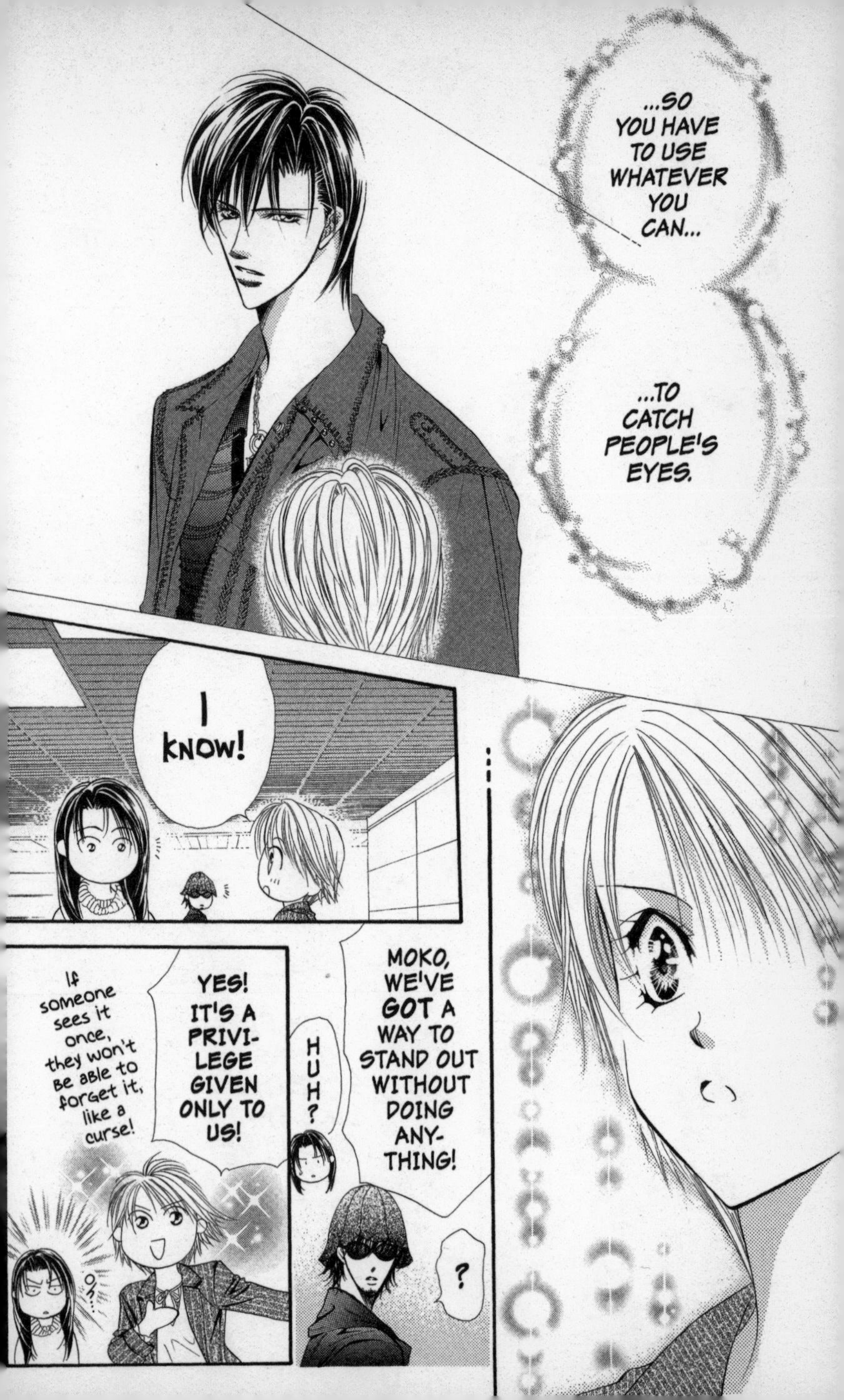
...SO YOU HAVE TO USE WHATEVER YOU CAN...
...TO CATCH PEOPLE'S EYES.
I KNOW!
MOKO, WE'VE GOT A WAY TO STAND OUT WITHOUT DOING ANYTHING!
HUH?
YES! IT'S A PRIVI-LEGE GIVEN ONLY TO US!
If someone sees it once, they won't be able to forget it, like a curse!
?
Oh...?

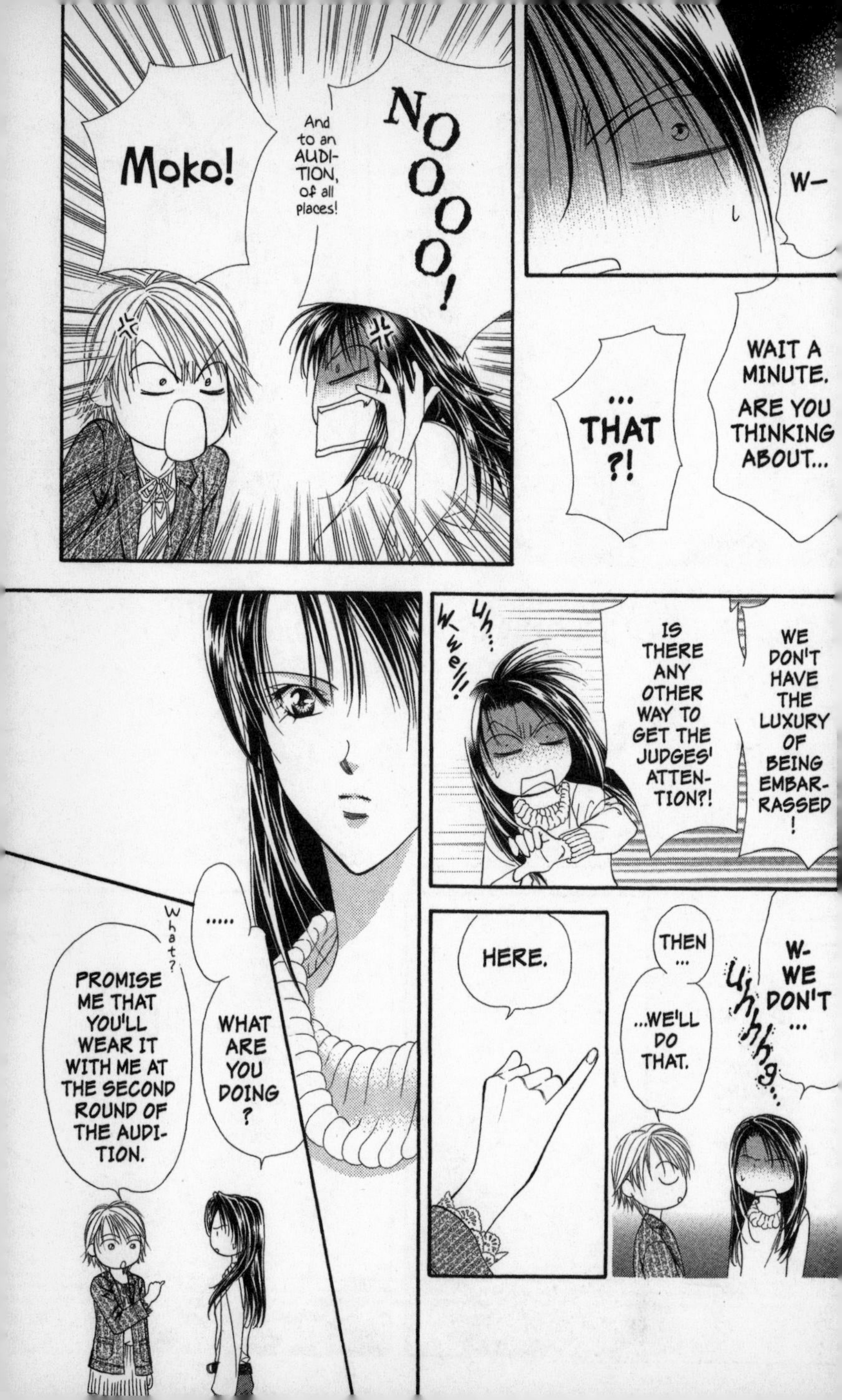
W-
WAIT A MINUTE. ARE YOU THINKING ABOUT...
... THAT ?!
NOOOO!
And to an AUDITION, of all places!
Moko!
WE DON'T HAVE THE LUXURY OF BEING EMBARRASSED!
IS THERE ANY OTHER WAY TO GET THE JUDGES' ATTENTION?!
Uh... W-well!!
W-WE DON'T ...
Uhhhg...
THEN ...
...WE'LL DO THAT.
HERE.
.....
What?
WHAT ARE YOU DOING?
PROMISE ME THAT YOU'LL WEAR IT WITH ME AT THE SECOND ROUND OF THE AUDITION.

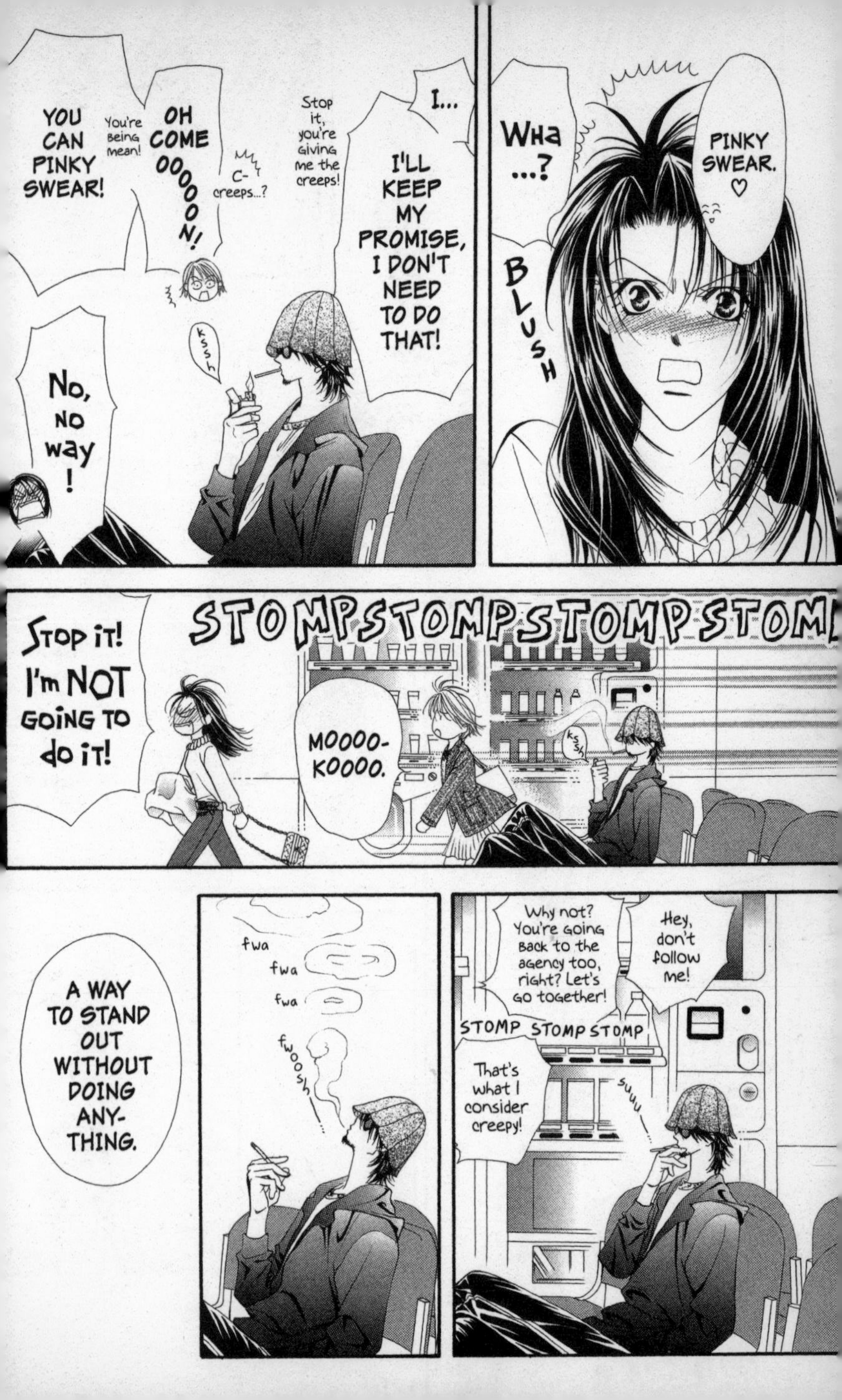
PINKY SWEAR. ♡
WHA ...?
BLUSH
I...
I'LL KEEP MY PROMISE, I DON'T NEED TO DO THAT!
Stop it, you're giving me the creeps!
C-creeps...?
OH COME OOOOOON!
You're being mean!
YOU CAN PINKY SWEAR!
kssh
No, no way!
STOMPSTOMPSTOMPSTOM
kssh
MOOOO-KOOOO.
Stop it! I'm NOT going to do it!
Hey, don't follow me!
Why not? You're going back to the agency too, right? Let's go together!
STOMP STOMP STOMP
suuu—
That's what I consider creepy!
fwa
fwa
fwa
fwoosh—
A WAY TO STAND OUT WITHOUT DOING ANY-THING.

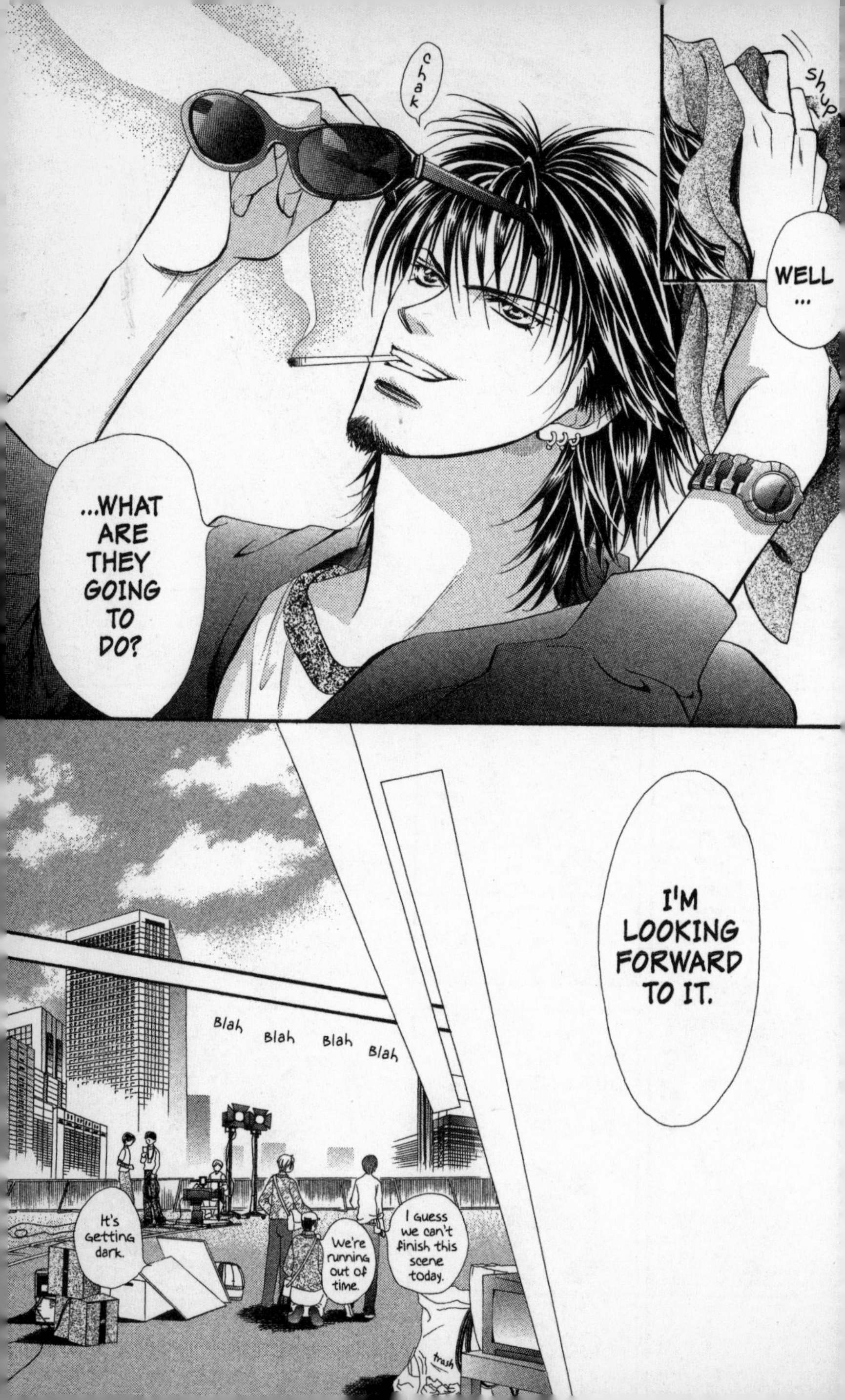
shup
WELL ...
chak
...WHAT ARE THEY GOING TO DO?
I'M LOOKING FORWARD TO IT.
Blah Blah Blah Blah
I guess we can't finish this scene today.
We're running out of time.
It's getting dark.
trash

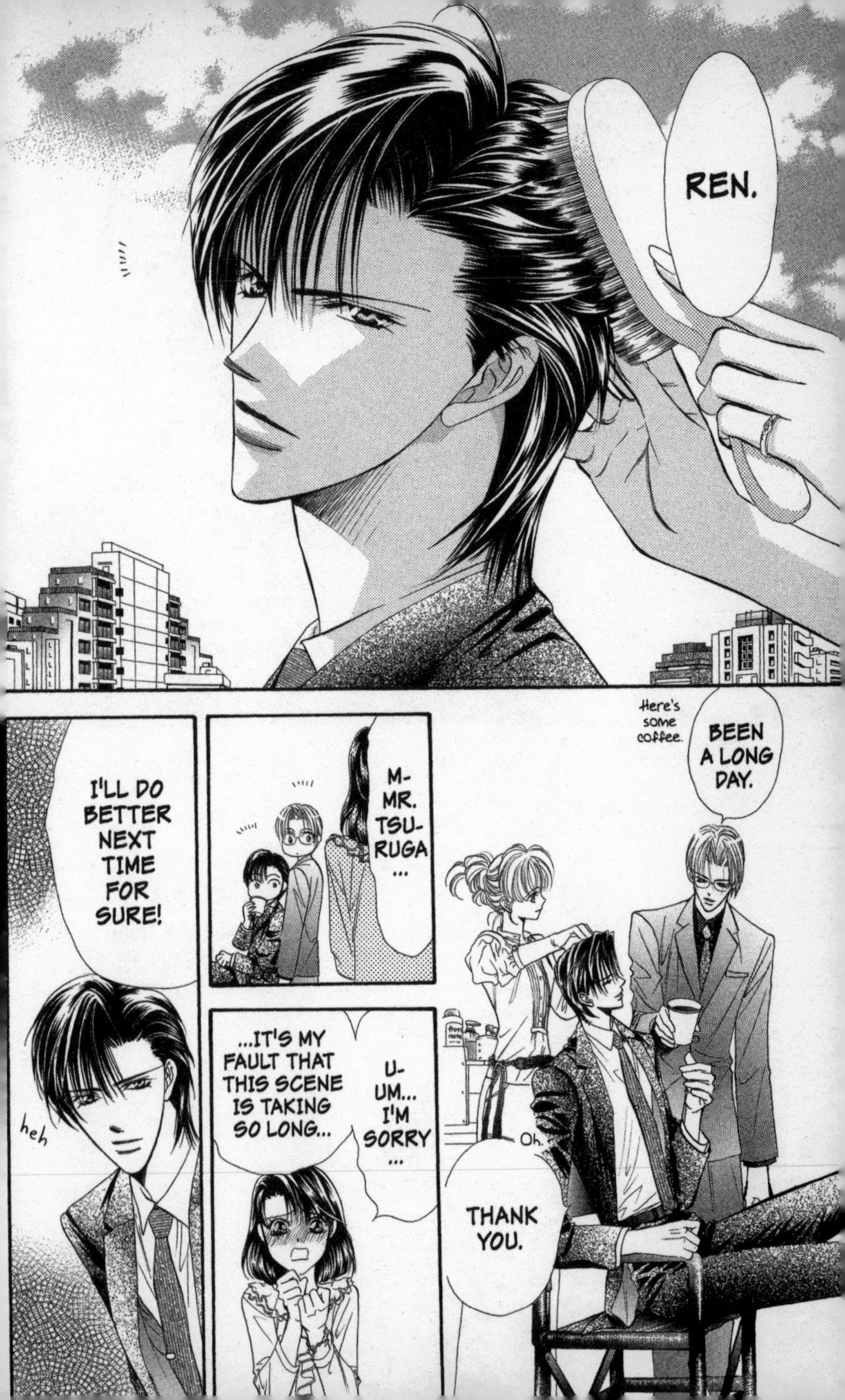

REN.
Here's some coffee.
BEEN A LONG DAY.
Oh.
THANK YOU.
M-MR. TSURUGA...
U-UM... I'M SORRY...
...IT'S MY FAULT THAT THIS SCENE IS TAKING SO LONG...
I'LL DO BETTER NEXT TIME FOR SURE!
heh

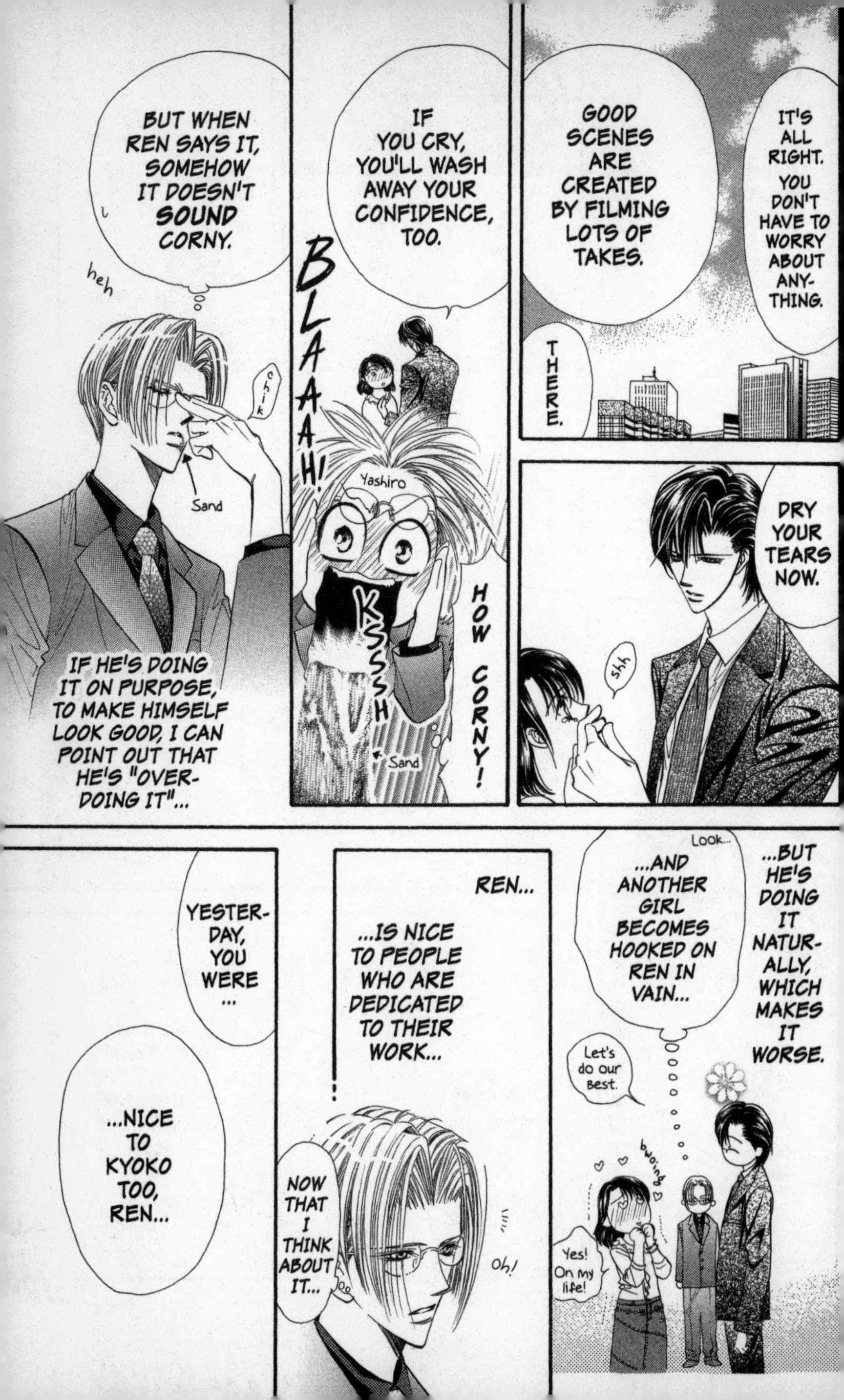
IT'S ALL RIGHT. YOU DON'T HAVE TO WORRY ABOUT ANYTHING.
GOOD SCENES ARE CREATED BY FILMING LOTS OF TAKES.
THERE.
DRY YOUR TEARS NOW.
shh
IF YOU CRY, YOU'LL WASH AWAY YOUR CONFIDENCE, TOO.
BLAAAAH!
Yashiro
KSSSH
Sand
HOW CORNY!
BUT WHEN REN SAYS IT, SOMEHOW IT DOESN'T SOUND CORNY.
heh
chik
Sand
IF HE'S DOING IT ON PURPOSE, TO MAKE HIMSELF LOOK GOOD, I CAN POINT OUT THAT HE'S "OVER-DOING IT"...
...BUT HE'S DOING IT NATURALLY, WHICH MAKES IT WORSE.
Look...
...AND ANOTHER GIRL BECOMES HOOKED ON REN IN VAIN...
Let's do our best.
bwoing
Yes! On my life!
REN...
...IS NICE TO PEOPLE WHO ARE DEDICATED TO THEIR WORK...
NOW THAT I THINK ABOUT IT...
Oh!
YESTER-DAY, YOU WERE...
...NICE TO KYOKO TOO, REN...

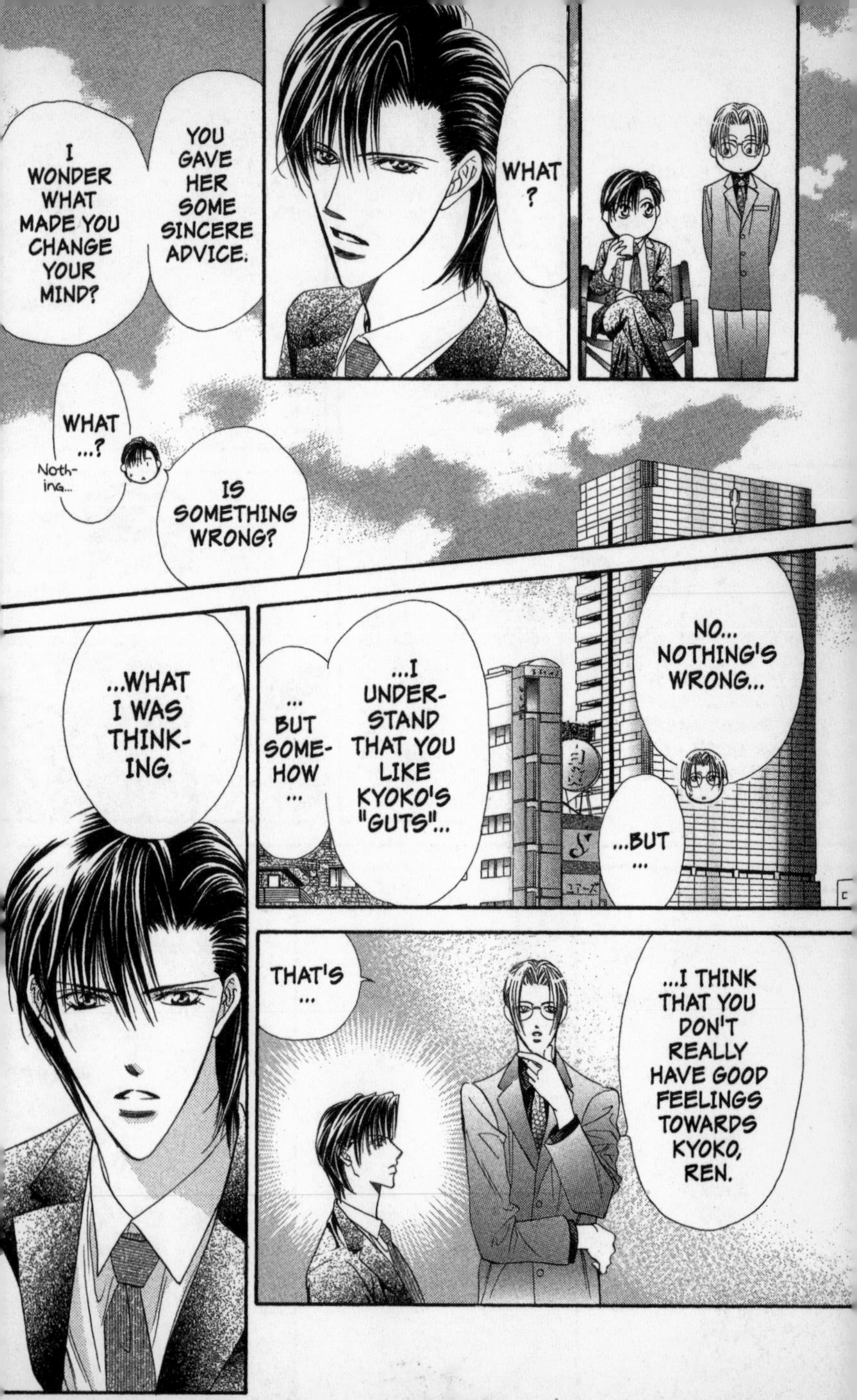
WHAT ?
YOU GAVE HER SOME SINCERE ADVICE.
I WONDER WHAT MADE YOU CHANGE YOUR MIND?
WHAT ...?
Noth-ing...
IS SOMETHING WRONG?
NO... NOTHING'S WRONG...
...BUT ...
...I UNDER-STAND THAT YOU LIKE KYOKO'S "GUTS"...
... BUT SOME-HOW ...
...I THINK THAT YOU DON'T REALLY HAVE GOOD FEELINGS TOWARDS KYOKO, REN.
THAT'S ...
...WHAT I WAS THINK-ING.

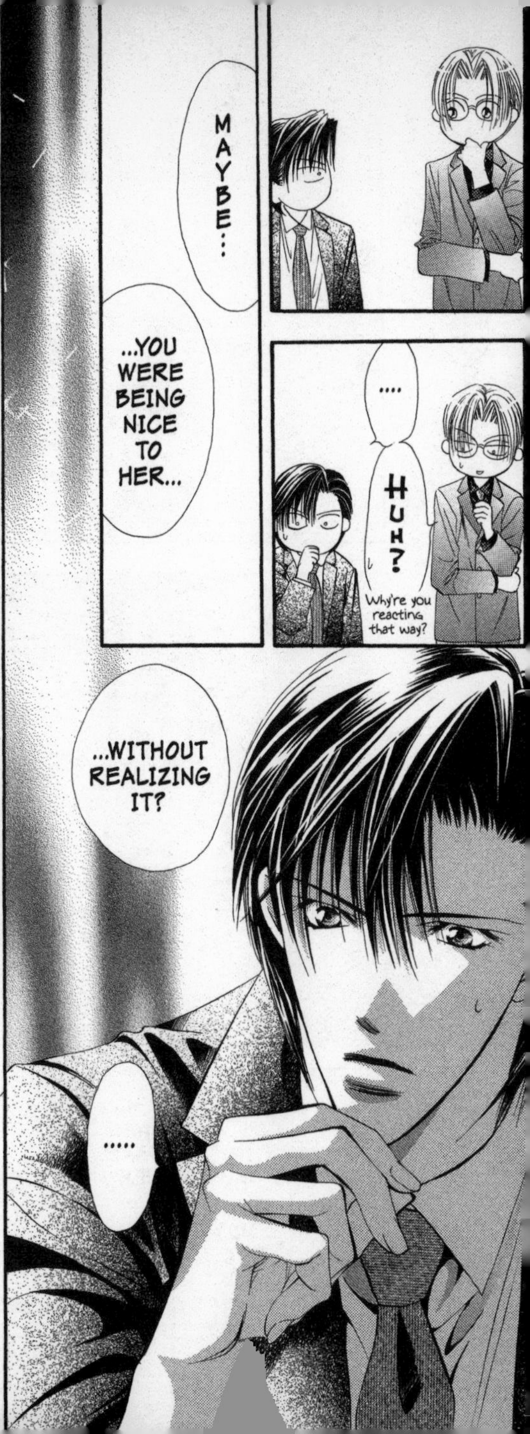
....
HUH?
Why're you reacting that way?
MAYBE...
...YOU WERE BEING NICE TO HER...
...WITHOUT REALIZING IT?
.....

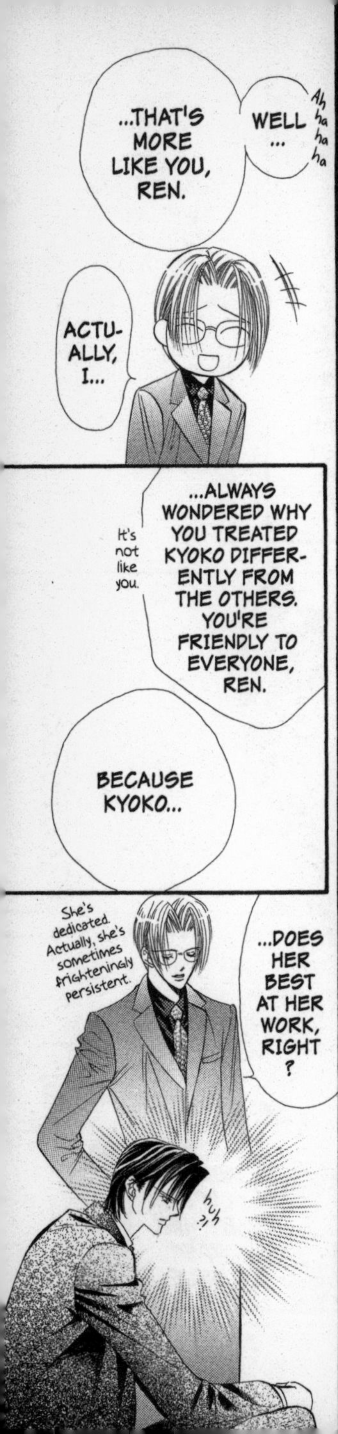
WELL...
Ah ha ha ha
...THAT'S MORE LIKE YOU, REN.
ACTU-ALLY, I...
...ALWAYS WONDERED WHY YOU TREATED KYOKO DIFFER-ENTLY FROM THE OTHERS. YOU'RE FRIENDLY TO EVERYONE, REN.
It's not like you.
BECAUSE KYOKO...
...DOES HER BEST AT HER WORK, RIGHT?
She's dedicated. Actually, she's sometimes frighteningly persistent.
huh!?

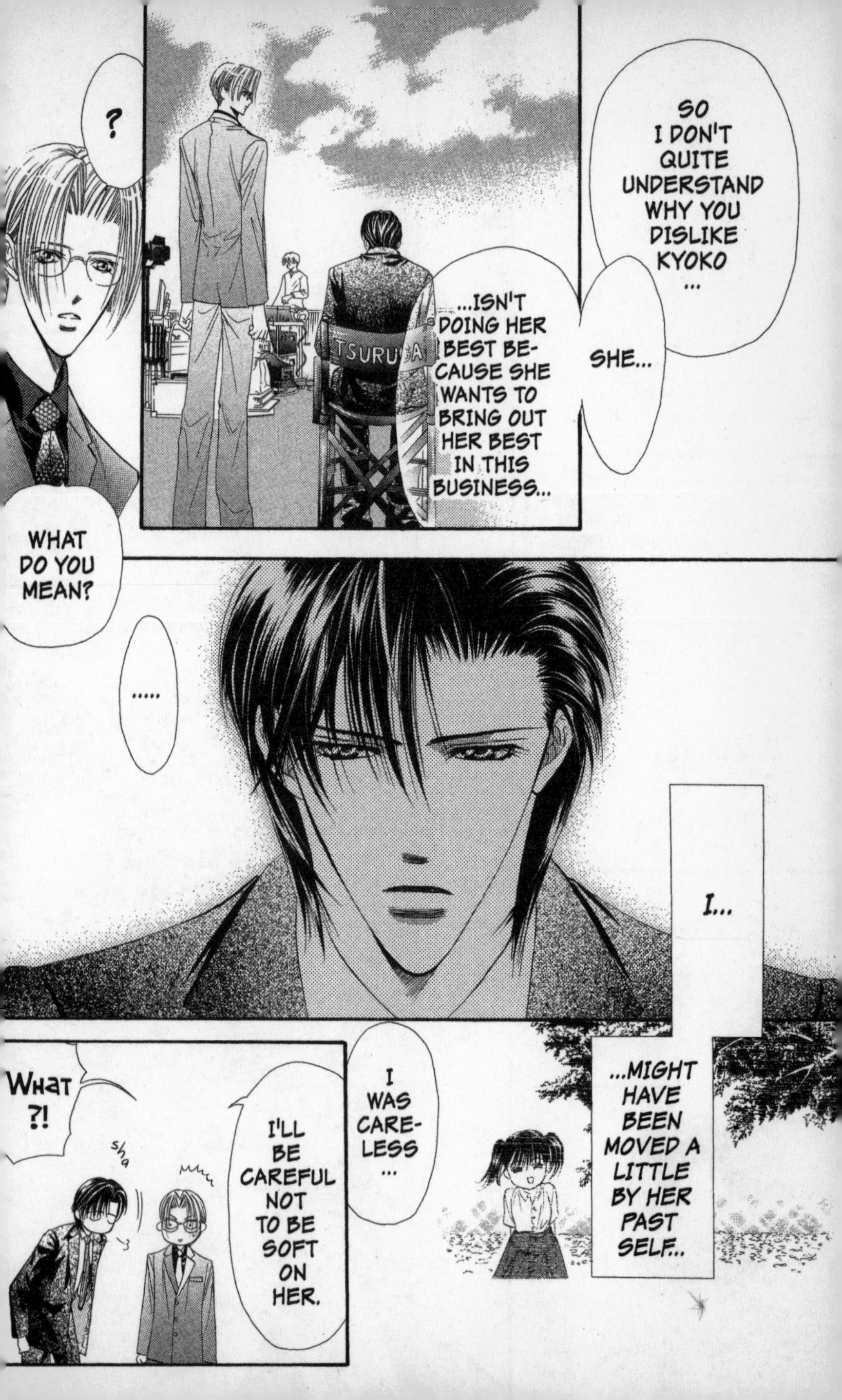
SO I DON'T QUITE UNDERSTAND WHY YOU DISLIKE KYOKO ...
SHE...
...ISN'T DOING HER BEST BE-CAUSE SHE WANTS TO BRING OUT HER BEST IN THIS BUSINESS...
TSURUGA
?
WHAT DO YOU MEAN?
.....
I...
...MIGHT HAVE BEEN MOVED A LITTLE BY HER PAST SELF..
I WAS CARE-LESS ...
I'LL BE CAREFUL NOT TO BE SOFT ON HER.
What ?!
sha

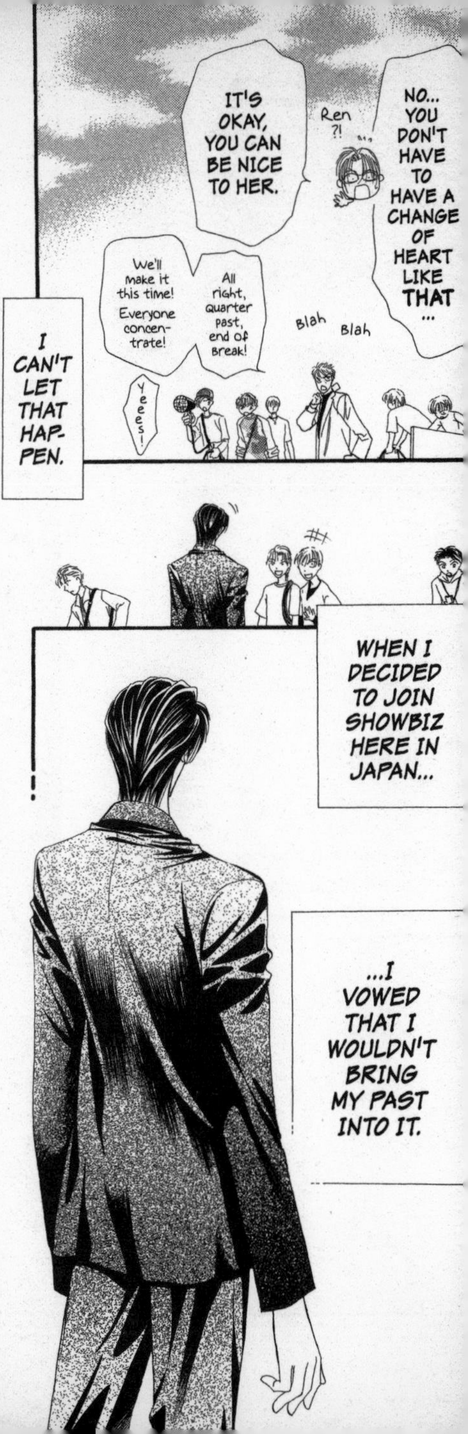
NO... YOU DON'T HAVE TO HAVE A CHANGE OF HEART LIKE THAT...
Ren ?!
IT'S OKAY, YOU CAN BE NICE TO HER.
Blah
Blah
All right, quarter past, end of break!
We'll make it this time! Everyone concentrate!
Yeees!
I CAN'T LET THAT HAPPEN.
WHEN I DECIDED TO JOIN SHOWBIZ HERE IN JAPAN...
...I VOWED THAT I WOULDN'T BRING MY PAST INTO IT.
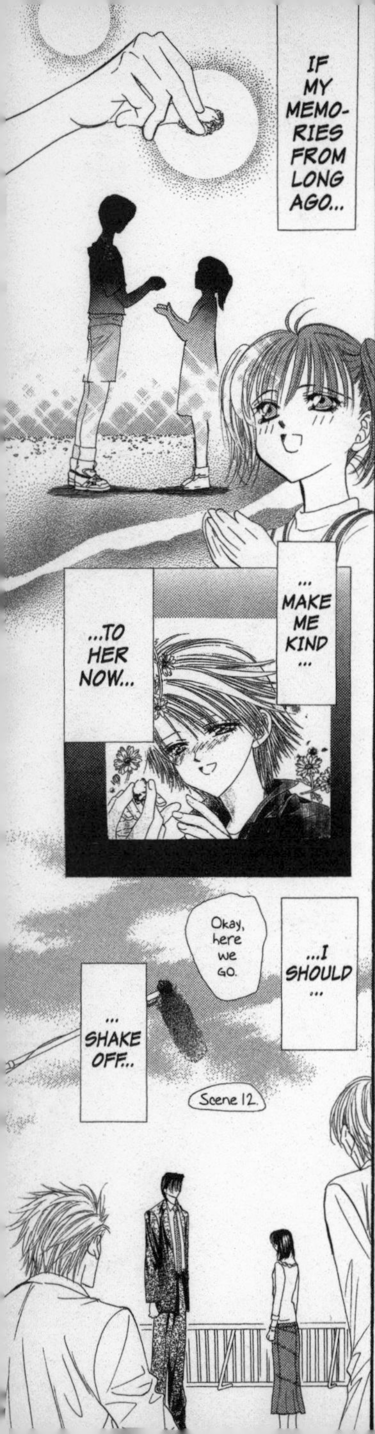
IF MY MEMORIES FROM LONG AGO...
... MAKE ME KIND ...
...TO HER NOW...
...I SHOULD ...
Okay, here we GO.
... SHAKE OFF...
Scene 12.

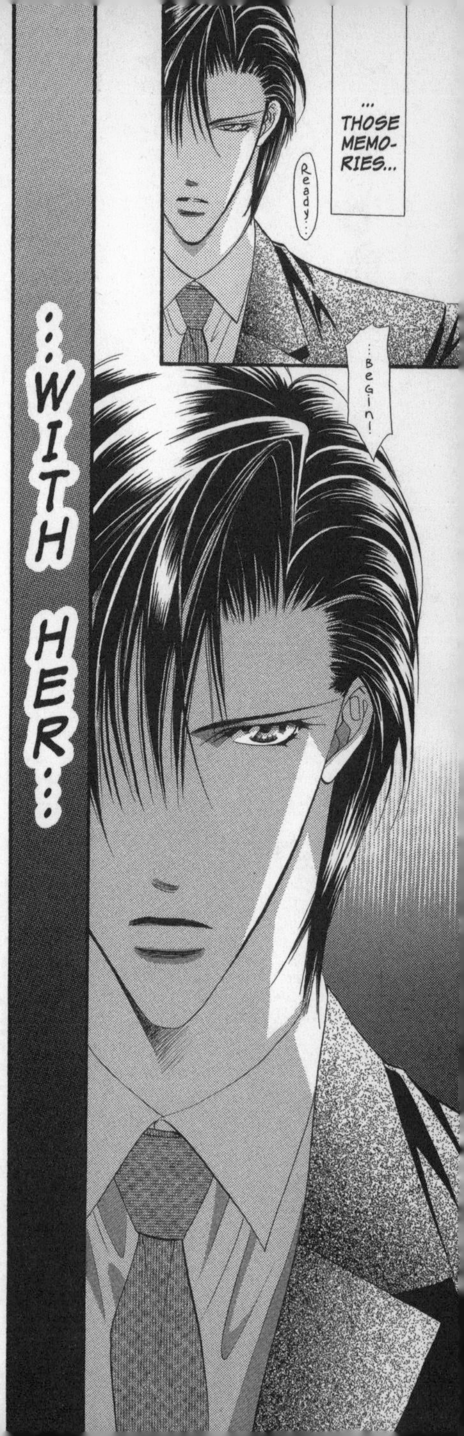
...THOSE MEMORIES...
Ready...
...Begin!
..WITH HER..

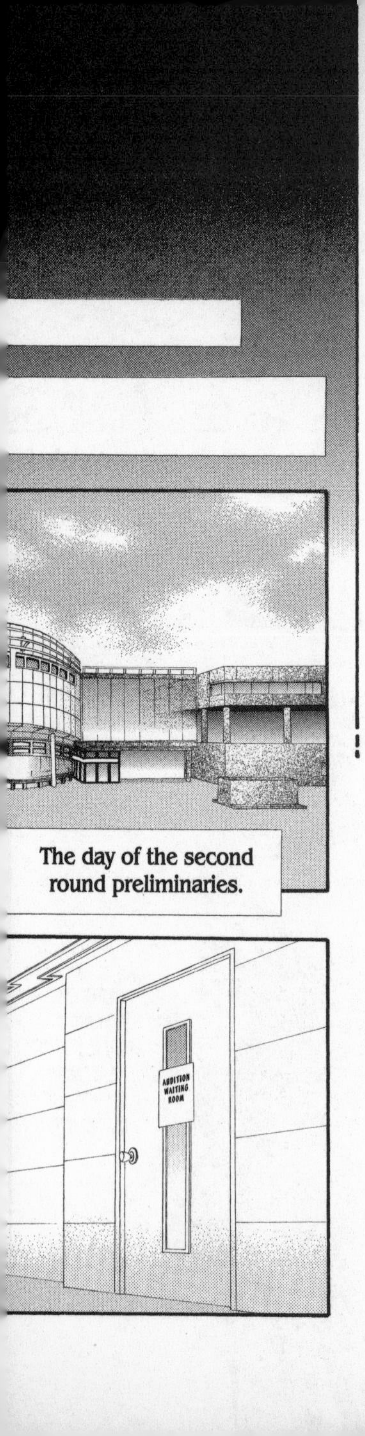
The day of the second round preliminaries.
AUDITION WAITING ROOM

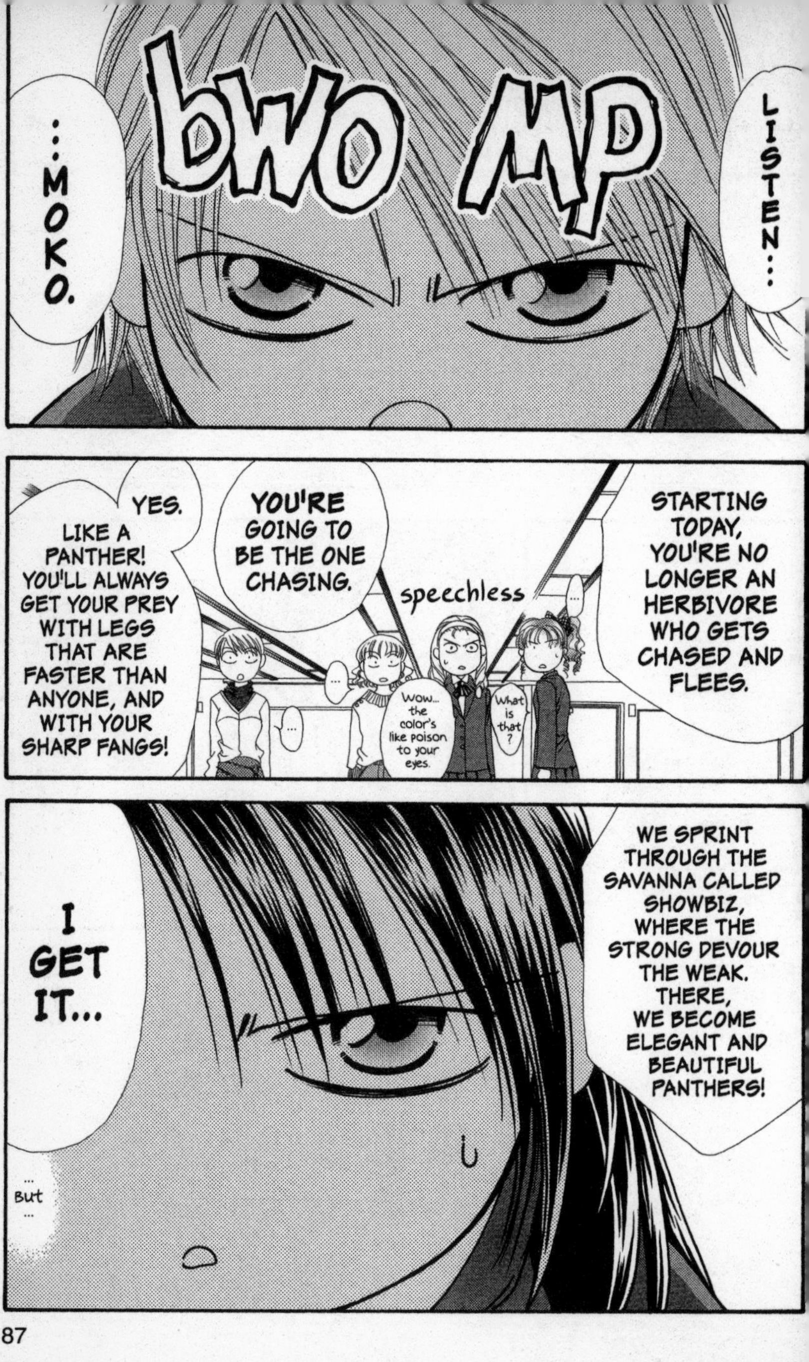
LISTEN...
BWOMP
...MOKO.
STARTING TODAY, YOU'RE NO LONGER AN HERBIVORE WHO GETS CHASED AND FLEES.
...
speechless
What is that?
Wow... the color's like poison to your eyes.
...
...
YOU'RE GOING TO BE THE ONE CHASING.
YES. LIKE A PANTHER! YOU'LL ALWAYS GET YOUR PREY WITH LEGS THAT ARE FASTER THAN ANYONE, AND WITH YOUR SHARP FANGS!
WE SPRINT THROUGH THE SAVANNA CALLED SHOWBIZ, WHERE THE STRONG DEVOUR THE WEAK. THERE, WE BECOME ELEGANT AND BEAUTIFUL PANTHERS!
I GET IT...
...But...

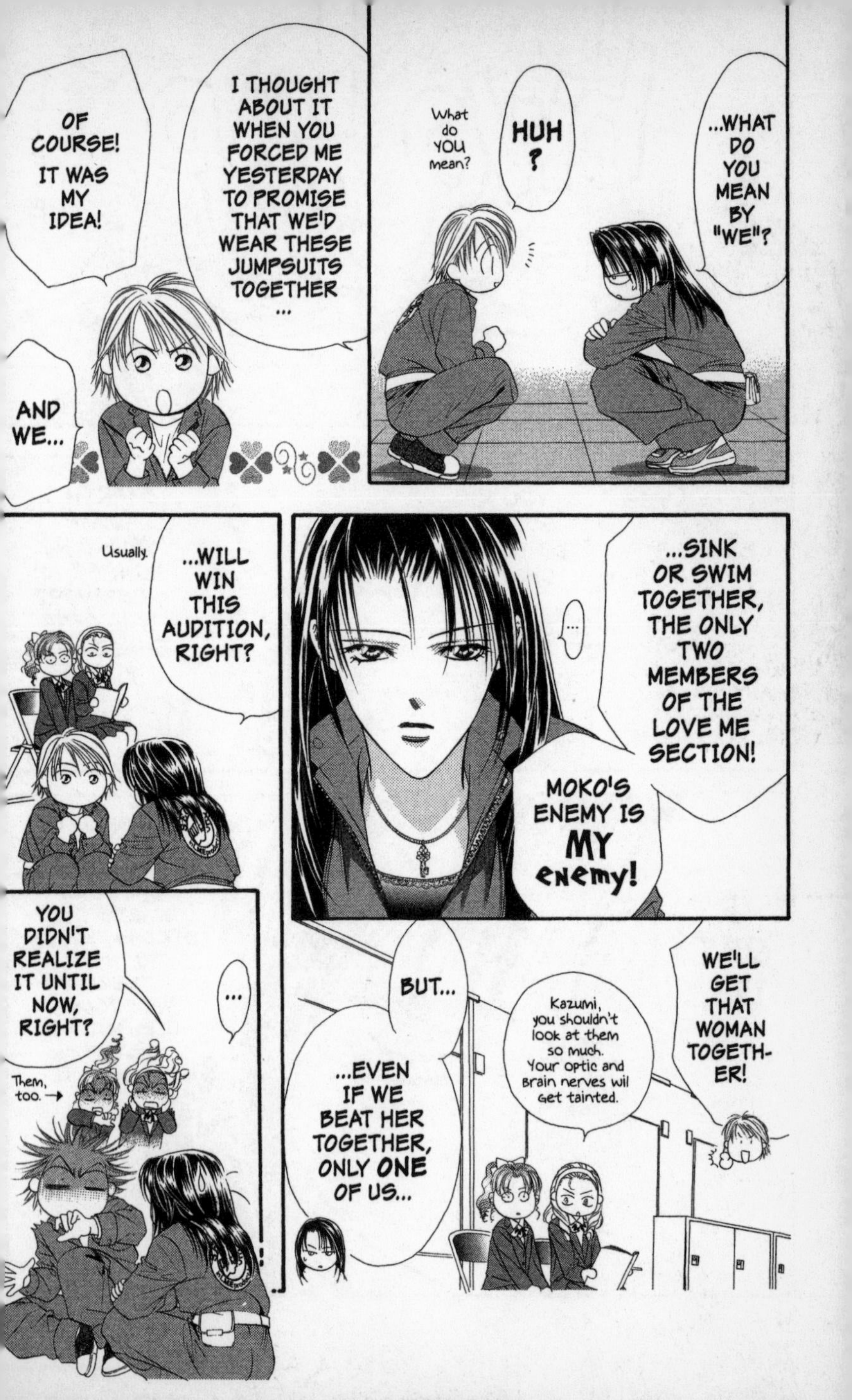

...WHAT DO YOU MEAN BY "WE"?
HUH?
What do YOU mean?
I THOUGHT ABOUT IT WHEN YOU FORCED ME YESTERDAY TO PROMISE THAT WE'D WEAR THESE JUMPSUITS TOGETHER...
OF COURSE! IT WAS MY IDEA!
AND WE...
...SINK OR SWIM TOGETHER, THE ONLY TWO MEMBERS OF THE LOVE ME SECTION!
...
MOKO'S ENEMY IS MY enemy!
...WILL WIN THIS AUDITION, RIGHT?
Usually.
YOU DIDN'T REALIZE IT UNTIL NOW, RIGHT?
...
Them, too. →
WE'LL GET THAT WOMAN TOGETHER!
Kazumi, you shouldn't look at them so much. Your optic and brain nerves wil get tainted.
BUT...
...EVEN IF WE BEAT HER TOGETHER, ONLY ONE OF US...

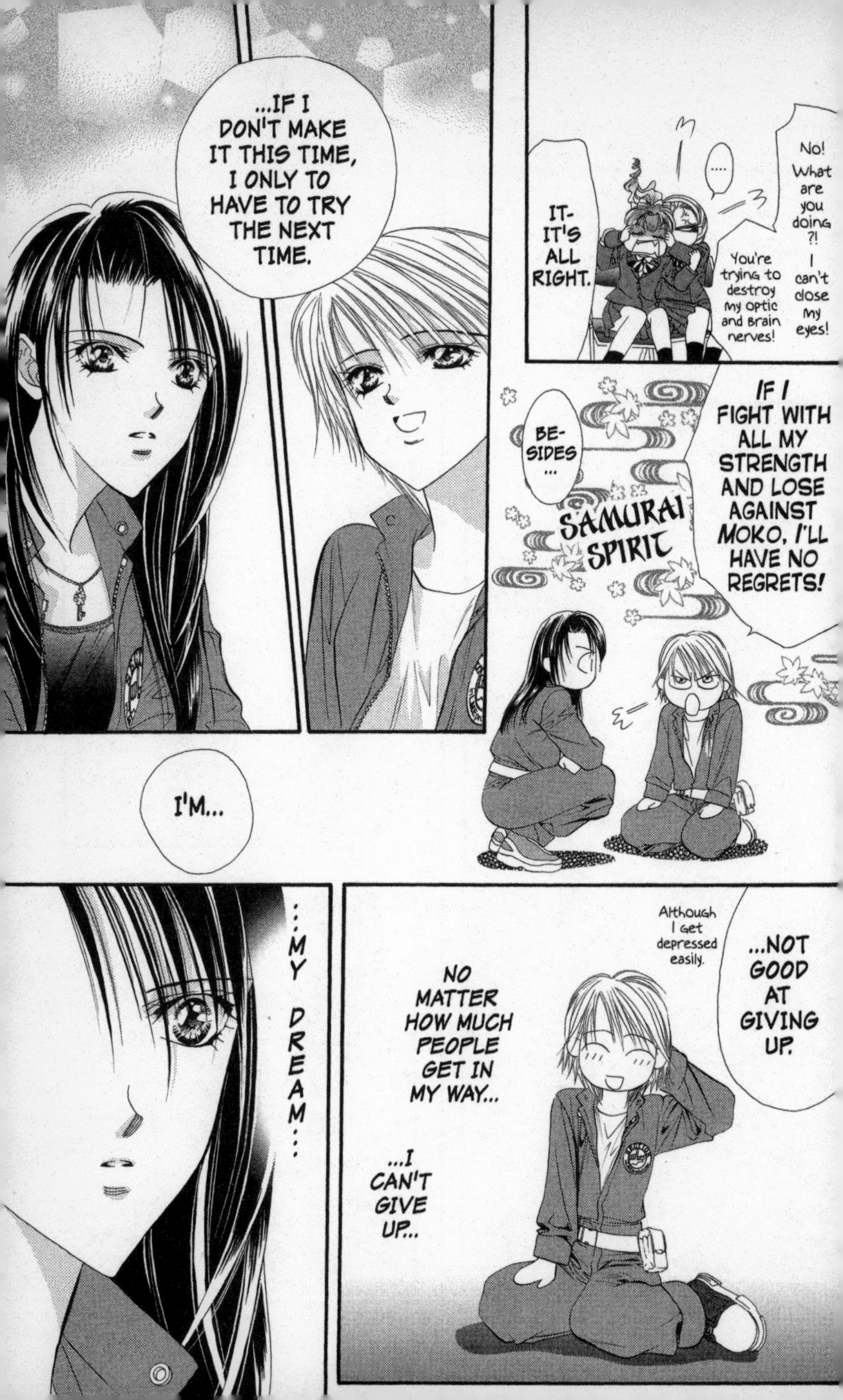

No! What are you doing?! I can't close my eyes!
....
You're trying to destroy my optic and brain nerves!
IT- IT'S ALL RIGHT.
IF I FIGHT WITH ALL MY STRENGTH AND LOSE AGAINST MOKO, I'LL HAVE NO REGRETS!
BE-SIDES...
SAMURAI SPIRIT
...IF I DON'T MAKE IT THIS TIME, I ONLY TO HAVE TO TRY THE NEXT TIME.
I'M...
Although I get depressed easily.
...NOT GOOD AT GIVING UP.
NO MATTER HOW MUCH PEOPLE GET IN MY WAY...
...I CAN'T GIVE UP...
...MY DREAM...

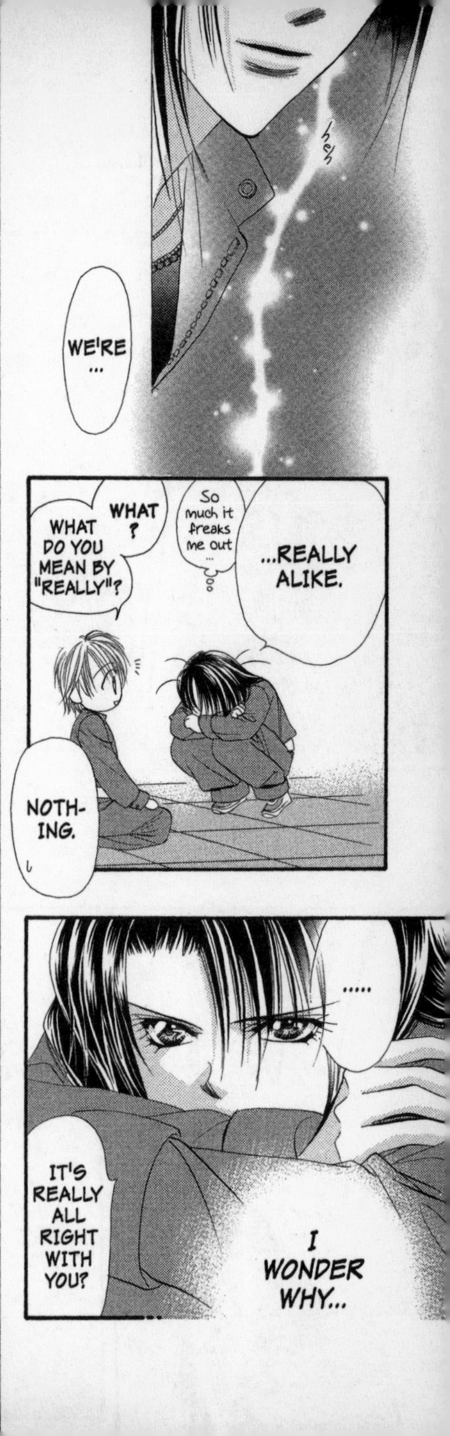
heh
WE'RE ...
...REALLY ALIKE.
So much it freaks me out ...
WHAT ?
WHAT DO YOU MEAN BY "REALLY"?
NOTH-ING.
.....
I WONDER WHY...
IT'S REALLY ALL RIGHT WITH YOU?
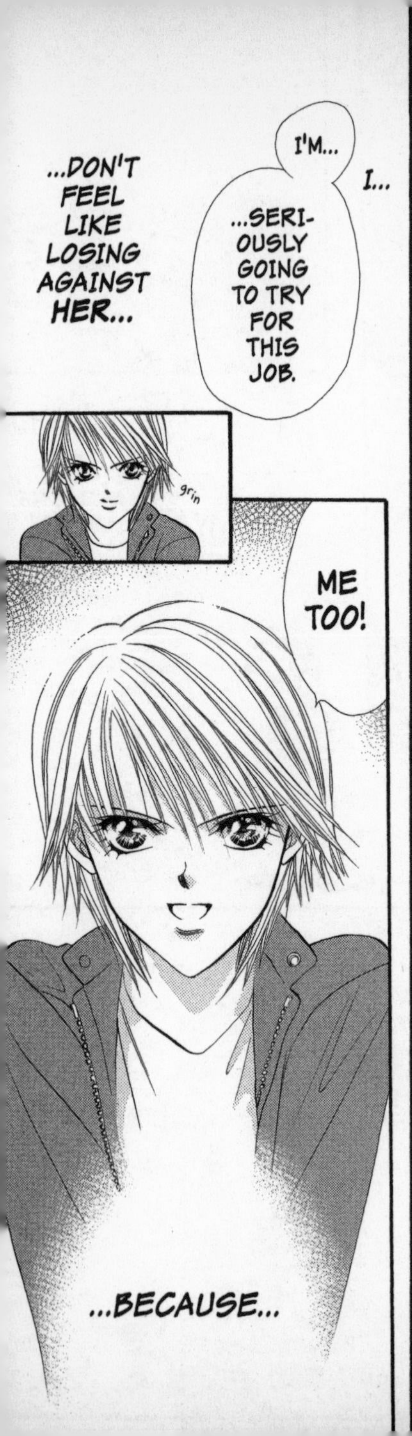
I...
I'M...
...SERI-OUSLY GOING TO TRY FOR THIS JOB.
...DON'T FEEL LIKE LOSING AGAINST HER...
grin
ME TOO!
...BECAUSE...

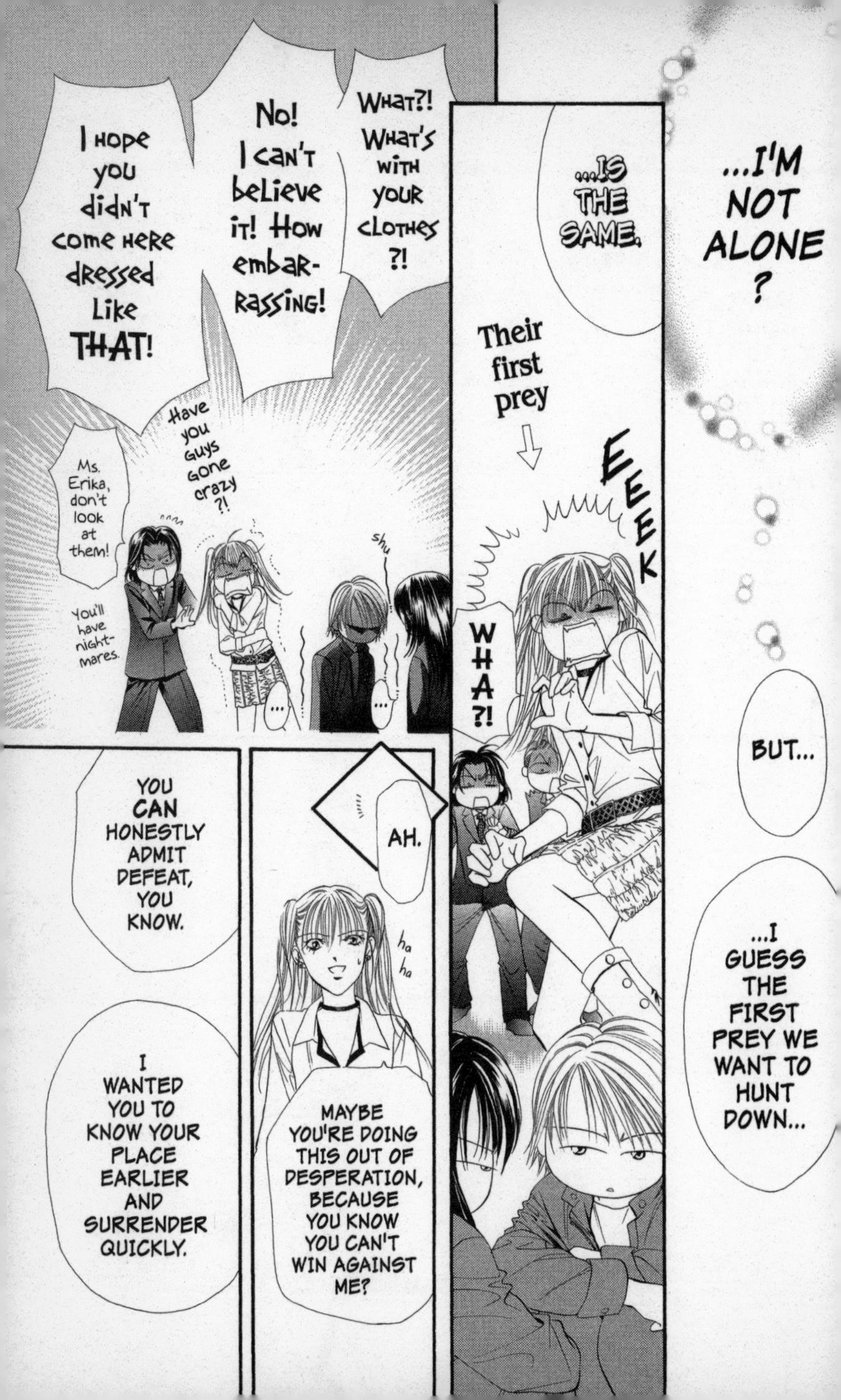
...I'M NOT ALONE?
BUT...
...I GUESS THE FIRST PREY WE WANT TO HUNT DOWN...
...IS THE SAME.
Their first prey
EEEK
WHA?!
WHAT?! WHAT'S WITH YOUR CLOTHES?!
No! I can't believe it! How embarrassing!
I hope you didn't come here dressed like THAT!
Have you guys gone crazy?!
Ms. Erika, don't look at them!
You'll have nightmares.
shu
...
...
AH.
ha ha
MAYBE YOU'RE DOING THIS OUT OF DESPERATION, BECAUSE YOU KNOW YOU CAN'T WIN AGAINST ME?
YOU CAN HONESTLY ADMIT DEFEAT, YOU KNOW.
I WANTED YOU TO KNOW YOUR PLACE EARLIER AND SURRENDER QUICKLY.

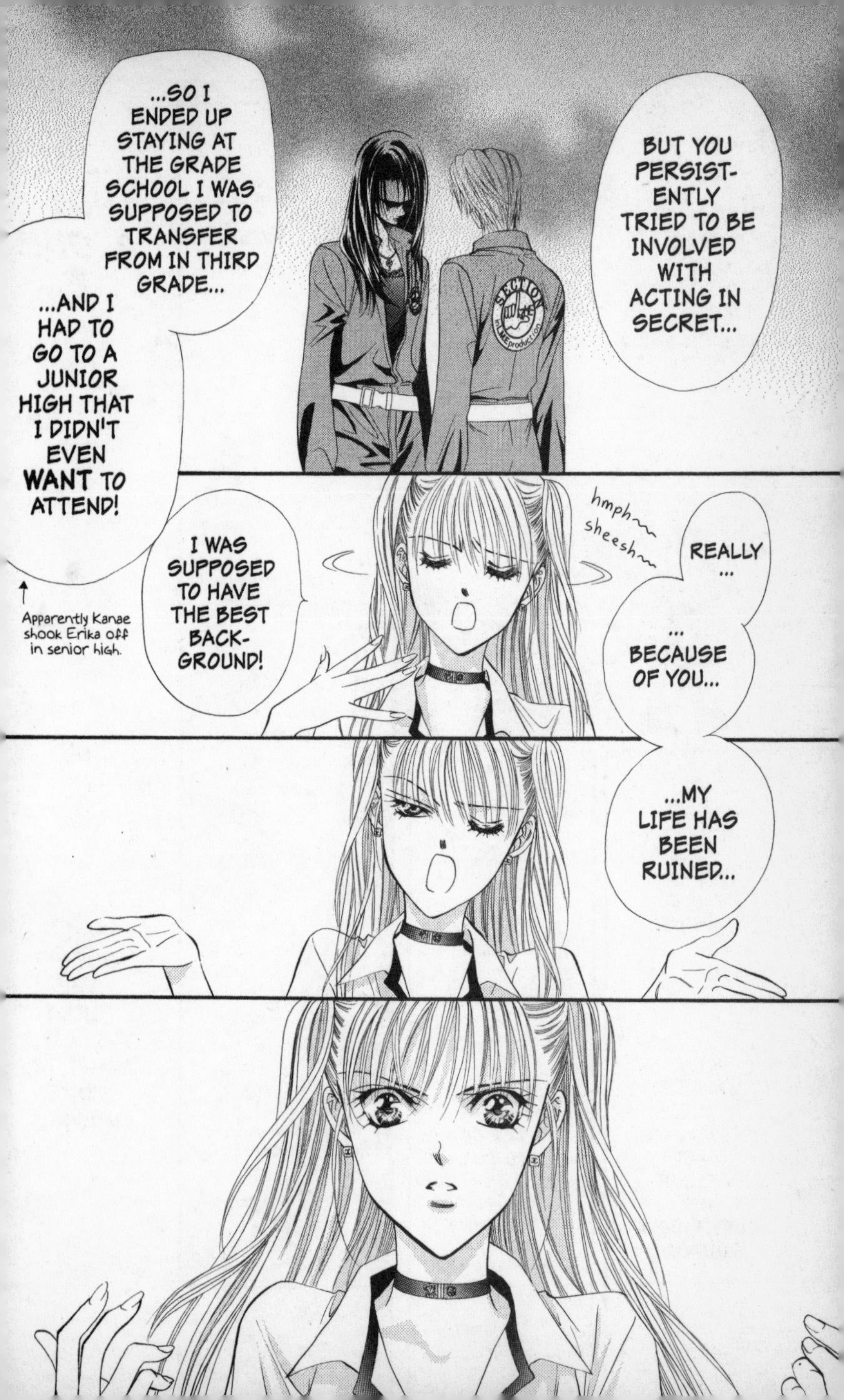
BUT YOU PERSISTENTLY TRIED TO BE INVOLVED WITH ACTING IN SECRET...
...SO I ENDED UP STAYING AT THE GRADE SCHOOL I WAS SUPPOSED TO TRANSFER FROM IN THIRD GRADE...
...AND I HAD TO GO TO A JUNIOR HIGH THAT I DIDN'T EVEN WANT TO ATTEND!
Apparently Kanae shook Erika off in senior high.
I WAS SUPPOSED TO HAVE THE BEST BACKGROUND!
hmph~ sheesh~
REALLY... ...BECAUSE OF YOU...
...MY LIFE HAS BEEN RUINED...

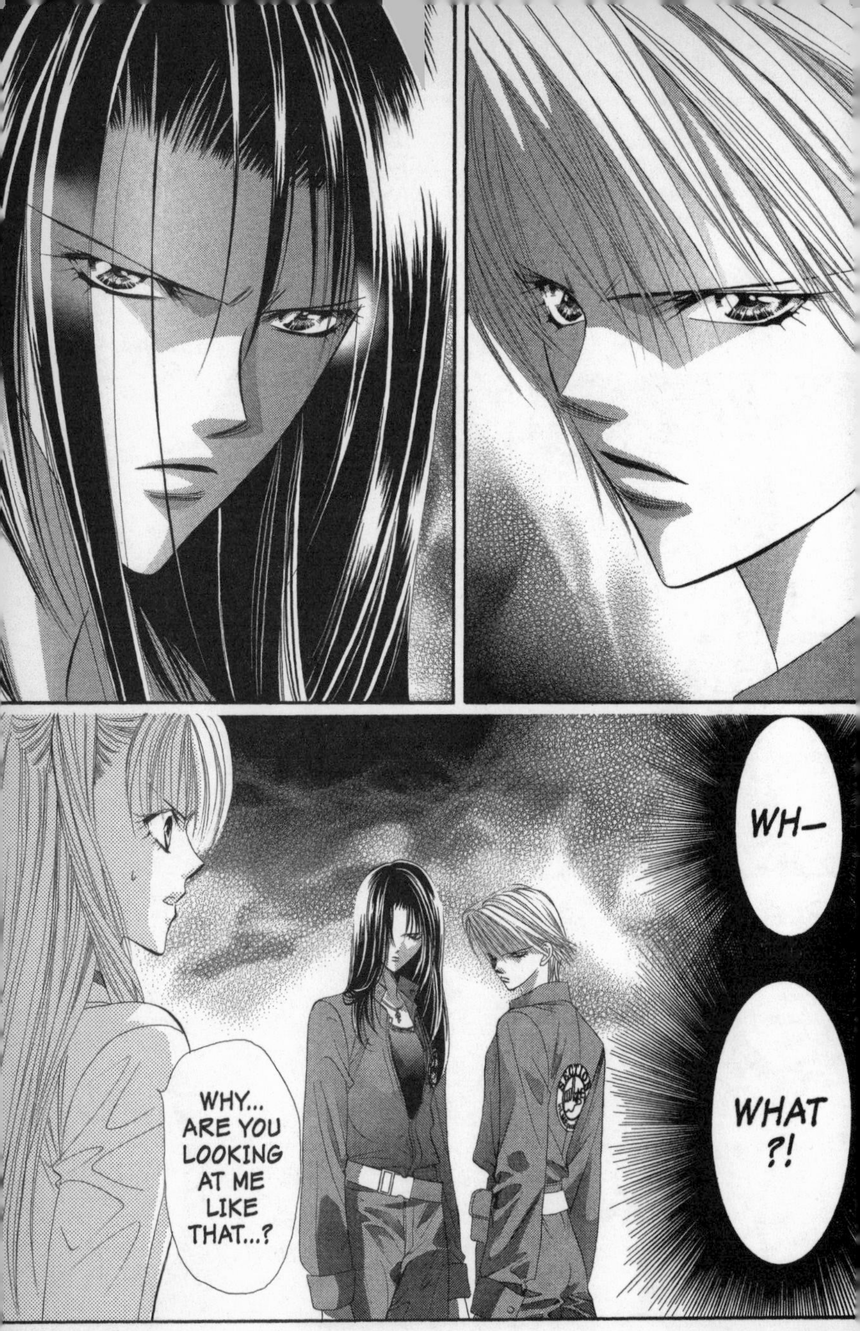
WH—
WHAT ?!
WHY... ARE YOU LOOKING AT ME LIKE THAT...?

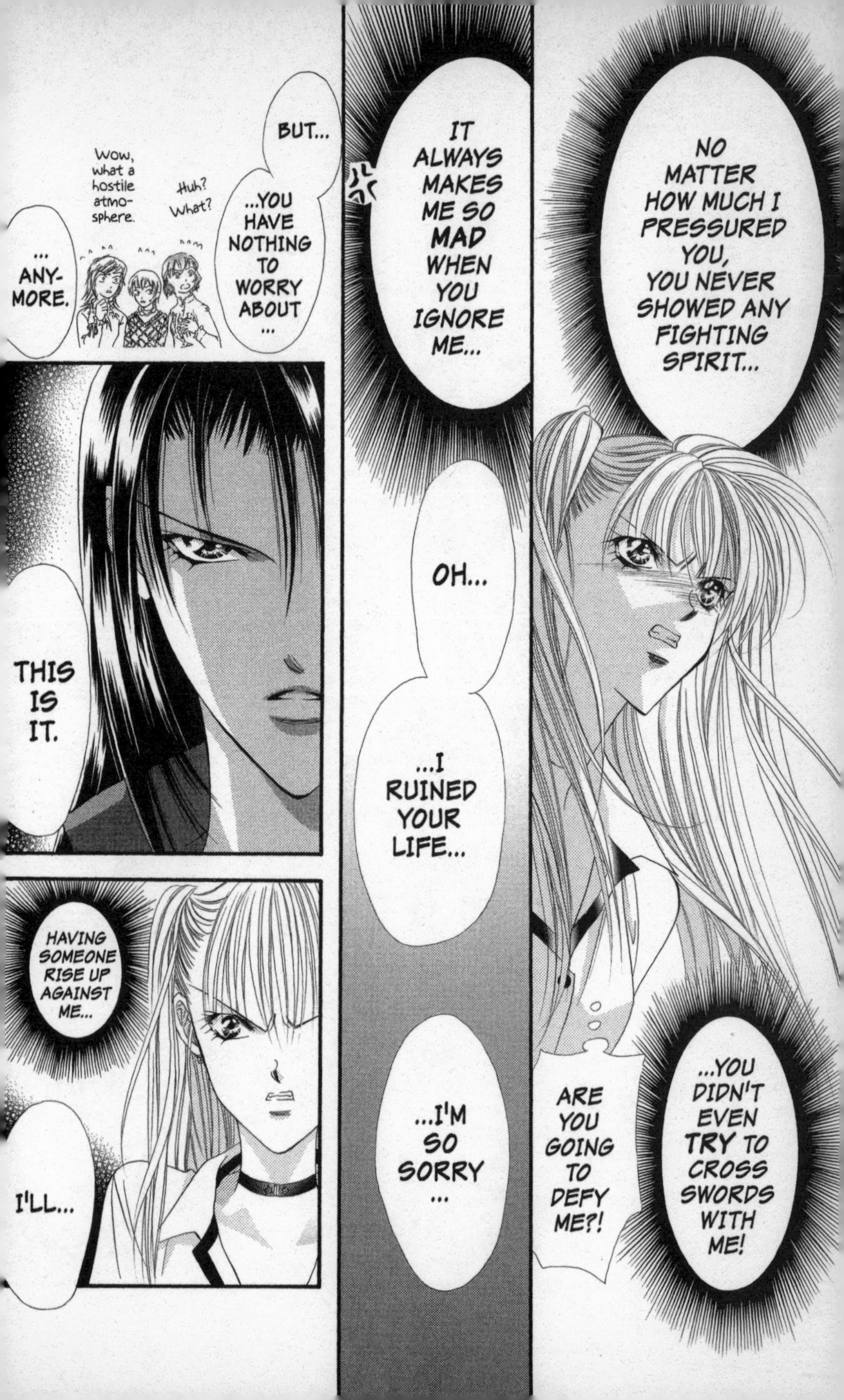
NO MATTER HOW MUCH I PRESSURED YOU, YOU NEVER SHOWED ANY FIGHTING SPIRIT...
...YOU DIDN'T EVEN TRY TO CROSS SWORDS WITH ME!
ARE YOU GOING TO DEFY ME?!
IT ALWAYS MAKES ME SO MAD WHEN YOU IGNORE ME...
OH...
...I RUINED YOUR LIFE...
...I'M SO SORRY...
BUT...
...YOU HAVE NOTHING TO WORRY ABOUT...
Huh? What?
Wow, what a hostile atmosphere.
...ANYMORE.
THIS IS IT.
HAVING SOMEONE RISE UP AGAINST ME...
I'LL...

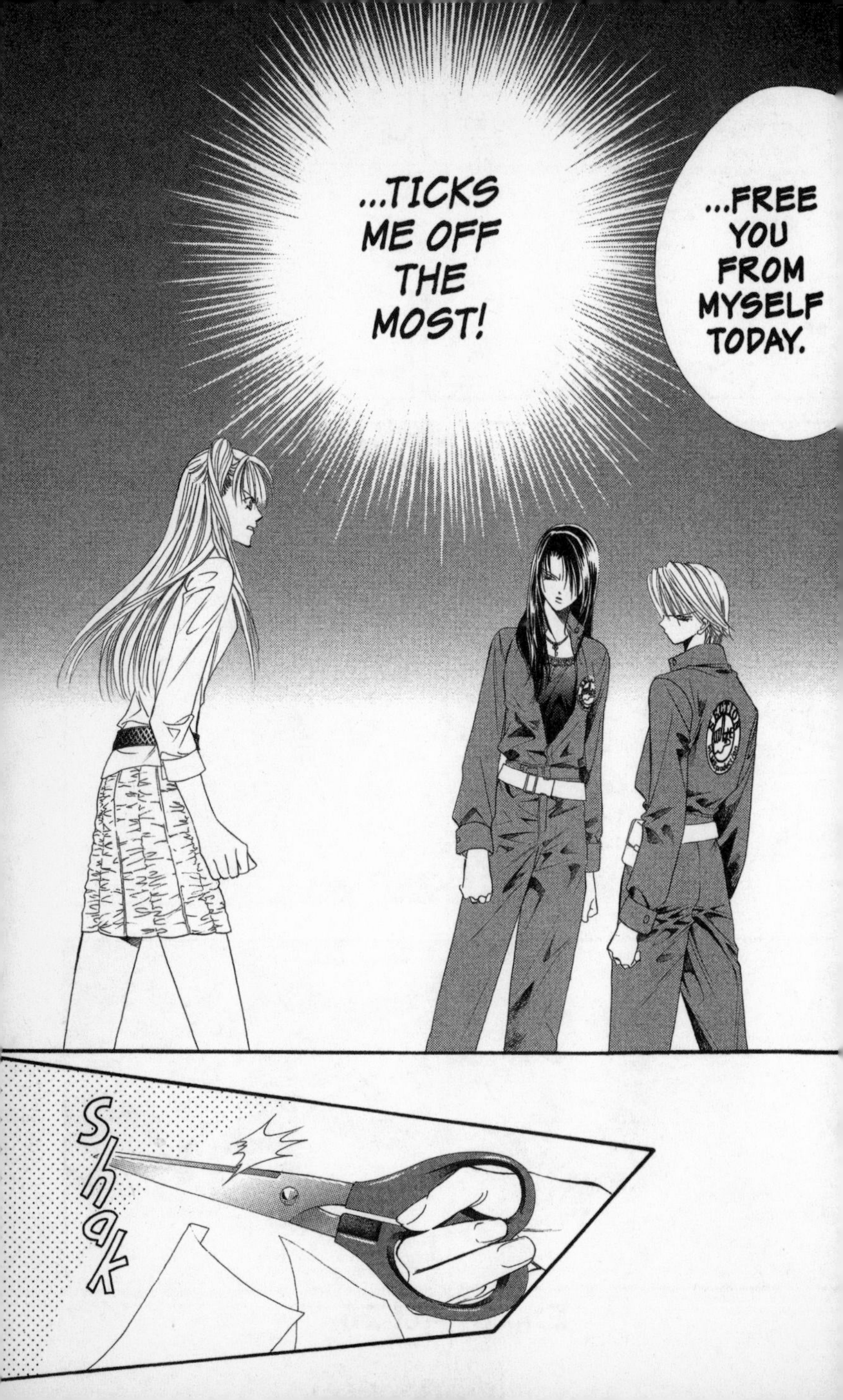
...FREE YOU FROM MYSELF TODAY.
...TICKS ME OFF THE MOST!
Shak

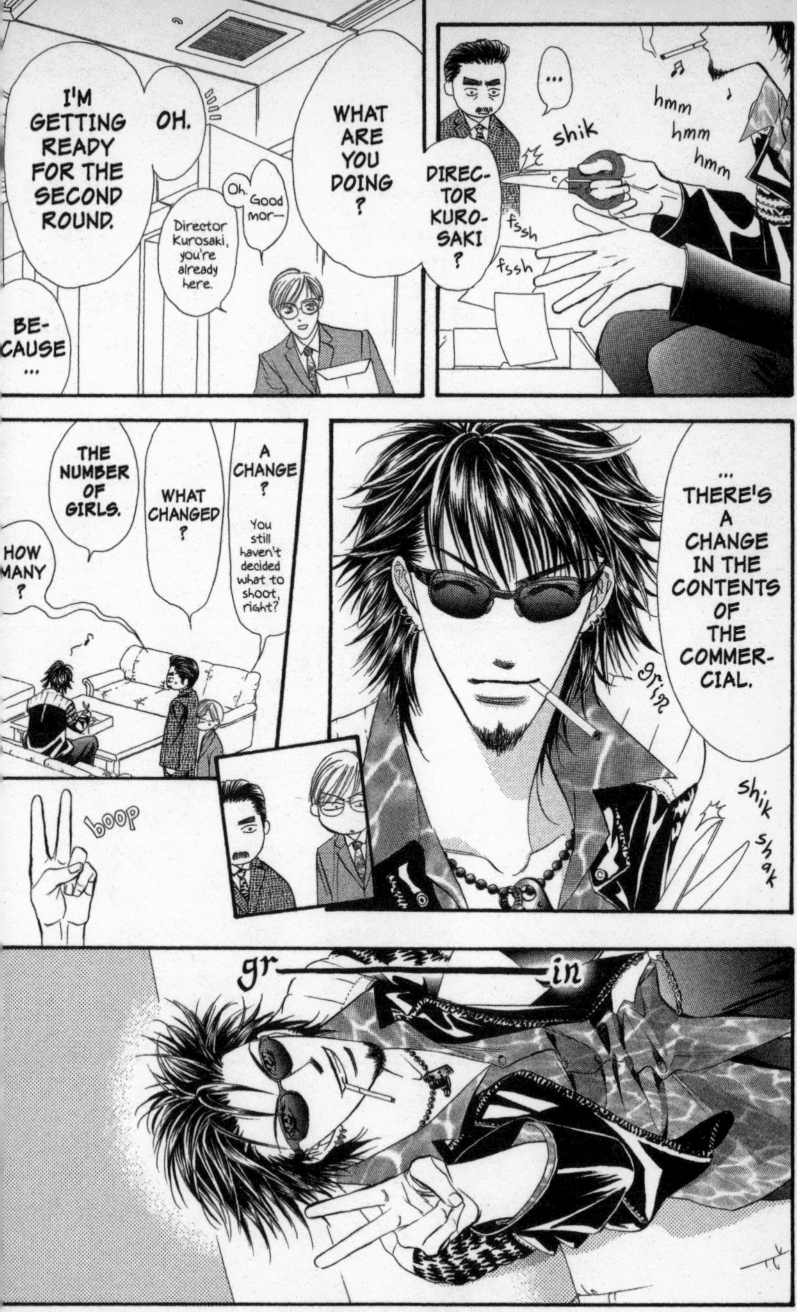
...
hmm hmm hmm
shik
DIRECTOR KUROSAKI?
fssh fssh
Oh. Good mor—
Director Kurosaki, you're already here.
WHAT ARE YOU DOING?
OH.
I'M GETTING READY FOR THE SECOND ROUND.
BECAUSE...
...THERE'S A CHANGE IN THE CONTENTS OF THE COMMERCIAL.
grin
shik shak
A CHANGE?
You still haven't decided what to shoot, right?
WHAT CHANGED?
THE NUMBER OF GIRLS.
HOW MANY?
boop
gr——in

End of Act 26

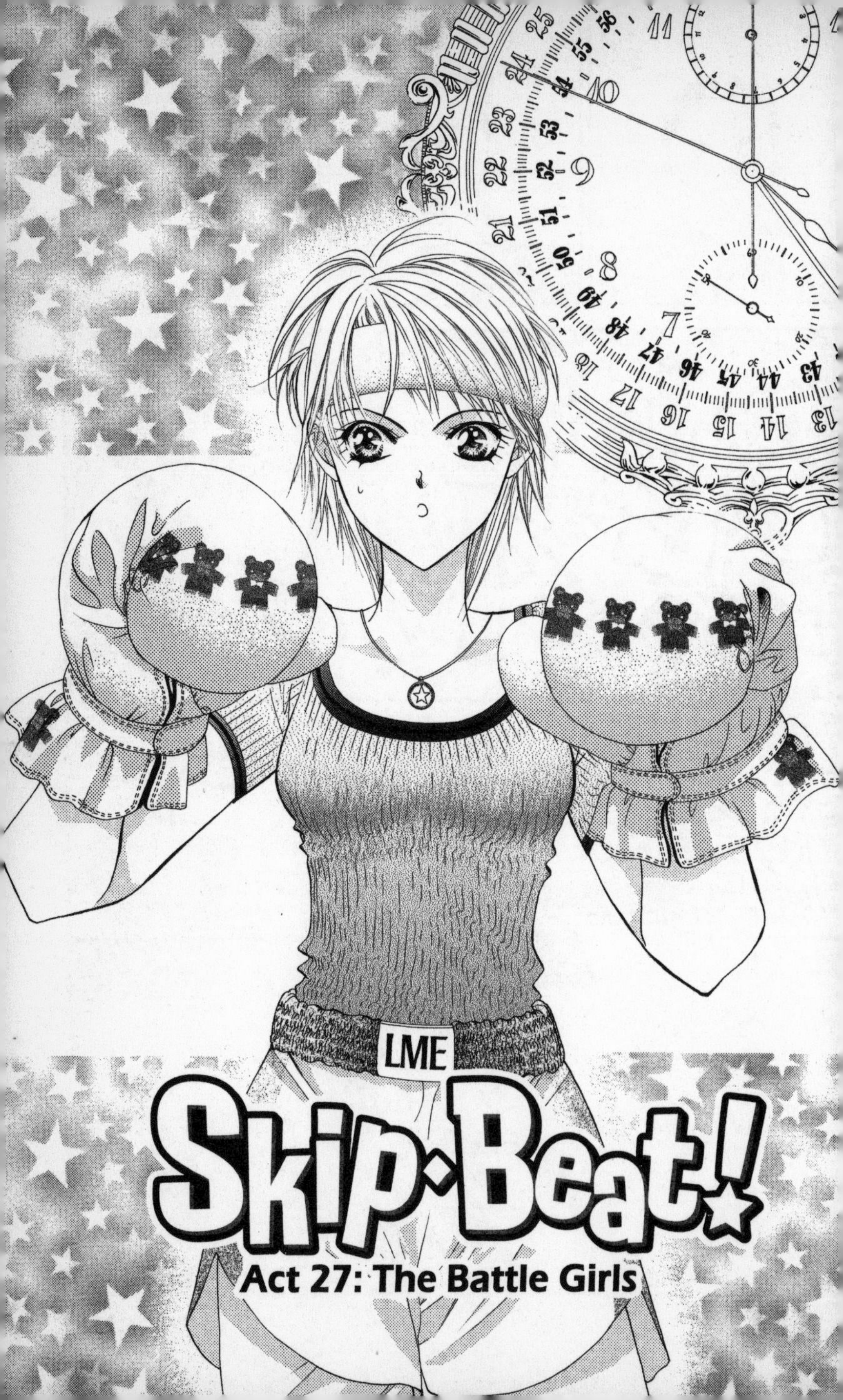
LME
Skip·Beat!
Act 27: The Battle Girls

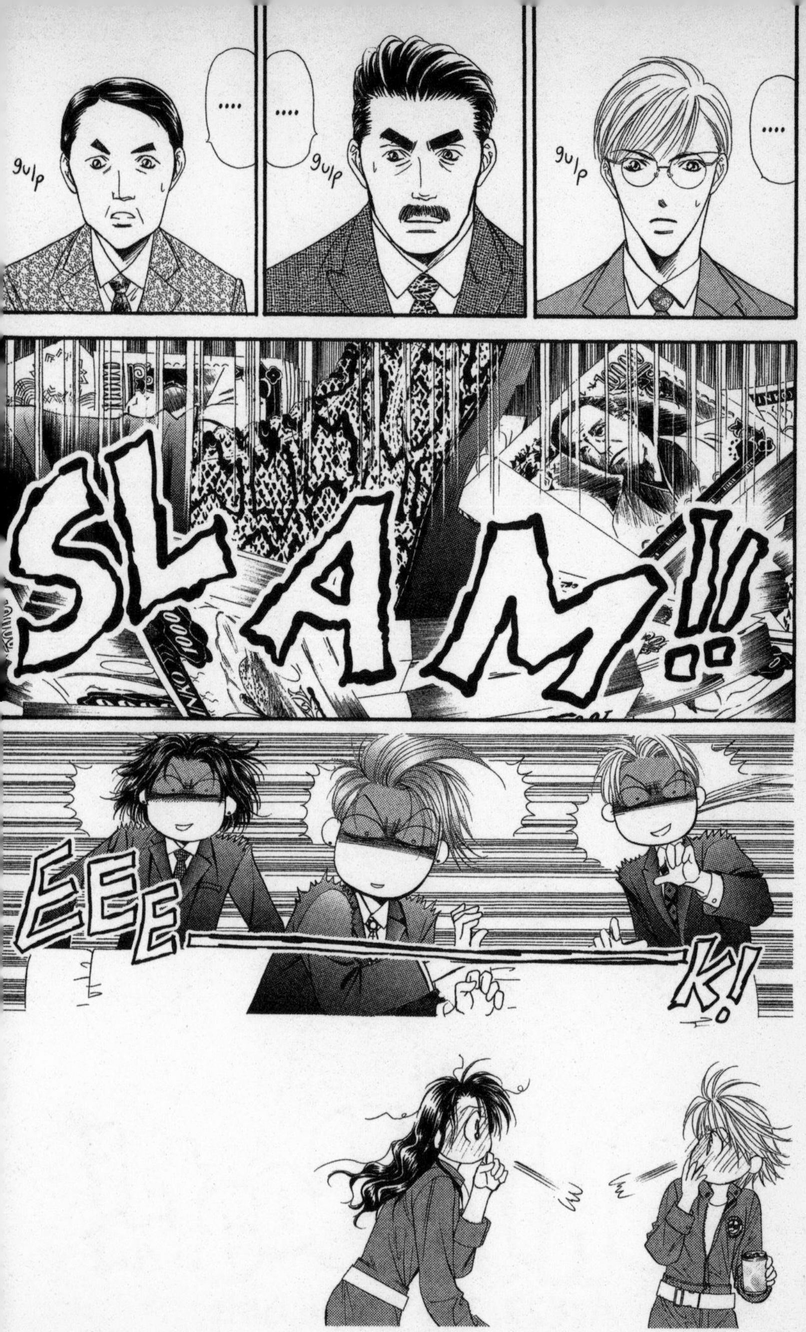
....
gulp
....
gulp
....
gulp
SLAM!!
EEE———K!

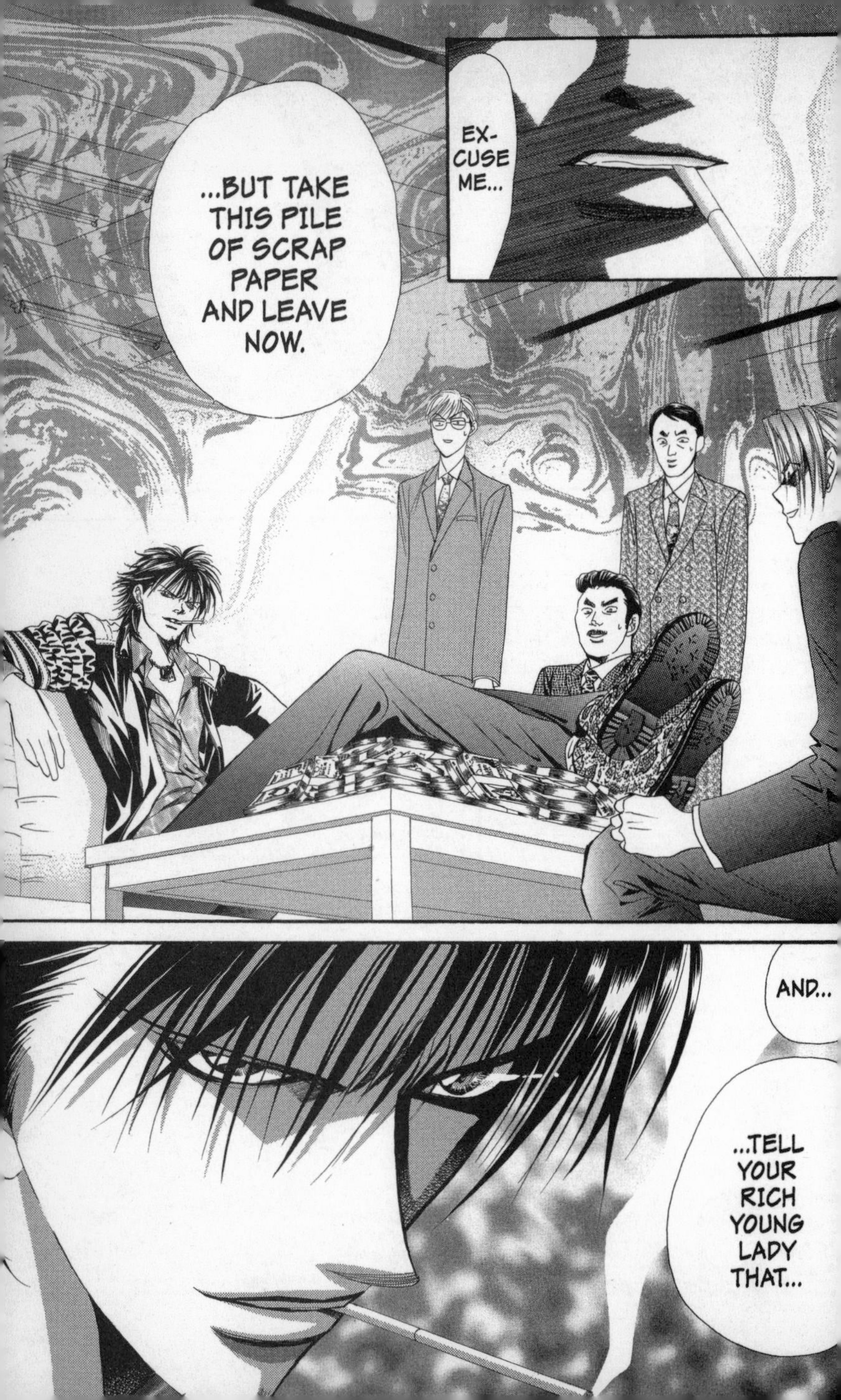
EX-CUSE ME...
...BUT TAKE THIS PILE OF SCRAP PAPER AND LEAVE NOW.
AND...
...TELL YOUR RICH YOUNG LADY THAT...

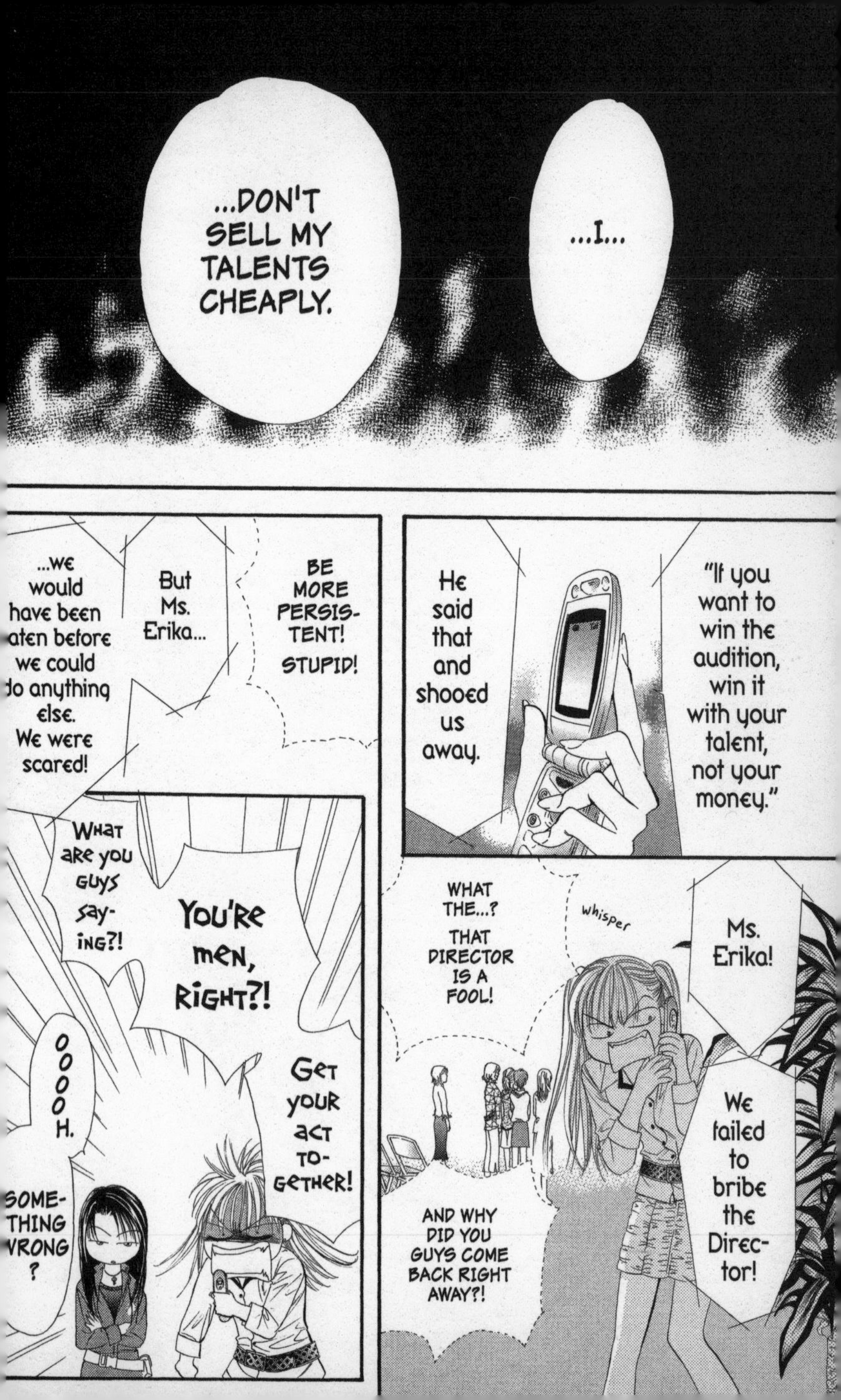
...I...
...DON'T SELL MY TALENTS CHEAPLY.
"If you want to win the audition, win it with your talent, not your money."
He said that and shooed us away.
Ms. Erika!
We failed to bribe the Director!
whisper
WHAT THE...? THAT DIRECTOR IS A FOOL!
AND WHY DID YOU GUYS COME BACK RIGHT AWAY?!
BE MORE PERSISTENT! STUPID!
But Ms. Erika...
...we would have been eaten before we could do anything else. We were scared!
WHAT are you GUYS say-ING?!
You're men, RIGHT?!
Get your act to-gether!
OOOOH.
SOME-THING WRONG?

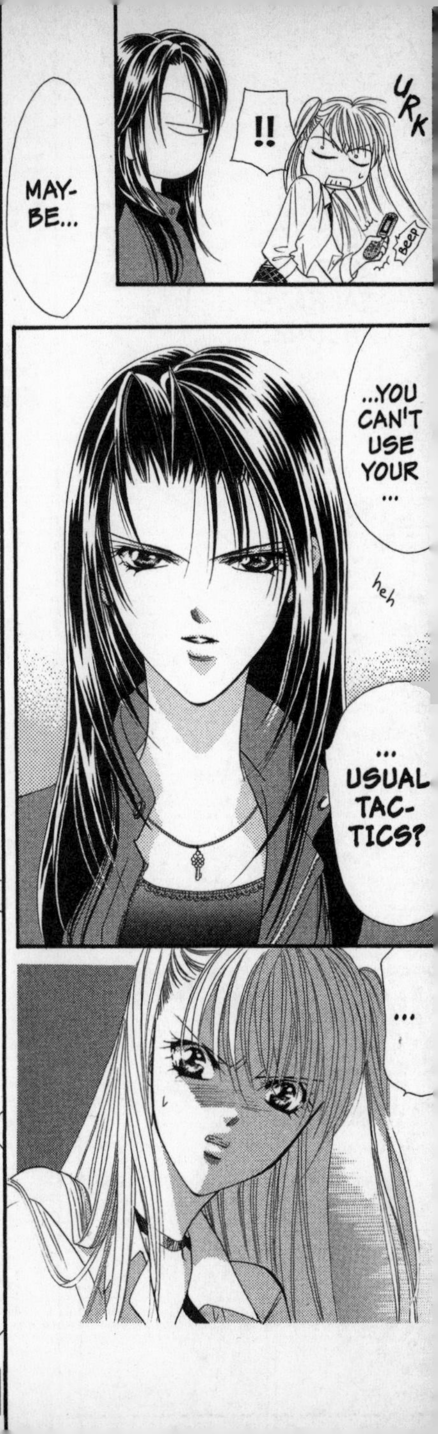
URK
!!
BEEP
MAY-BE...
...YOU CAN'T USE YOUR ...
heh
... USUAL TAC-TICS?
...

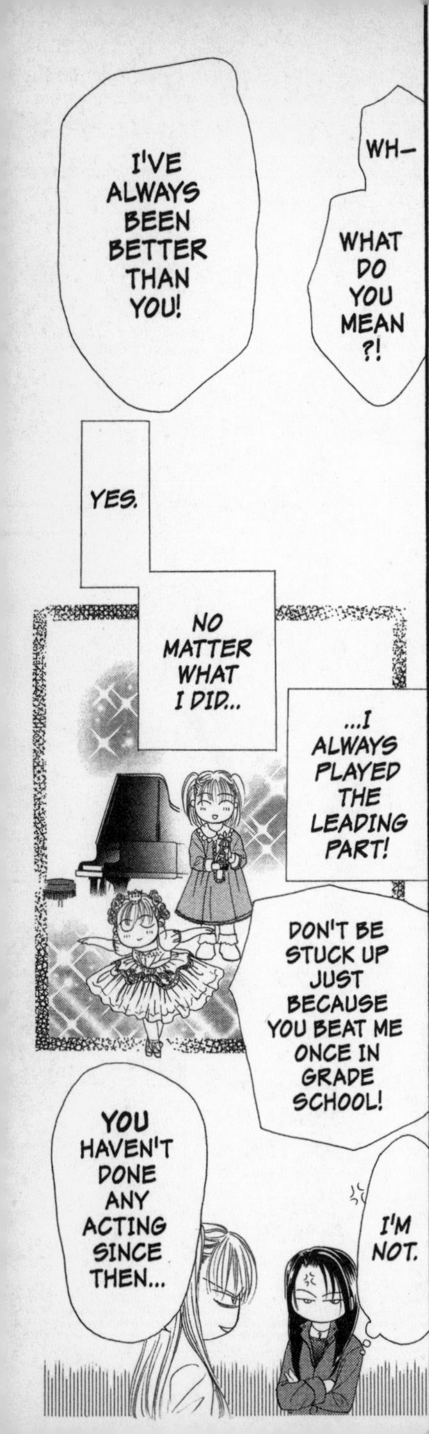
WH— WHAT DO YOU MEAN ?!
I'VE ALWAYS BEEN BETTER THAN YOU!
YES.
NO MATTER WHAT I DID...
...I ALWAYS PLAYED THE LEADING PART!
DON'T BE STUCK UP JUST BECAUSE YOU BEAT ME ONCE IN GRADE SCHOOL!
I'M NOT.
YOU HAVEN'T DONE ANY ACTING SINCE THEN...

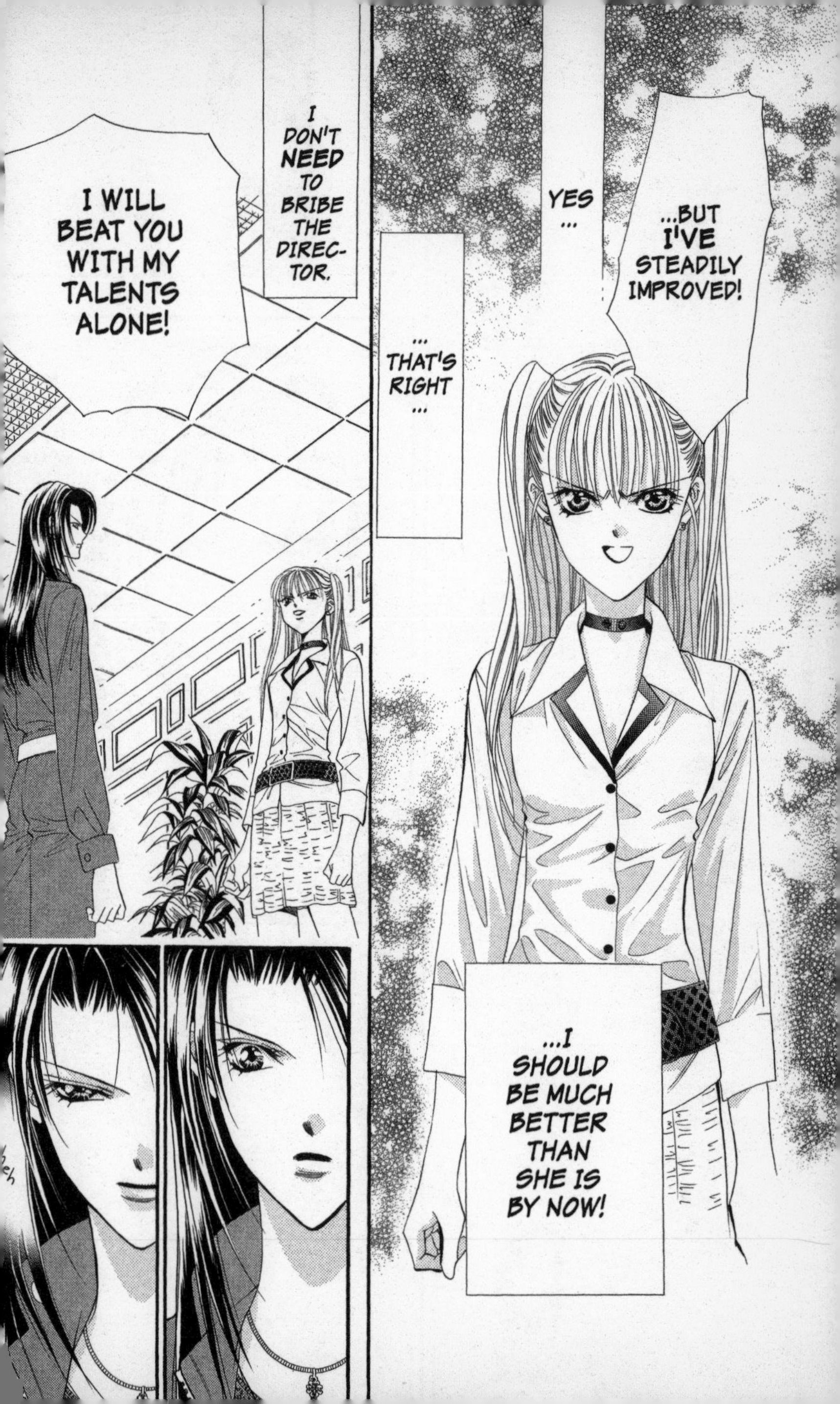
YES ...
...BUT I'VE STEADILY IMPROVED!
... THAT'S RIGHT ...
...I SHOULD BE MUCH BETTER THAN SHE IS BY NOW!
I DON'T NEED TO BRIBE THE DIRECTOR.
I WILL BEAT YOU WITH MY TALENTS ALONE!

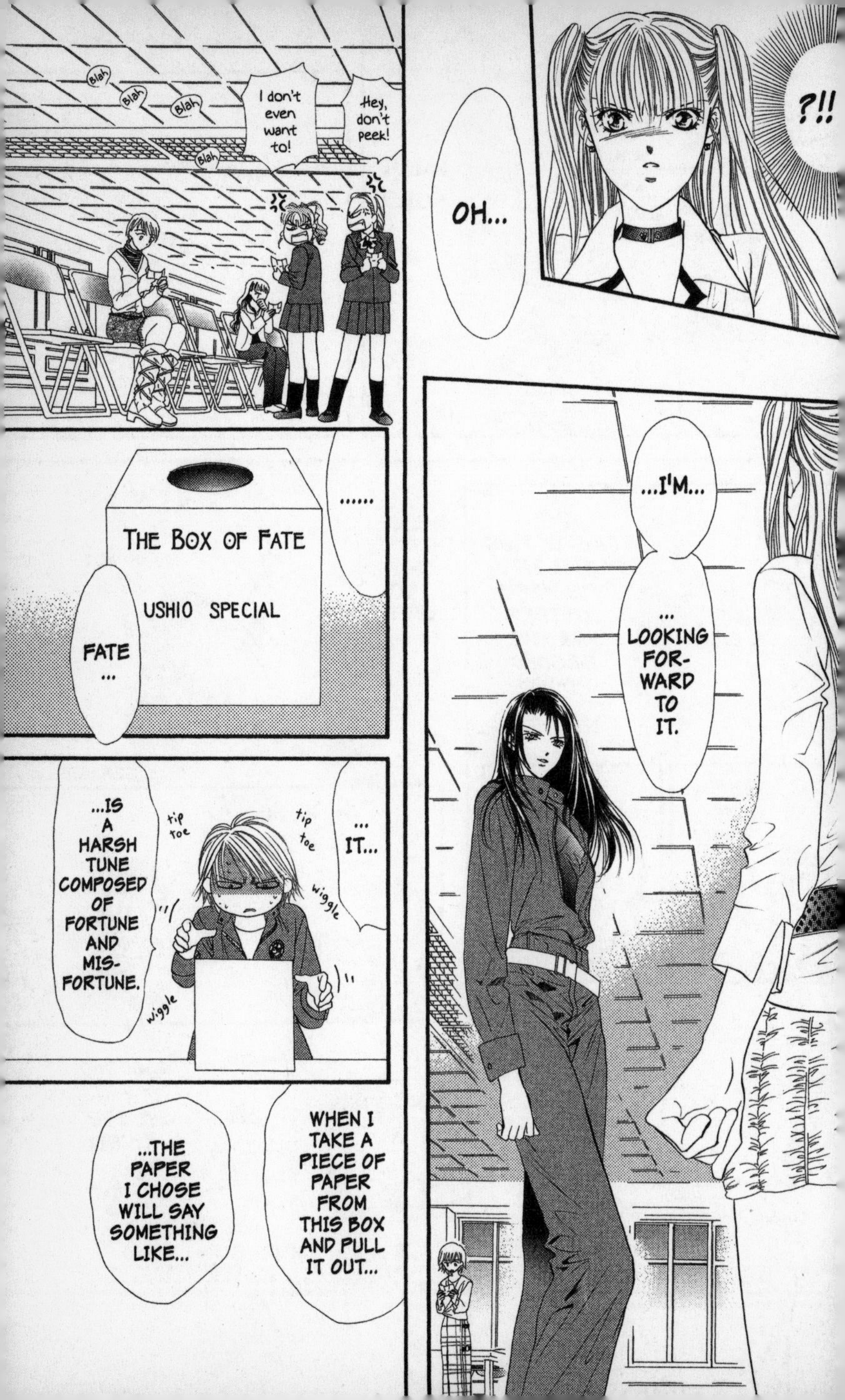
?!!
OH...
...I'M...
...LOOKING FORWARD TO IT.
Hey, don't peek!
I don't even want to!
Blah
Blah
Blah
Blah
......
THE BOX OF FATE
USHIO SPECIAL
FATE...
...IT...
tip toe
wiggle
tip toe
...IS A HARSH TUNE COMPOSED OF FORTUNE AND MIS-FORTUNE.
wiggle
WHEN I TAKE A PIECE OF PAPER FROM THIS BOX AND PULL IT OUT...
...THE PAPER I CHOSE WILL SAY SOMETHING LIKE...

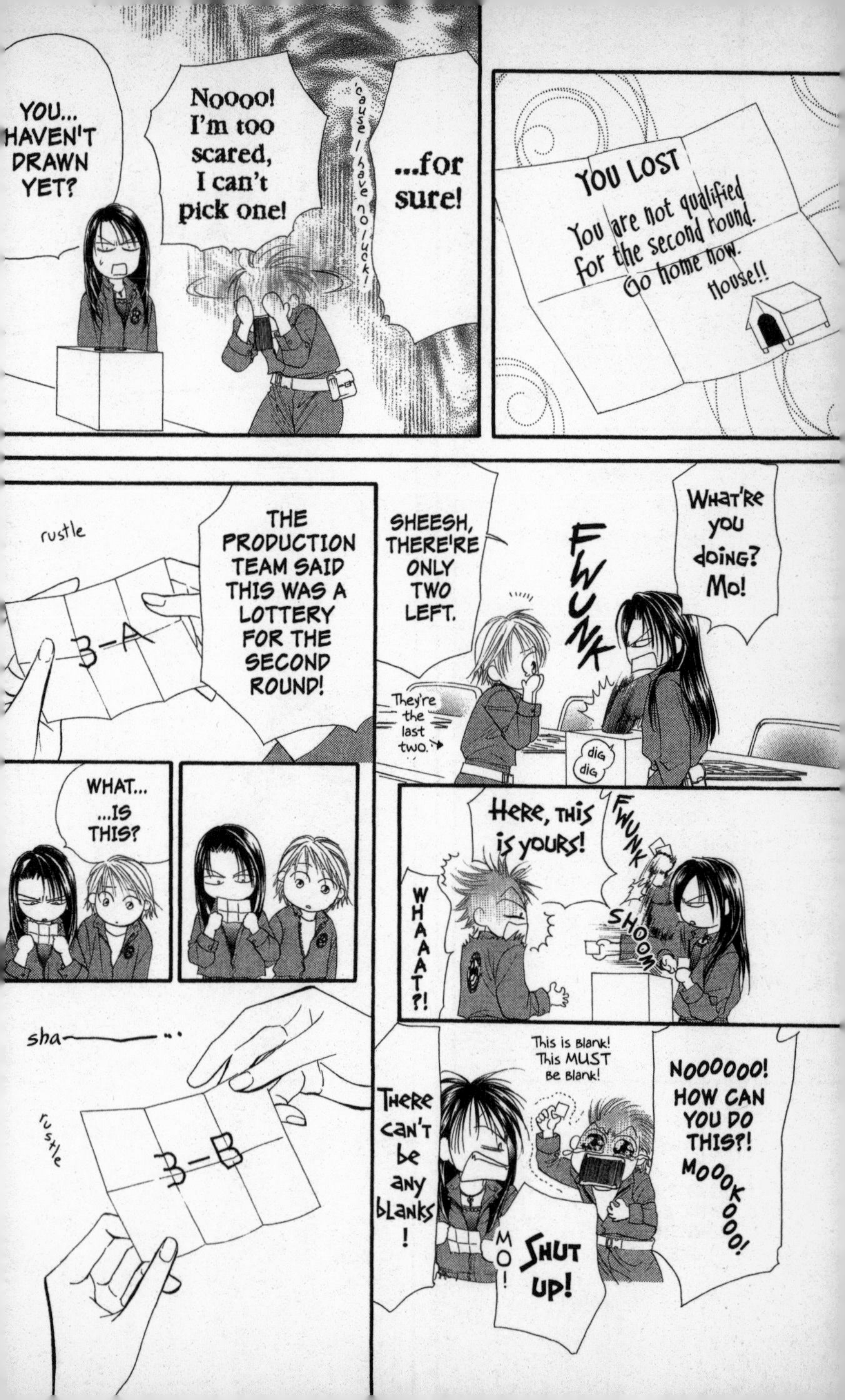
YOU LOST
You are not qualified for the second round. Go home now.
House!!
...for sure!
'cause I have no luck!
Noooo! I'm too scared, I can't pick one!
YOU... HAVEN'T DRAWN YET?
What're you doing? Mo!
FWUNK
SHEESH, THERE'RE ONLY TWO LEFT.
They're the last two.
dig dig
THE PRODUCTION TEAM SAID THIS WAS A LOTTERY FOR THE SECOND ROUND!
rustle
3-A
WHAT... ...IS THIS?
Here, this is yours!
FWUNK
SHOOM
WHAAAAT?!
NOOOOOO! HOW CAN YOU DO THIS?! MOOOKOOOO!
This is Blank! This MUST Be Blank!
SHUT UP!
MO!
There can't be any blanks!
sha——— ..
rustle
3-B

THE BOX OF

USHIO SPECIAL

Kaindo
Dorinko
President

anabu
unada

Account
Planner

Minoru
Imai

····

····

····

····

····

····

····

····

·····

·····

···

···

····

...WHAT
THIS
IS...?

I
WON-
DER...

BWA
HA
HA

URK

EEK

EEK

EEK

EEK

SECTION
in the production

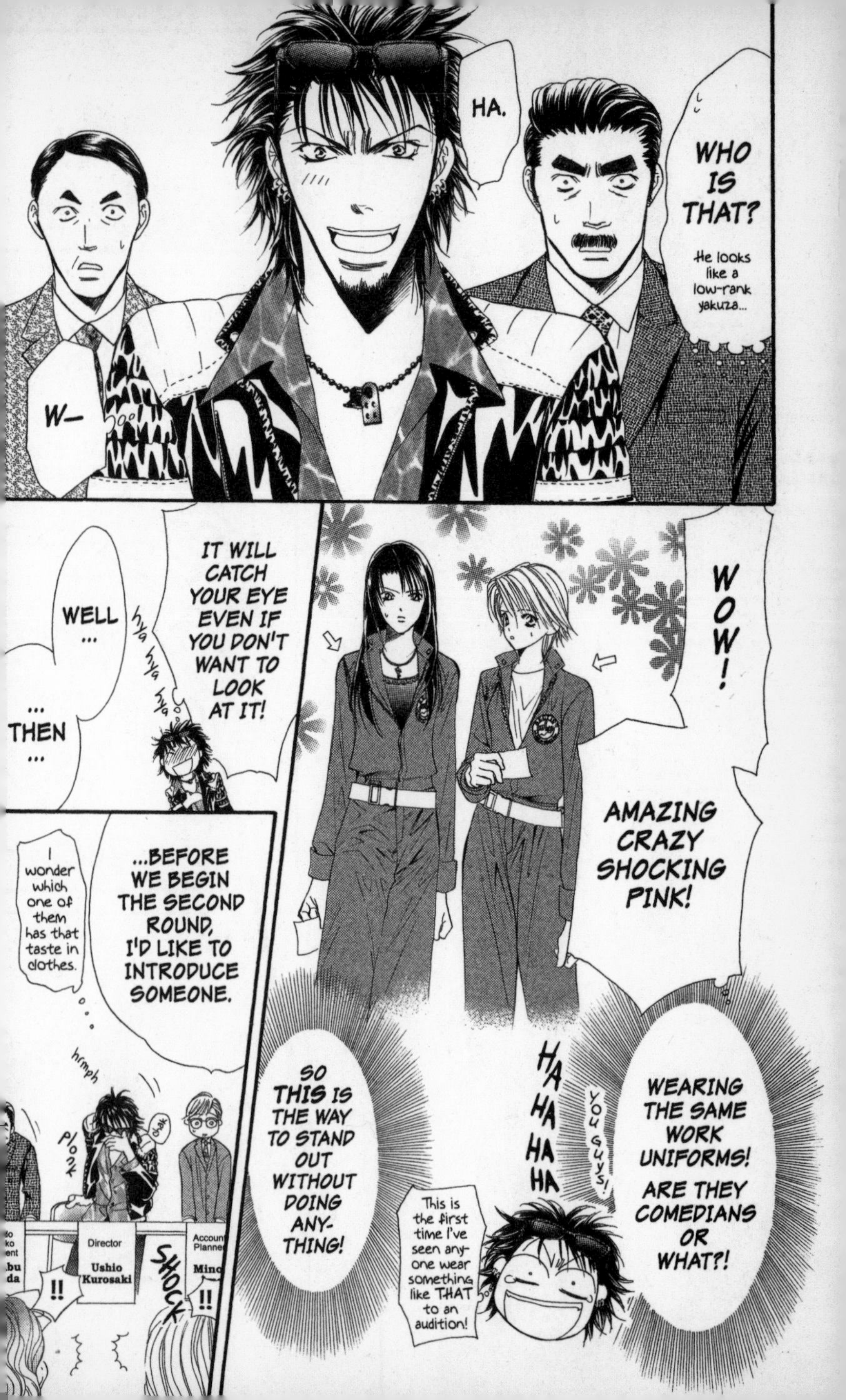
WHO IS THAT?
He looks like a low-rank yakuza...
HA.
W—
WOW!
AMAZING CRAZY SHOCKING PINK!
WEARING THE SAME WORK UNIFORMS! ARE THEY COMEDIANS OR WHAT?!
YOU GUYS!
HA HA HA HA HA
This is the first time I've seen anyone wear something like THAT to an audition!
SO THIS IS THE WAY TO STAND OUT WITHOUT DOING ANYTHING!
IT WILL CATCH YOUR EYE EVEN IF YOU DON'T WANT TO LOOK AT IT!
hya hya hya hya
WELL...
...THEN...
...BEFORE WE BEGIN THE SECOND ROUND, I'D LIKE TO INTRODUCE SOMEONE.
I wonder which one of them has that taste in clothes.
hrmph
plonk
chak
Director
Ushio Kurosaki
SHOCK
!!
!!

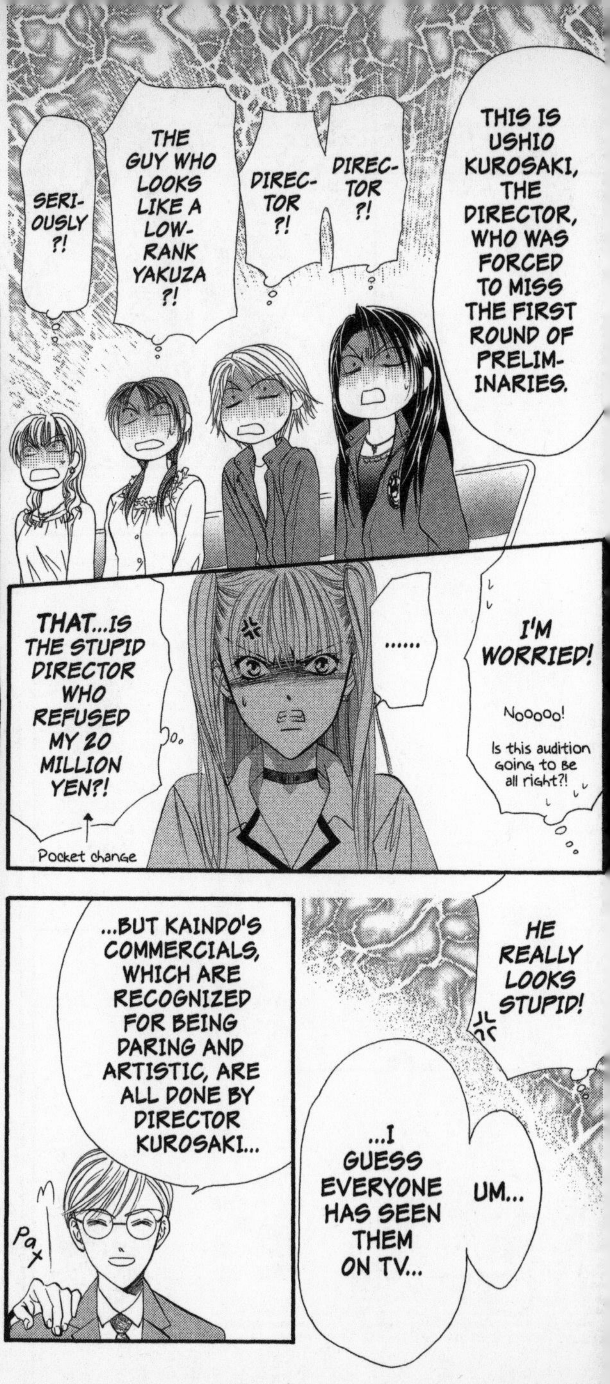
THIS IS USHIO KUROSAKI, THE DIRECTOR, WHO WAS FORCED TO MISS THE FIRST ROUND OF PRELIMINARIES.
DIREC-TOR?!
DIREC-TOR?!
THE GUY WHO LOOKS LIKE A LOW-RANK YAKUZA?!
SERI-OUSLY?!
I'M WORRIED!
Noooo!
Is this audition going to be all right?!
......
THAT...IS THE STUPID DIRECTOR WHO REFUSED MY 20 MILLION YEN?!
Pocket change
HE REALLY LOOKS STUPID!
UM...
...I GUESS EVERYONE HAS SEEN THEM ON TV...
...BUT KAINDO'S COMMERCIALS, WHICH ARE RECOGNIZED FOR BEING DARING AND ARTISTIC, ARE ALL DONE BY DIRECTOR KUROSAKI...
Pat

Ushio Kurosaki

In the business, he's known as "Kuroshio." I picked his name because I wanted to use this nickname... However, I couldn't use it in the story, and I regret it...

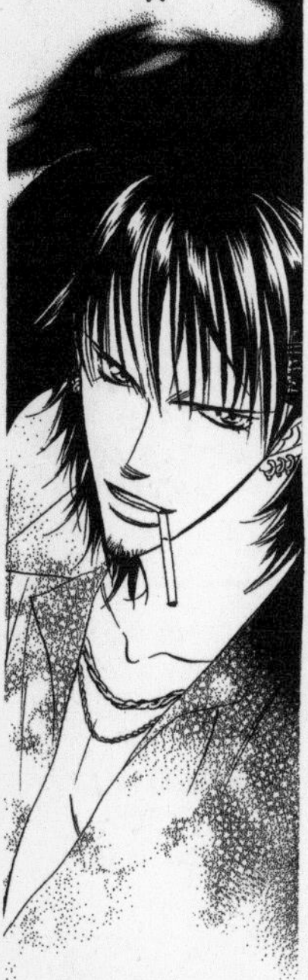

Personally, I wanted to make him more like a hardcore low-rank yakuza...a wild man who cuts you like a knife if you touch him (Ah...I love that type of guy...( ) He didn't turn out perfectly. Maybe he'd have looked more yakuza-like if his hair went straight back and his bangs were hanging lazily...but...a guy who obviously looks like a yakuza... My editor has...gently forbidden yakuza... My editor knows well that I go berserk... Ho ho ho...

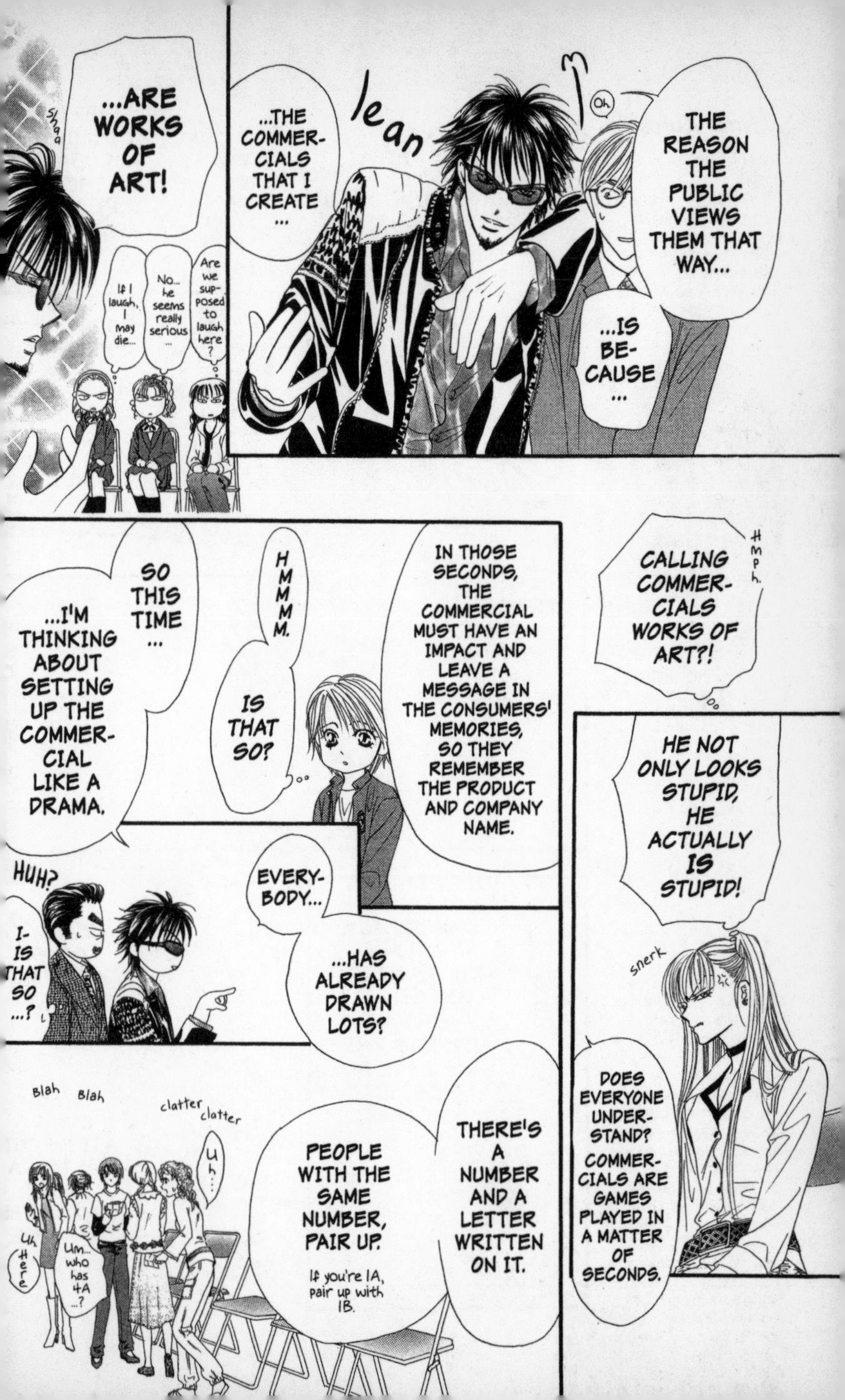
THE REASON THE PUBLIC VIEWS THEM THAT WAY...
Oh.
...IS BE-CAUSE...
lean
...THE COMMER-CIALS THAT I CREATE...
...ARE WORKS OF ART!
Shaa
Are we sup-posed to laugh here?
No... he seems really serious...
If I laugh, I may die...
CALLING COMMER-CIALS WORKS OF ART?!
Hmph.
HE NOT ONLY LOOKS STUPID, HE ACTUALLY IS STUPID!
IN THOSE SECONDS, THE COMMERCIAL MUST HAVE AN IMPACT AND LEAVE A MESSAGE IN THE CONSUMERS' MEMORIES, SO THEY REMEMBER THE PRODUCT AND COMPANY NAME.
HMMMM.
IS THAT SO?
SO THIS TIME...
...I'M THINKING ABOUT SETTING UP THE COMMER-CIAL LIKE A DRAMA.
snerk
DOES EVERYONE UNDER-STAND? COMMER-CIALS ARE GAMES PLAYED IN A MATTER OF SECONDS.
EVERY-BODY...
...HAS ALREADY DRAWN LOTS?
HUH?
I-IS THAT SO...?
THERE'S A NUMBER AND A LETTER WRITTEN ON IT.
PEOPLE WITH THE SAME NUMBER, PAIR UP.
If you're 1A, pair up with 1B.
clatter clatter
Uh...
Blah Blah
Um... who has 4A...?
Uh here

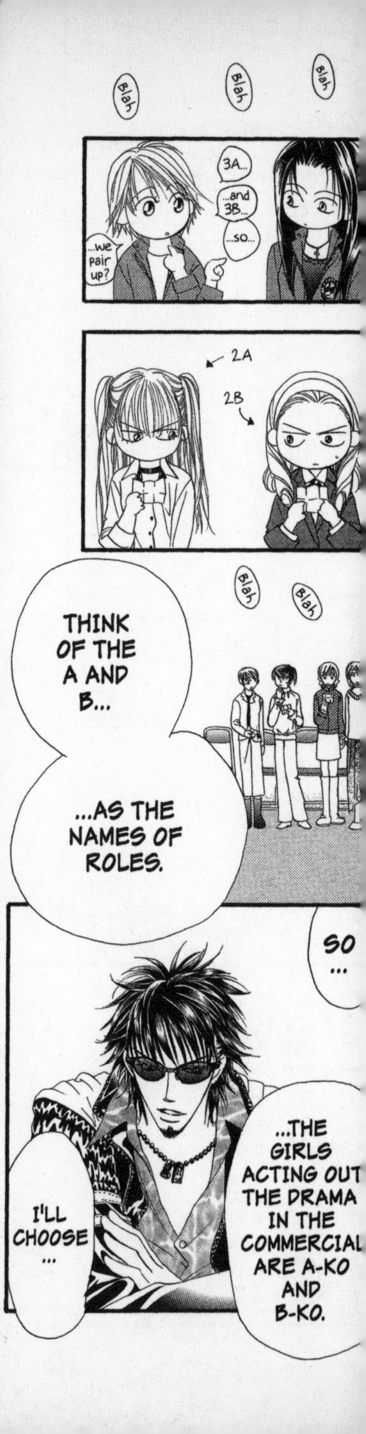
Blah
Blah
Blah
3A...
...and 3B...
...so...
...we pair up?
2A
2B
Blah
Blah
THINK OF THE A AND B...
...AS THE NAMES OF ROLES.
SO...
...THE GIRLS ACTING OUT THE DRAMA IN THE COMMERCIAL ARE A-KO AND B-KO.
I'LL CHOOSE...

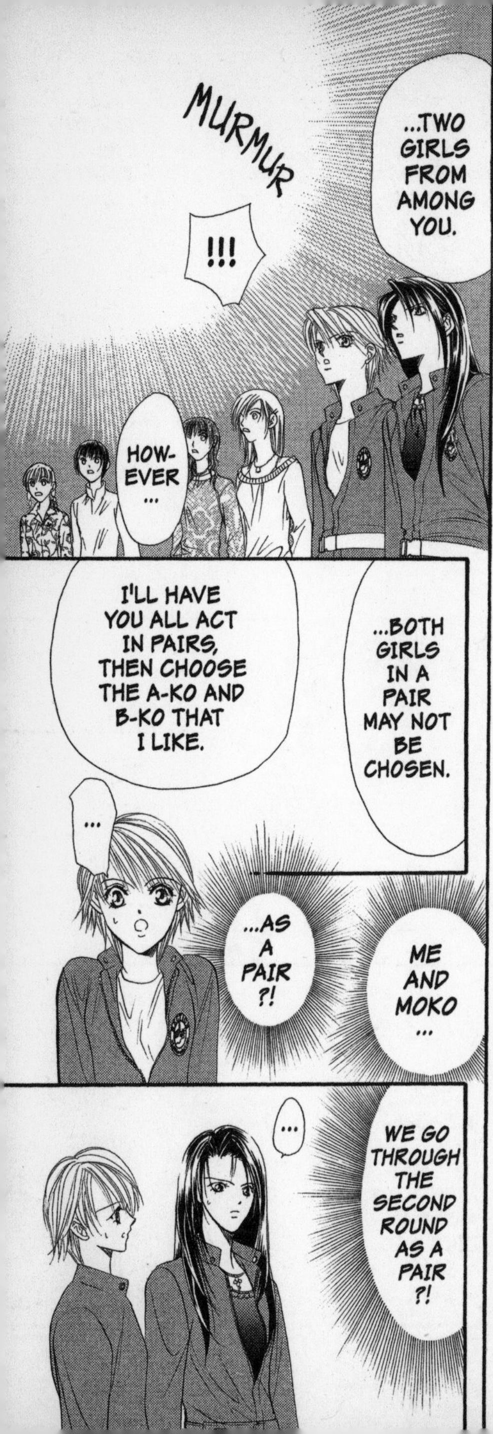
...TWO GIRLS FROM AMONG YOU.
MURMUR
!!!
HOW-EVER...
...BOTH GIRLS IN A PAIR MAY NOT BE CHOSEN.
I'LL HAVE YOU ALL ACT IN PAIRS, THEN CHOOSE THE A-KO AND B-KO THAT I LIKE.
ME AND MOKO...
...AS A PAIR?!
...
WE GO THROUGH THE SECOND ROUND AS A PAIR?!
...

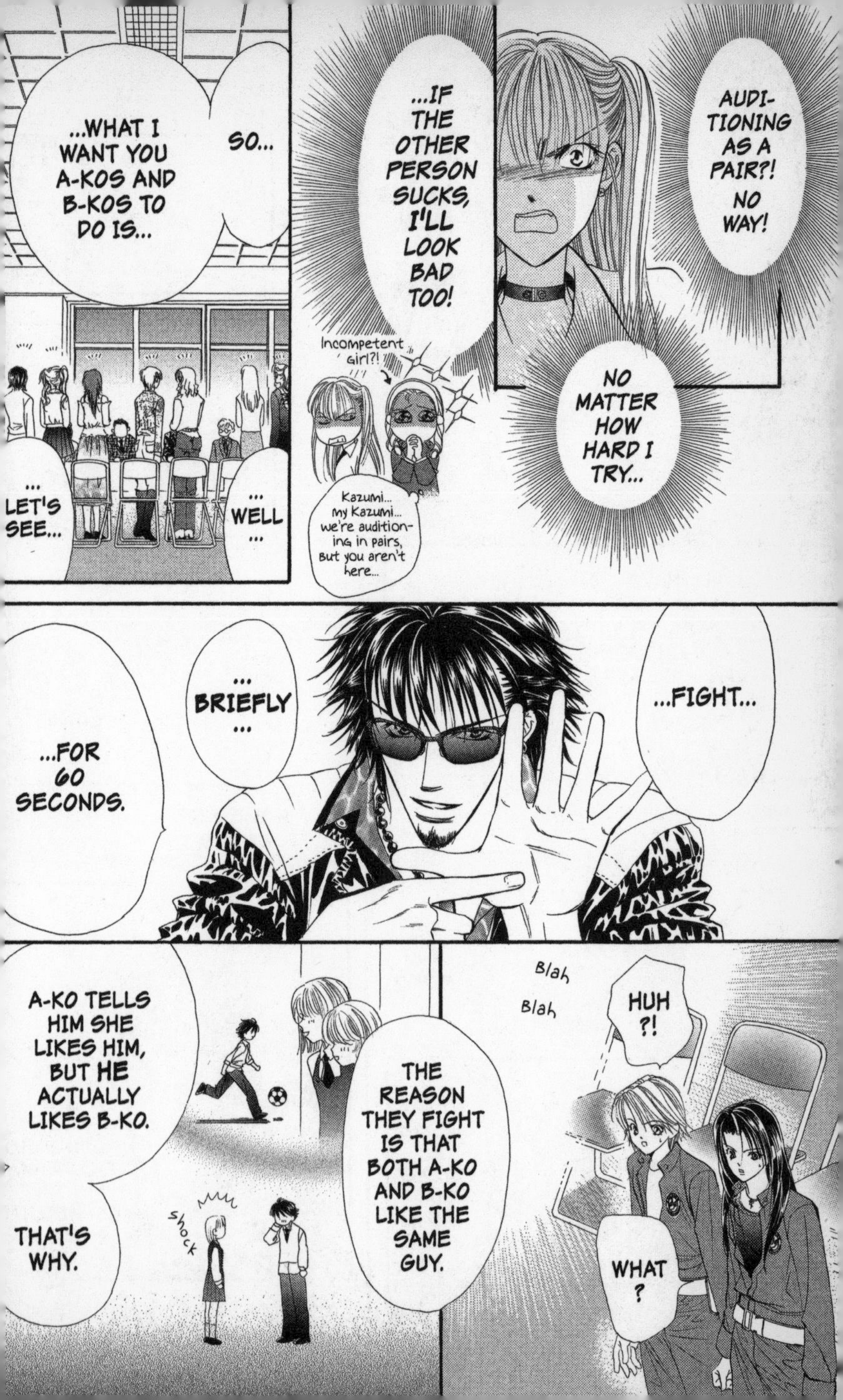
AUDITIONING AS A PAIR?! NO WAY!
NO MATTER HOW HARD I TRY...
...IF THE OTHER PERSON SUCKS, I'LL LOOK BAD TOO!
Incompetent girl?!
Kazumi... my Kazumi... we're auditioning in pairs, but you aren't here...
SO...
...WHAT I WANT YOU A-KOS AND B-KOS TO DO IS...
...WELL...
...LET'S SEE...
...FIGHT...
...BRIEFLY...
...FOR 60 SECONDS.
Blah
Blah
HUH?!
WHAT?
THE REASON THEY FIGHT IS THAT BOTH A-KO AND B-KO LIKE THE SAME GUY.
A-KO TELLS HIM SHE LIKES HIM, BUT HE ACTUALLY LIKES B-KO.
shock
THAT'S WHY.

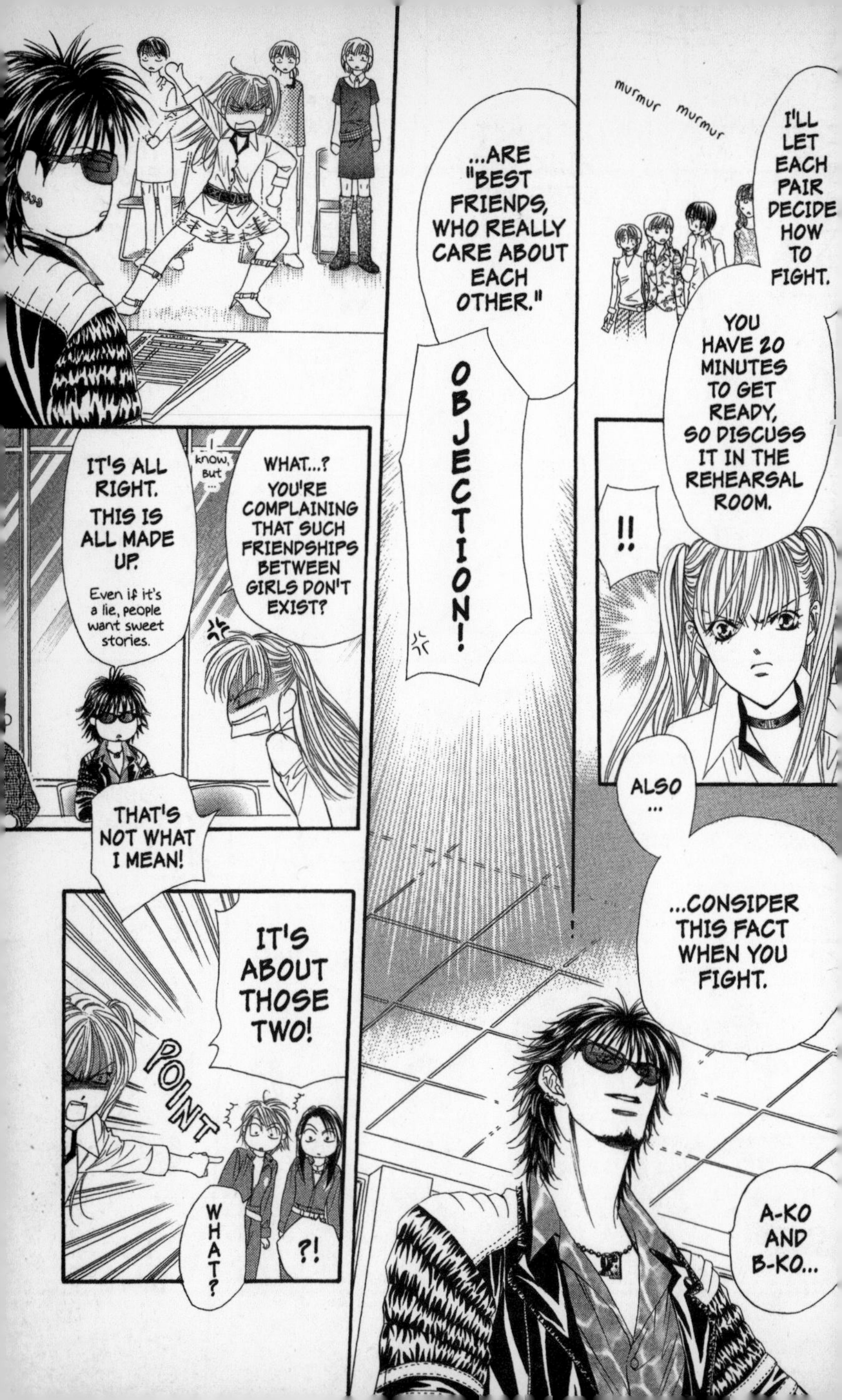
murmur murmur
I'LL LET EACH PAIR DECIDE HOW TO FIGHT.
YOU HAVE 20 MINUTES TO GET READY, SO DISCUSS IT IN THE REHEARSAL ROOM.
!!
ALSO...
...CONSIDER THIS FACT WHEN YOU FIGHT.
A-KO AND B-KO...
...ARE "BEST FRIENDS, WHO REALLY CARE ABOUT EACH OTHER."
OBJECTION!
WHAT...? YOU'RE COMPLAINING THAT SUCH FRIENDSHIPS BETWEEN GIRLS DON'T EXIST?
I know, but...
IT'S ALL RIGHT. THIS IS ALL MADE UP.
Even if it's a lie, people want sweet stories.
THAT'S NOT WHAT I MEAN!
IT'S ABOUT THOSE TWO!
POINT
?!
WHAT?

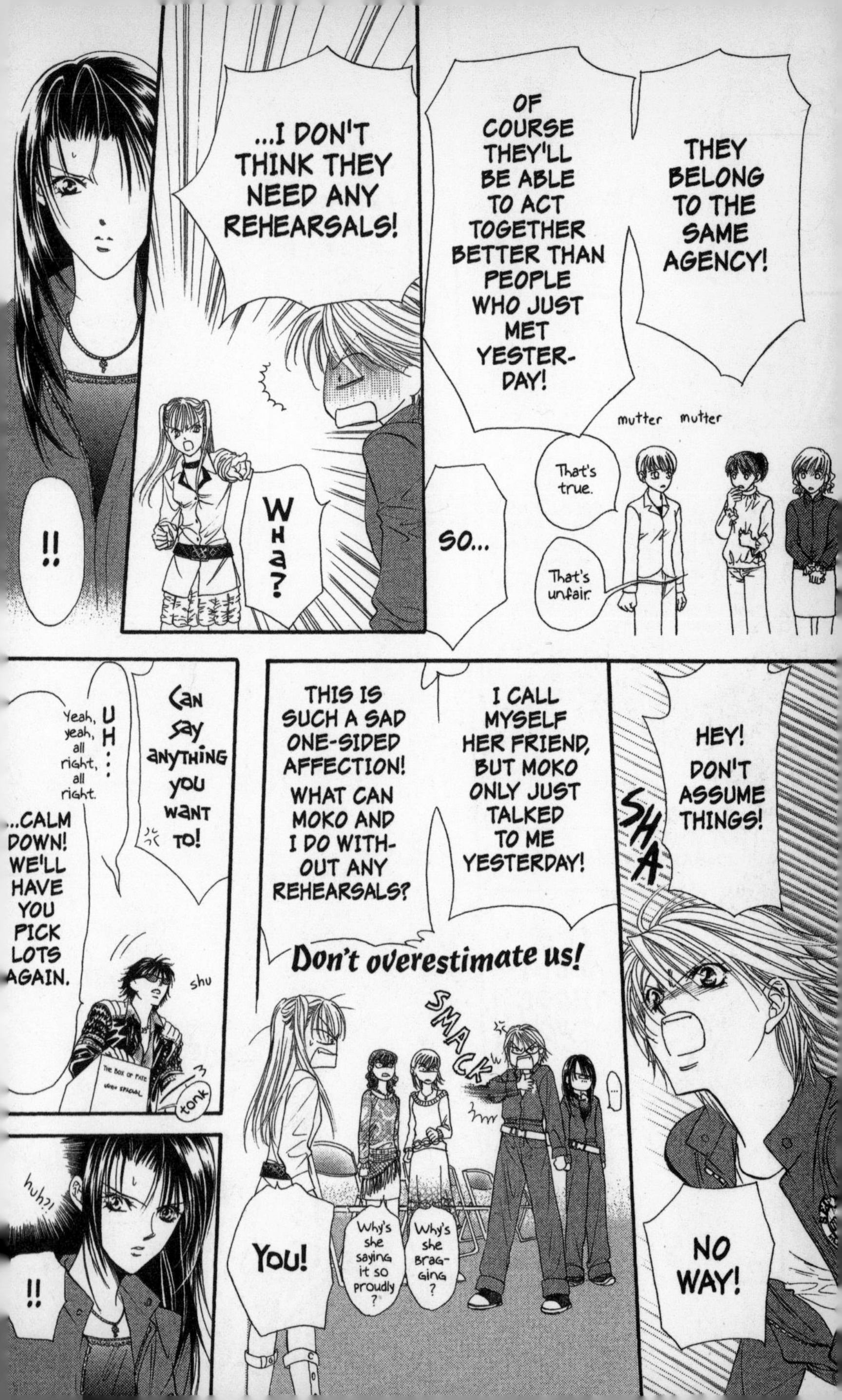
THEY BELONG TO THE SAME AGENCY!
OF COURSE THEY'LL BE ABLE TO ACT TOGETHER BETTER THAN PEOPLE WHO JUST MET YESTER-DAY!
mutter mutter
That's true.
That's unfair.
SO...
...I DON'T THINK THEY NEED ANY REHEARSALS!
WHa?
!!
HEY! DON'T ASSUME THINGS!
SHA
NO WAY!
I CALL MYSELF HER FRIEND, BUT MOKO ONLY JUST TALKED TO ME YESTERDAY!
THIS IS SUCH A SAD ONE-SIDED AFFECTION! WHAT CAN MOKO AND I DO WITH-OUT ANY REHEARSALS?
Don't overestimate us!
SMACK
...
YOU!
Why's she brag-ging?
Why's she saying it so proudly?
CAN SAY ANYTHING YOU WANT TO!
UH...
Yeah, yeah, all right, all right.
...CALM DOWN! WE'LL HAVE YOU PICK LOTS AGAIN.
shu
THE BOX OF FATE
tonk
huh?!
!!

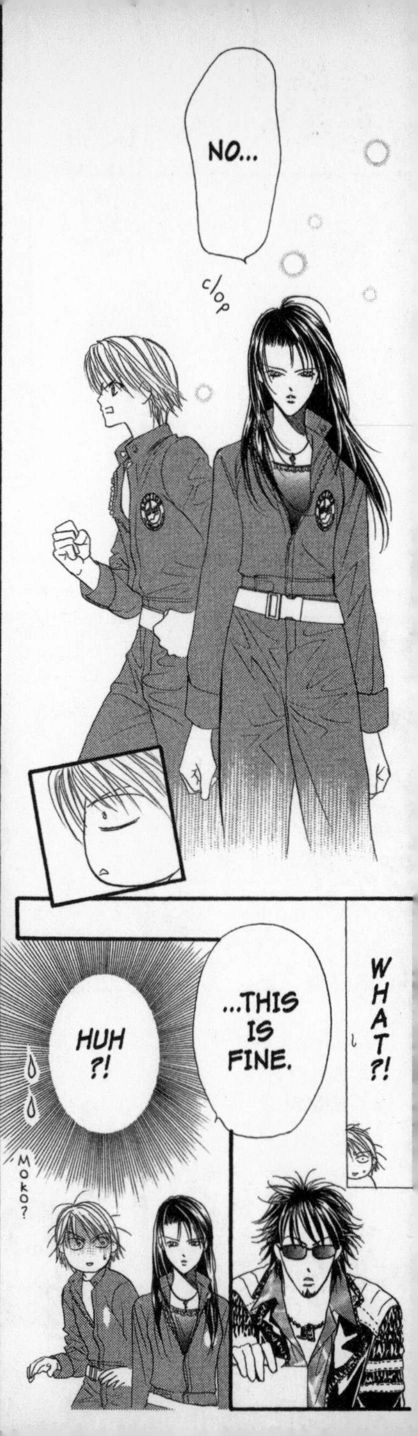
NO...
clop
WHAT?!
...THIS IS FINE.
HUH?!
MOKO?

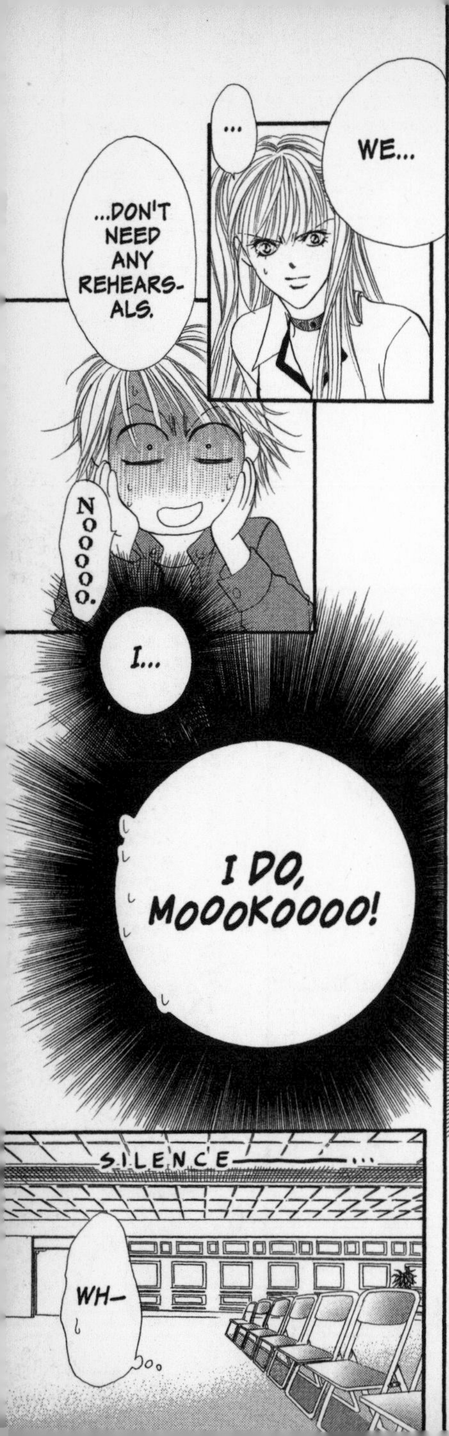
WE...
...
...DON'T NEED ANY REHEARS-ALS.
NOOOOOO.
I...
I DO, MOOOKOOOO!
SILENCE——...
WH—

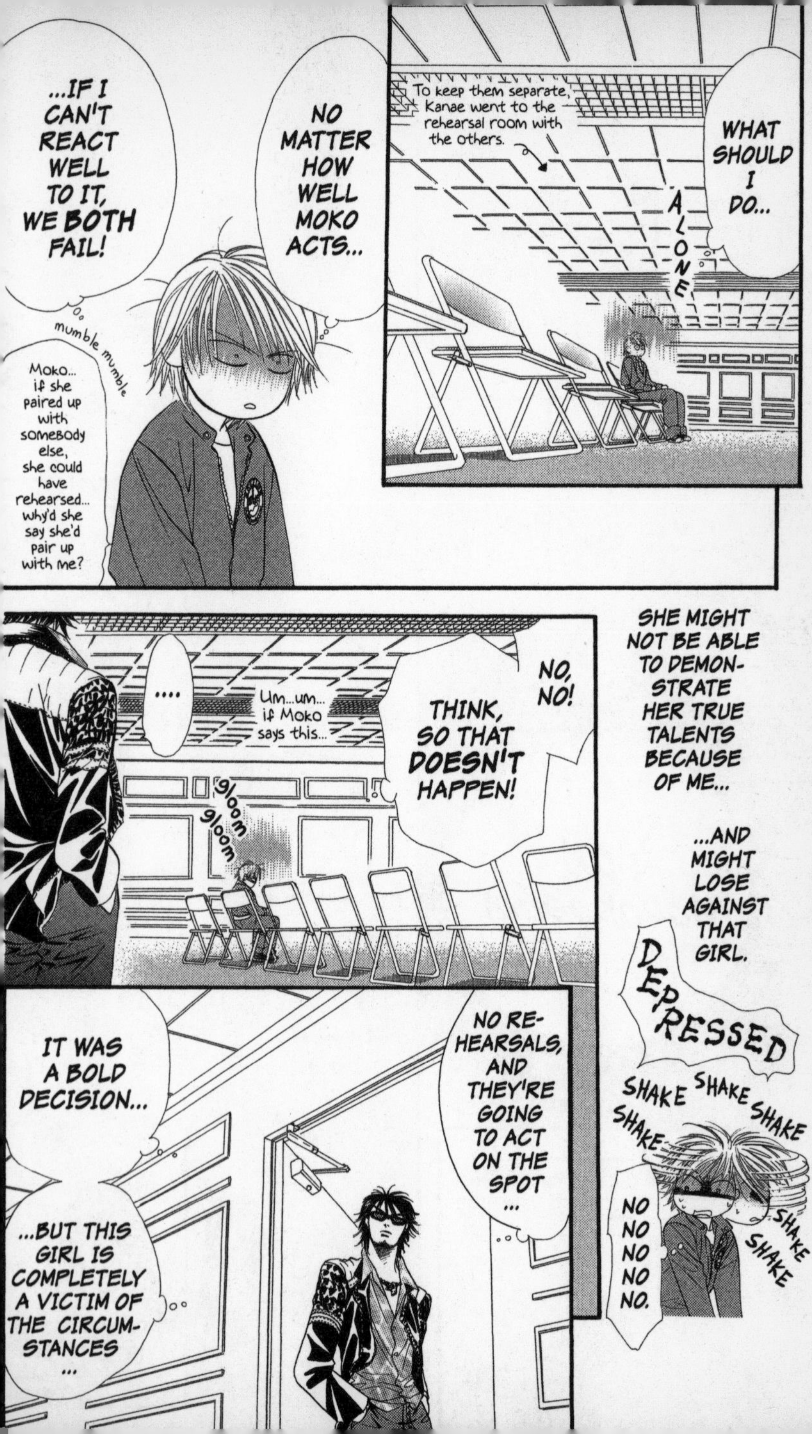
WHAT SHOULD I DO...
ALONE
To keep them separate, Kanae went to the rehearsal room with the others.
NO MATTER HOW WELL MOKO ACTS...
...IF I CAN'T REACT WELL TO IT, WE BOTH FAIL!
mumble mumble
Moko... if she paired up with somebody else, she could have rehearsed... why'd she say she'd pair up with me?
SHE MIGHT NOT BE ABLE TO DEMON-STRATE HER TRUE TALENTS BECAUSE OF ME...
...AND MIGHT LOSE AGAINST THAT GIRL.
DEPRESSED
SHAKE SHAKE SHAKE SHAKE SHAKE SHAKE
NO NO NO NO NO.
NO, NO!
THINK, SO THAT DOESN'T HAPPEN!
Um...um... if Moko says this...
....
gloom gloom
NO RE-HEARSALS, AND THEY'RE GOING TO ACT ON THE SPOT ...
IT WAS A BOLD DECISION...
...BUT THIS GIRL IS COMPLETELY A VICTIM OF THE CIRCUM-STANCES ...

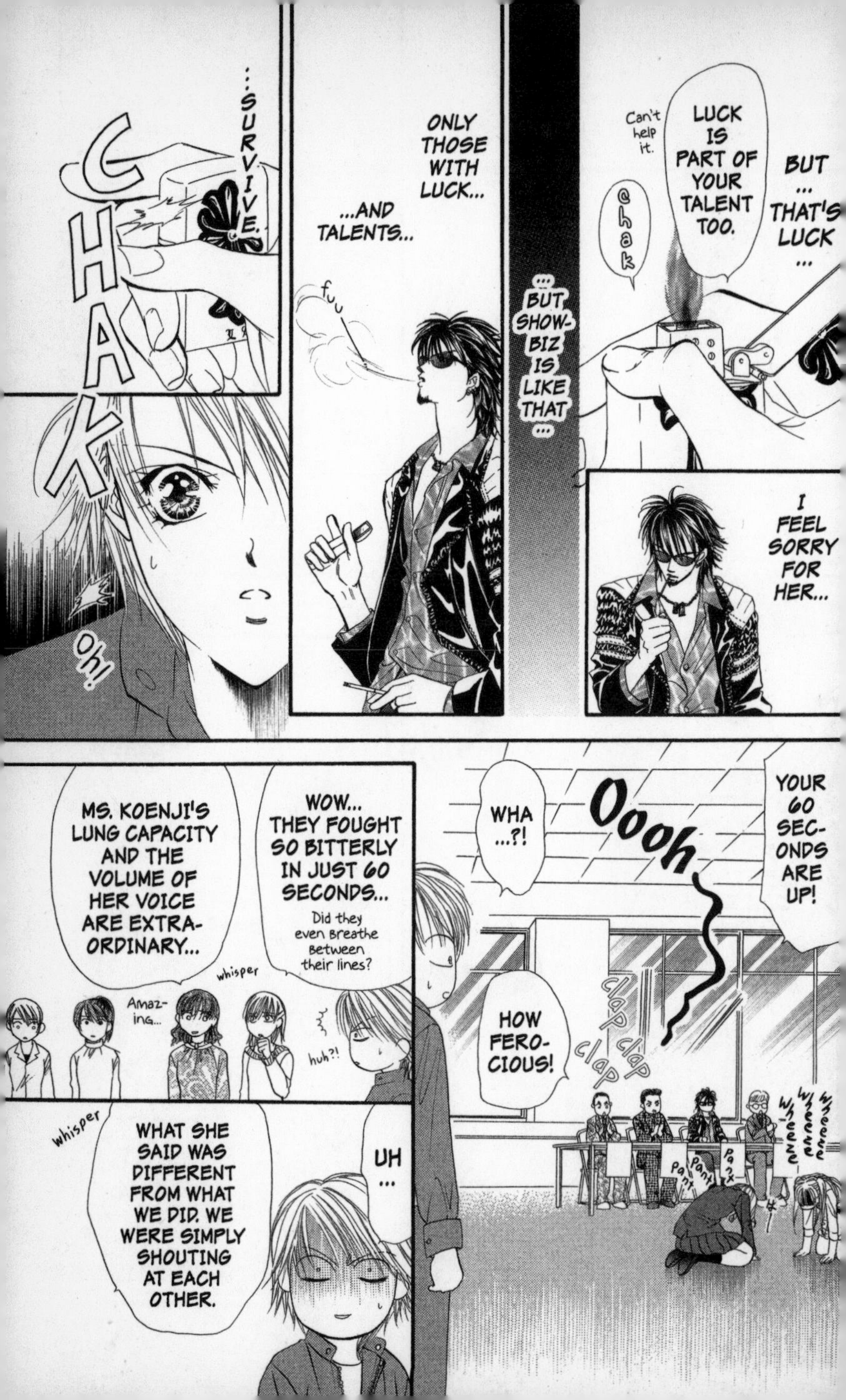
BUT ... THAT'S LUCK ...
LUCK IS PART OF YOUR TALENT TOO.
Can't help it.
chak
I FEEL SORRY FOR HER...
... BUT SHOW-BIZ IS LIKE THAT ...
ONLY THOSE WITH LUCK...
...AND TALENTS...
fuu
...SURVIVE.
CHAK
Oh!
YOUR 60 SECONDS ARE UP!
Oooh
WHA ...?!
HOW FEROCIOUS!
clap clap clap
wheeze wheeze wheeze
pant pant
WOW... THEY FOUGHT SO BITTERLY IN JUST 60 SECONDS...
Did they even breathe between their lines?
MS. KOENJI'S LUNG CAPACITY AND THE VOLUME OF HER VOICE ARE EXTRA-ORDINARY...
whisper
Amazing...
huh?!
UH ...
whisper
WHAT SHE SAID WAS DIFFERENT FROM WHAT WE DID. WE WERE SIMPLY SHOUTING AT EACH OTHER.

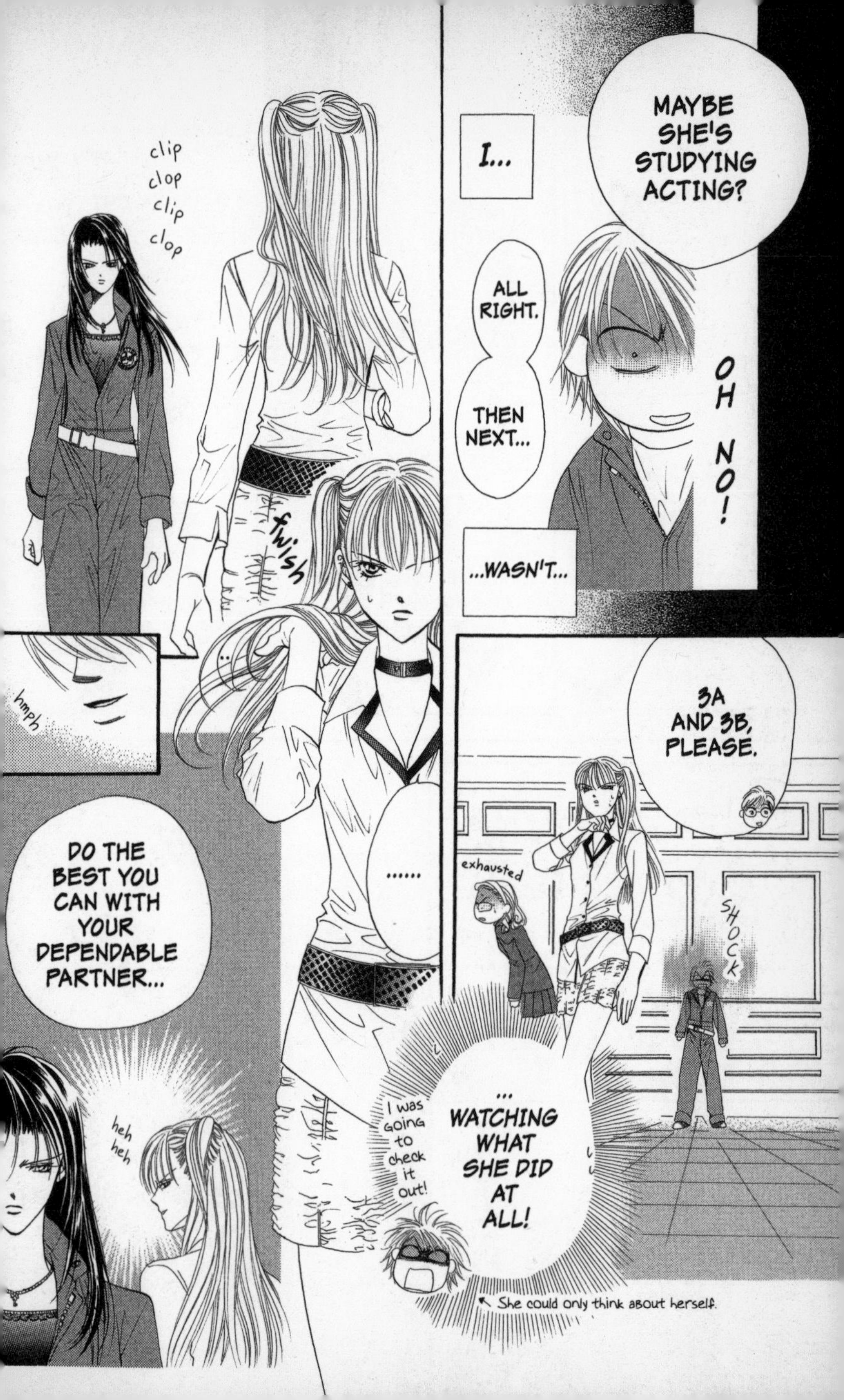
MAYBE SHE'S STUDYING ACTING?
I...
ALL RIGHT.
THEN NEXT...
OH NO!
...WASN'T...
clip clop clip clop
fwish
3A AND 3B, PLEASE.
SHOCK
exhausted
...WATCHING WHAT SHE DID AT ALL!
I was going to check it out!
She could only think about herself.
......
..
hmph
DO THE BEST YOU CAN WITH YOUR DEPENDABLE PARTNER...
heh heh

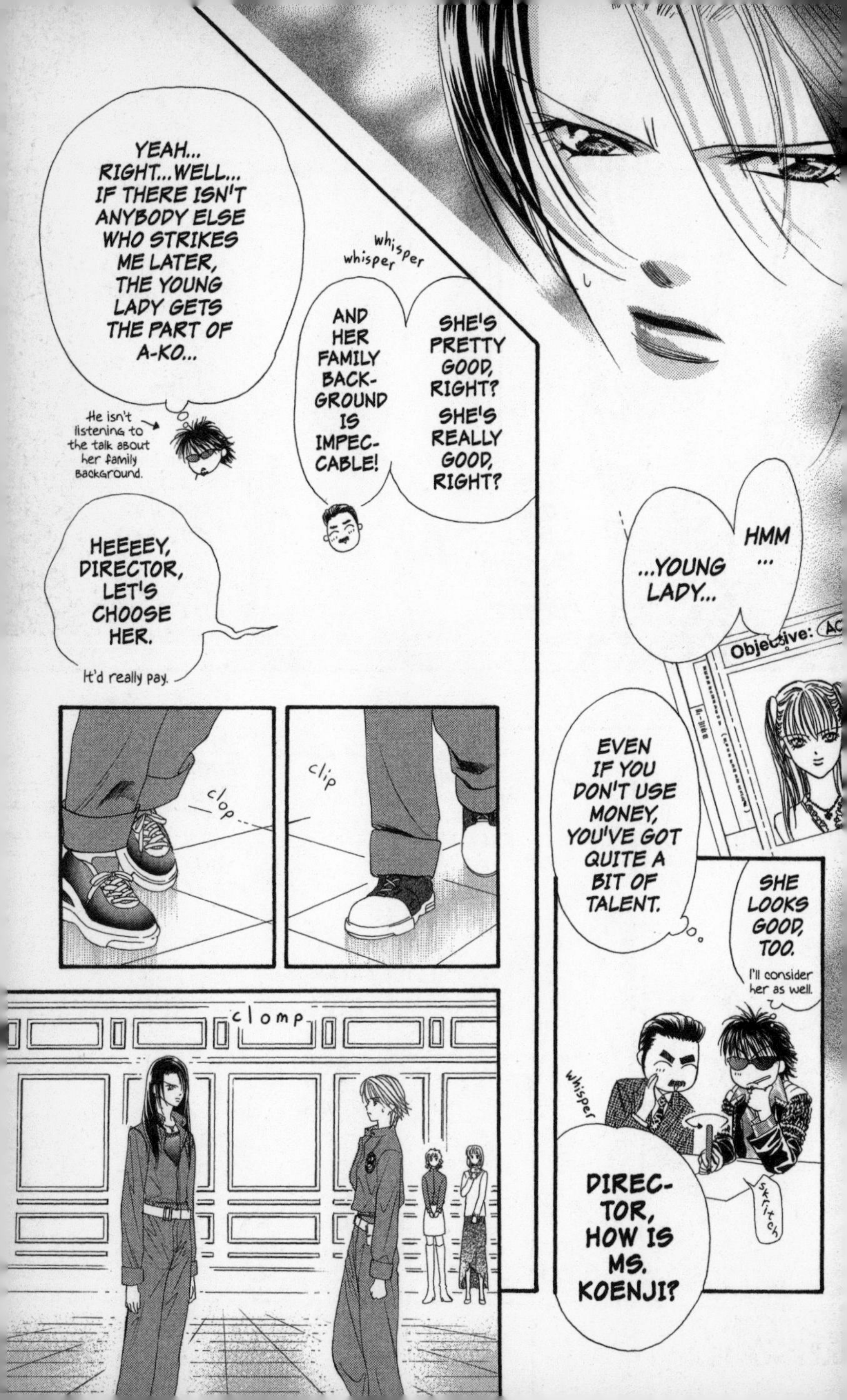
HMM...
...YOUNG LADY...
Objective: AC
EVEN IF YOU DON'T USE MONEY, YOU'VE GOT QUITE A BIT OF TALENT.
SHE LOOKS GOOD, TOO.
I'll consider her as well.
whisper
DIRECTOR, HOW IS MS. KOENJI?
skritch
SHE'S PRETTY GOOD, RIGHT? SHE'S REALLY GOOD, RIGHT?
AND HER FAMILY BACKGROUND IS IMPECCABLE!
whisper whisper
YEAH... RIGHT...WELL... IF THERE ISN'T ANYBODY ELSE WHO STRIKES ME LATER, THE YOUNG LADY GETS THE PART OF A-KO...
He isn't listening to the talk about her family background.
HEEEEY, DIRECTOR, LET'S CHOOSE HER.
It'd really pay.
clip
clop...
clomp

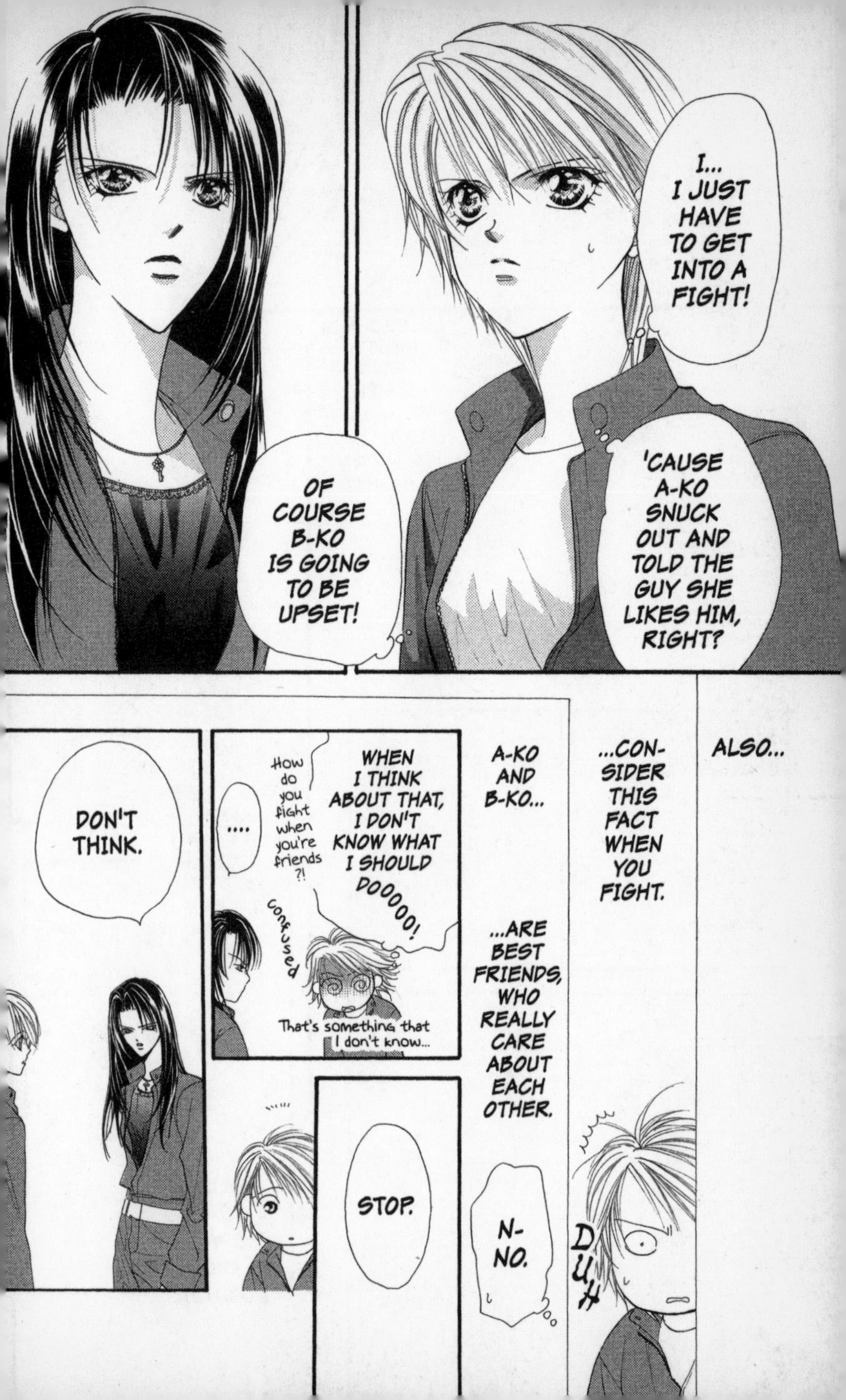
I... I JUST HAVE TO GET INTO A FIGHT!
'CAUSE A-KO SNUCK OUT AND TOLD THE GUY SHE LIKES HIM, RIGHT?
OF COURSE B-KO IS GOING TO BE UPSET!
ALSO...
...CON-SIDER THIS FACT WHEN YOU FIGHT.
A-KO AND B-KO...
...ARE BEST FRIENDS, WHO REALLY CARE ABOUT EACH OTHER.
DUH
N-NO.
WHEN I THINK ABOUT THAT, I DON'T KNOW WHAT I SHOULD DOOOOO!
How do you fight when you're friends?!
....
confused
That's something that I don't know...
STOP.
DON'T THINK.

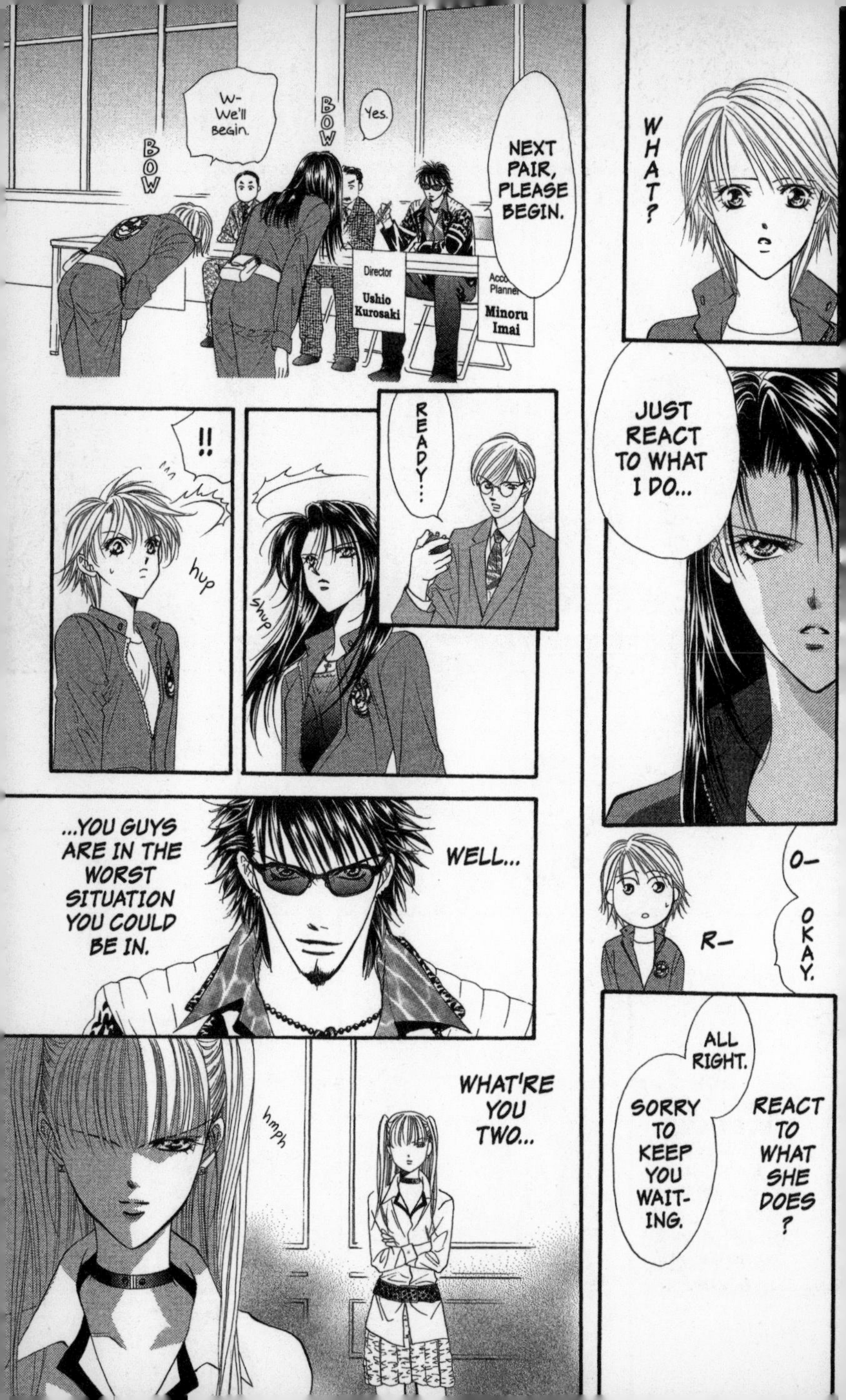
WHAT?
JUST REACT TO WHAT I DO...
O-OKAY.
R-
REACT TO WHAT SHE DOES?
ALL RIGHT.
SORRY TO KEEP YOU WAITING.
NEXT PAIR, PLEASE BEGIN.
Yes.
BOW
W- We'll begin.
BOW
Accou Planner Minoru Imai
Director Ushio Kurosaki
READY...
shup
!!
hup
WELL...
...YOU GUYS ARE IN THE WORST SITUATION YOU COULD BE IN.
WHAT'RE YOU TWO...
hmph

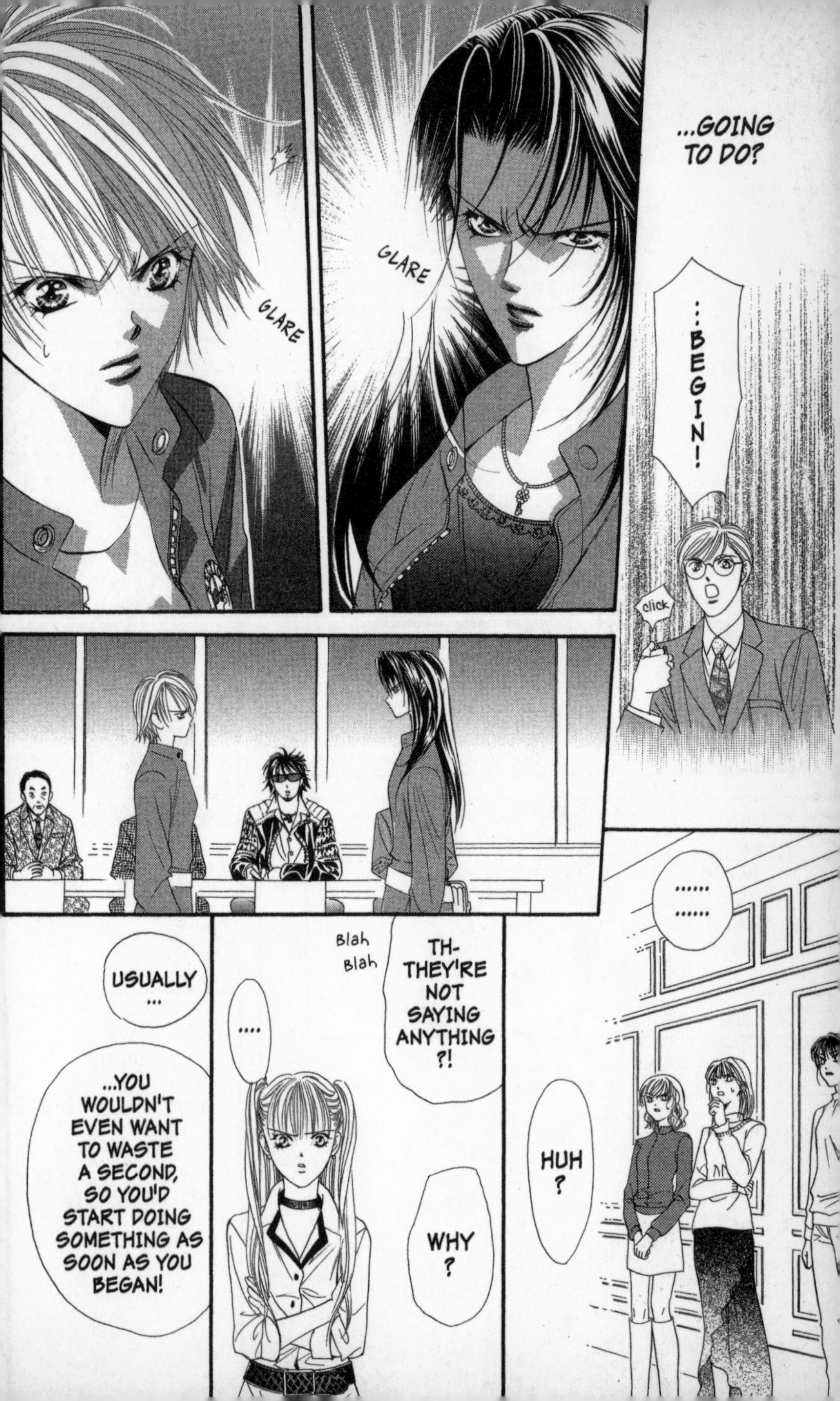
...GOING TO DO?
...BEGIN!
click
GLARE
GLARE
......
......
HUH?
WHY?
Blah Blah
TH-THEY'RE NOT SAYING ANYTHING?!
....
USUALLY...
...YOU WOULDN'T EVEN WANT TO WASTE A SECOND, SO YOU'D START DOING SOMETHING AS SOON AS YOU BEGAN!

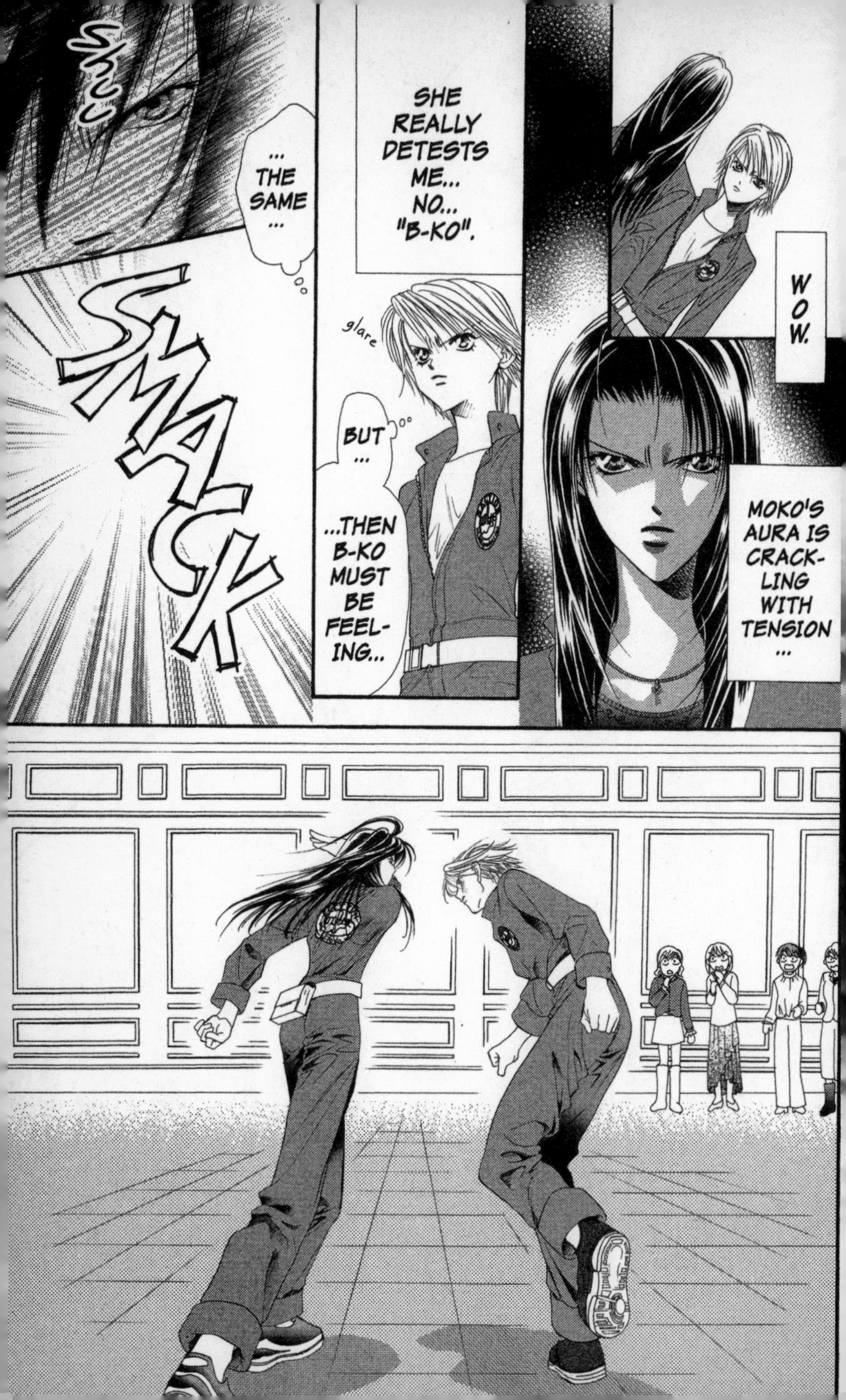
WOW.
MOKO'S AURA IS CRACKLING WITH TENSION...
SHE REALLY DETESTS ME... NO... "B-KO".
glare
BUT...
...THEN B-KO MUST BE FEELING...
Shuu
...THE SAME...
SMACK

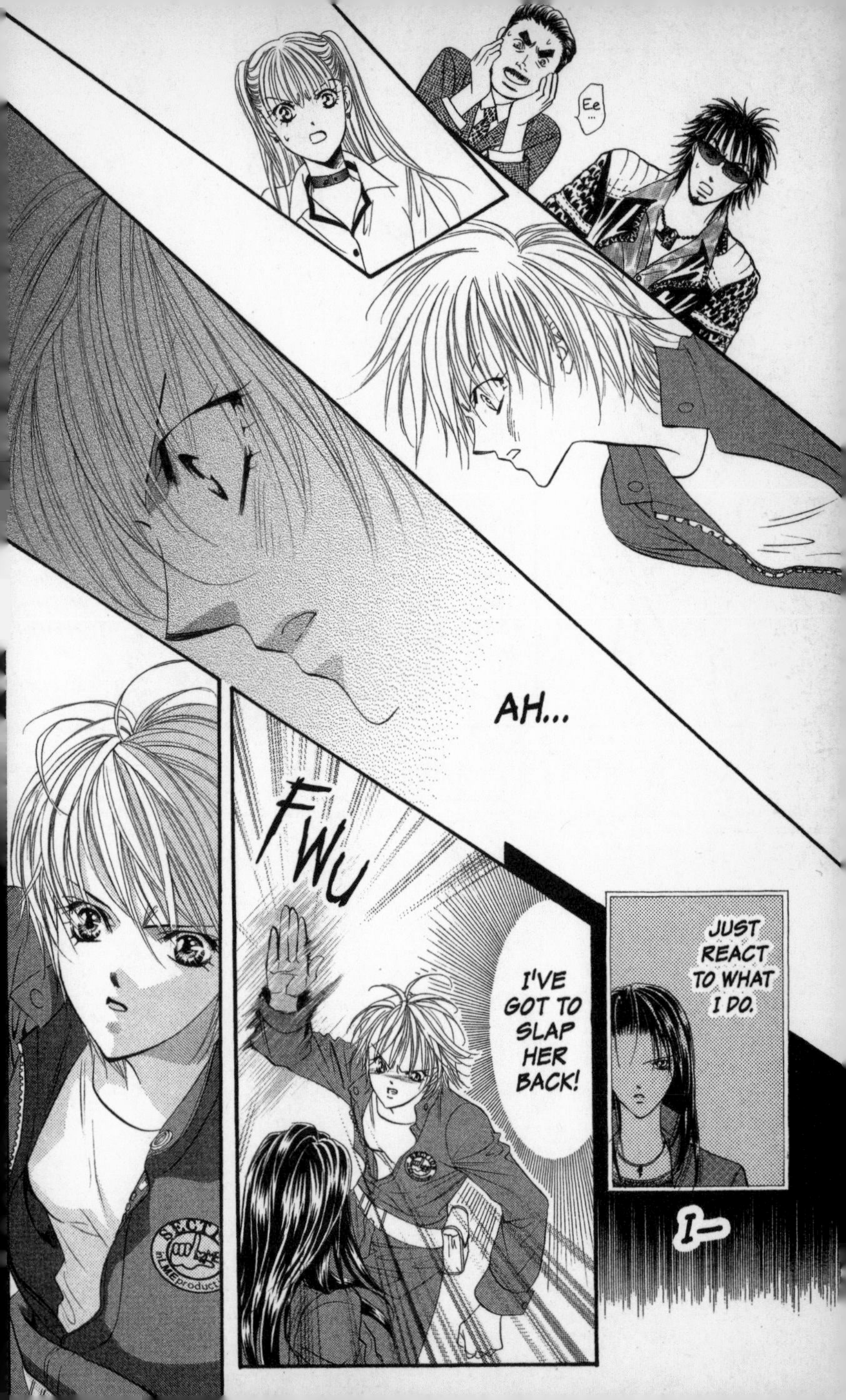
Ee...
AH...
JUST REACT TO WHAT I DO.
I—
I'VE GOT TO SLAP HER BACK!
FWU

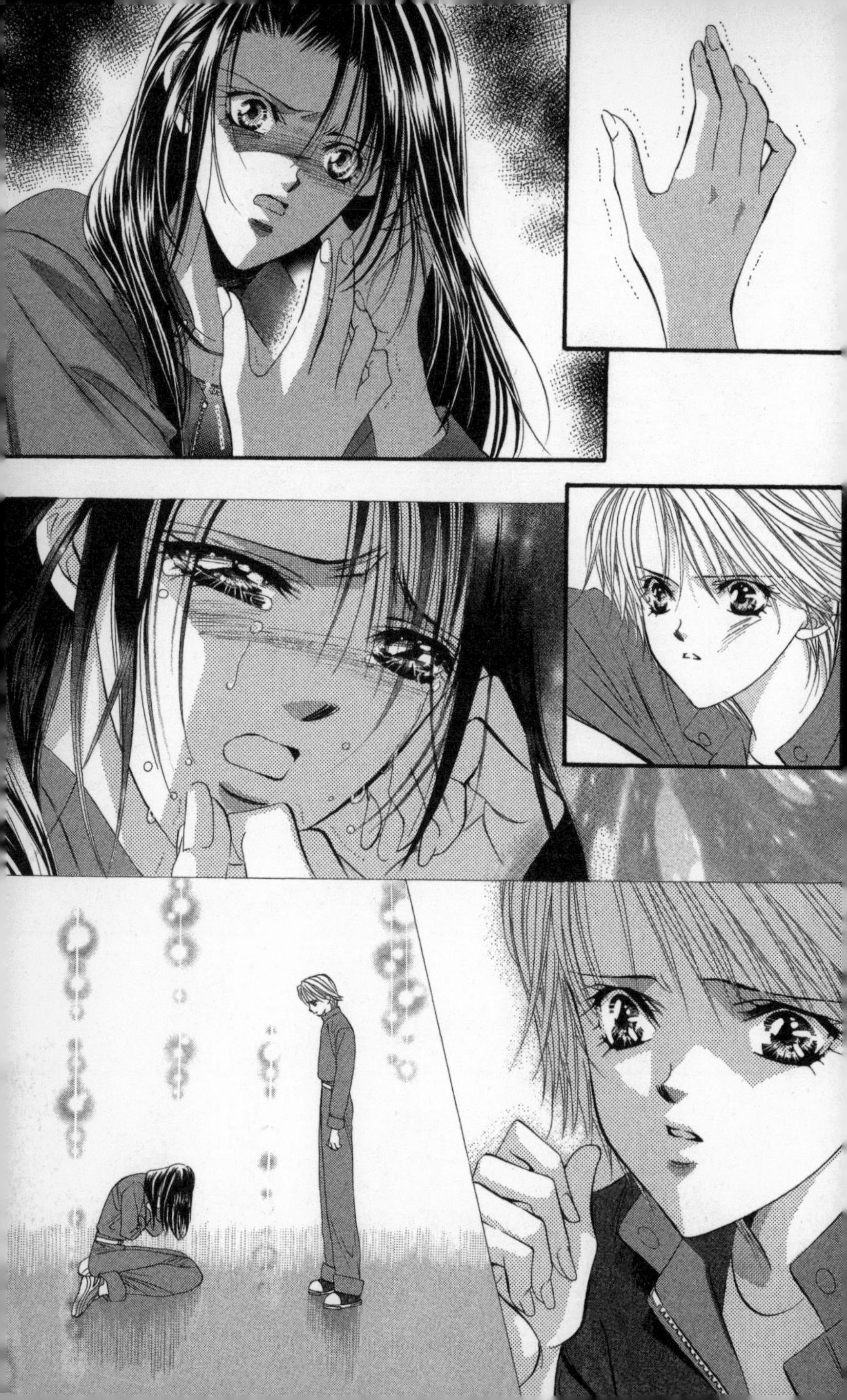

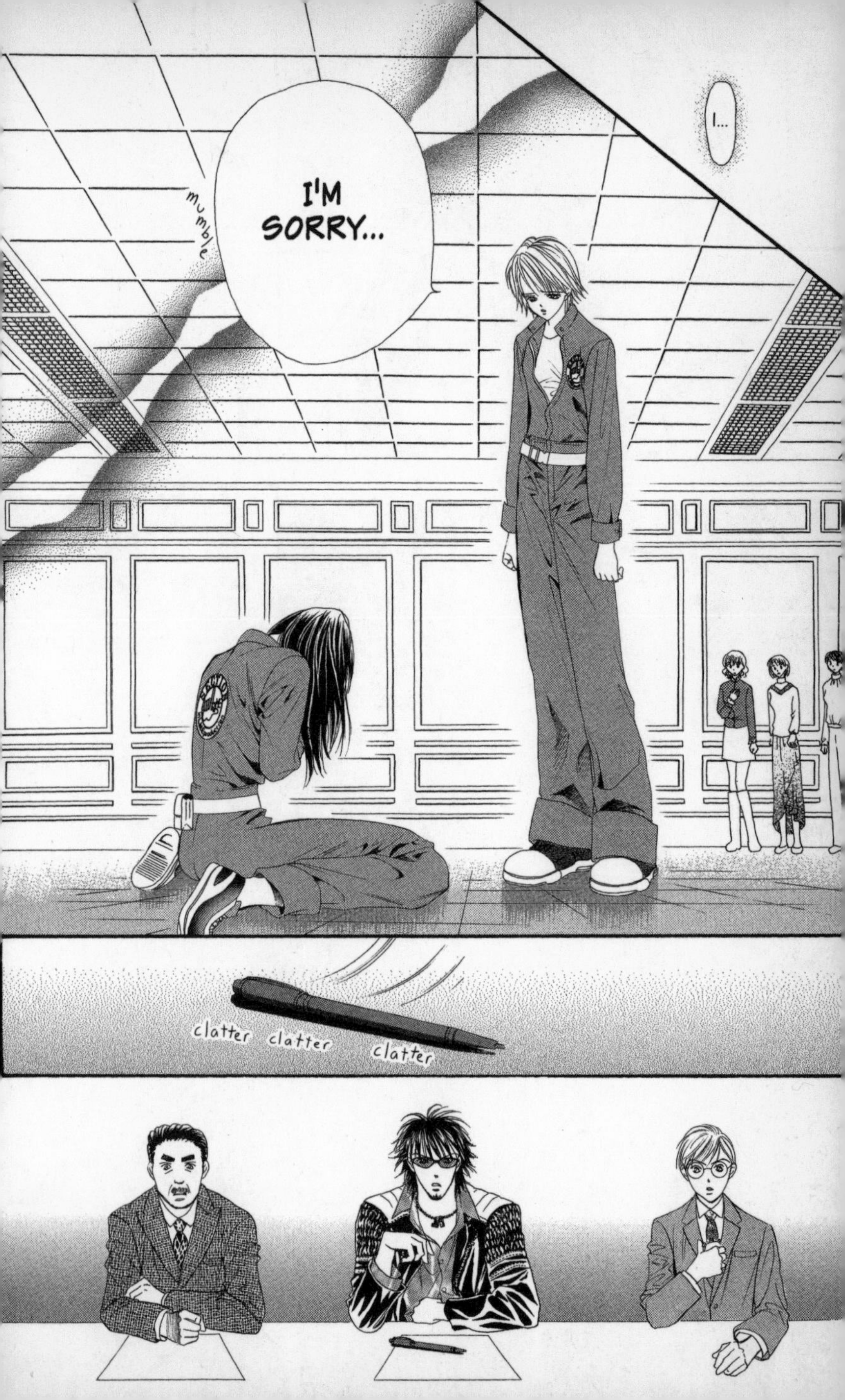
I...
I'M SORRY...
mumble
clatter
clatter
clatter

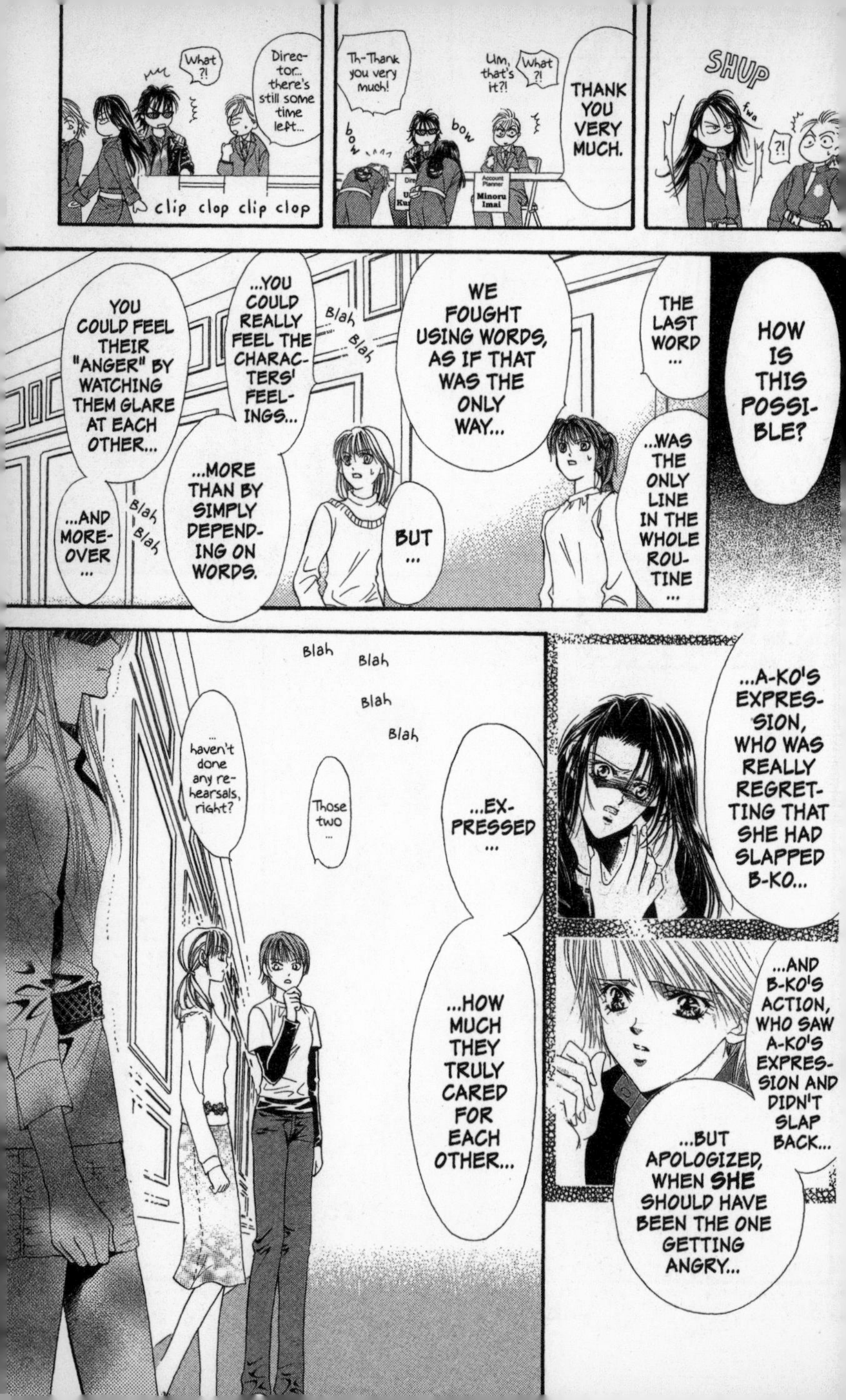
SHUP
fwa
?!
THANK YOU VERY MUCH.
Um, that's it?!
What ?!
Th-Thank you very much!
bow
bow
Account Planner
Minoru Imai
Director... there's still some time left...
What ?!
clip clop clip clop
HOW IS THIS POSSIBLE?
THE LAST WORD ...
...WAS THE ONLY LINE IN THE WHOLE ROUTINE ...
WE FOUGHT USING WORDS, AS IF THAT WAS THE ONLY WAY...
BUT ...
...YOU COULD REALLY FEEL THE CHARACTERS' FEELINGS...
Blah Blah
YOU COULD FEEL THEIR "ANGER" BY WATCHING THEM GLARE AT EACH OTHER...
...MORE THAN BY SIMPLY DEPENDING ON WORDS.
...AND MOREOVER ...
Blah Blah
...A-KO'S EXPRESSION, WHO WAS REALLY REGRETTING THAT SHE HAD SLAPPED B-KO...
...AND B-KO'S ACTION, WHO SAW A-KO'S EXPRESSION AND DIDN'T SLAP BACK...
...BUT APOLOGIZED, WHEN SHE SHOULD HAVE BEEN THE ONE GETTING ANGRY...
...EXPRESSED ...
...HOW MUCH THEY TRULY CARED FOR EACH OTHER...
Blah Blah Blah Blah
Those two ...
... haven't done any rehearsals, right?

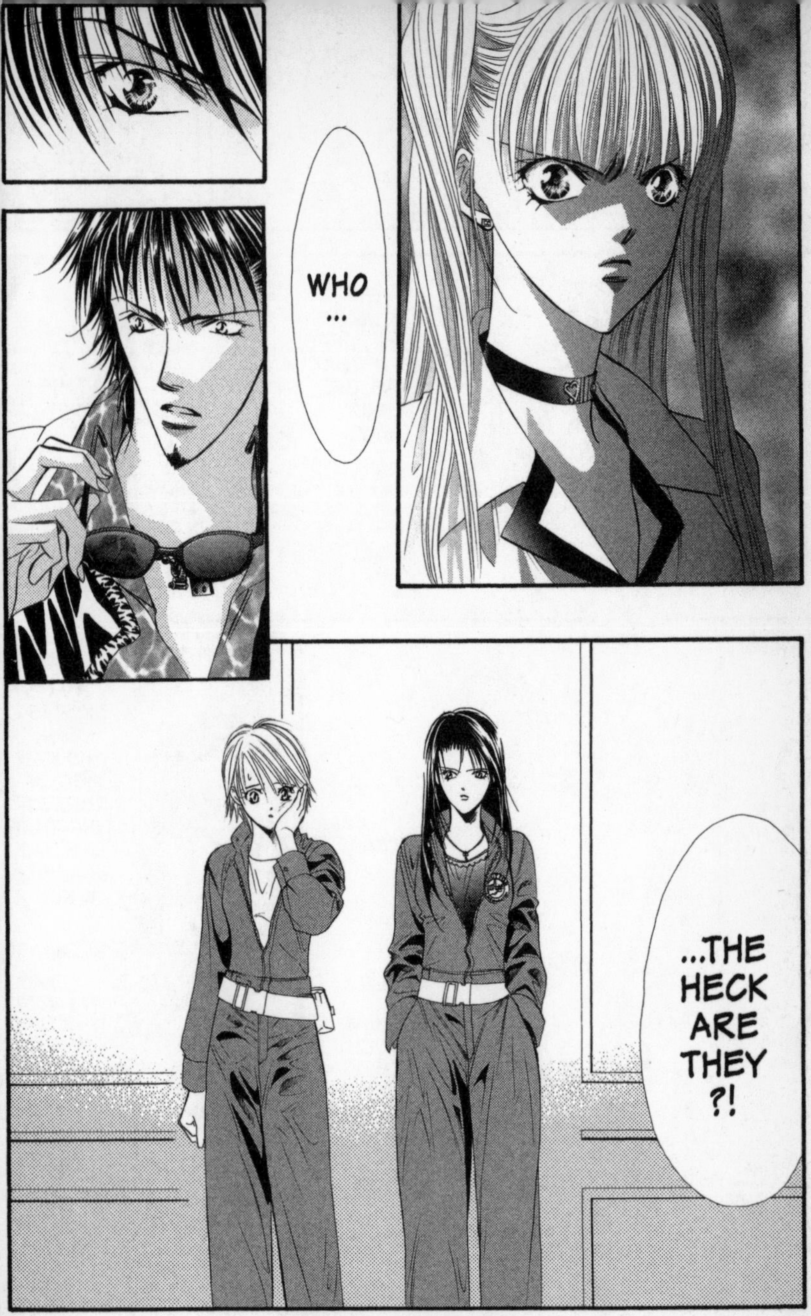
WHO ...
...THE HECK ARE THEY ?!

End of Act 27

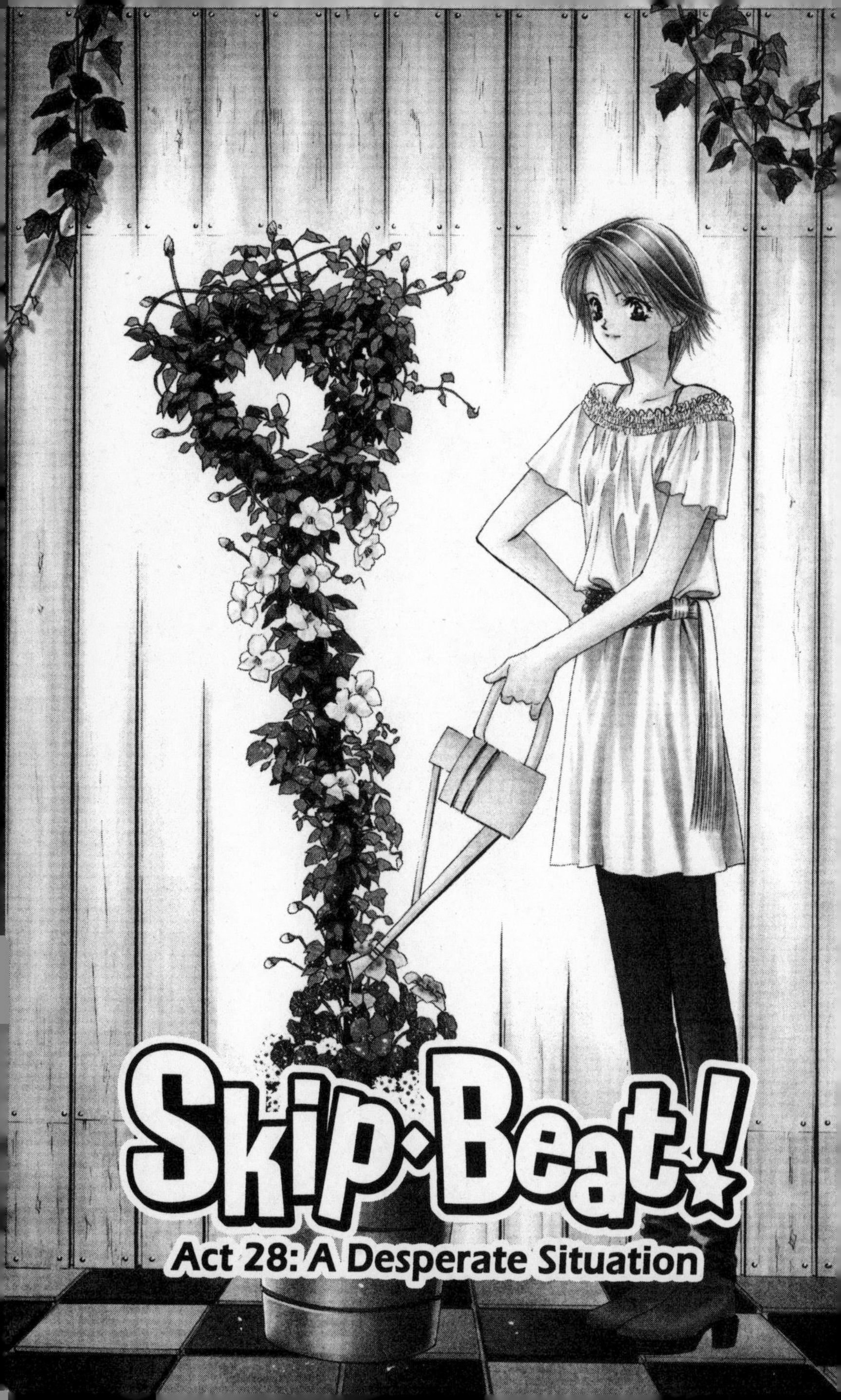
Skip·Beat!
Act 28: A Desperate Situation

Skip•Beat!

Volume 5

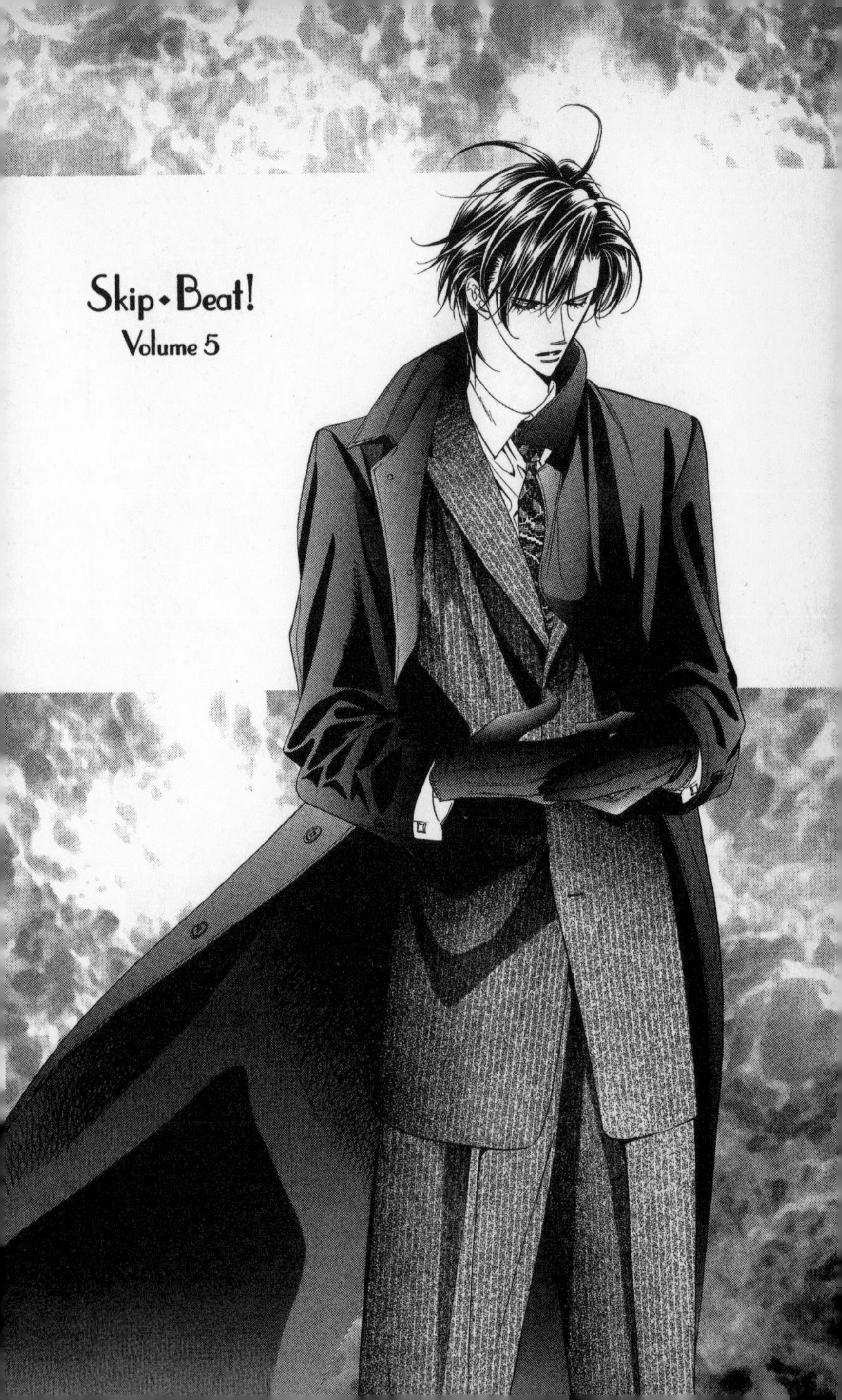

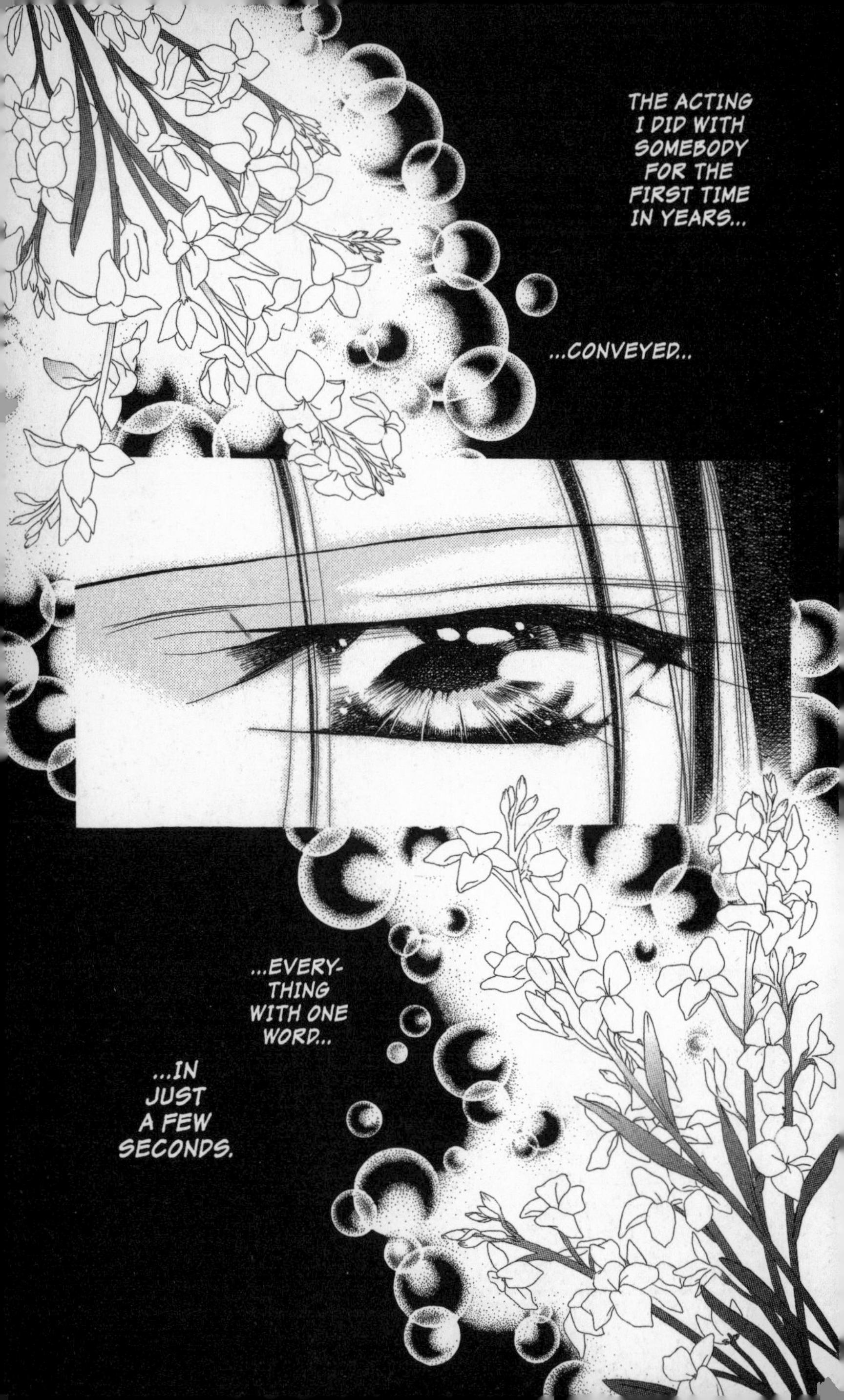
THE ACTING I DID WITH SOMEBODY FOR THE FIRST TIME IN YEARS...
...CONVEYED...
...EVERY-THING WITH ONE WORD...
...IN JUST A FEW SECONDS.

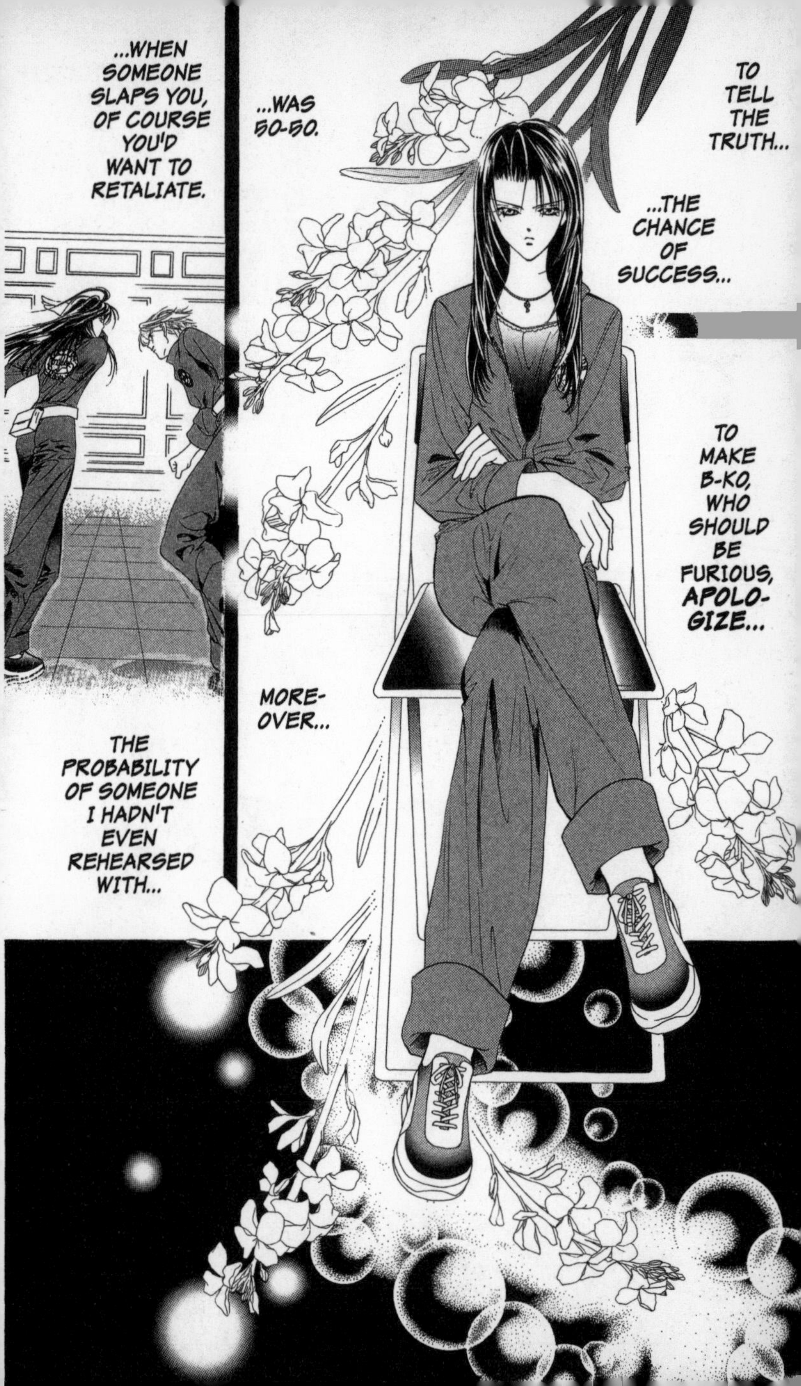
TO TELL THE TRUTH...
...THE CHANCE OF SUCCESS...
...WAS 50-50.
TO MAKE B-KO, WHO SHOULD BE FURIOUS, APOLO-GIZE...
MORE-OVER...
...WHEN SOMEONE SLAPS YOU, OF COURSE YOU'D WANT TO RETALIATE.
THE PROBABILITY OF SOMEONE I HADN'T EVEN REHEARSED WITH...

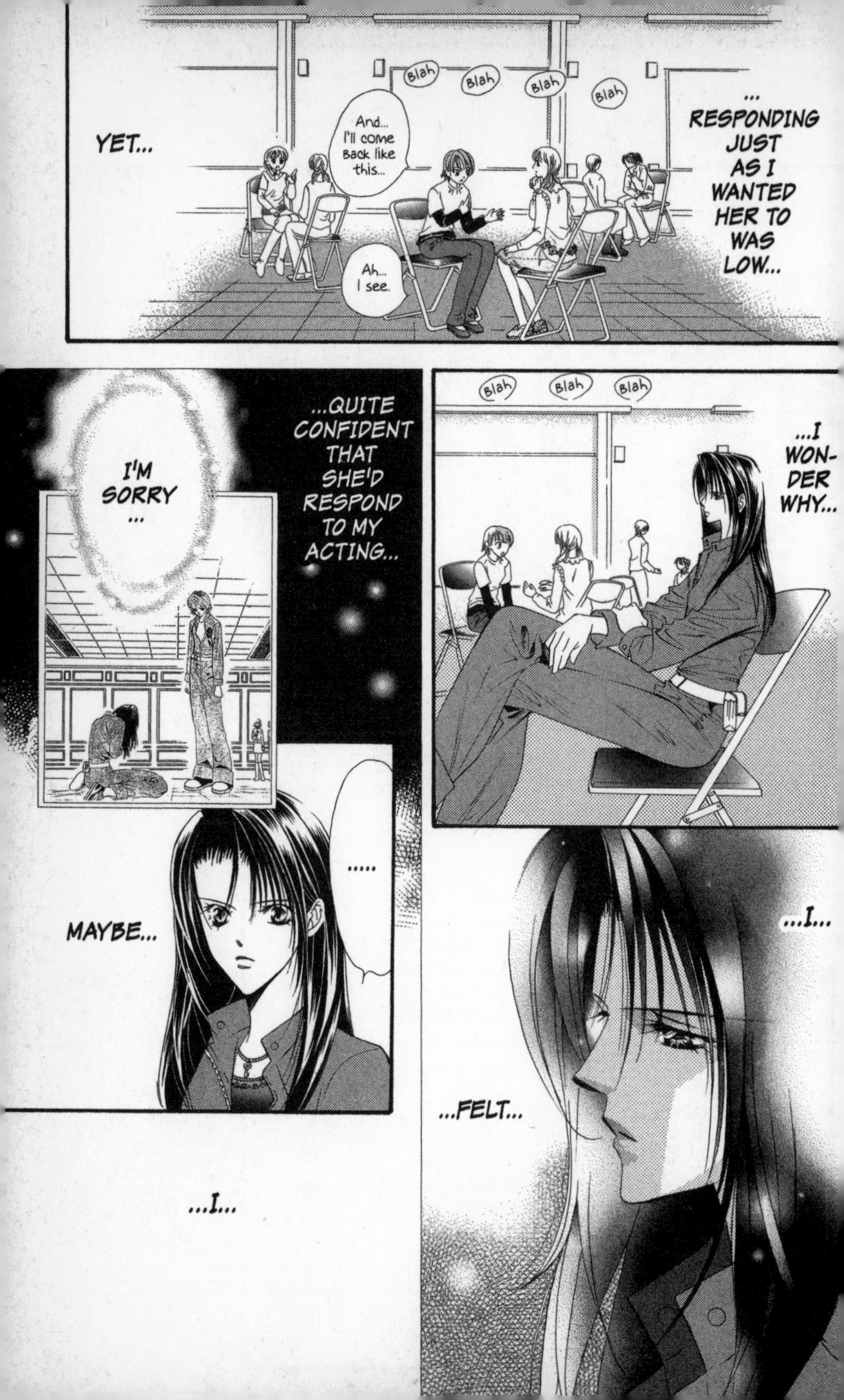
...RESPONDING JUST AS I WANTED HER TO WAS LOW...
Blah
Blah
Blah
Blah
And... I'll come back like this...
YET...
Ah... I see.
Blah
Blah
Blah
...I WONDER WHY...
...QUITE CONFIDENT THAT SHE'D RESPOND TO MY ACTING...
I'M SORRY ...
...I...
...FELT...
.....
MAYBE...
...I...

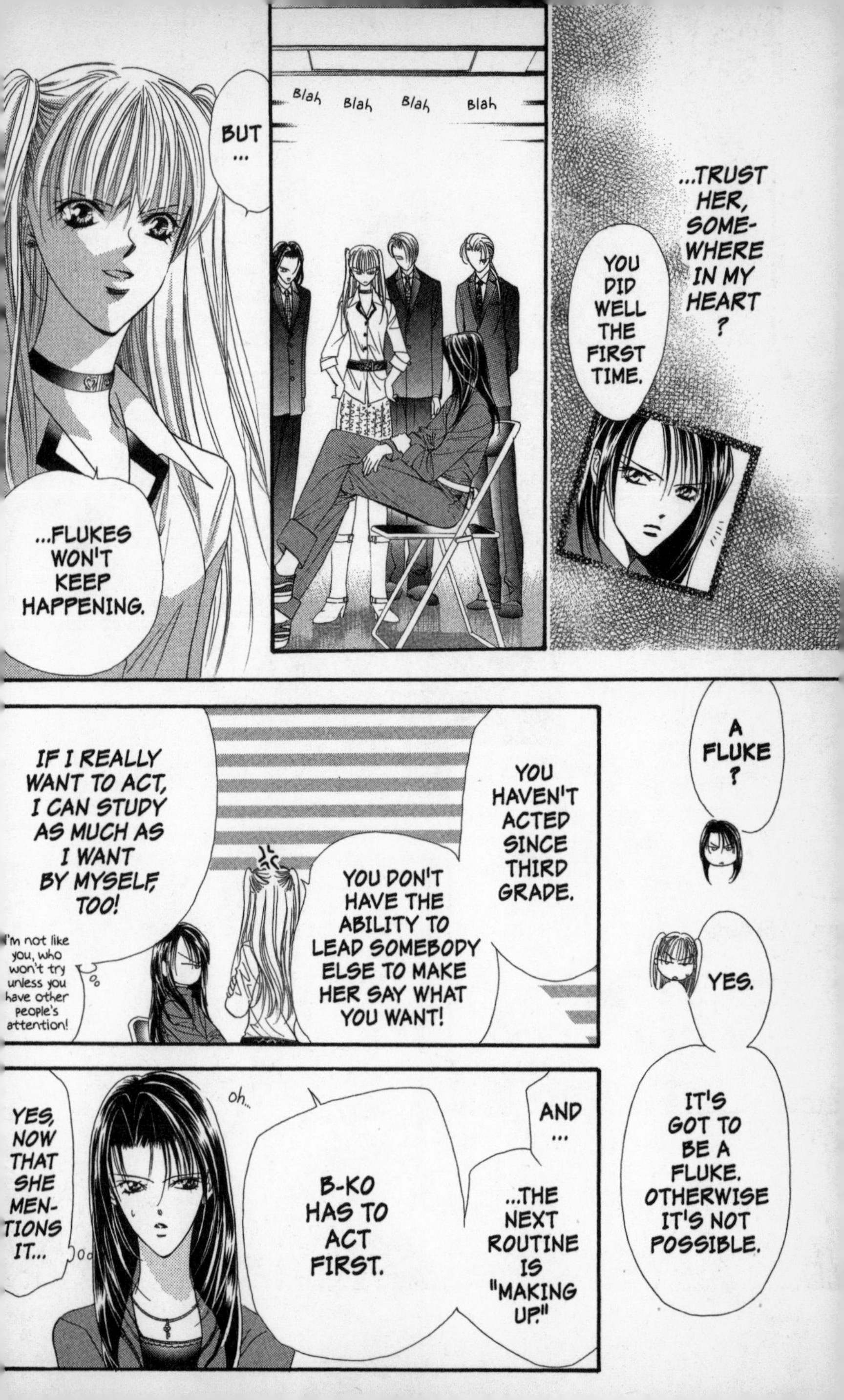
...TRUST HER, SOMEWHERE IN MY HEART?
YOU DID WELL THE FIRST TIME.
Blah Blah Blah Blah
BUT ...
...FLUKES WON'T KEEP HAPPENING.
A FLUKE?
YES.
IT'S GOT TO BE A FLUKE. OTHERWISE IT'S NOT POSSIBLE.
YOU HAVEN'T ACTED SINCE THIRD GRADE.
YOU DON'T HAVE THE ABILITY TO LEAD SOMEBODY ELSE TO MAKE HER SAY WHAT YOU WANT!
IF I REALLY WANT TO ACT, I CAN STUDY AS MUCH AS I WANT BY MYSELF, TOO!
I'm not like you, who won't try unless you have other people's attention!
AND ...
...THE NEXT ROUTINE IS "MAKING UP."
B-KO HAS TO ACT FIRST.
oh...
YES, NOW THAT SHE MENTIONS IT...

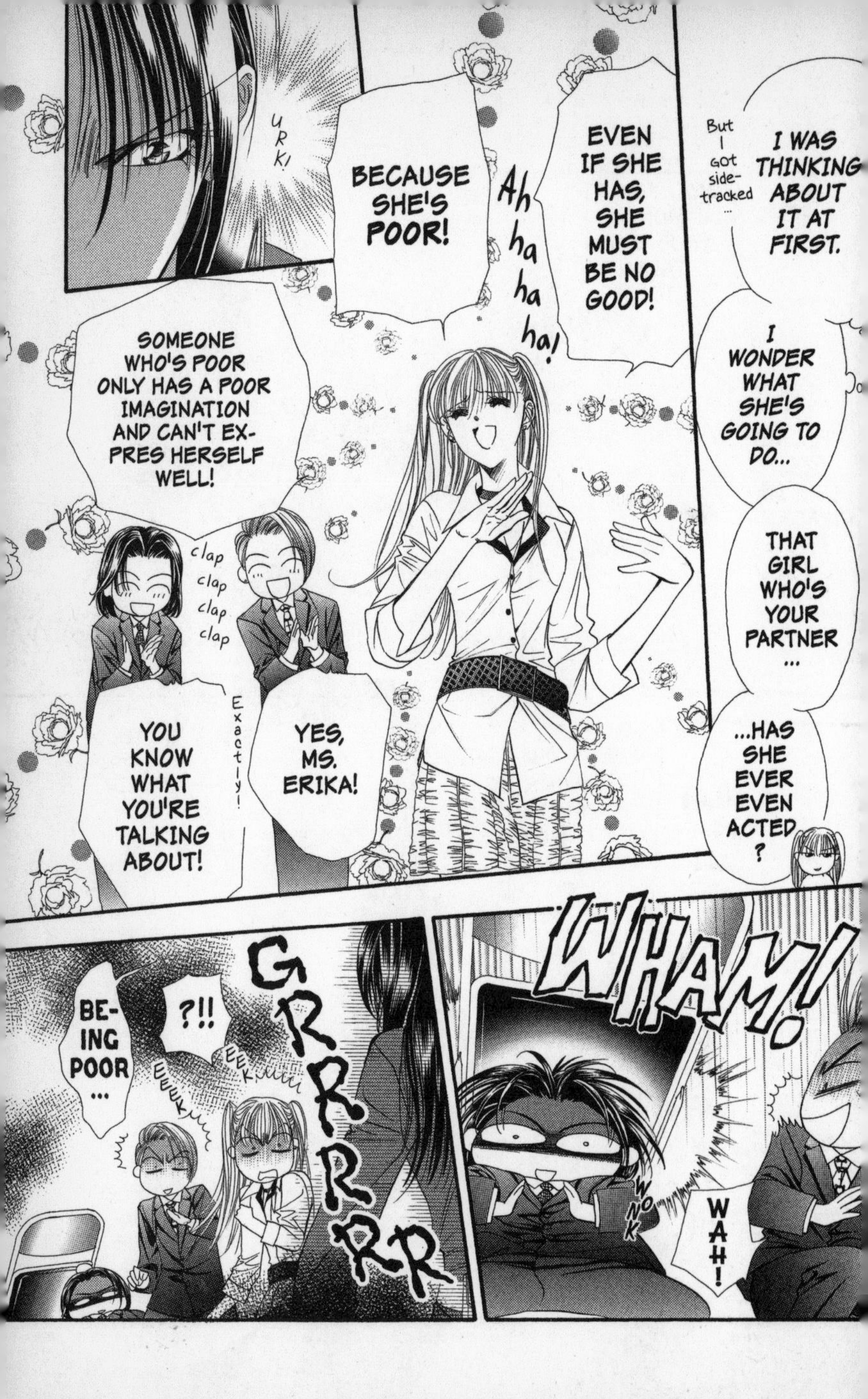

I WAS THINKING ABOUT IT AT FIRST.
But I got side-tracked...
I WONDER WHAT SHE'S GOING TO DO...
THAT GIRL WHO'S YOUR PARTNER...
...HAS SHE EVER EVEN ACTED?
EVEN IF SHE HAS, SHE MUST BE NO GOOD!
Ah ha ha ha!
BECAUSE SHE'S POOR!
URK!
SOMEONE WHO'S POOR ONLY HAS A POOR IMAGINATION AND CAN'T EX-PRES HERSELF WELL!
clap clap clap clap
YES, MS. ERIKA!
Exactly!
YOU KNOW WHAT YOU'RE TALKING ABOUT!
WHAM!
WAH!
WONK
GRRRRR
?!!
BE-ING POOR...
EEEK
EEEK

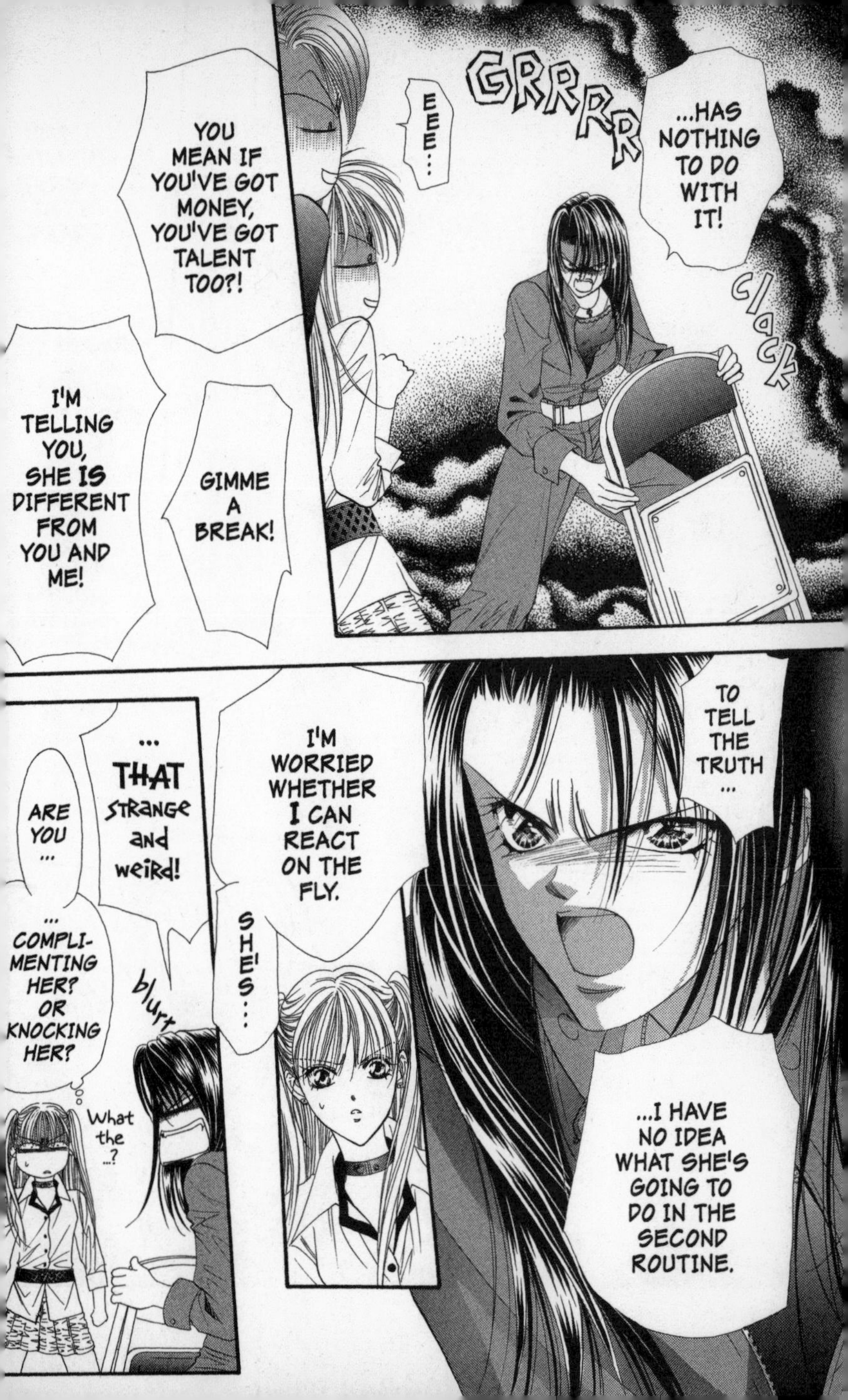
GRRRR
...HAS NOTHING TO DO WITH IT!
clack
EEE...
YOU MEAN IF YOU'VE GOT MONEY, YOU'VE GOT TALENT TOO?!
GIMME A BREAK!
I'M TELLING YOU, SHE IS DIFFERENT FROM YOU AND ME!
TO TELL THE TRUTH...
...I HAVE NO IDEA WHAT SHE'S GOING TO DO IN THE SECOND ROUTINE.
I'M WORRIED WHETHER I CAN REACT ON THE FLY.
SHE'S...
...THAT strange and weird!
blurt
ARE YOU...
...COMPLIMENTING HER? OR KNOCKING HER?
What the ...?

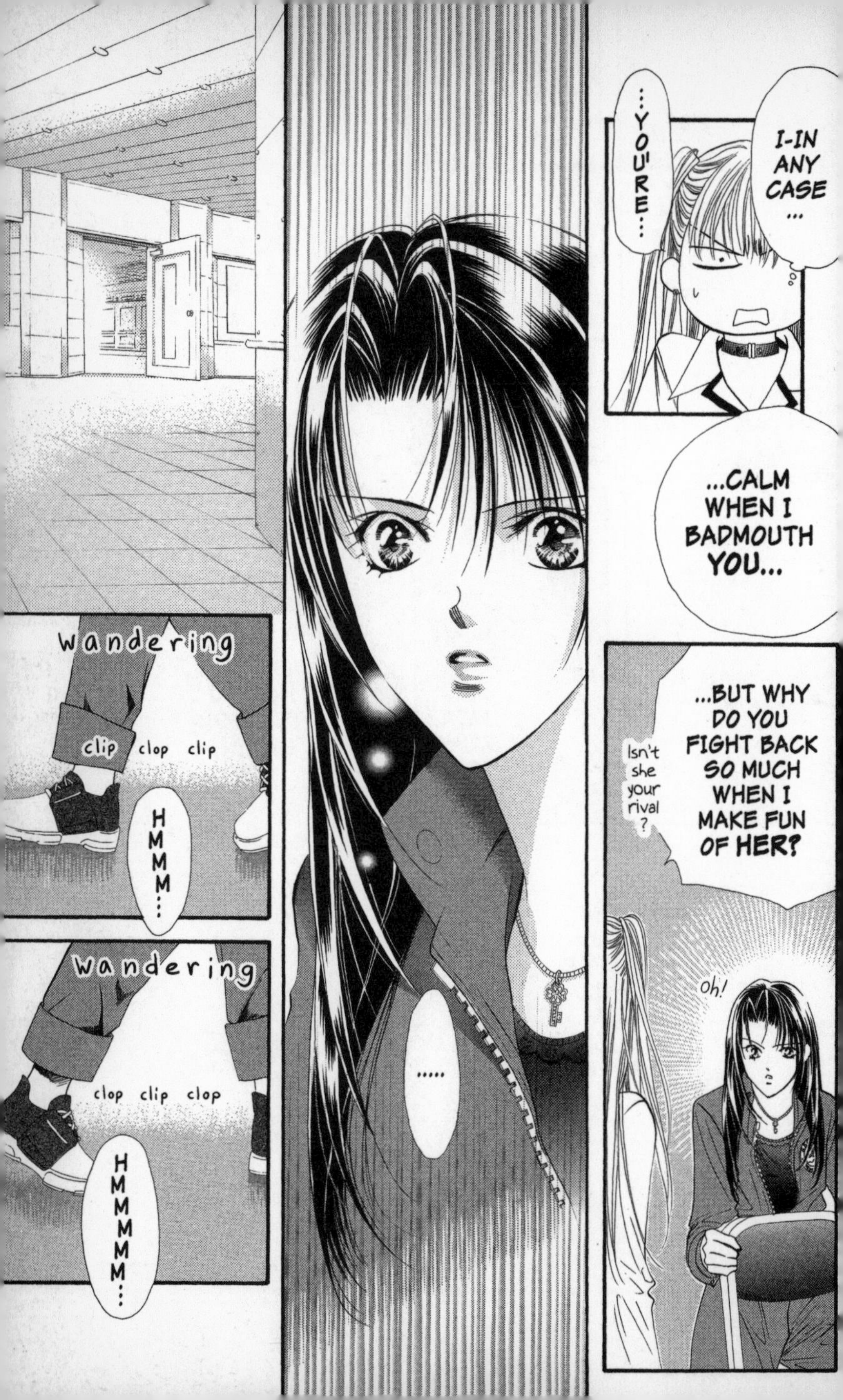

I-IN ANY CASE ...
...YOU'RE...
...CALM WHEN I BADMOUTH YOU...
...BUT WHY DO YOU FIGHT BACK SO MUCH WHEN I MAKE FUN OF HER?
Isn't she your rival?
oh!
......
wandering
clip clop clip
HMMM...
wandering
clop clip clop
HMMMMM...

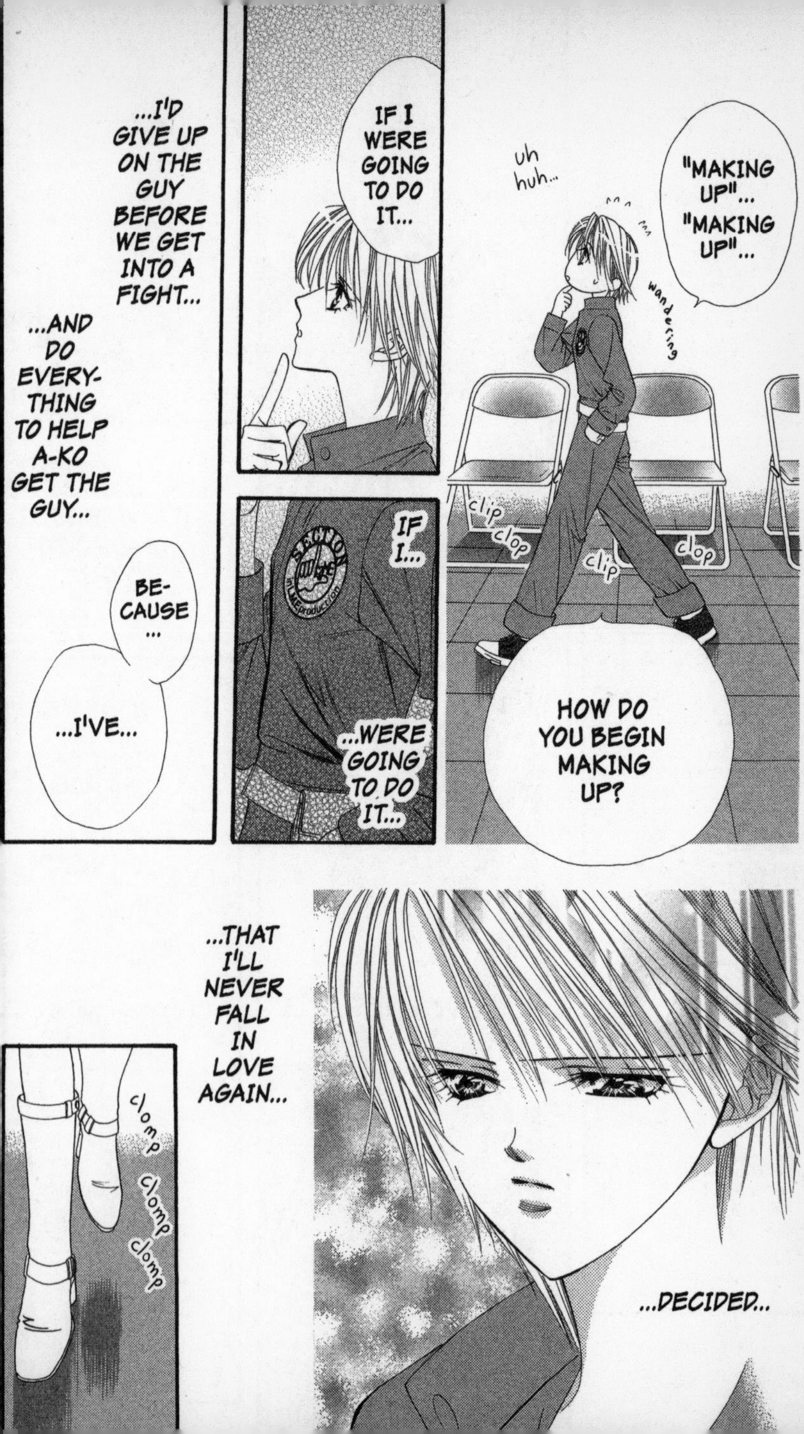
uh huh...
"MAKING UP"... "MAKING UP"...
wandering
clip clop
clip clop
HOW DO YOU BEGIN MAKING UP?
IF I WERE GOING TO DO IT...
IF I...
...WERE GOING TO DO IT...
...I'D GIVE UP ON THE GUY BEFORE WE GET INTO A FIGHT...
...AND DO EVERY-THING TO HELP A-KO GET THE GUY...
BE-CAUSE...
...I'VE...
...DECIDED...
...THAT I'LL NEVER FALL IN LOVE AGAIN...
clomp clomp clomp clomp

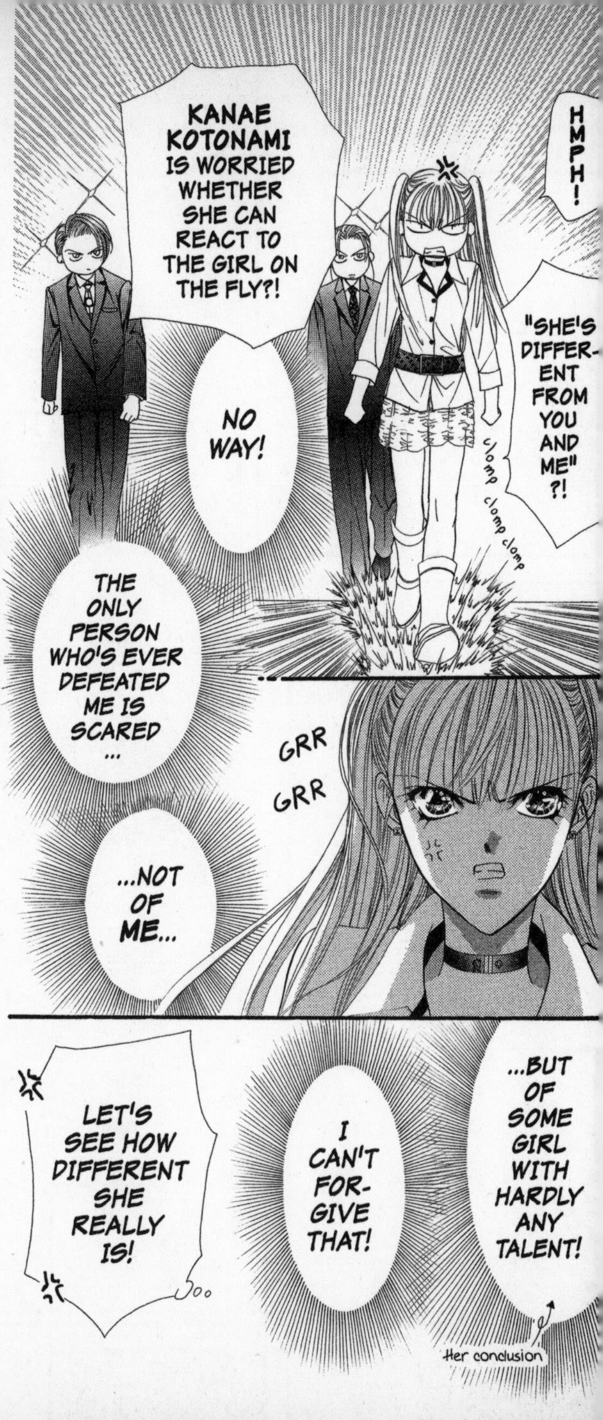
HMPH!
KANAE KOTONAMI IS WORRIED WHETHER SHE CAN REACT TO THE GIRL ON THE FLY?!
"SHE'S DIFFERENT FROM YOU AND ME"?!
NO WAY!
clomp clomp clomp
THE ONLY PERSON WHO'S EVER DEFEATED ME IS SCARED...
GRR GRR
...NOT OF ME...
...BUT OF SOME GIRL WITH HARDLY ANY TALENT!
I CAN'T FORGIVE THAT!
LET'S SEE HOW DIFFERENT SHE REALLY IS!
Her conclusion

Curara

I don't drink soda much, so I don't know much about them...I didn't even know that plastic bottles containing soda and non-soda drinks are shaped differently...(the body and the bottom of the bottle are different) In the story, when Kyoko realizes that Curara is a soda, my assistant noticed "What, Curara was a soda?!"

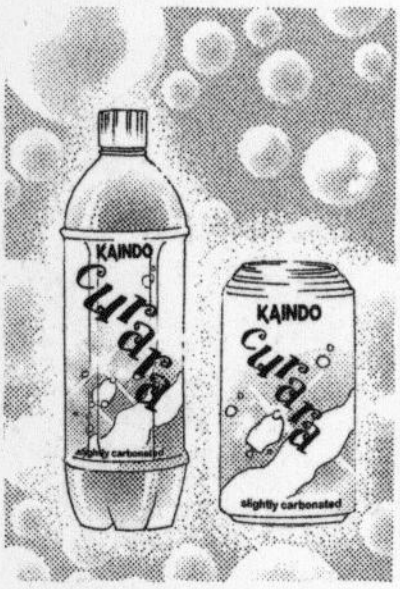
KAINDO
Curara
KAINDO
Curara
slightly carbonated

and told me about the difference in the bottom of the container eh heh heh. So the Curara that first appeared in the magazine is not a soda container...Because I really didn't know... And I thought "soft drinks" were soda... Because the dictionary said they were cold drinks containing carbonic acid for example...I thought they were called cooling drinks because you feel refreshed after you drink them... I was really convinced... But on sodas, it says "carbonated drink" and drinks labeled "soft drinks" are...

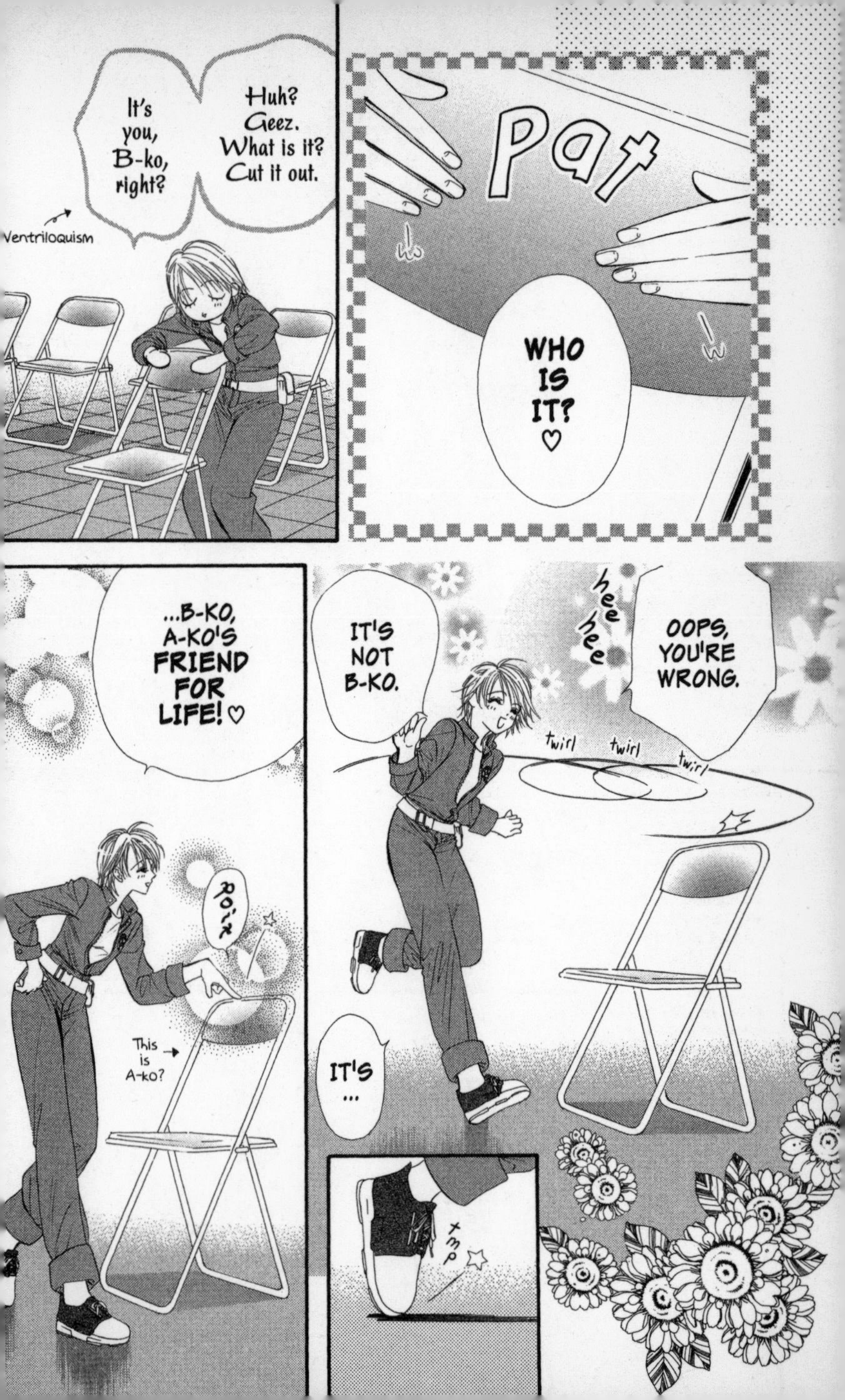

Pat
WHO IS IT? ♡
Huh? Geez. What is it? Cut it out.
It's you, B-ko, right?
Ventriloquism
OOPS, YOU'RE WRONG.
hee hee
IT'S NOT B-KO.
twirl twirl twirl
IT'S ...
tmp
...B-KO, A-KO'S FRIEND FOR LIFE! ♡
poit
This is A-ko?

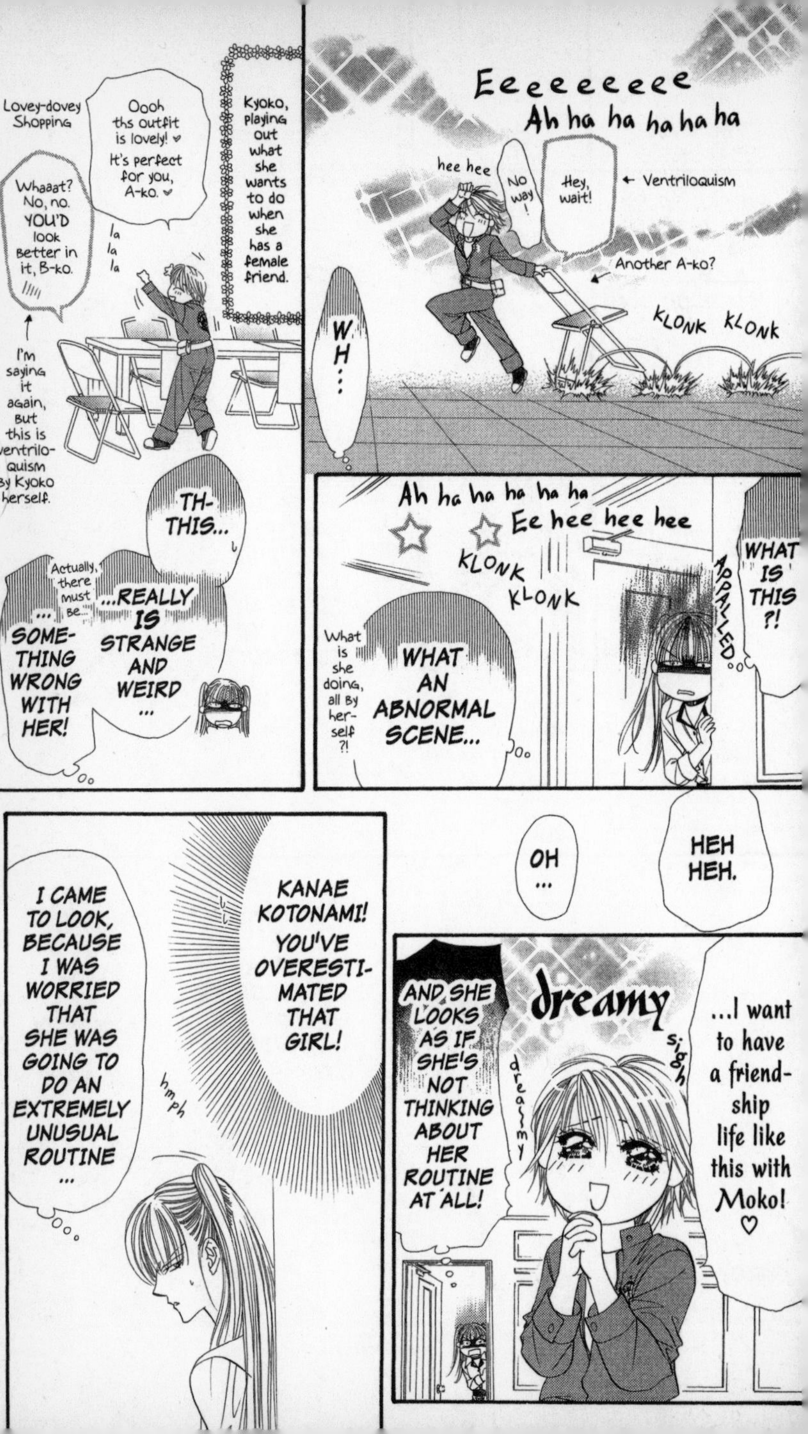
Eeeeeeeee
Ah ha ha ha ha ha
Hey, wait!
← Ventriloquism
No way!
hee hee
Another A-ko?
KLONK KLONK
WH...
WHAT IS THIS?!
APPALLED
Ah ha ha ha ha ha
Ee hee hee hee
KLONK KLONK
WHAT AN ABNORMAL SCENE...
What is she doing, all by herself?!
Kyoko, playing out what she wants to do when she has a female friend.
Oooh ths outfit is lovely! ♥ It's perfect for you, A-ko. ♥
Lovey-dovey Shopping
Whaaat? No, no. YOU'D look better in it, B-ko.
la la la
I'm saying it again, but this is ventriloquism by Kyoko herself.
TH-THIS...
...REALLY IS STRANGE AND WEIRD...
Actually, there must be...
...SOMETHING WRONG WITH HER!
HEH HEH.
OH...
...I want to have a friendship life like this with Moko! ♡
dreamy
sigh
dreamy
AND SHE LOOKS AS IF SHE'S NOT THINKING ABOUT HER ROUTINE AT ALL!
KANAE KOTONAMI! YOU'VE OVERESTIMATED THAT GIRL!
I CAME TO LOOK, BECAUSE I WAS WORRIED THAT SHE WAS GOING TO DO AN EXTREMELY UNUSUAL ROUTINE...
hmph

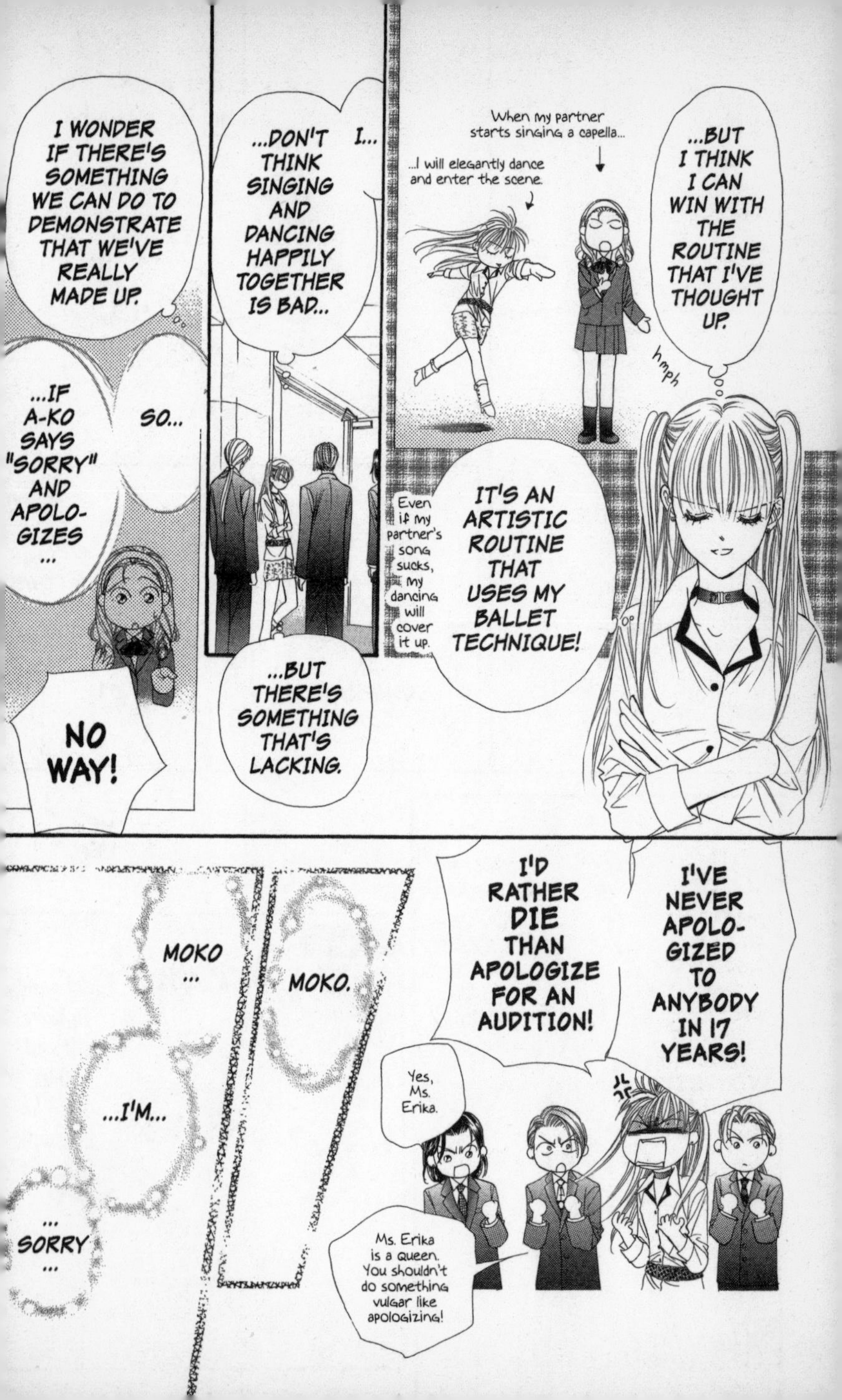
...BUT I THINK I CAN WIN WITH THE ROUTINE THAT I'VE THOUGHT UP.
When my partner starts singing a capella...
...I will elegantly dance and enter the scene.
hmph
IT'S AN ARTISTIC ROUTINE THAT USES MY BALLET TECHNIQUE!
Even if my partner's song sucks, my dancing will cover it up.
I...
...DON'T THINK SINGING AND DANCING HAPPILY TOGETHER IS BAD...
...BUT THERE'S SOMETHING THAT'S LACKING.
I WONDER IF THERE'S SOMETHING WE CAN DO TO DEMONSTRATE THAT WE'VE REALLY MADE UP.
SO...
...IF A-KO SAYS "SORRY" AND APOLOGIZES...
NO WAY!
I'VE NEVER APOLOGIZED TO ANYBODY IN 17 YEARS!
I'D RATHER DIE THAN APOLOGIZE FOR AN AUDITION!
Yes, Ms. Erika.
Ms. Erika is a queen. You shouldn't do something vulgar like apologizing!
MOKO.
MOKO...
...I'M...
...SORRY...

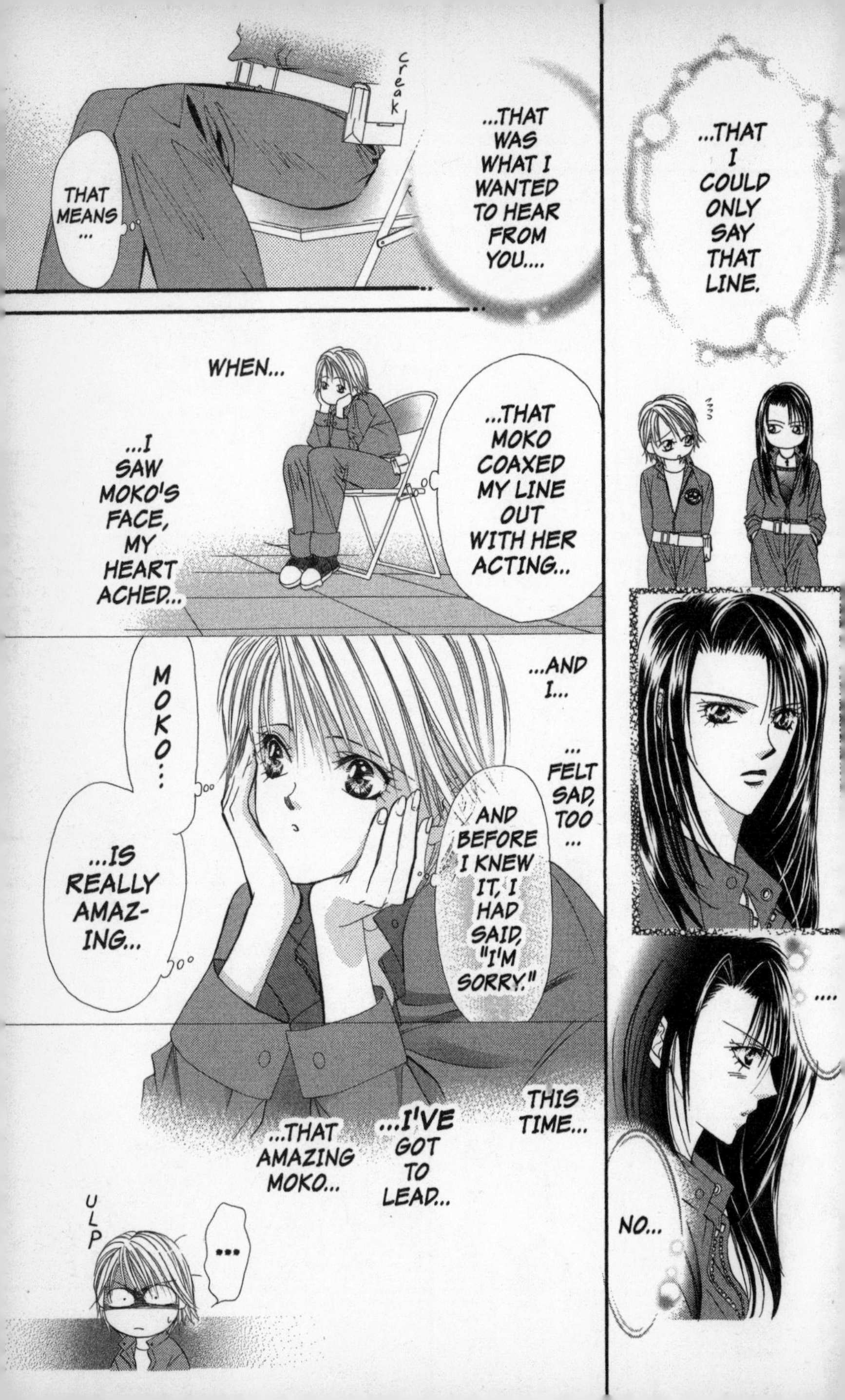
...THAT I COULD ONLY SAY THAT LINE.
....
NO...
creak
...THAT WAS WHAT I WANTED TO HEAR FROM YOU....
THAT MEANS...
WHEN...
...THAT MOKO COAXED MY LINE OUT WITH HER ACTING...
...I SAW MOKO'S FACE, MY HEART ACHED...
...AND I...
...FELT SAD, TOO...
AND BEFORE I KNEW IT, I HAD SAID, "I'M SORRY."
MOKO...
...IS REALLY AMAZING...
THIS TIME...
...I'VE GOT TO LEAD...
...THAT AMAZING MOKO...
ULP
...

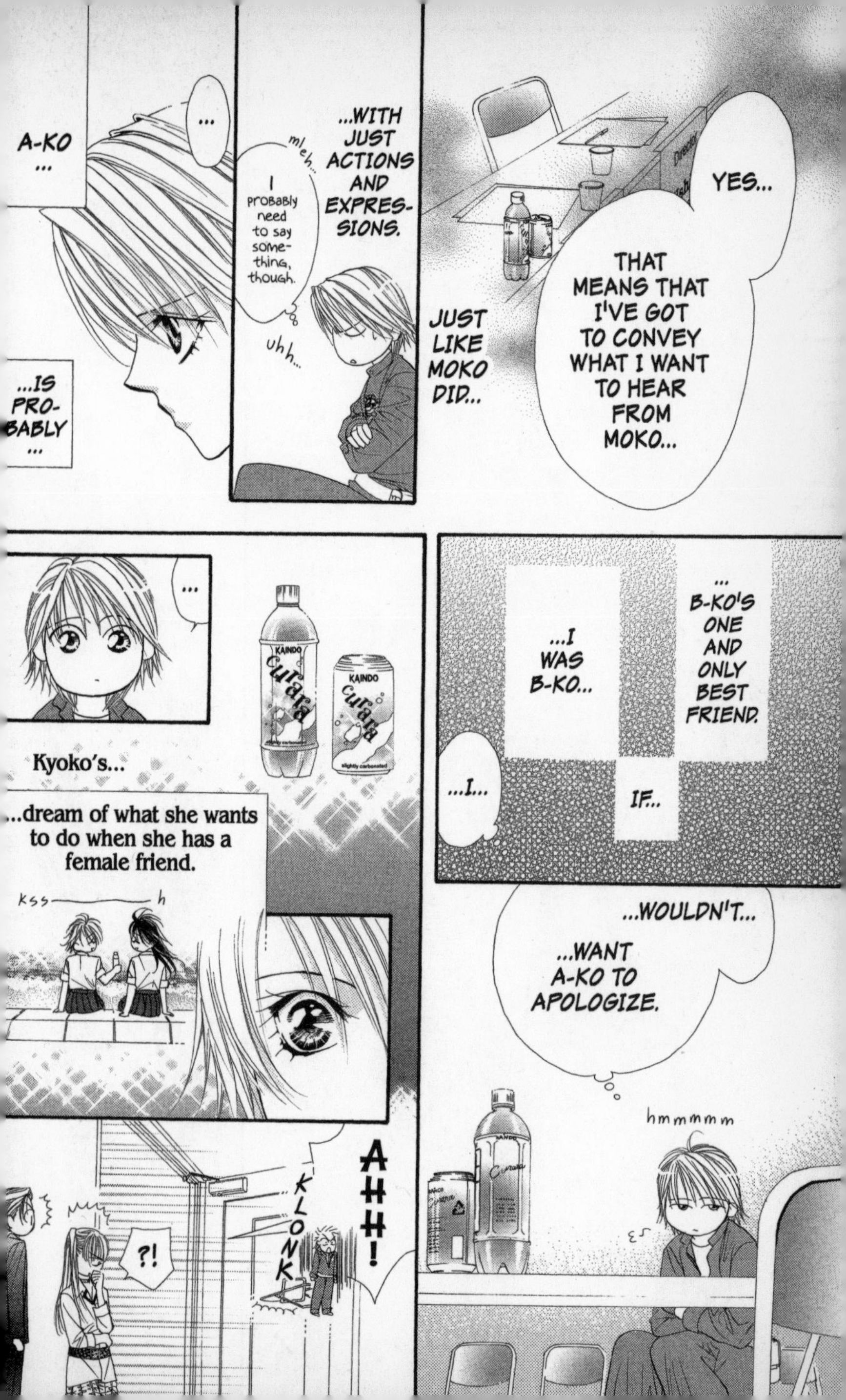

YES...
THAT MEANS THAT I'VE GOT TO CONVEY WHAT I WANT TO HEAR FROM MOKO...
JUST LIKE MOKO DID...
...WITH JUST ACTIONS AND EXPRESSIONS.
mleh...
I probably need to say some-thing, though.
uhh...
...
A-KO ...
...IS PRO-BABLY ...
... B-KO'S ONE AND ONLY BEST FRIEND.
...I WAS B-KO...
IF...
...I...
...WOULDN'T...
...WANT A-KO TO APOLOGIZE.
hmmmmm
...
KAINDO Curara
slightly carbonated
Kyoko's...
...dream of what she wants to do when she has a female friend.
kss———h
AHH!
KLONK
?!

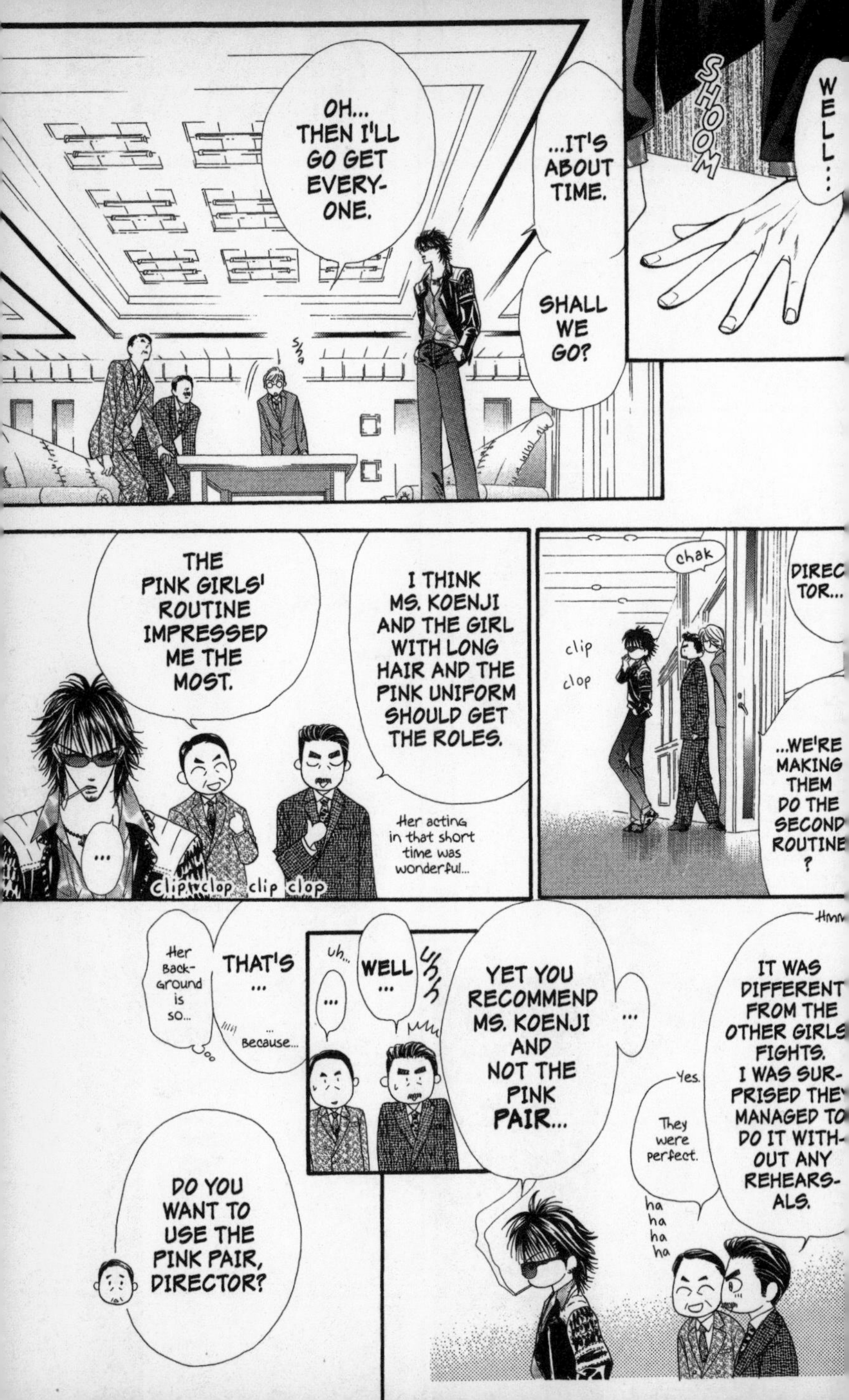
WELL...
SHOOM
...IT'S ABOUT TIME.
SHALL WE GO?
OH... THEN I'LL GO GET EVERYONE.
sha
DIRECTOR...
...WE'RE MAKING THEM DO THE SECOND ROUTINE?
chak
clip
clop
I THINK MS. KOENJI AND THE GIRL WITH LONG HAIR AND THE PINK UNIFORM SHOULD GET THE ROLES.
Her acting in that short time was wonderful...
THE PINK GIRLS' ROUTINE IMPRESSED ME THE MOST.
...
clip clop clip clop
Hmm
IT WAS DIFFERENT FROM THE OTHER GIRLS' FIGHTS. I WAS SURPRISED THEY MANAGED TO DO IT WITHOUT ANY REHEARSALS.
Yes.
They were perfect.
ha ha ha ha
...
YET YOU RECOMMEND MS. KOENJI AND NOT THE PINK PAIR...
WELL ...
uh...
...
THAT'S ...
... Because...
Her Background is so...
DO YOU WANT TO USE THE PINK PAIR, DIRECTOR?

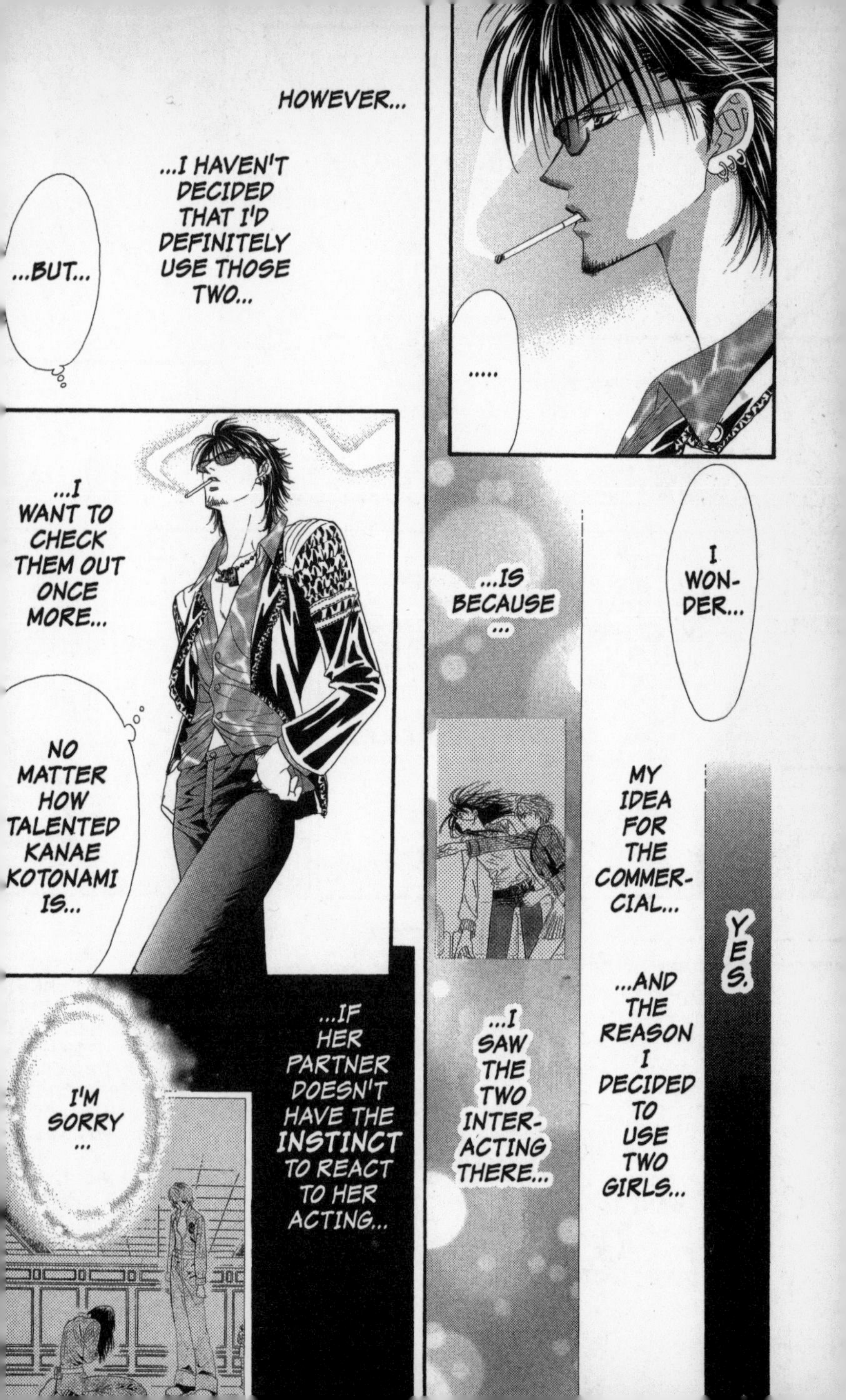

.....
I WONDER...
YES.
MY IDEA FOR THE COMMERCIAL...
...AND THE REASON I DECIDED TO USE TWO GIRLS...
...IS BECAUSE...
...I SAW THE TWO INTERACTING THERE...
HOWEVER...
...I HAVEN'T DECIDED THAT I'D DEFINITELY USE THOSE TWO...
...BUT...
...I WANT TO CHECK THEM OUT ONCE MORE...
NO MATTER HOW TALENTED KANAE KOTONAMI IS...
...IF HER PARTNER DOESN'T HAVE THE INSTINCT TO REACT TO HER ACTING...
I'M SORRY...

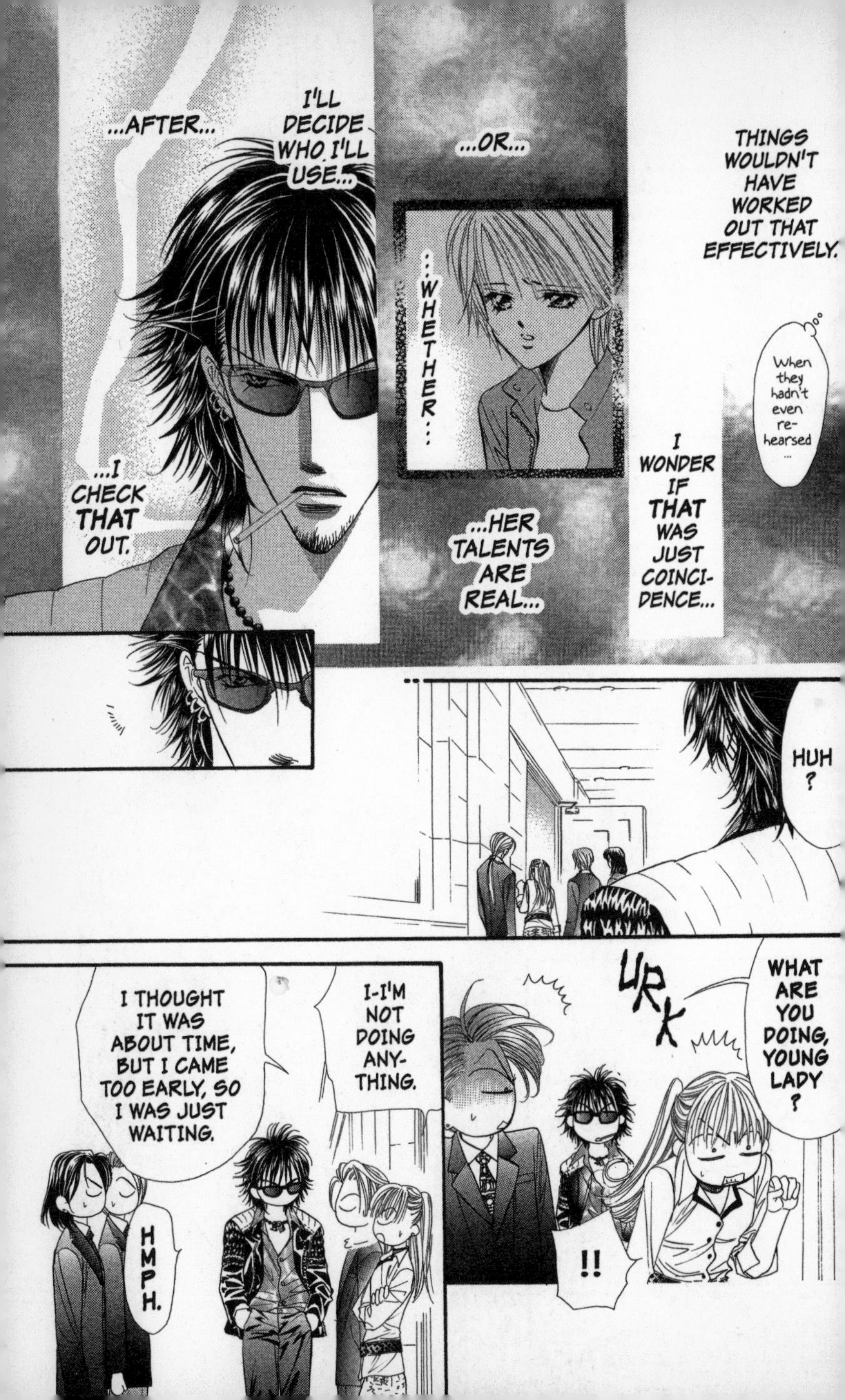
THINGS WOULDN'T HAVE WORKED OUT THAT EFFECTIVELY.
When they hadn't even re-hearsed ...
I WONDER IF THAT WAS JUST COINCIDENCE...
...OR...
...WHETHER...
...HER TALENTS ARE REAL...
I'LL DECIDE WHO I'LL USE...
...AFTER...
...I CHECK THAT OUT.
HUH?
WHAT ARE YOU DOING, YOUNG LADY?
URK
!!
I-I'M NOT DOING ANYTHING.
I THOUGHT IT WAS ABOUT TIME, BUT I CAME TOO EARLY, SO I WAS JUST WAITING.
HMPH.

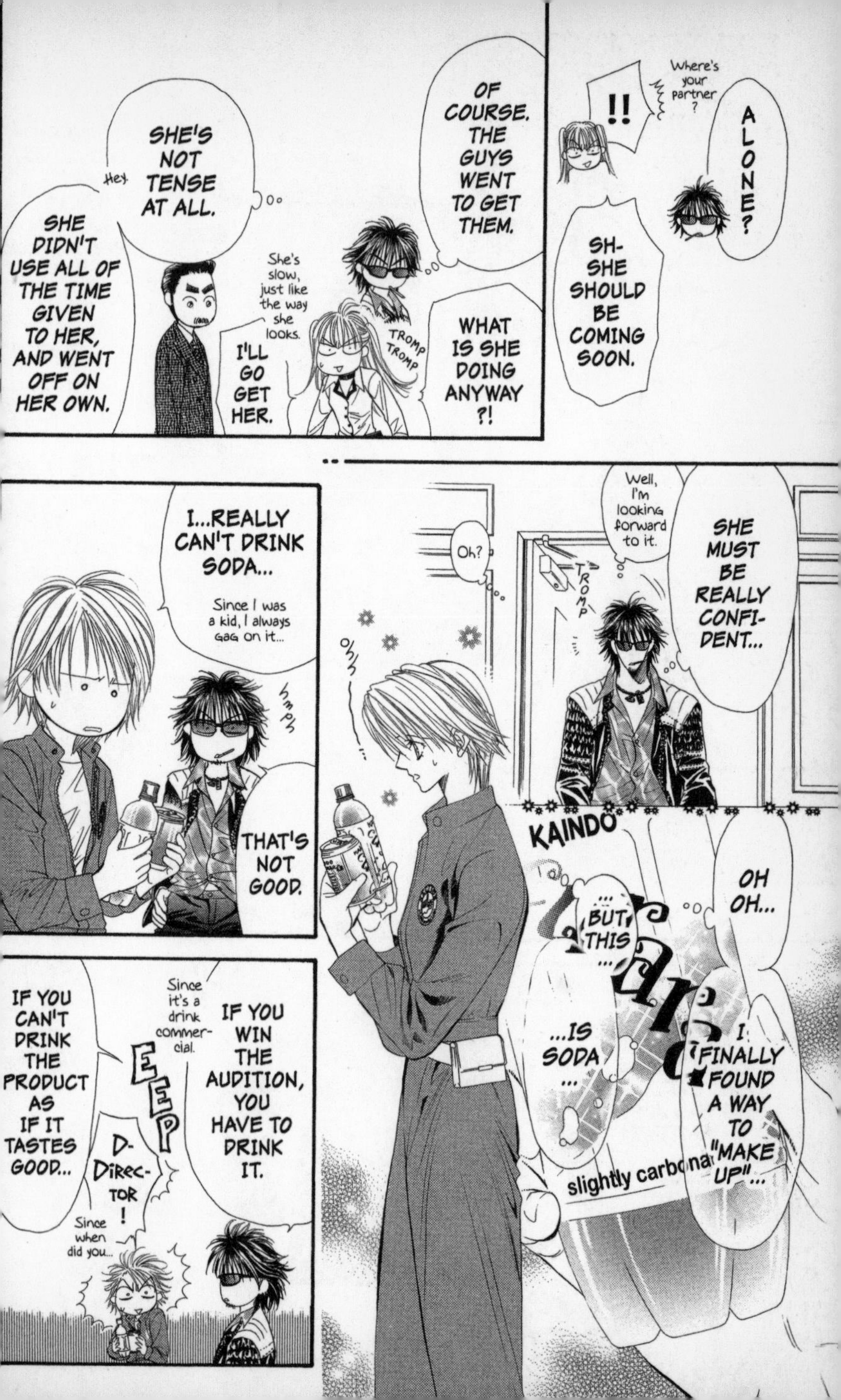
Where's your partner?
ALONE?
!!
SH-SHE SHOULD BE COMING SOON.
OF COURSE. THE GUYS WENT TO GET THEM.
WHAT IS SHE DOING ANYWAY?!
She's slow, just like the way she looks.
TROMP TROMP
I'LL GO GET HER.
SHE'S NOT TENSE AT ALL.
Hey.
SHE DIDN'T USE ALL OF THE TIME GIVEN TO HER, AND WENT OFF ON HER OWN.
Well, I'm looking forward to it.
SHE MUST BE REALLY CONFIDENT...
TROMP
Oh?
OH OH...
I FINALLY FOUND A WAY TO "MAKE UP"...
...BUT THIS...
...IS SODA...
KAINDO
slightly carbona
I...REALLY CAN'T DRINK SODA...
Since I was a kid, I always GAG on it...
hmph
THAT'S NOT GOOD.
IF YOU WIN THE AUDITION, YOU HAVE TO DRINK IT.
Since it's a drink commercial.
IF YOU CAN'T DRINK THE PRODUCT AS IF IT TASTES GOOD...
EEP
D-DIRECTOR!
Since when did you...

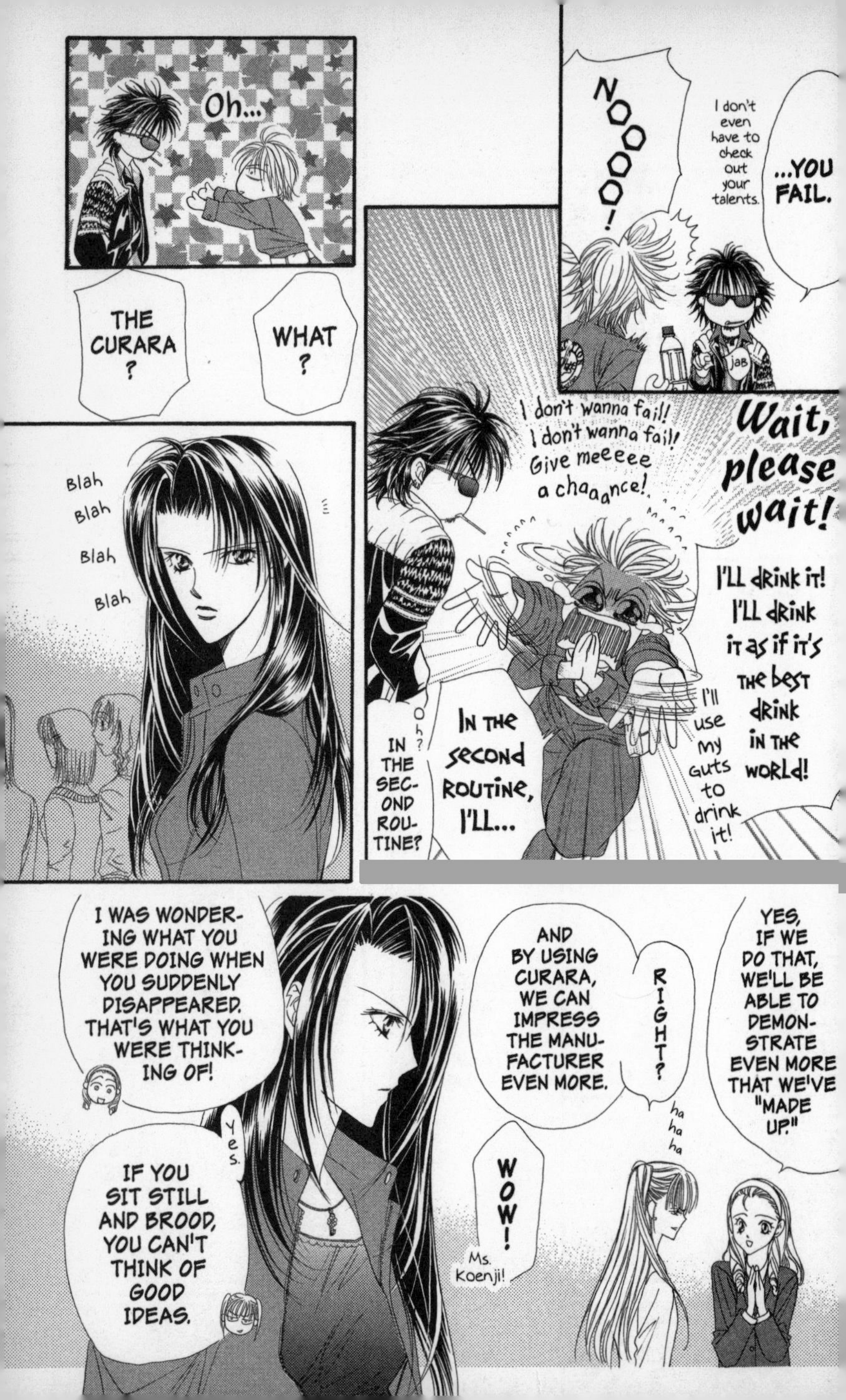
I don't even have to check out your talents.
...YOU FAIL.
jab
NOOOOO!
Wait, please wait!
I don't wanna fail! I don't wanna fail! Give meeeee a chaaaance!
I'LL dRink it! I'LL dRink it as if it's the best dRink in the woRLd!
I'll use my guts to drink it!
In the second routine, I'll...
Oh?
IN THE SECOND ROUTINE?
Oh...
WHAT?
THE CURARA?
Blah Blah Blah Blah
YES, IF WE DO THAT, WE'LL BE ABLE TO DEMONSTRATE EVEN MORE THAT WE'VE "MADE UP."
ha ha ha
RIGHT?
AND BY USING CURARA, WE CAN IMPRESS THE MANUFACTURER EVEN MORE.
WOW!
Ms. Koenji!
I WAS WONDERING WHAT YOU WERE DOING WHEN YOU SUDDENLY DISAPPEARED. THAT'S WHAT YOU WERE THINKING OF!
Yes.
IF YOU SIT STILL AND BROOD, YOU CAN'T THINK OF GOOD IDEAS.

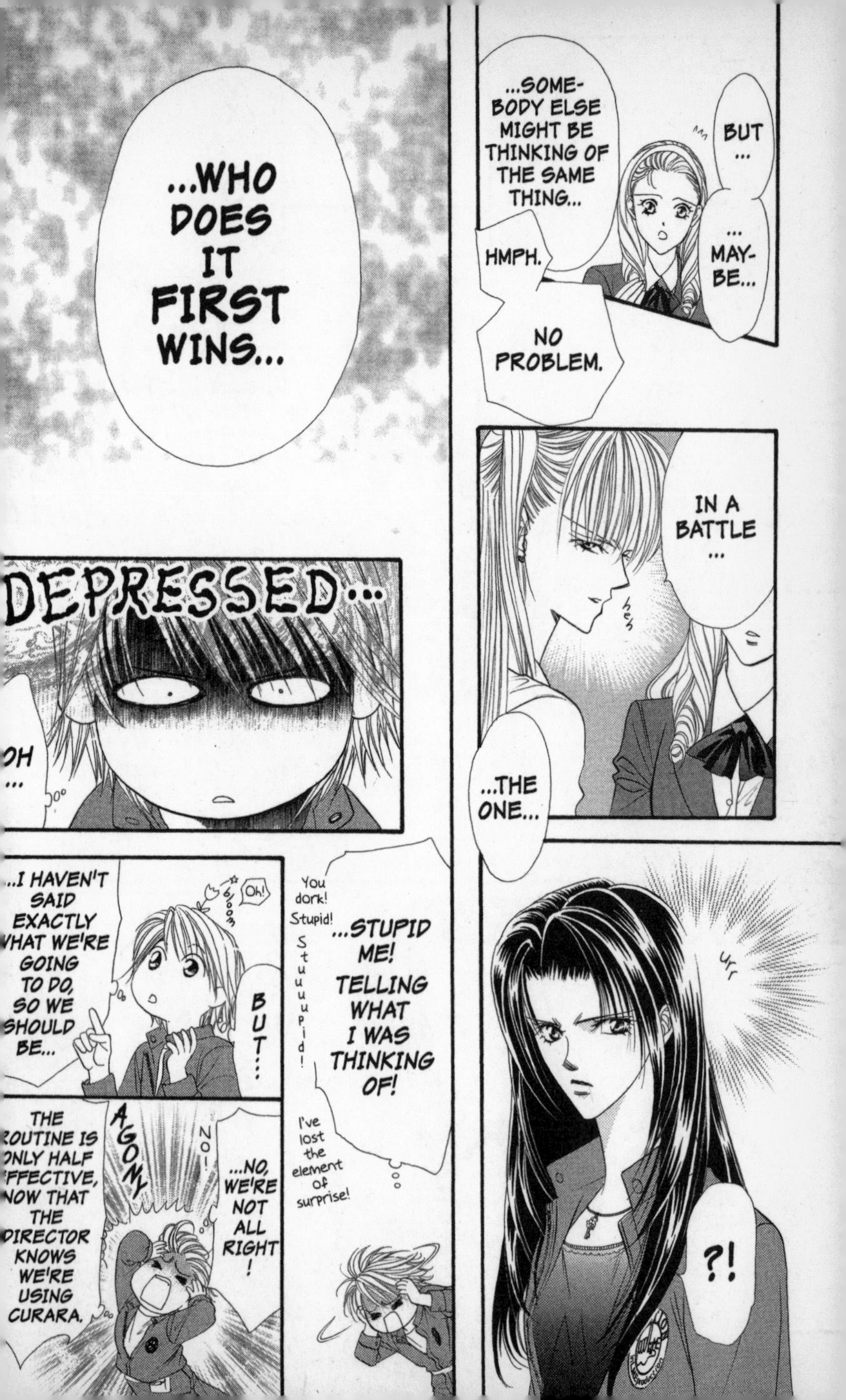

BUT...
...MAY-BE...
...SOME-BODY ELSE MIGHT BE THINKING OF THE SAME THING...
HMPH.
NO PROBLEM.
IN A BATTLE...
heh
...THE ONE...
...WHO DOES IT FIRST WINS...
urr
?!
DEPRESSED...
OH...
...I HAVEN'T SAID EXACTLY WHAT WE'RE GOING TO DO, SO WE SHOULD BE...
bloom
Oh!
BUT...
...NO, WE'RE NOT ALL RIGHT!
NO!
AGONY
THE ROUTINE IS ONLY HALF EFFECTIVE, NOW THAT THE DIRECTOR KNOWS WE'RE USING CURARA.
You dork! Stupid!
Stuuuupid!
...STUPID ME! TELLING WHAT I WAS THINKING OF!
I've lost the element of surprise!

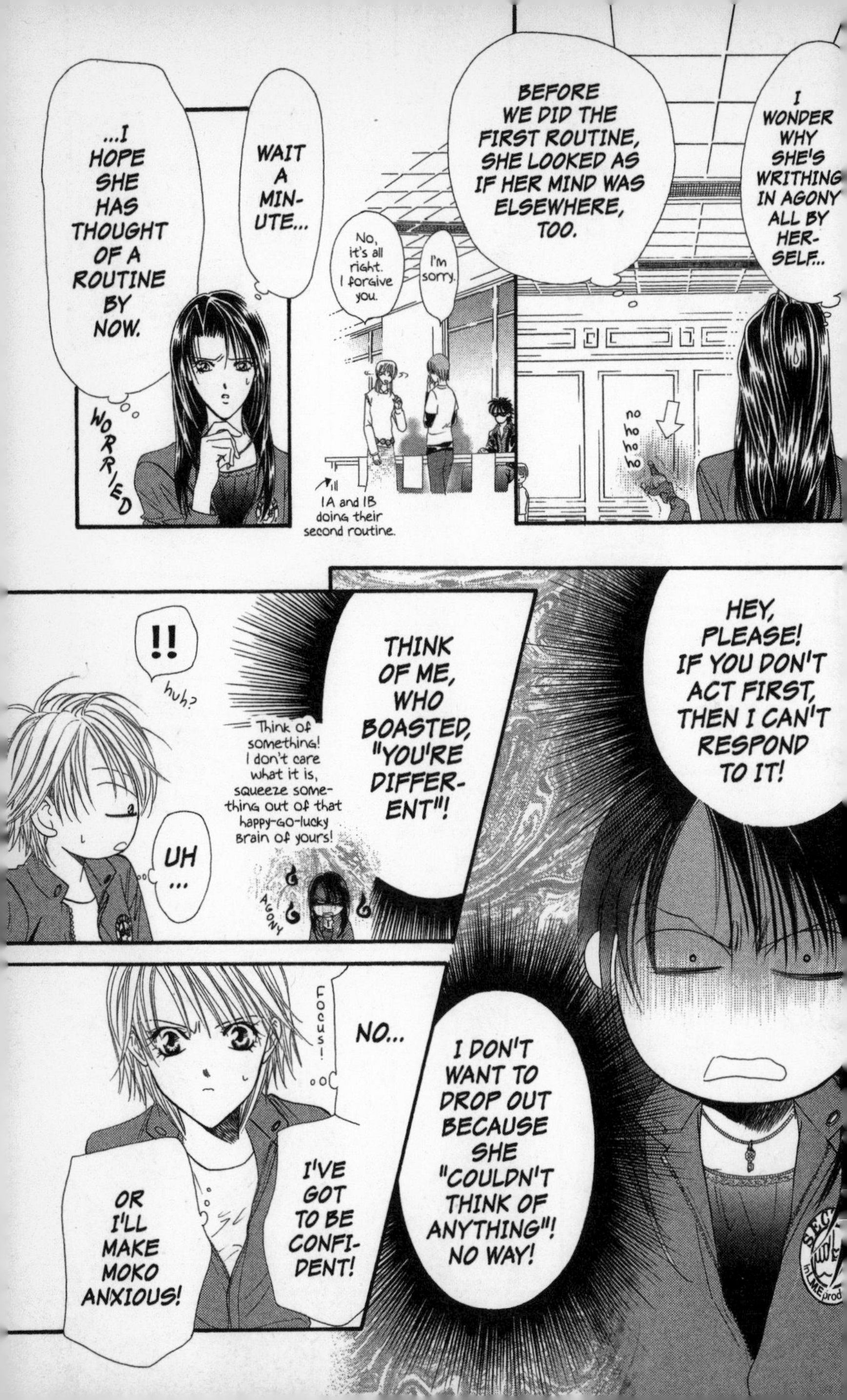
I WONDER WHY SHE'S WRITHING IN AGONY ALL BY HERSELF...
BEFORE WE DID THE FIRST ROUTINE, SHE LOOKED AS IF HER MIND WAS ELSEWHERE, TOO.
no ho ho ho
I'm sorry.
No, it's all right. I forgive you.
1A and 1B doing their second routine.
WAIT A MINUTE...
...I HOPE SHE HAS THOUGHT OF A ROUTINE BY NOW.
WORRIED
HEY, PLEASE! IF YOU DON'T ACT FIRST, THEN I CAN'T RESPOND TO IT!
THINK OF ME, WHO BOASTED, "YOU'RE DIFFERENT"!
!!
huh?
Think of something! I don't care what it is, squeeze something out of that happy-go-lucky brain of yours!
UH ...
AGONY
I DON'T WANT TO DROP OUT BECAUSE SHE "COULDN'T THINK OF ANYTHING"! NO WAY!
NO...
Focus!
I'VE GOT TO BE CONFIDENT!
OR I'LL MAKE MOKO ANXIOUS!

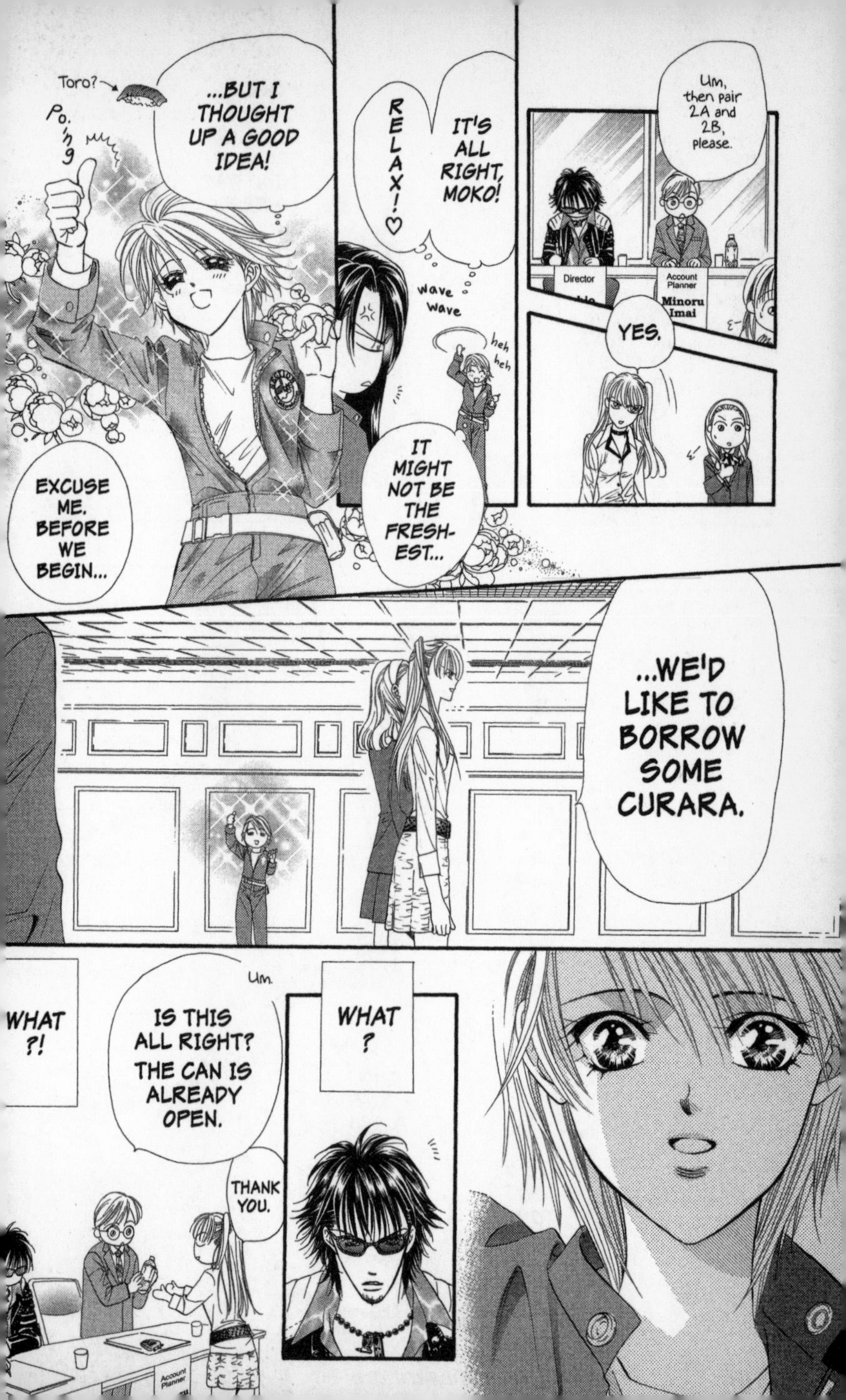
Um, then pair 2A and 2B, please.
Director
Account Planner
Minoru Imai
YES.
IT'S ALL RIGHT, MOKO!
RELAX!♡
wave wave
heh heh
IT MIGHT NOT BE THE FRESHEST...
...BUT I THOUGHT UP A GOOD IDEA!
Toro?
Po.ng
EXCUSE ME. BEFORE WE BEGIN...
...WE'D LIKE TO BORROW SOME CURARA.
WHAT?
Um.
IS THIS ALL RIGHT? THE CAN IS ALREADY OPEN.
THANK YOU.
WHAT?!
Account Planner

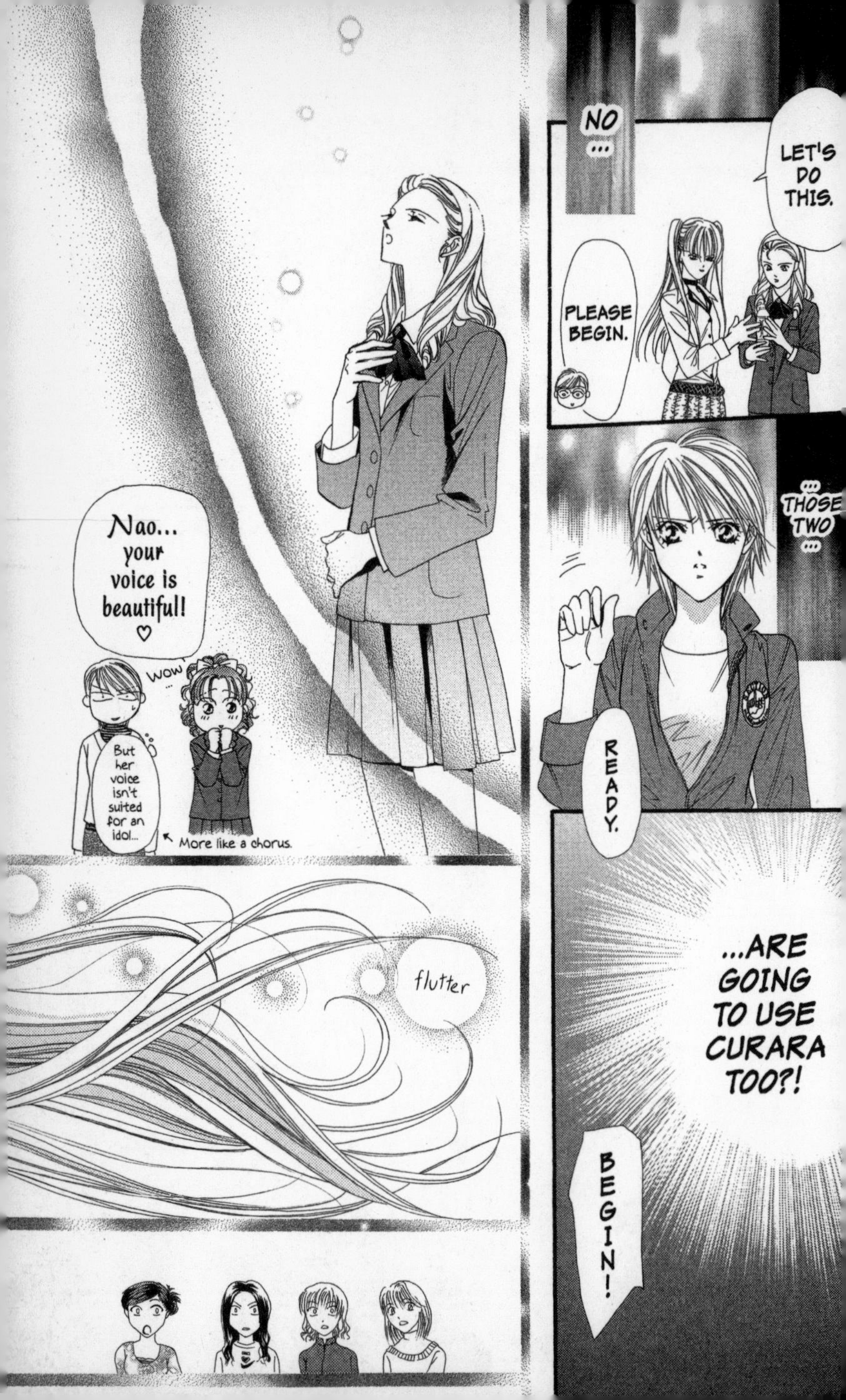
NO...
LET'S DO THIS.
PLEASE BEGIN.
...THOSE TWO...
READY.
...ARE GOING TO USE CURARA TOO?!
BEGIN!
Nao... your voice is beautiful! ♡
Wow...
But her voice isn't suited for an idol...
More like a chorus.
flutter

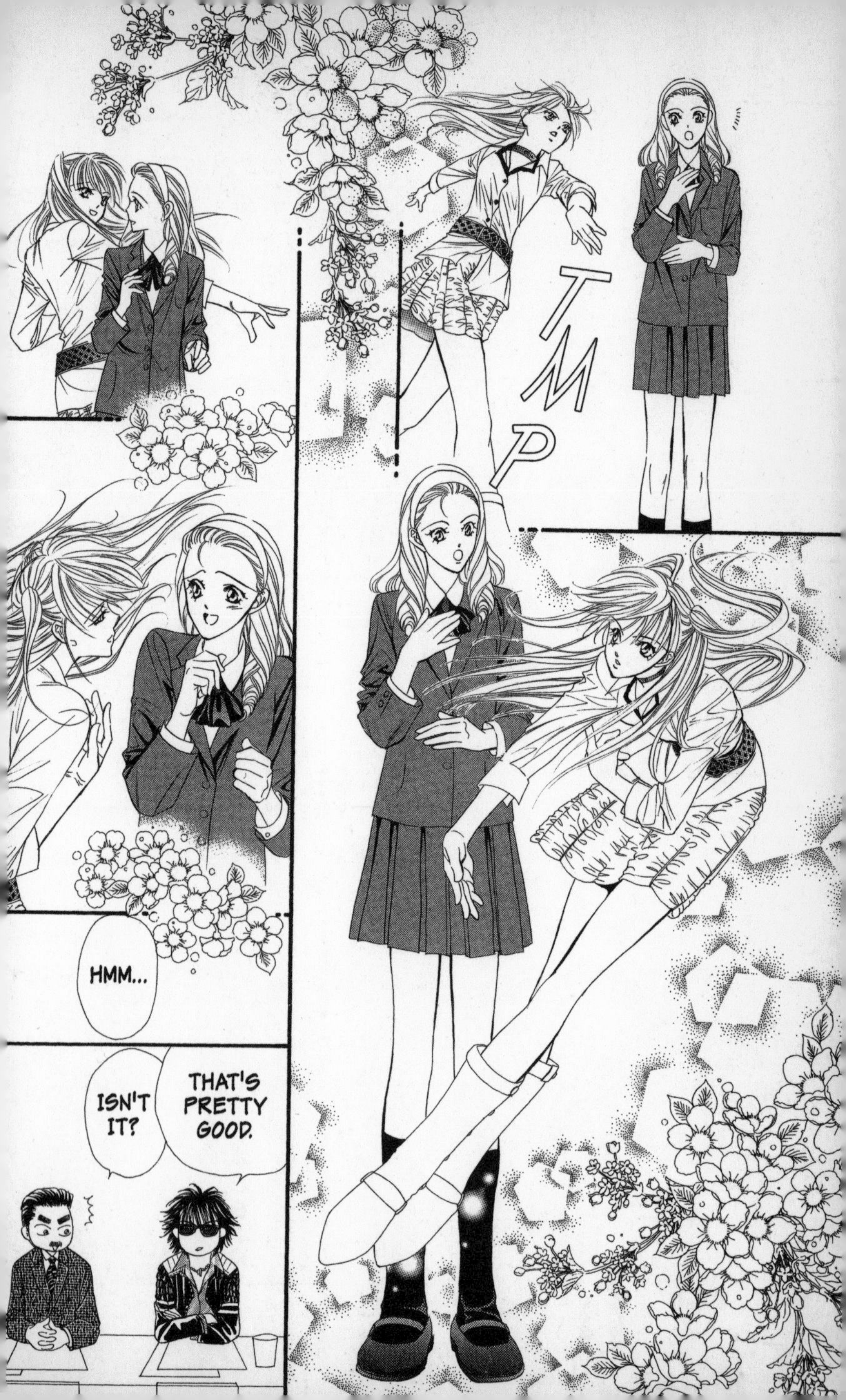
TMP
HMM...
THAT'S PRETTY GOOD.
ISN'T IT?

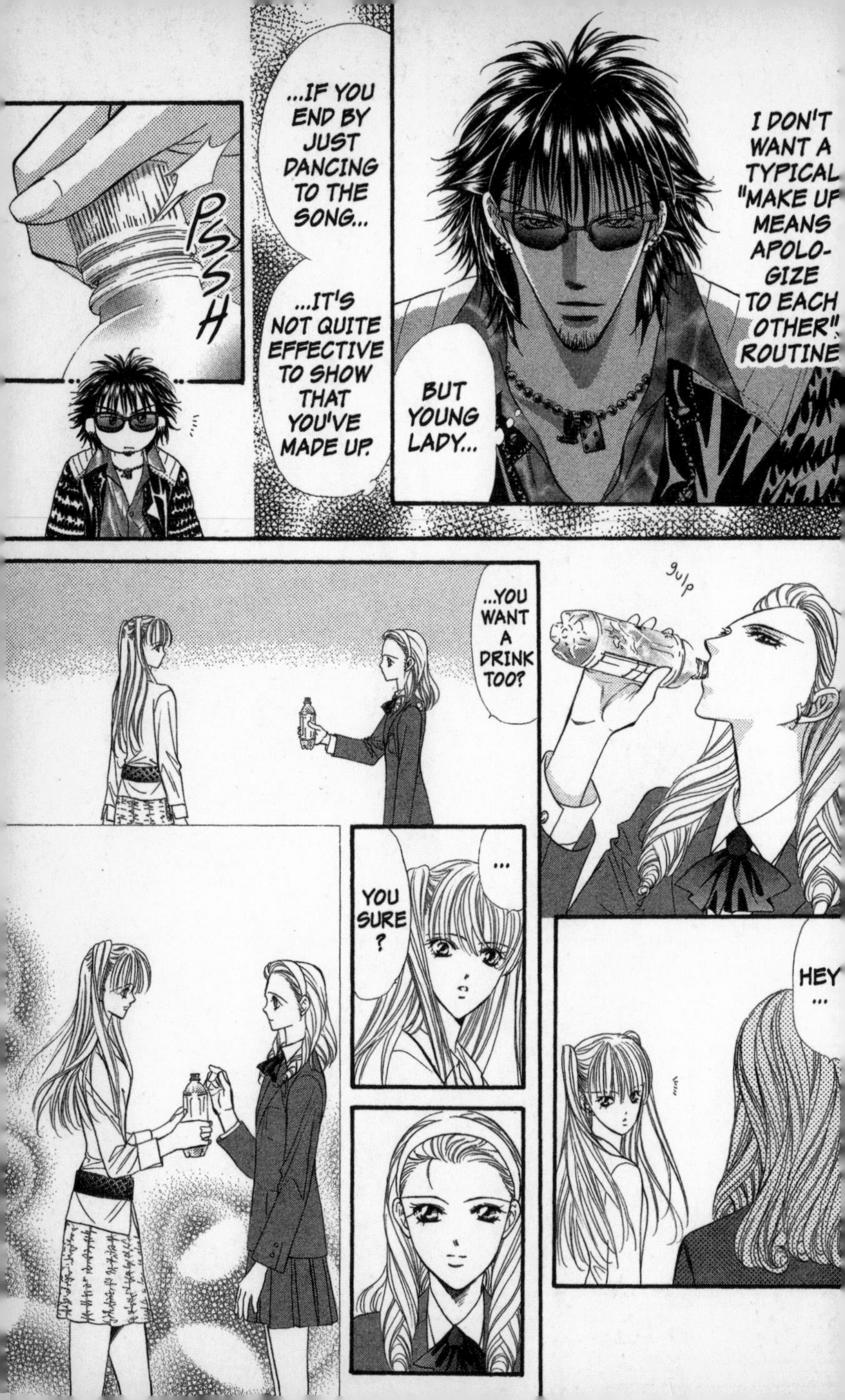

I DON'T WANT A TYPICAL "MAKE UP MEANS APOLOGIZE TO EACH OTHER" ROUTINE
BUT YOUNG LADY...
...IF YOU END BY JUST DANCING TO THE SONG...
...IT'S NOT QUITE EFFECTIVE TO SHOW THAT YOU'VE MADE UP.
PSSH
gulp
...YOU WANT A DRINK TOO?
HEY ...
...
YOU SURE ?

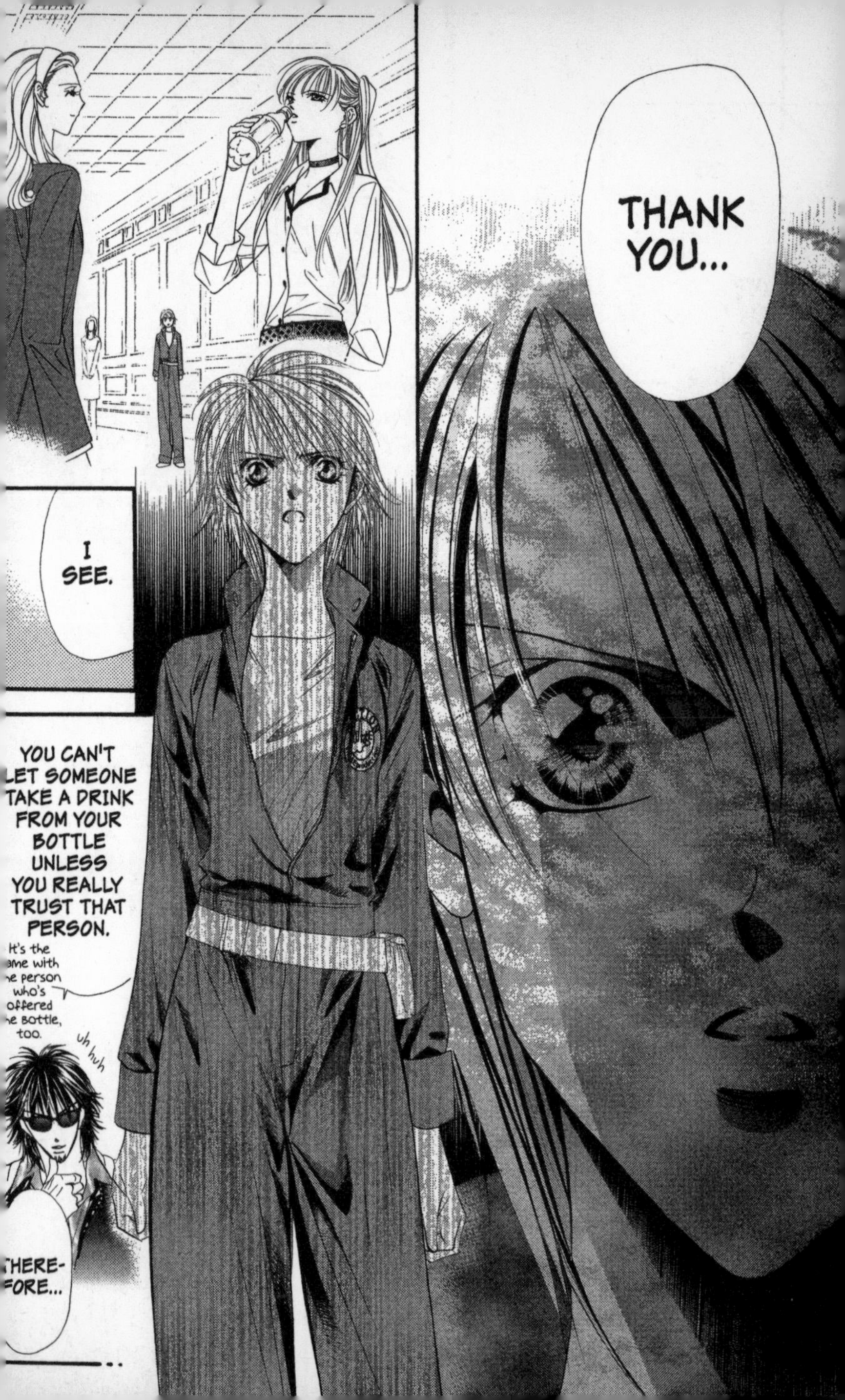
THANK YOU...
I SEE.
YOU CAN'T LET SOMEONE TAKE A DRINK FROM YOUR BOTTLE UNLESS YOU REALLY TRUST THAT PERSON.
It's the ame with ne person who's offered ne bottle, too.
uh huh
THERE-FORE...

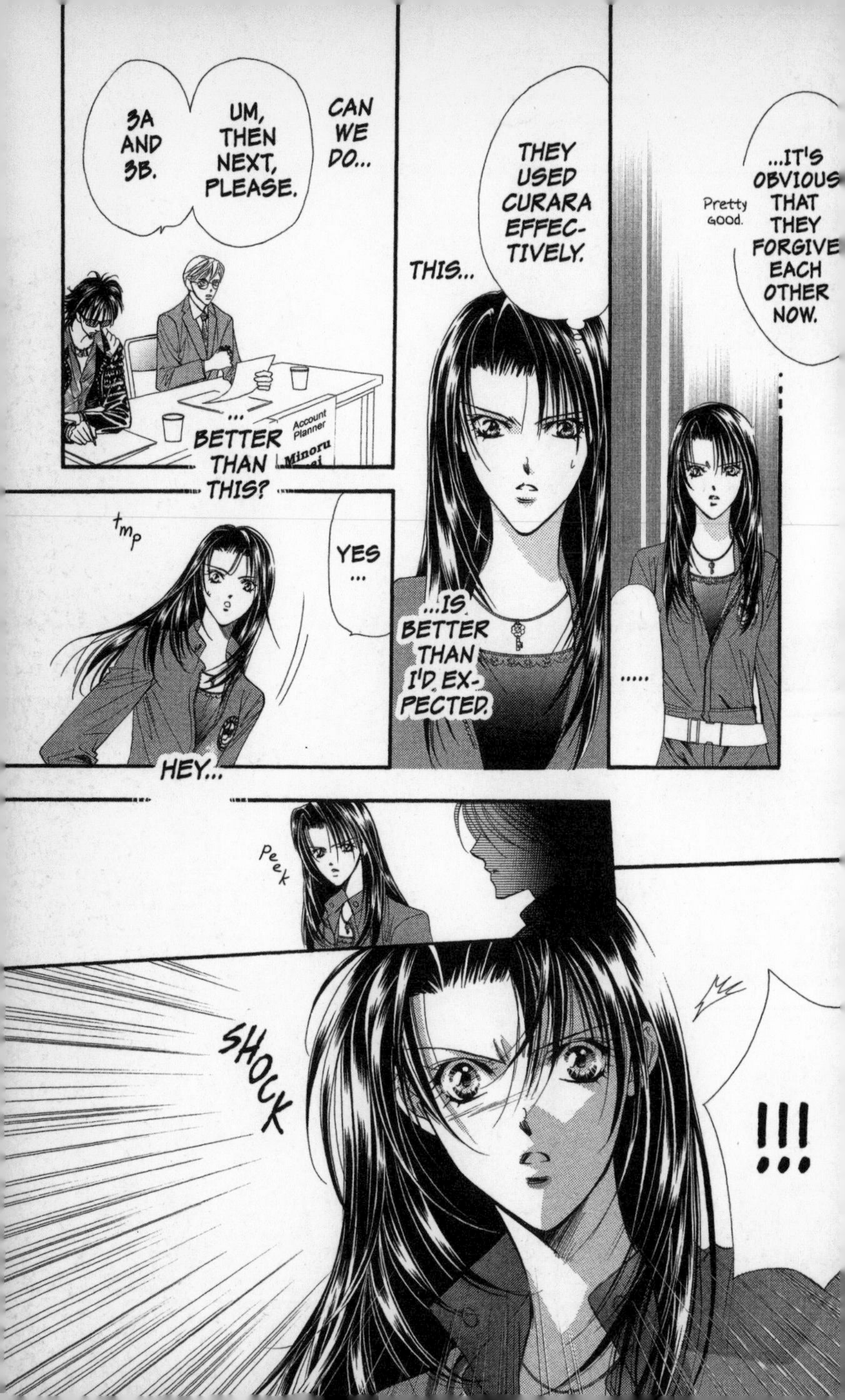
Pretty good.
...IT'S OBVIOUS THAT THEY FORGIVE EACH OTHER NOW.
.....
THEY USED CURARA EFFEC-TIVELY.
THIS...
...IS BETTER THAN I'D EX-PECTED.
CAN WE DO...
UM, THEN NEXT, PLEASE.
3A AND 3B.
Account Planner
Minoru
...BETTER THAN THIS?
YES...
tmp
HEY...
Peek
SHOCK
!!!

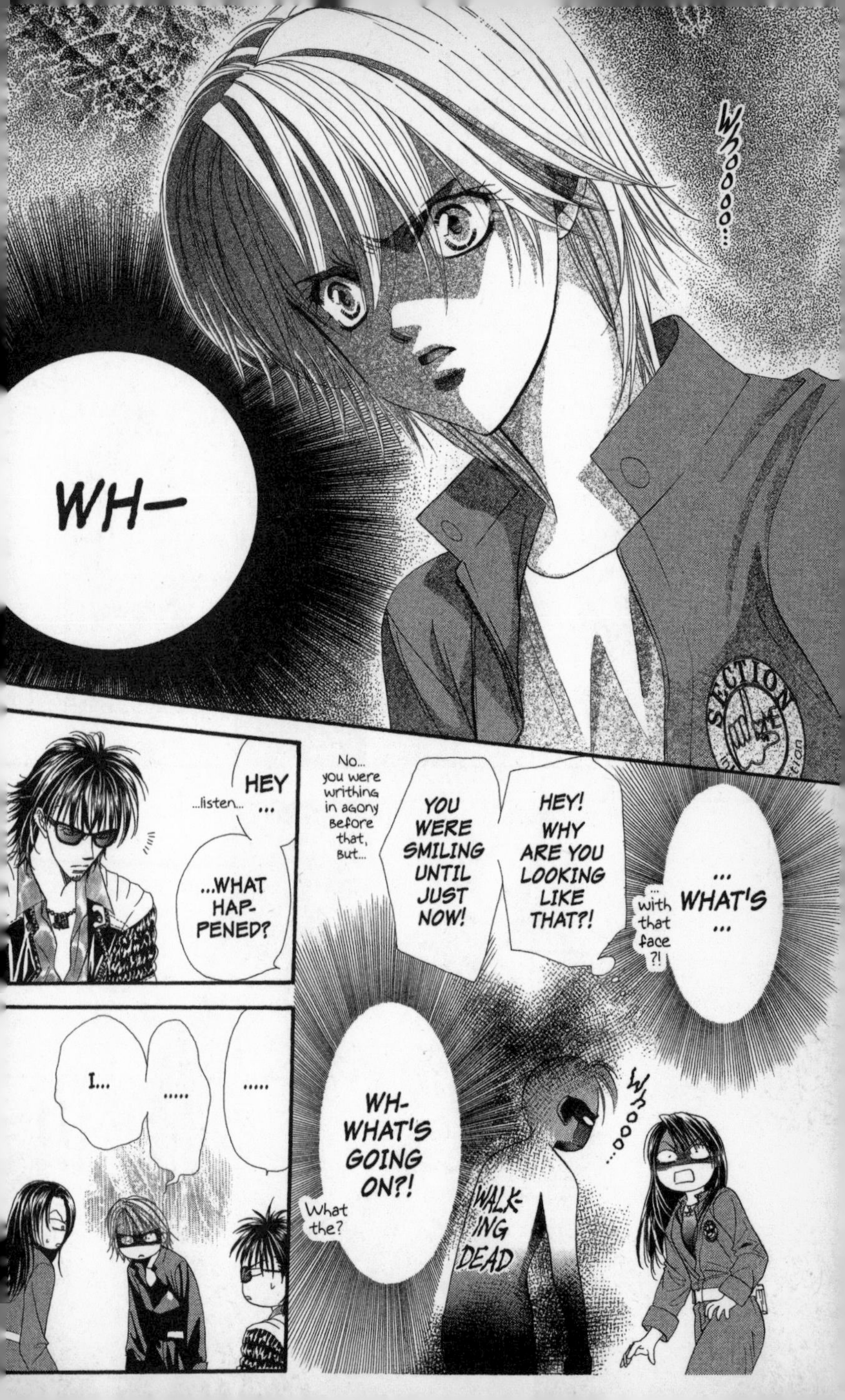
Whoooo...
WH—
... WHAT'S ...
... with that face ?!
HEY! WHY ARE YOU LOOKING LIKE THAT?!
YOU WERE SMILING UNTIL JUST NOW!
No... you were writhing in agony before that, but...
Whooo...
WALK-ING DEAD
WH-WHAT'S GOING ON?!
What the?
HEY ...
...listen...
...WHAT HAP-PENED?
.....
.....
I...

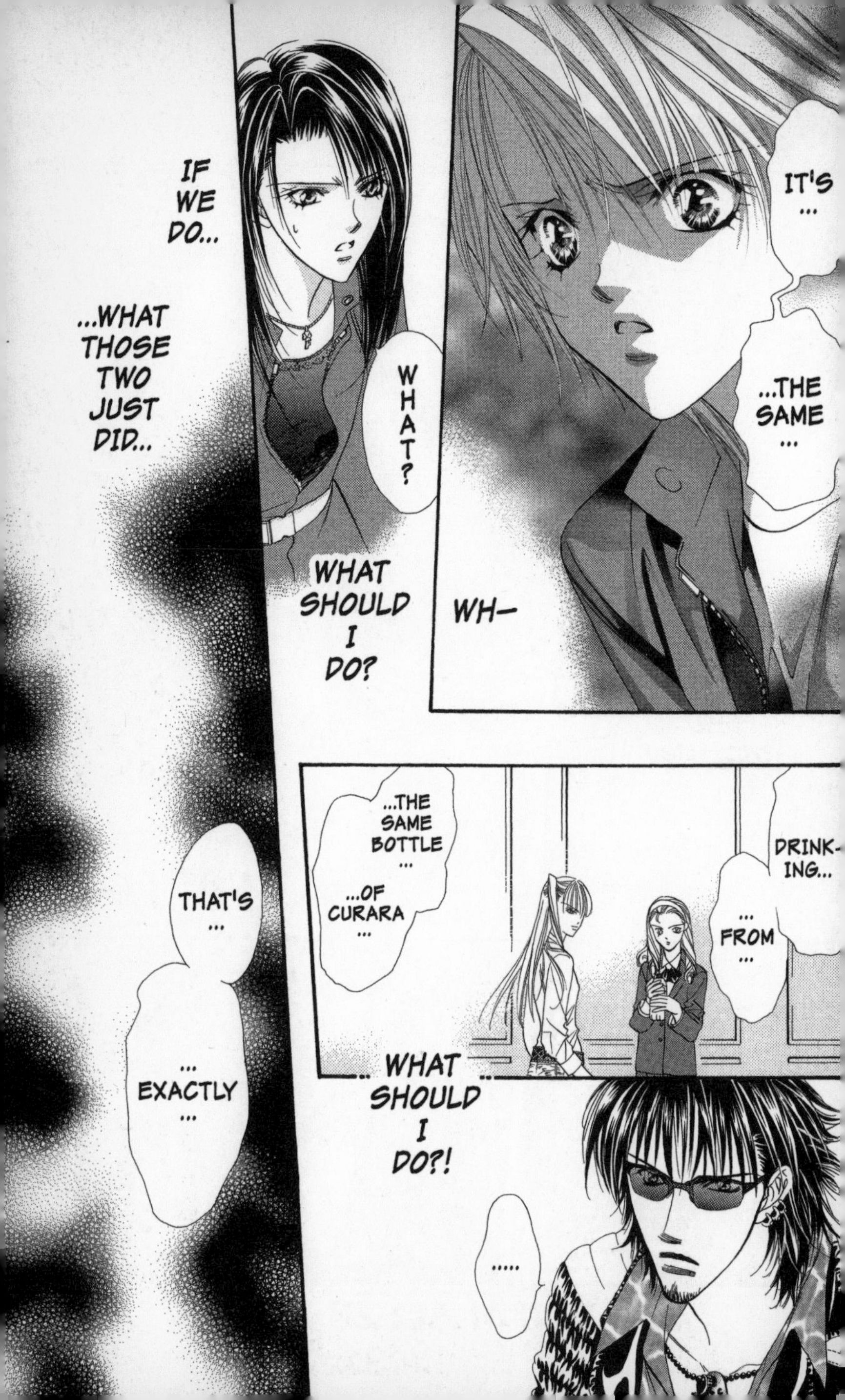

IT'S ...
...THE SAME ...
WH-
WHAT?
WHAT SHOULD I DO?
DRINKING...
... FROM ...
...THE SAME BOTTLE ...
...OF CURARA ...
...WHAT SHOULD I DO?!
.....
IF WE DO...
...WHAT THOSE TWO JUST DID...
THAT'S ...
... EXACTLY ...

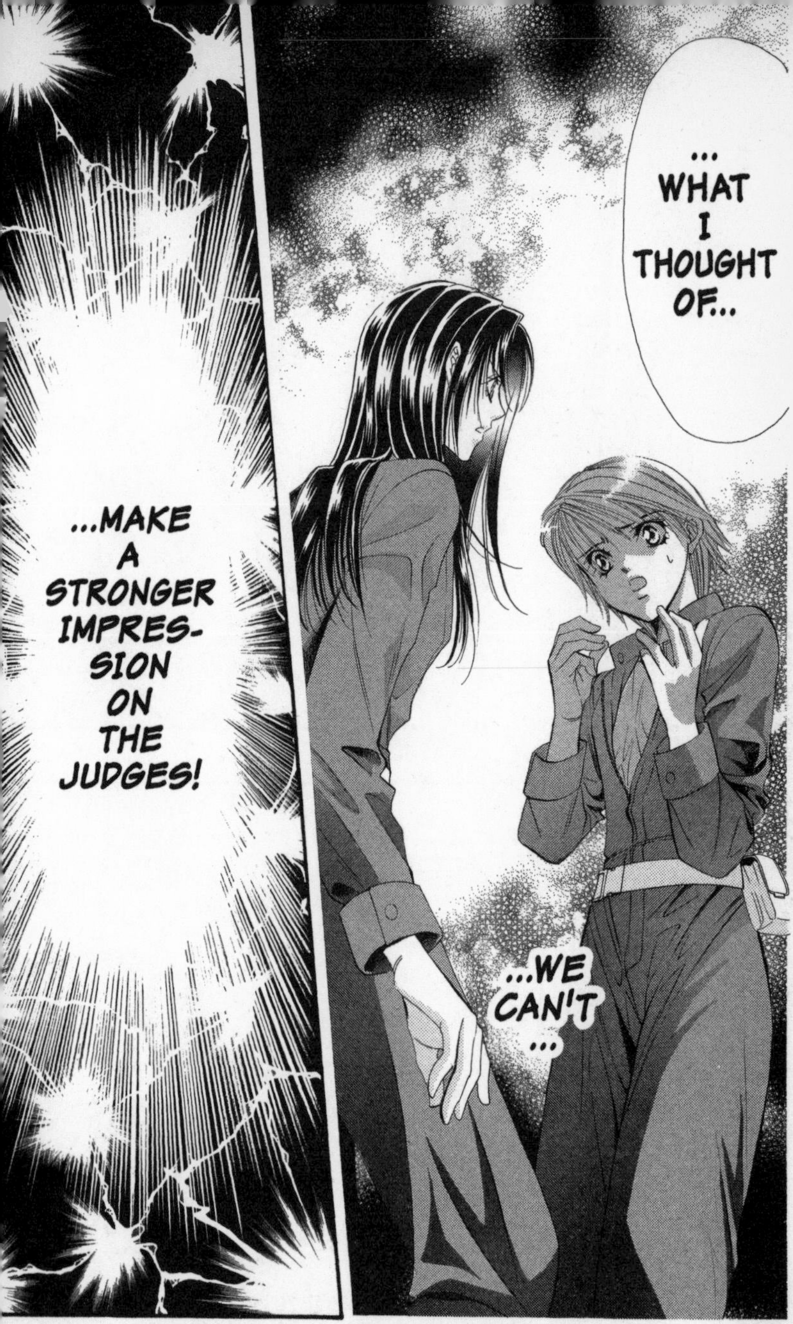
... WHAT I THOUGHT OF...
...WE CAN'T ...
...MAKE A STRONGER IMPRES- SION ON THE JUDGES!

End of Act 28

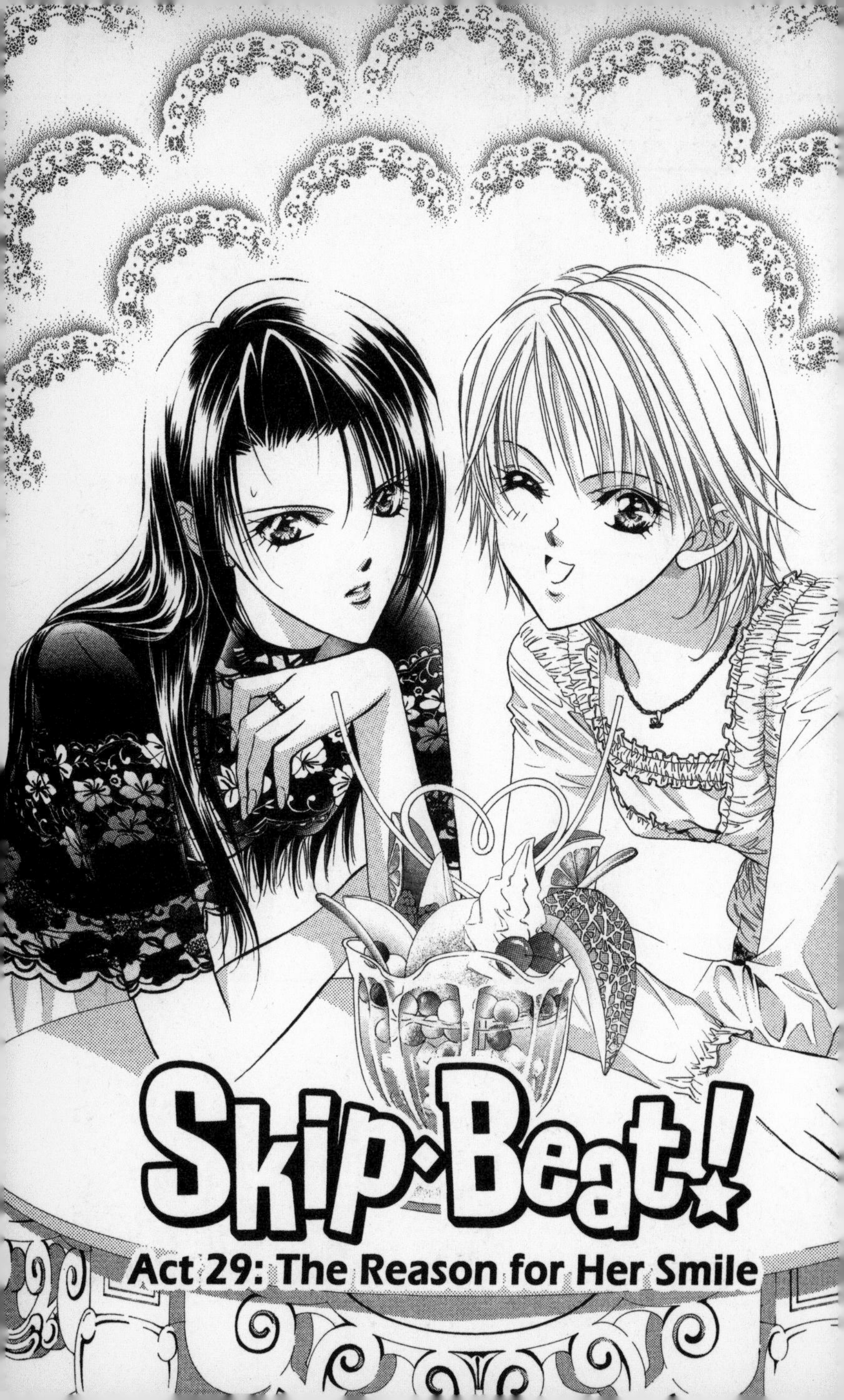
Skip·Beat!
Act 29: The Reason for Her Smile

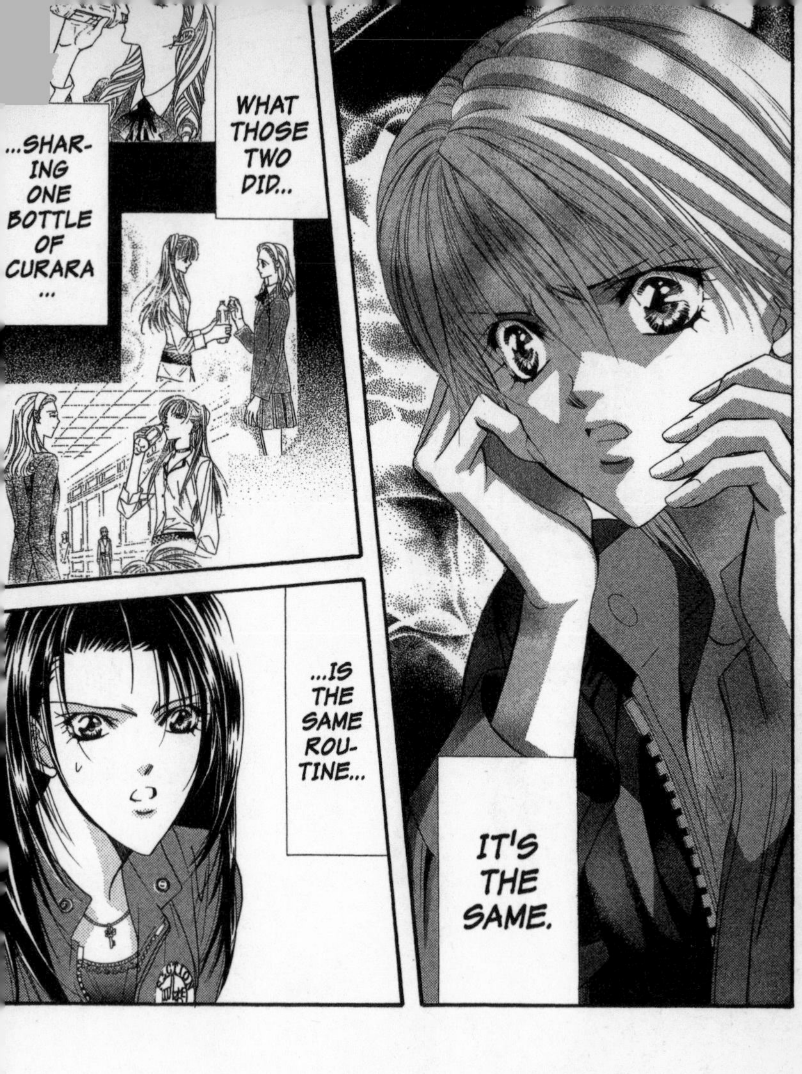
WHAT THOSE TWO DID...
...SHARING ONE BOTTLE OF CURARA ...
...IS THE SAME ROUTINE...
IT'S THE SAME.

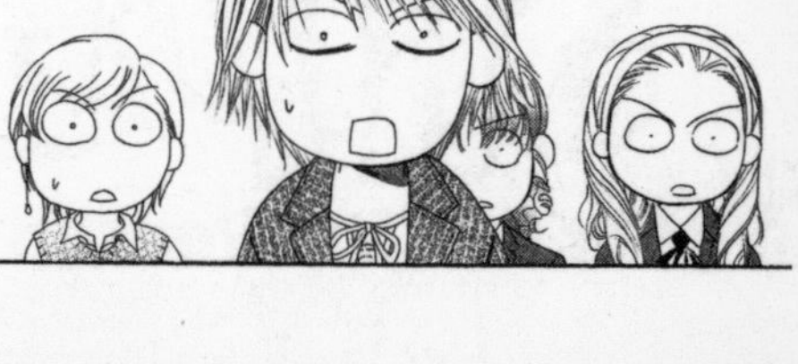

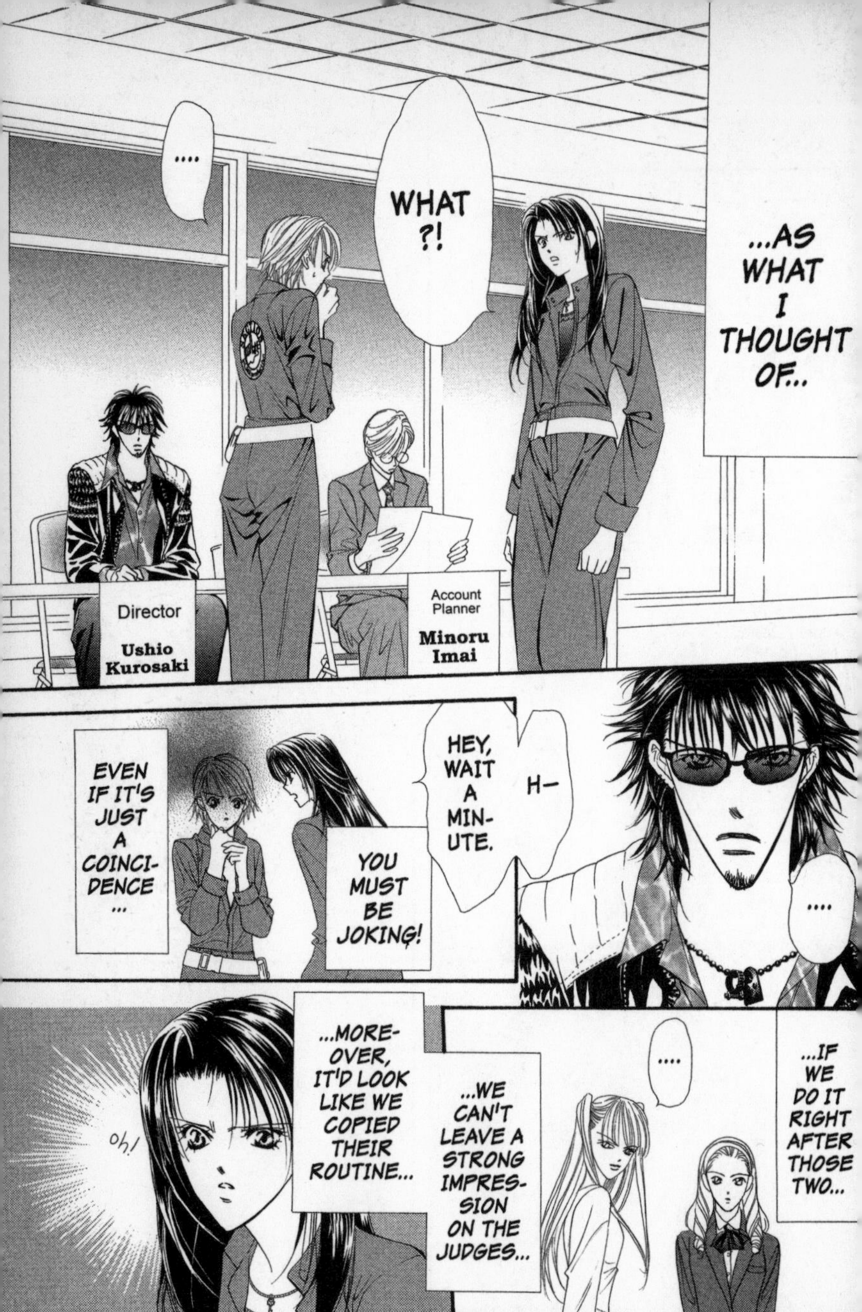
...AS WHAT I THOUGHT OF...
WHAT ?!
....
Account Planner
Minoru Imai
Director
Ushio Kurosaki
H—
....
HEY, WAIT A MIN-UTE.
YOU MUST BE JOKING!
EVEN IF IT'S JUST A COINCI-DENCE ...
...IF WE DO IT RIGHT AFTER THOSE TWO...
....
...WE CAN'T LEAVE A STRONG IMPRES-SION ON THE JUDGES...
...MORE-OVER, IT'D LOOK LIKE WE COPIED THEIR ROUTINE...
oh!

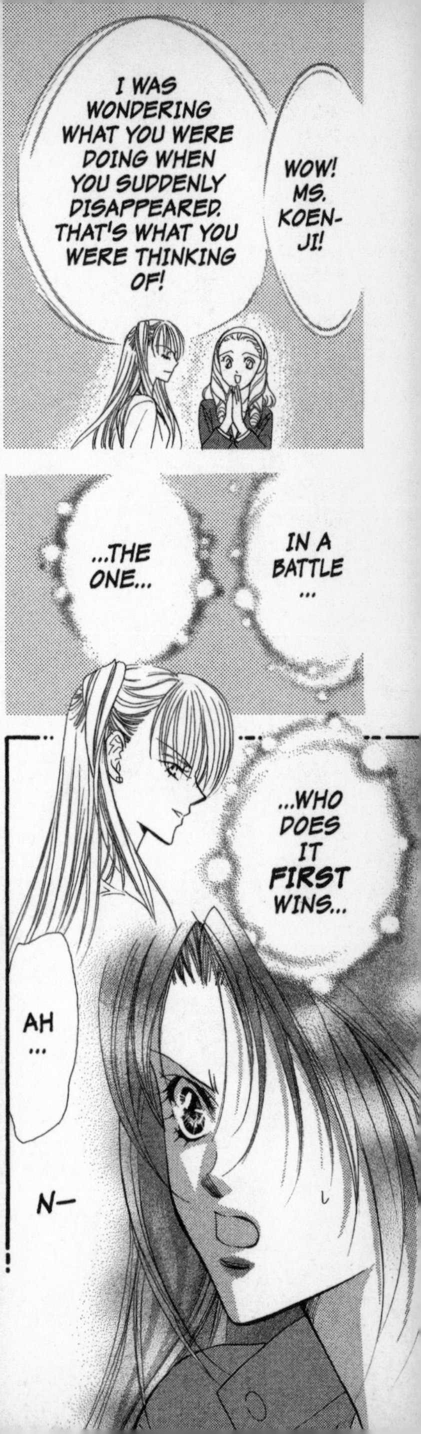
WOW! MS. KOEN-JI!
I WAS WONDERING WHAT YOU WERE DOING WHEN YOU SUDDENLY DISAPPEARED. THAT'S WHAT YOU WERE THINKING OF!
IN A BATTLE ...
...THE ONE...
...WHO DOES IT FIRST WINS...
AH ...
N—

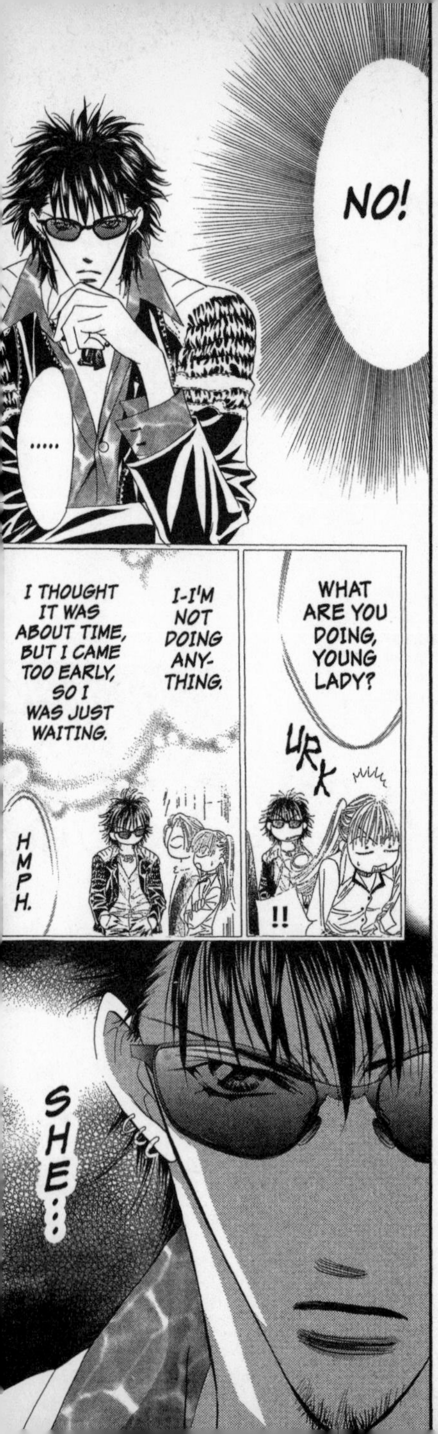
NO!
.....
WHAT ARE YOU DOING, YOUNG LADY?
URK
!!
I-I'M NOT DOING ANY-THING.
I THOUGHT IT WAS ABOUT TIME, BUT I CAME TOO EARLY, SO I WAS JUST WAITING.
HMPH.
SHE...

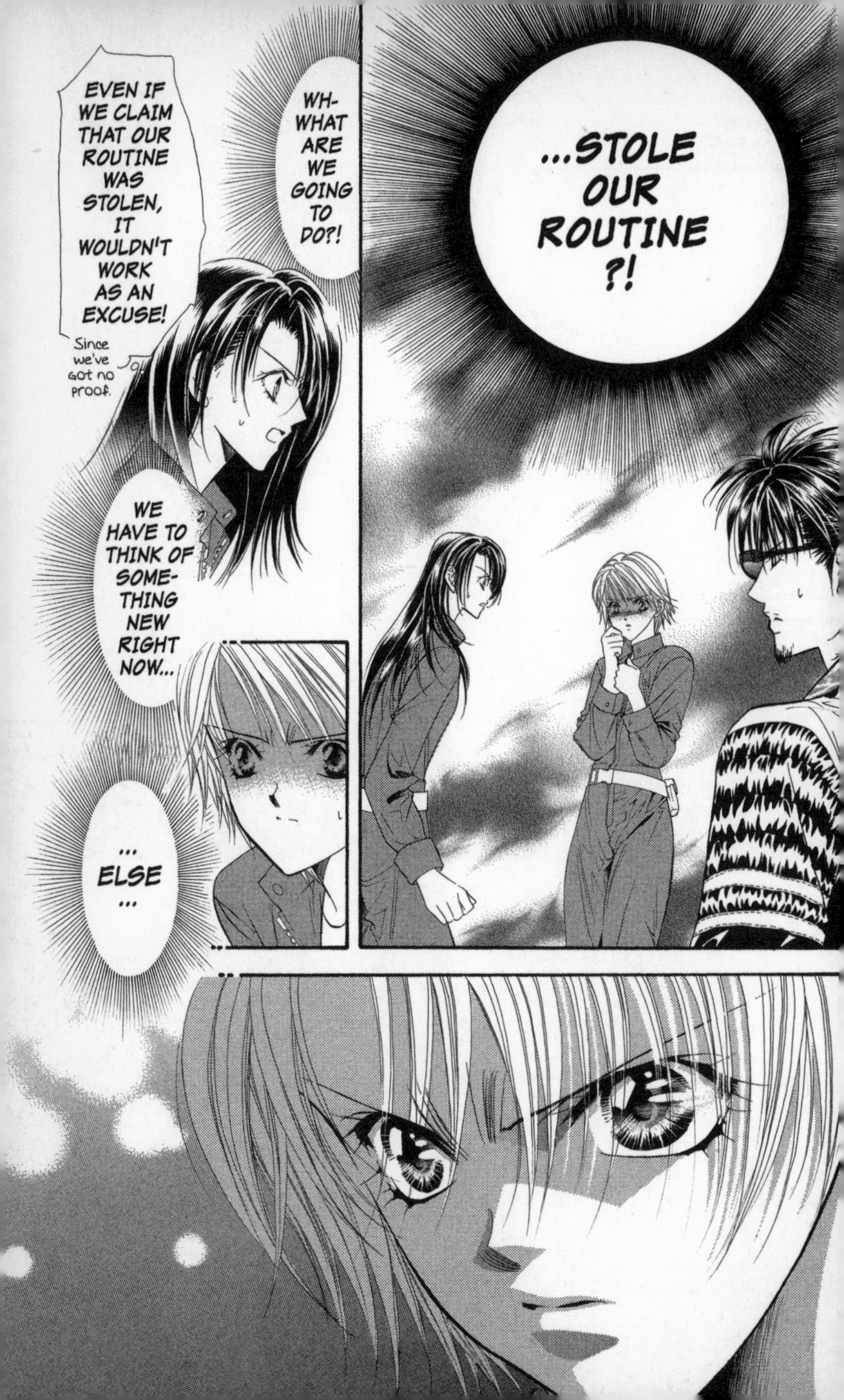
...STOLE OUR ROUTINE?!
WH-WHAT ARE WE GOING TO DO?!
EVEN IF WE CLAIM THAT OUR ROUTINE WAS STOLEN, IT WOULDN'T WORK AS AN EXCUSE!
Since we've got no proof.
WE HAVE TO THINK OF SOME-THING NEW RIGHT NOW...
...ELSE...

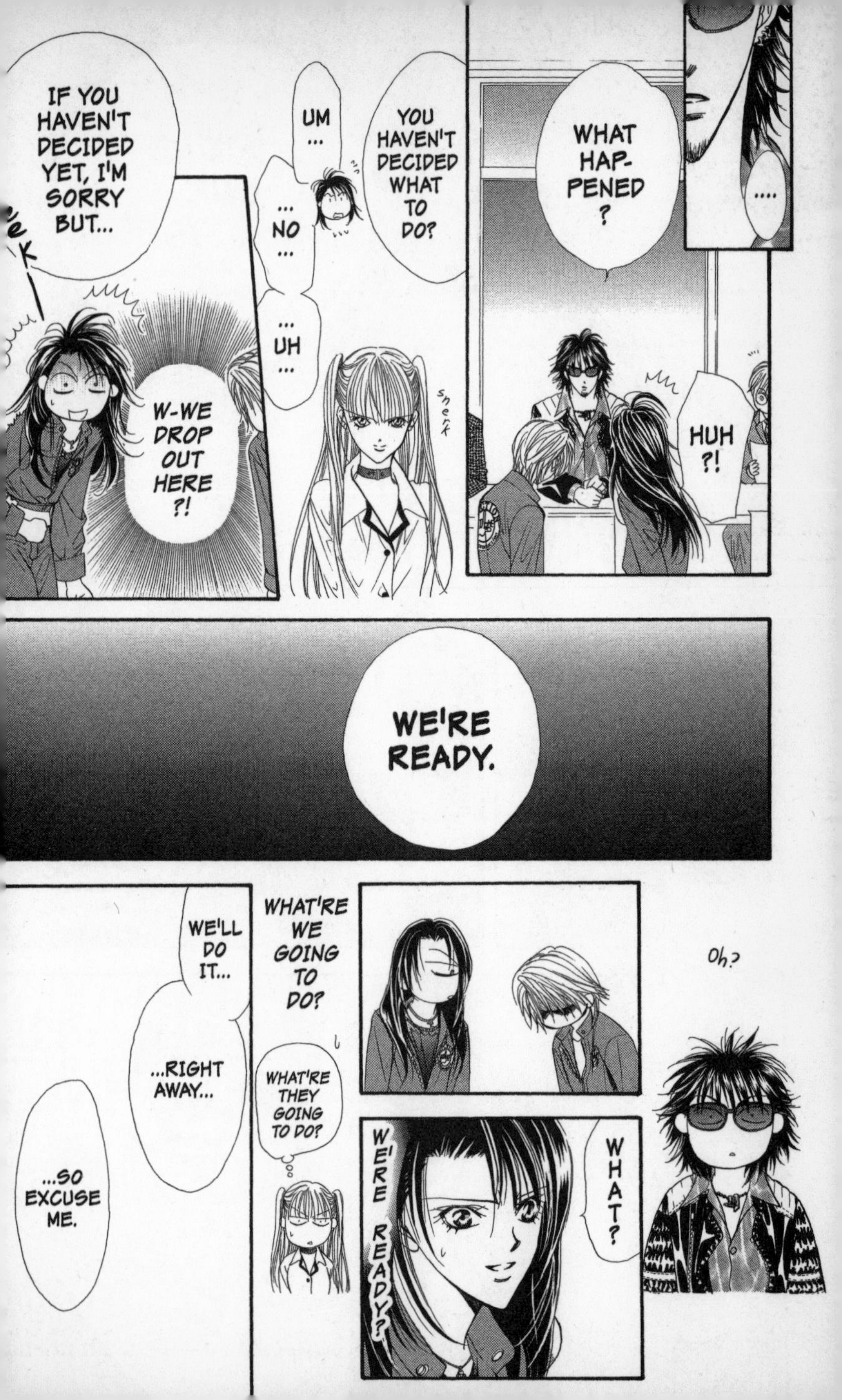
....
WHAT HAP-PENED?
HUH?!
YOU HAVEN'T DECIDED WHAT TO DO?
UM...
...NO...
...UH...
snerk
IF YOU HAVEN'T DECIDED YET, I'M SORRY BUT...
W-WE DROP OUT HERE?!
WE'RE READY.
Oh?
WHAT'RE WE GOING TO DO?
WHAT?
WE'RE READY?
WHAT'RE THEY GOING TO DO?
WE'LL DO IT...
...RIGHT AWAY...
...SO EXCUSE ME.

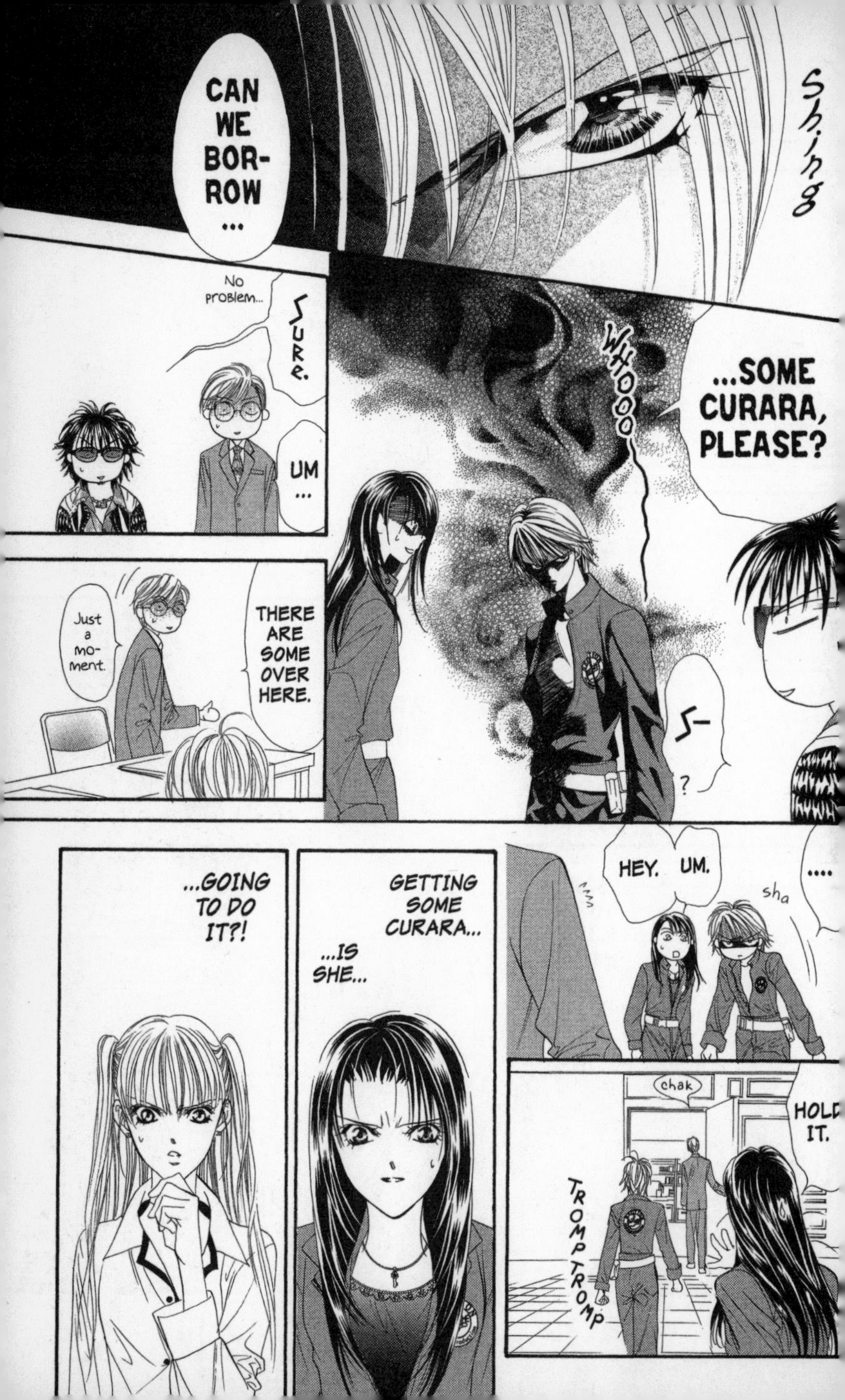
Shing
CAN WE BORROW...
...SOME CURARA, PLEASE?
WHOOO
S-
?
UM...
Sure.
No problem...
THERE ARE SOME OVER HERE.
Just a moment.
....
sha
HEY.
UM.
HOLD IT.
chak
TROMP TROMP
GETTING SOME CURARA...
...IS SHE...
...GOING TO DO IT?!

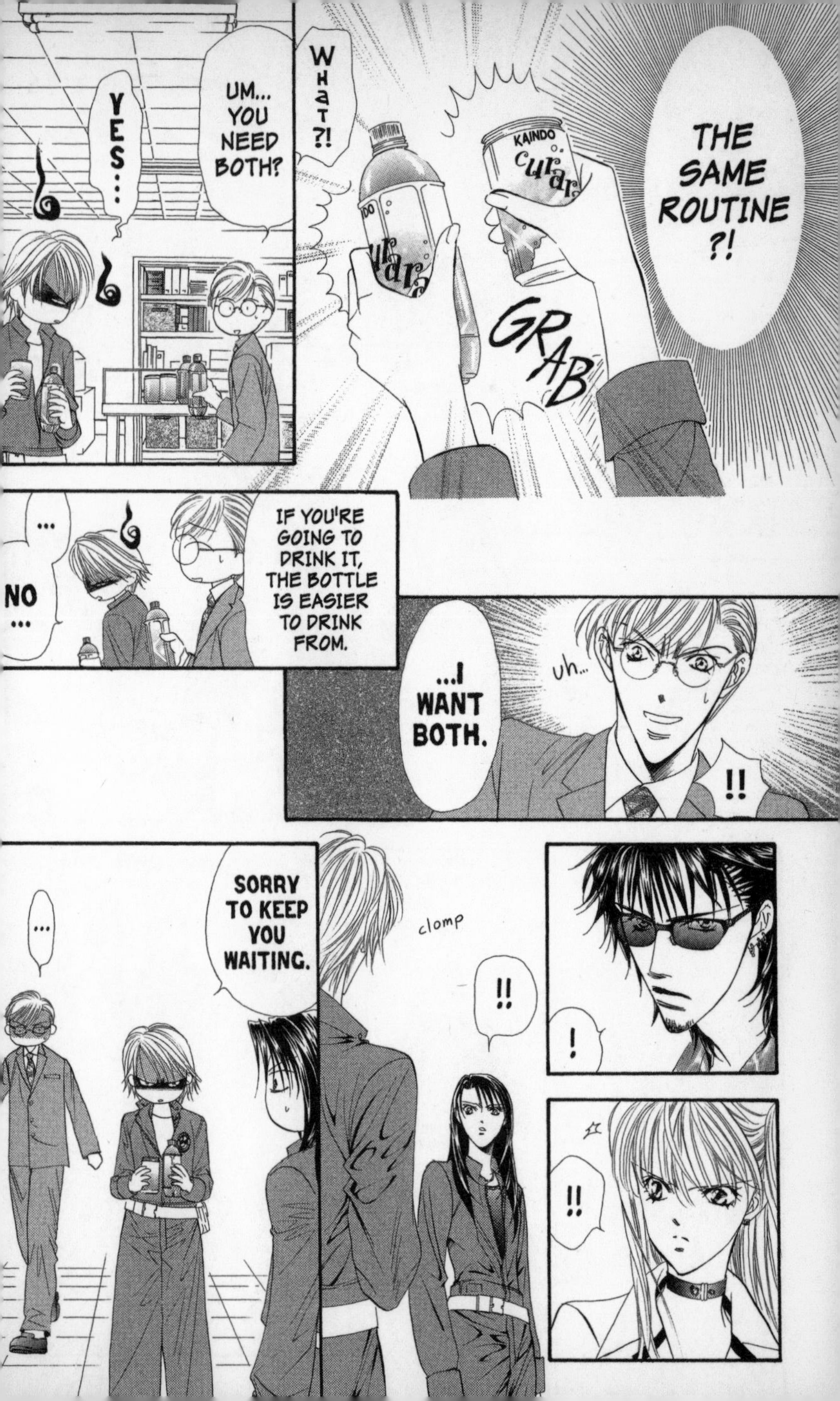
THE SAME ROUTINE ?!
KAINDO curara
WHAT?!
curara
GRAB
UM... YOU NEED BOTH?
YES...
IF YOU'RE GOING TO DRINK IT, THE BOTTLE IS EASIER TO DRINK FROM.
...
NO ...
...I WANT BOTH.
uh...
!!
!
!!
SORRY TO KEEP YOU WAITING.
clomp
!!
...

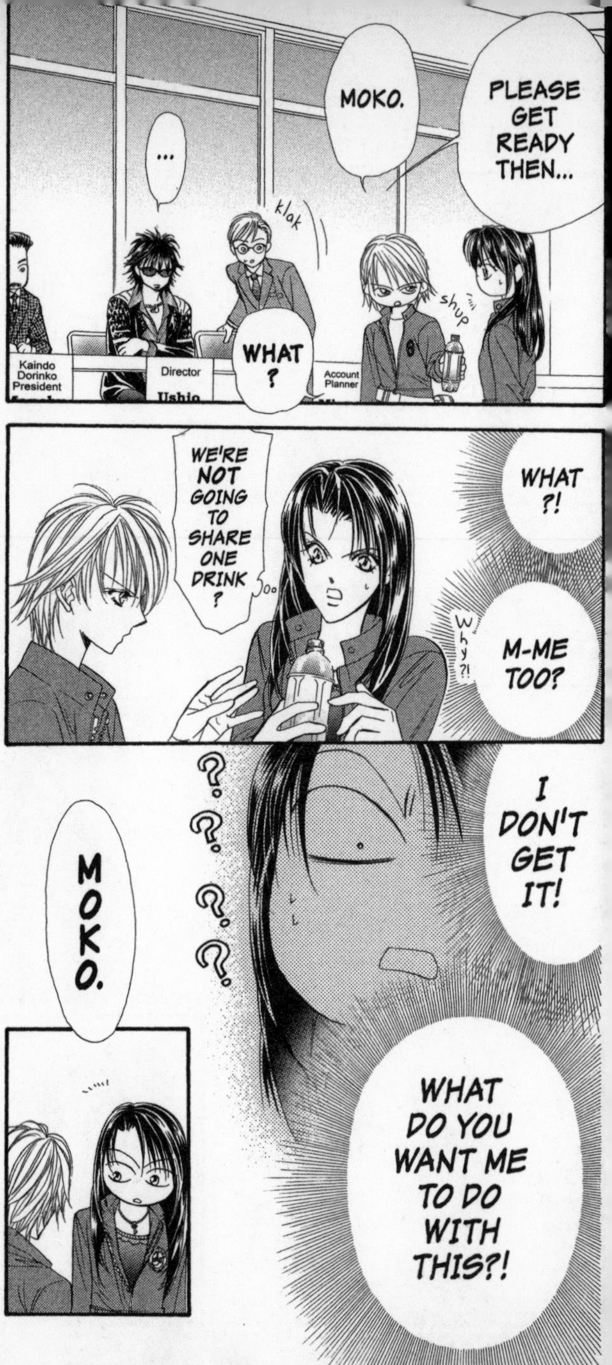
PLEASE GET READY THEN...
MOKO.
klak
...
shup
WHAT?
Kaindo Dorinko President
Director
Ushio
Account Planner
WHAT?!
M-ME TOO?
Why?!
WE'RE NOT GOING TO SHARE ONE DRINK?
I DON'T GET IT!
WHAT DO YOU WANT ME TO DO WITH THIS?!
MOKO.

...drinks like tea and sports drinks...And like Kanae, I thought that soda that comes in plastic bottles spurts out like canned soda...at work, we bought cans and plastic bottles (slightly carbonated) and all the staff tested how the liquid spurts out... well, well...so we were bustling about while working on the commercial audition arc. I never really have sufficient time to do my work... It's probably because I take twice as much time as other people to do the storyboards... I won't say that's the only reason, but I really haven't studied enough about showbiz. I gathered materials since I was going to draw a showbiz story, but there are too many things that I don't understand yet...so those of you who know the ins and outs of showbiz...please give me information!! Please, please.

Apology

About Kyoko's lines in Act 26 about panthers. It might seem that cheetahs are more appropriate, but I chose panthers because it sounded better, and when I was working on the storyboard, I wanted to make the subtitle "The Pink Panthers' Counterattack" so I used panthers... But the subtitle wasn't used in the end...well, it wasn't much of a counterattack, so...

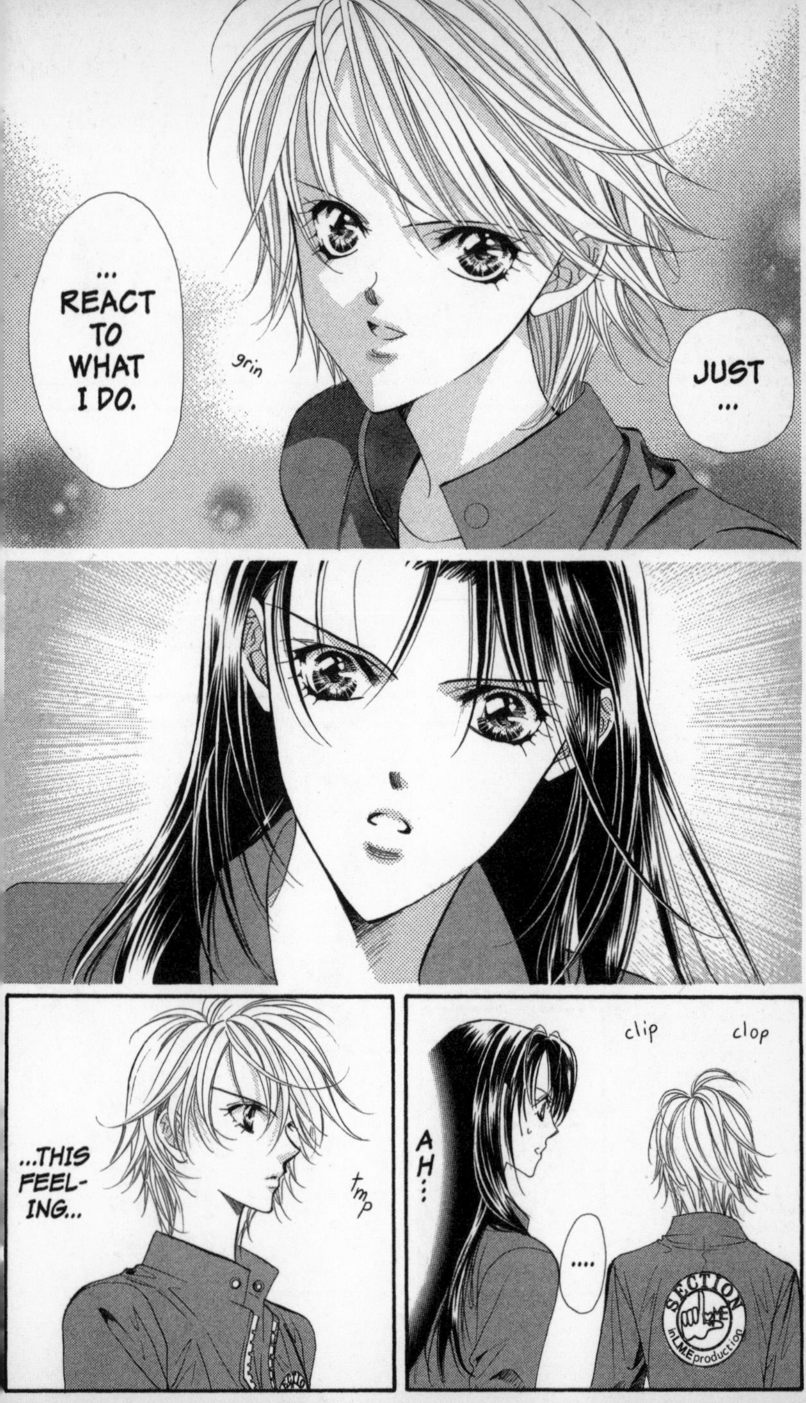
JUST ...
grin
... REACT TO WHAT I DO.
clip
clop
AH...
....
SECTION
in L.M.E production
...THIS FEEL-ING...
tmp

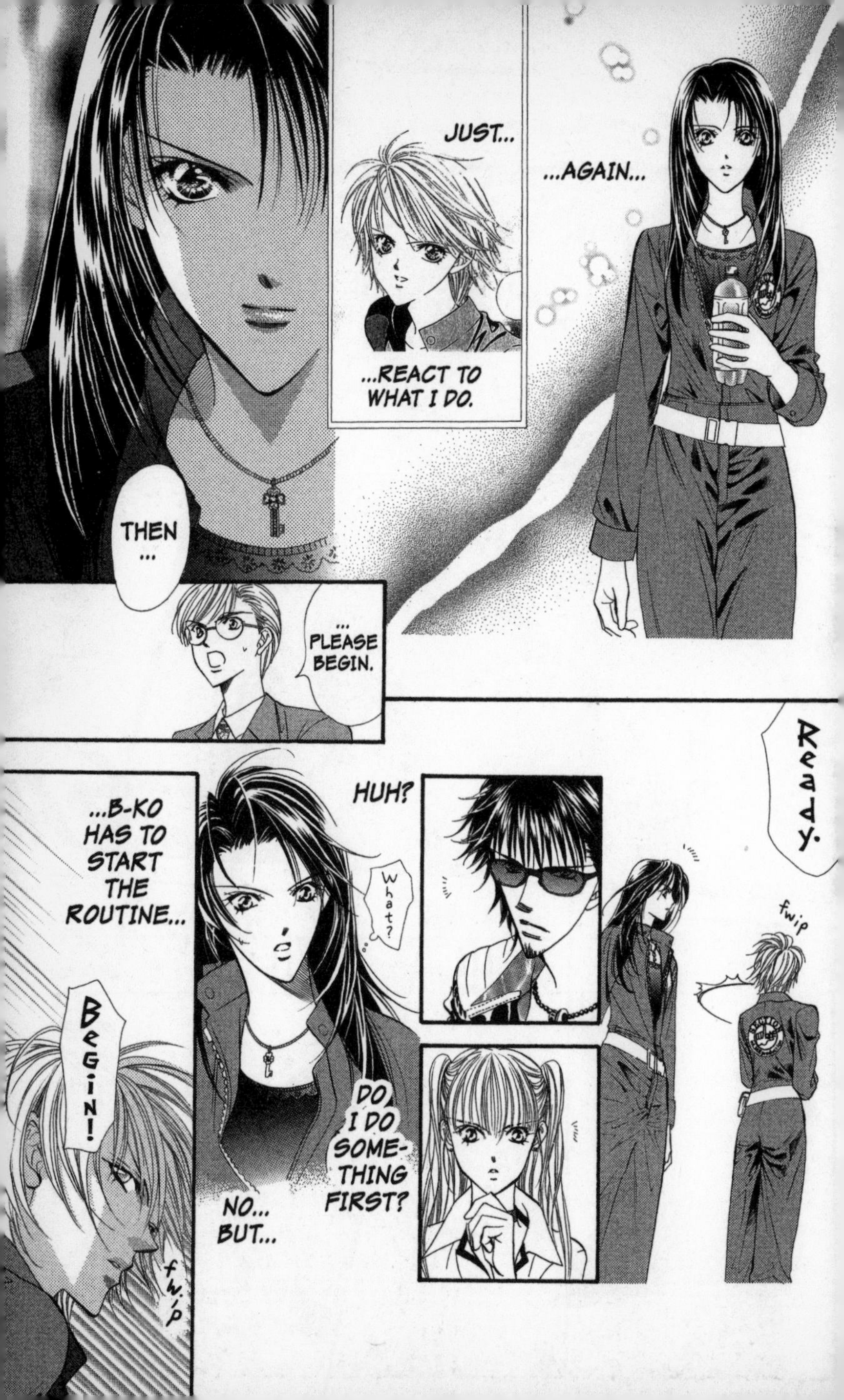
...AGAIN...
JUST...
...REACT TO WHAT I DO.
THEN...
...PLEASE BEGIN.
Ready.
fwip
HUH?
DO I DO SOMETHING FIRST?
What?
NO... BUT...
...B-KO HAS TO START THE ROUTINE...
Begin!
fwip

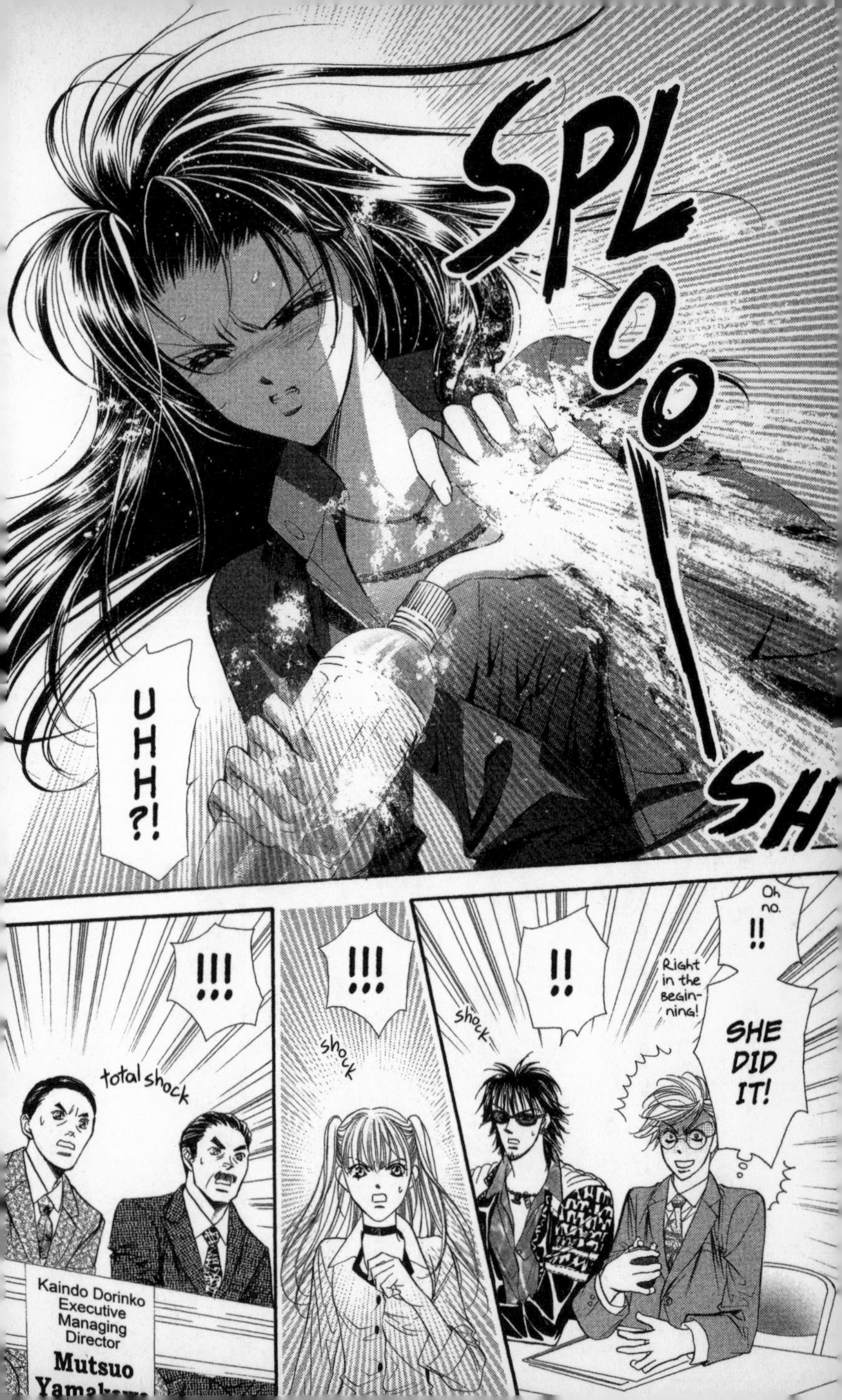
SPLOOOOSH
UHH?!
Oh no.
!!
Right in the Begin-ning!
SHE DID IT!
!!
shock
!!!
shock
!!!
total shock
Kaindo Dorinko Executive Managing Director
Mutsuo

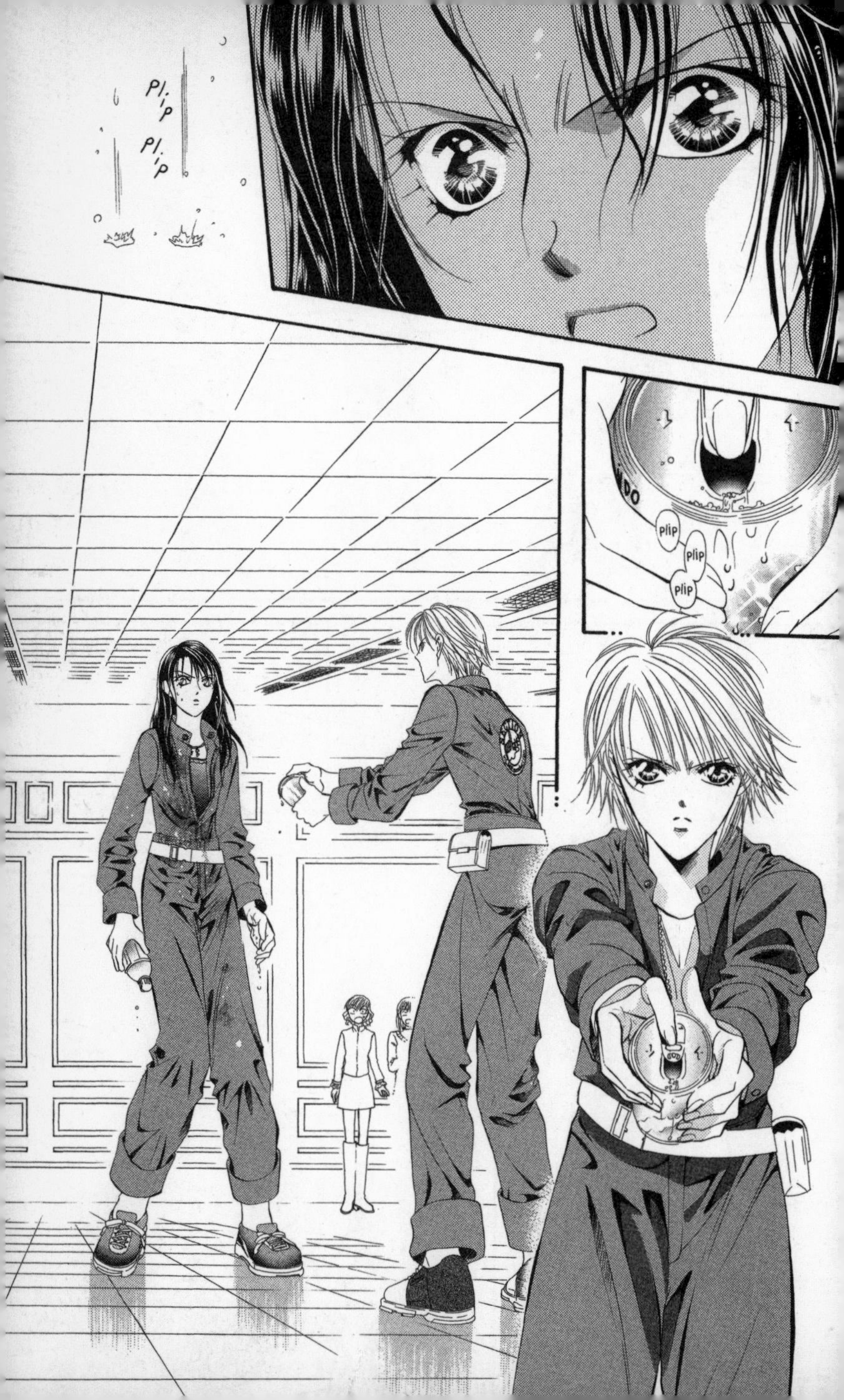
Plip
Plip
plip
plip
plip

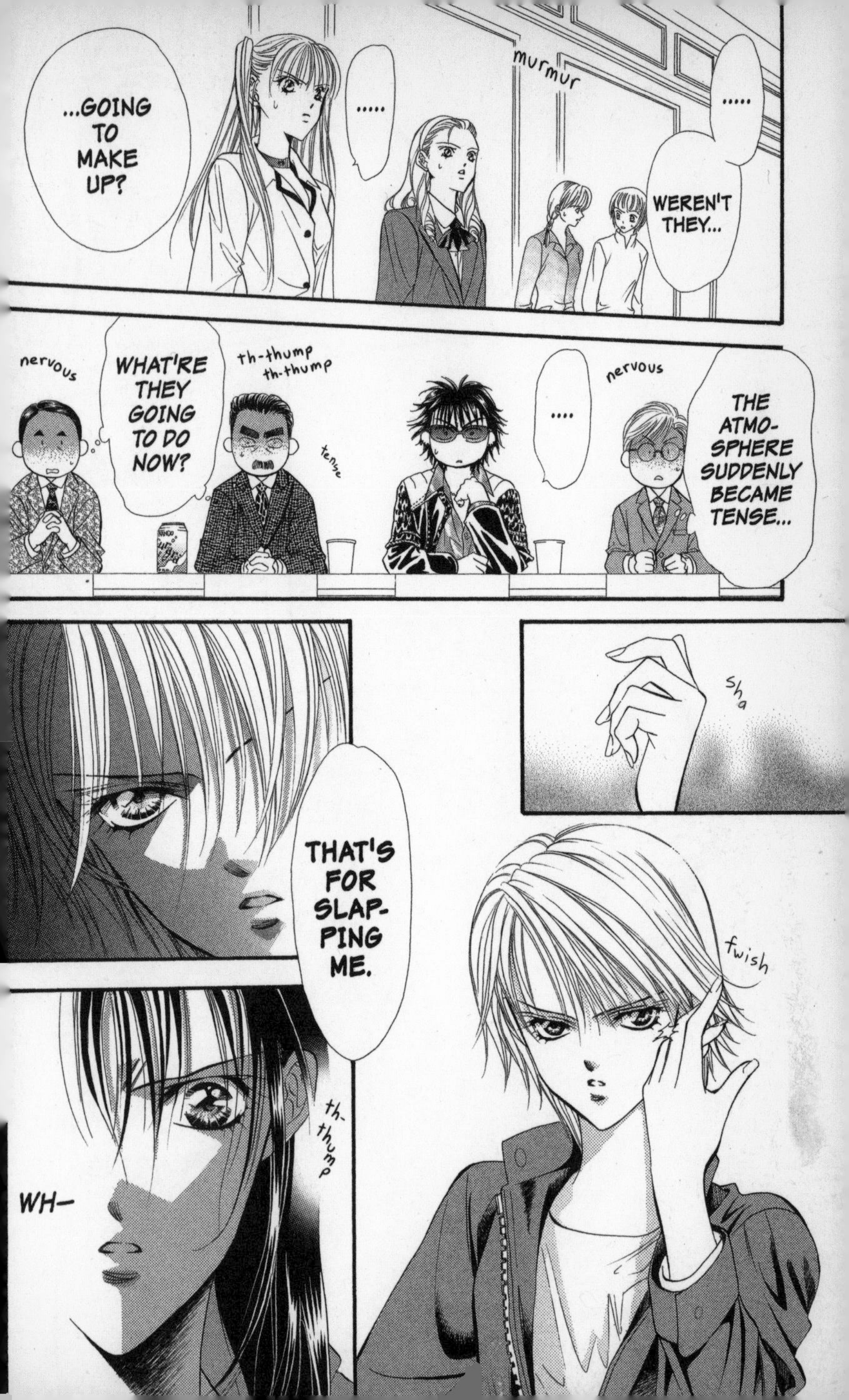
.....
WEREN'T THEY...
murmur
.....
...GOING TO MAKE UP?
THE ATMOSPHERE SUDDENLY BECAME TENSE...
nervous
....
tense
th-thump th-thump
WHAT'RE THEY GOING TO DO NOW?
nervous
sha
fwish
THAT'S FOR SLAPPING ME.
th-thump
WH-

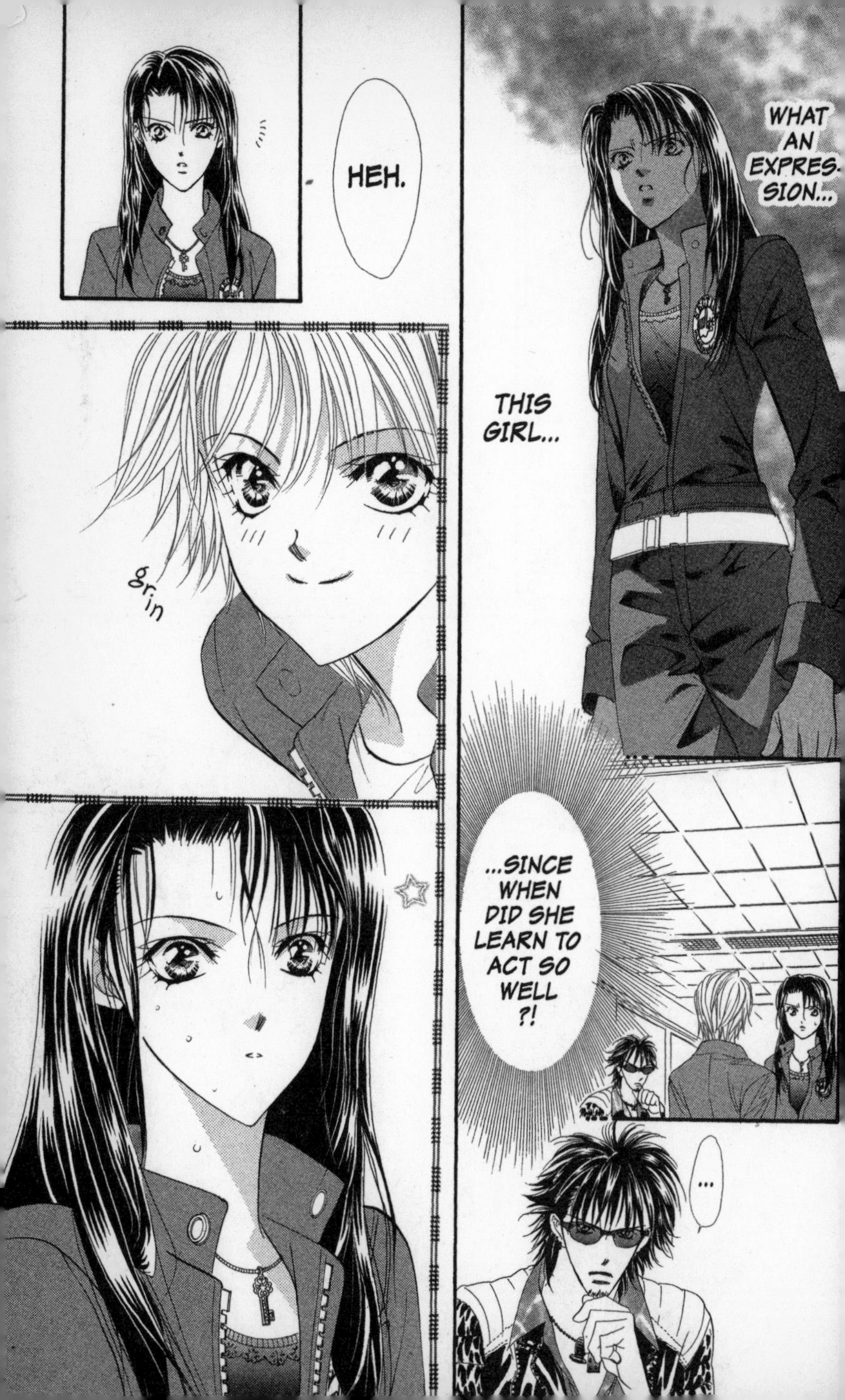
WHAT AN EXPRES-SION...
THIS GIRL...
...SINCE WHEN DID SHE LEARN TO ACT SO WELL ?!
...
HEH.
grin

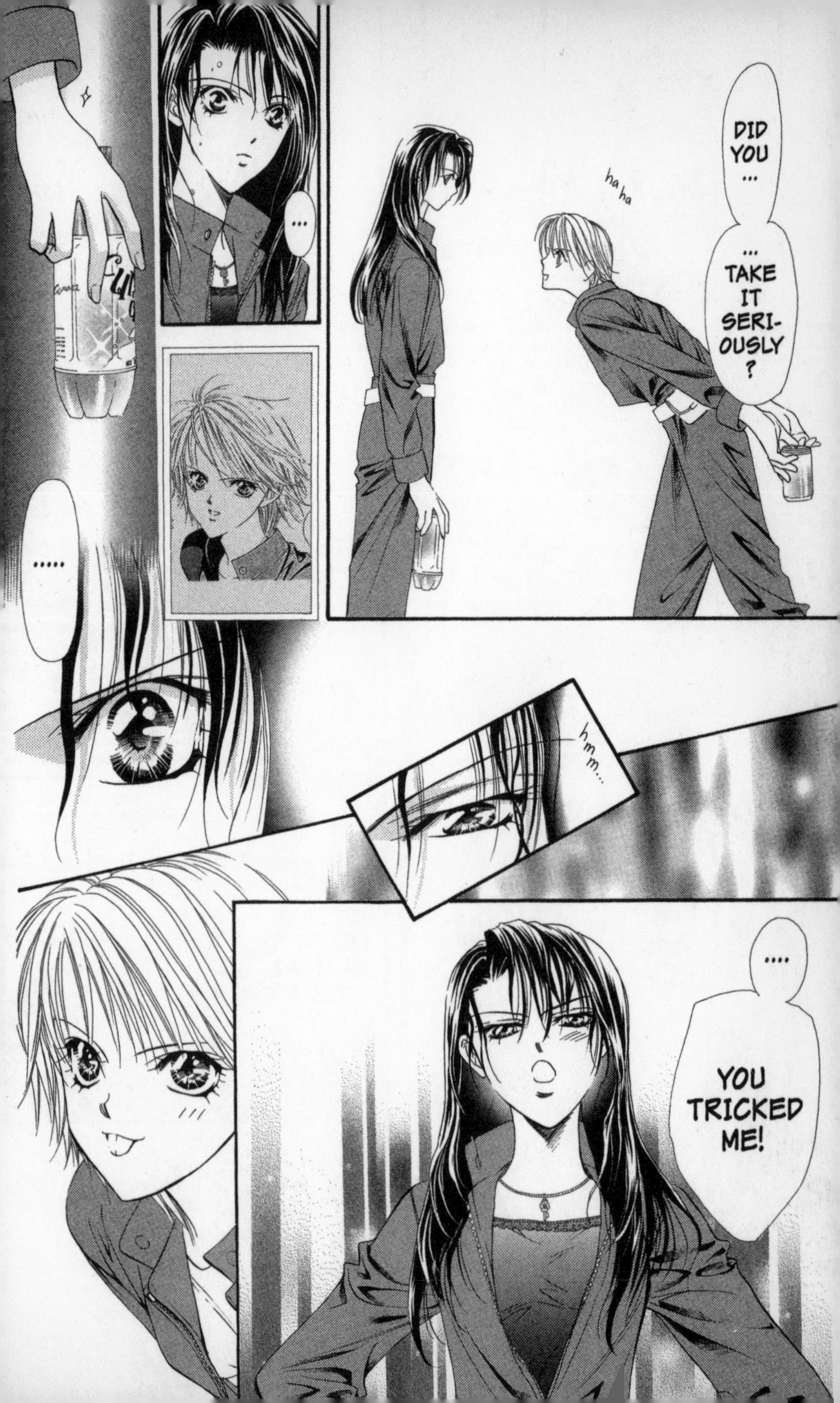
DID YOU ...
... TAKE IT SERIOUSLY?
ha ha
...
.....
hmm...
....
YOU TRICKED ME!

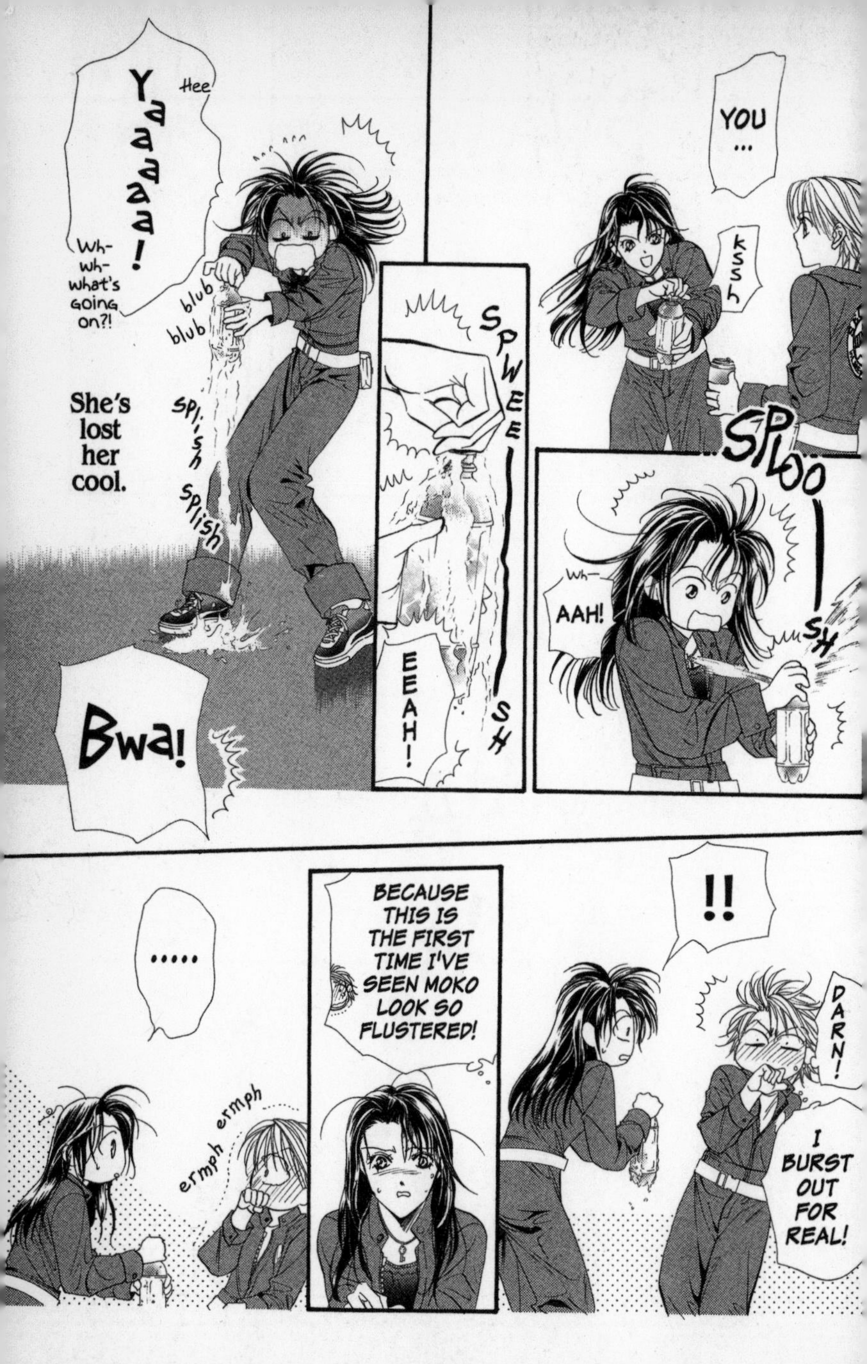
YOU ...
kssh
SPLOOSH
Wh-
AAH!
SPWEESH
EEAH!
Yaaaaa!
Hee
Wh-wh-what's going on?!
blub blub
splish
splish
She's lost her cool.
Bwa!
!!
DARN!
I BURST OUT FOR REAL!
BECAUSE THIS IS THE FIRST TIME I'VE SEEN MOKO LOOK SO FLUSTERED!
.....
ermph ermph

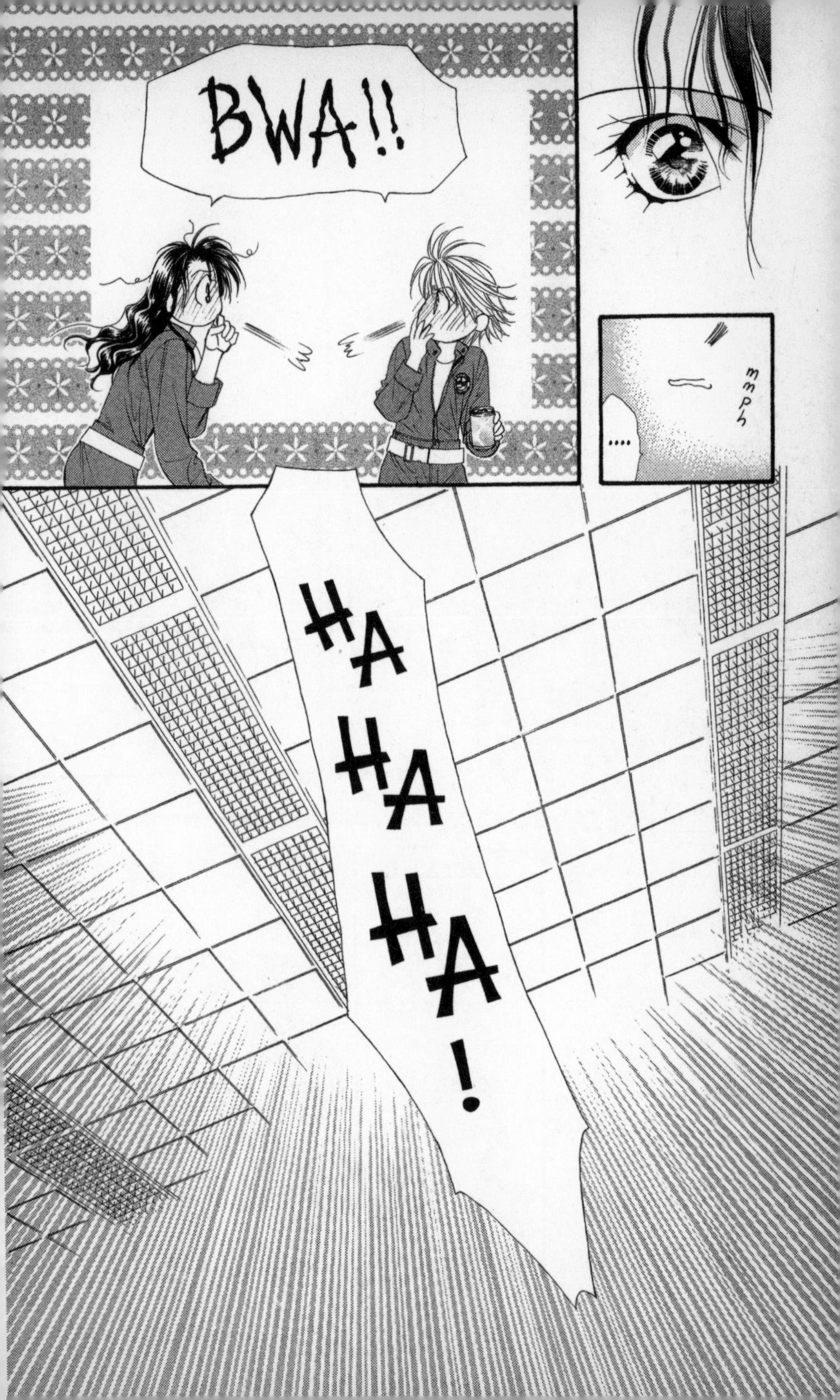

mmph
....
BWA!!
HA HA HA!

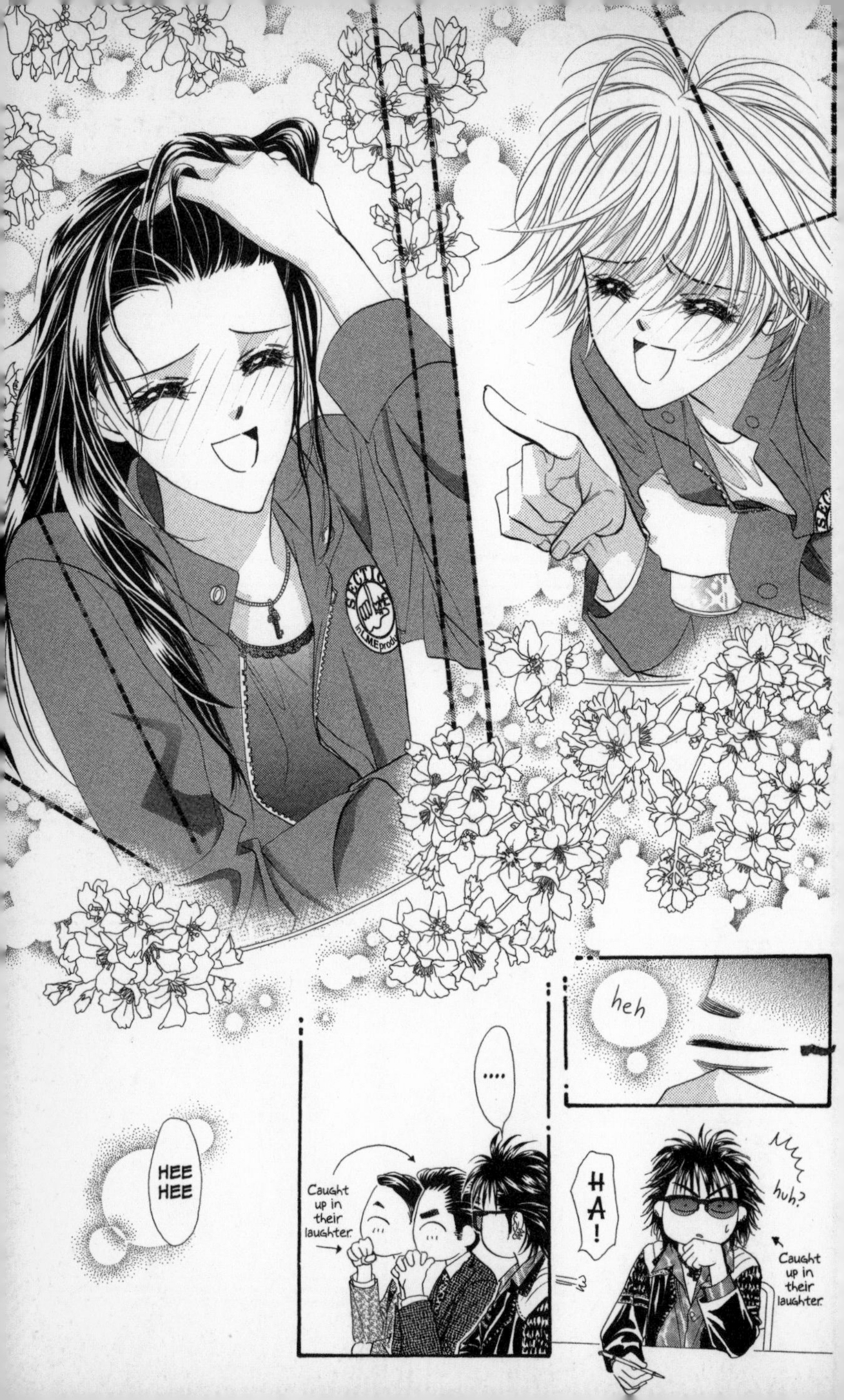
heh
HA!
huh?
Caught up in their laughter.
....
Caught up in their laughter.
HEE HEE

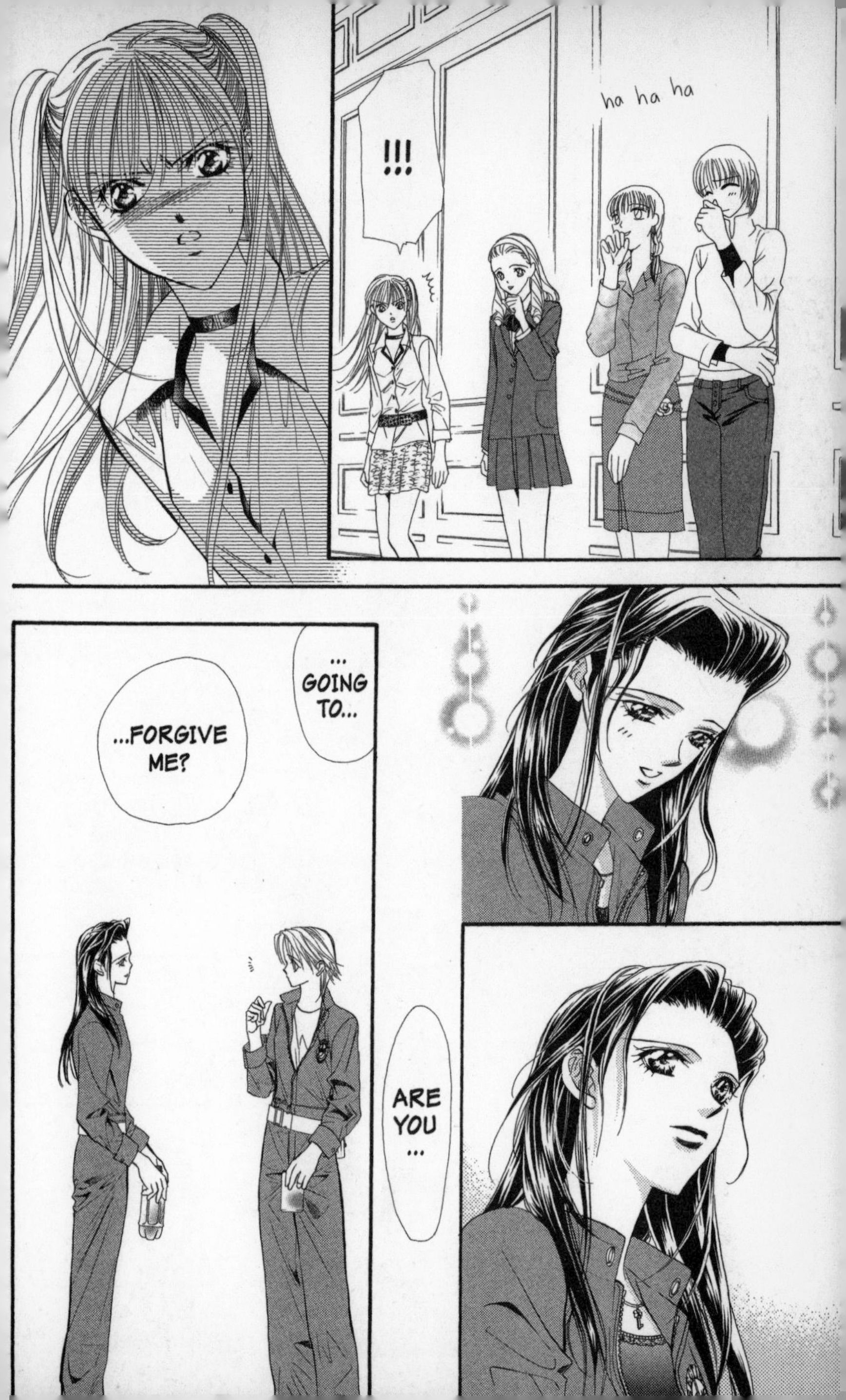

ha ha ha
!!!
ARE YOU ...
... GOING TO...
...FORGIVE ME?

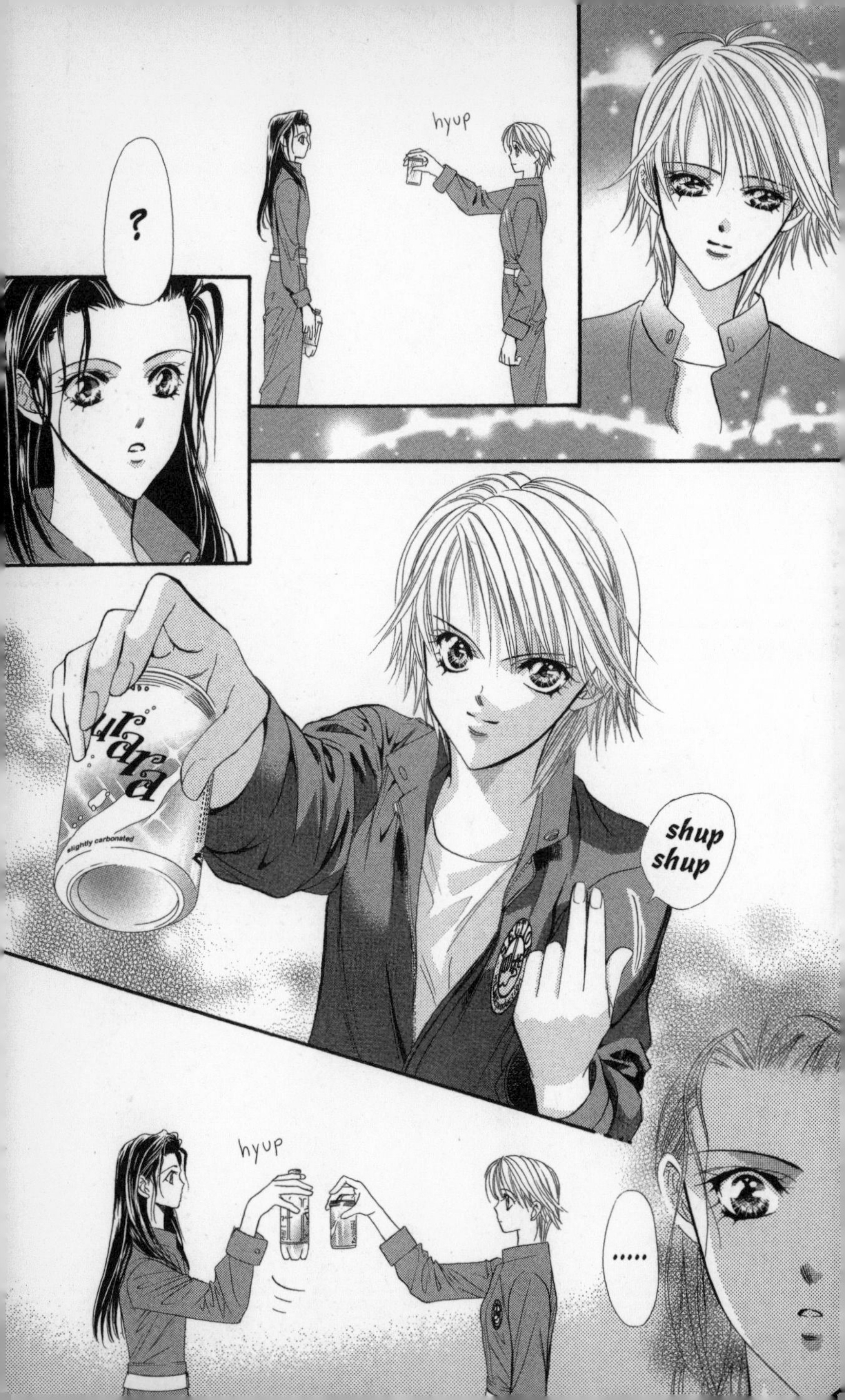
hyup
?
slightly carbonated
shup shup
......
hyup

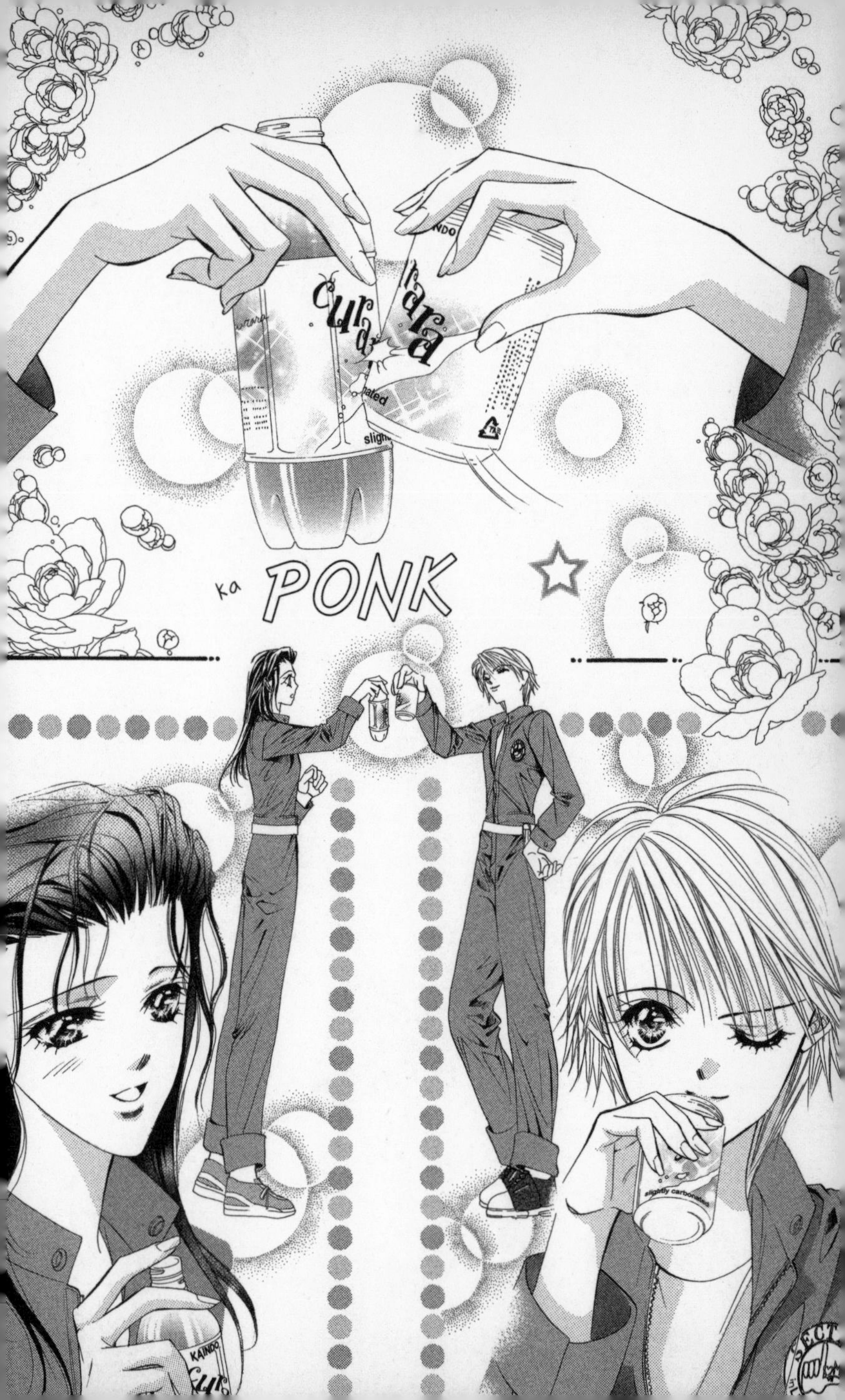
ka PONK
slightly carbonated
KAINDO

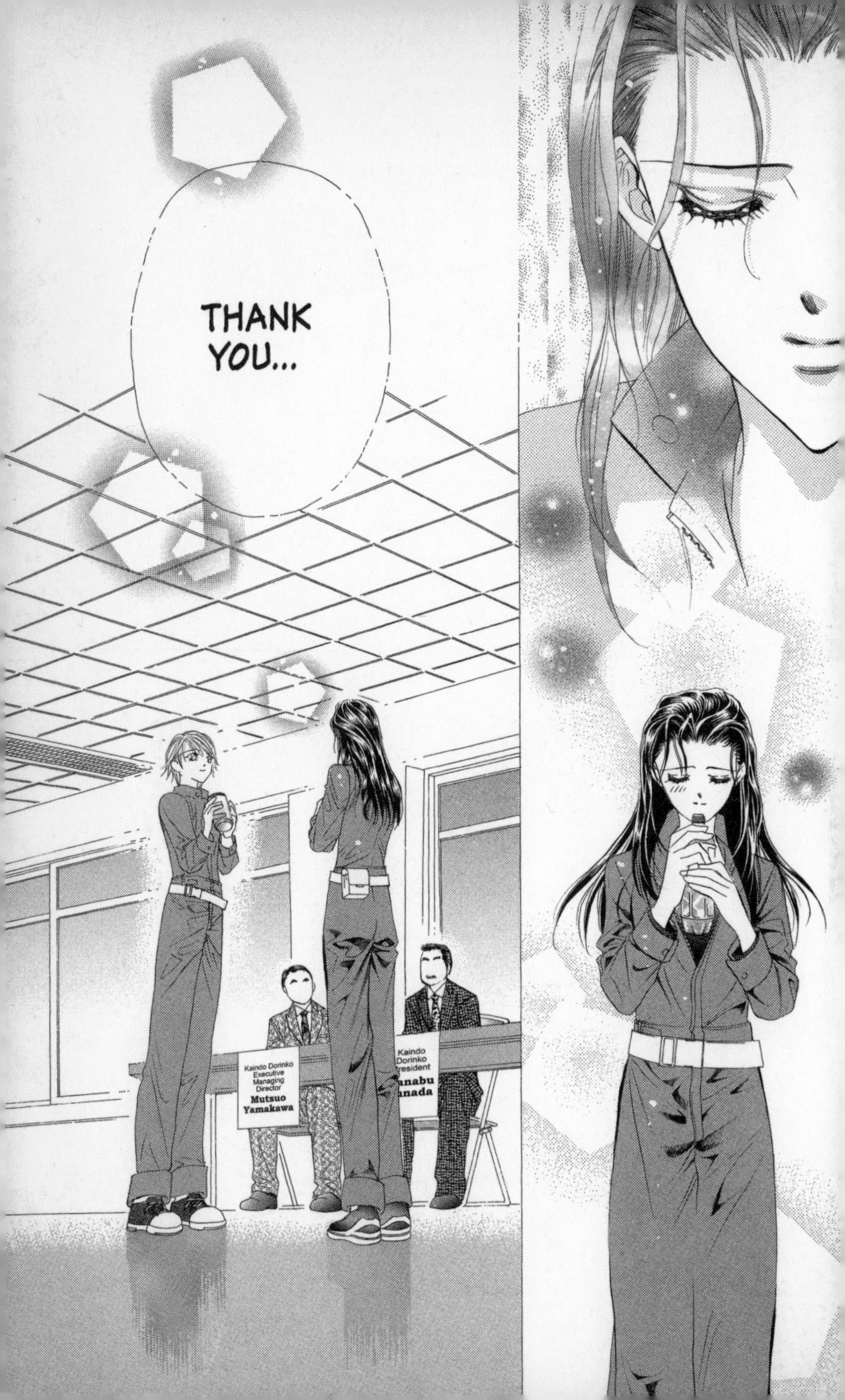
THANK YOU...
Kaindo Dorinko Executive Managing Director Mutsuo Yamakawa
Kaindo Dorinko President

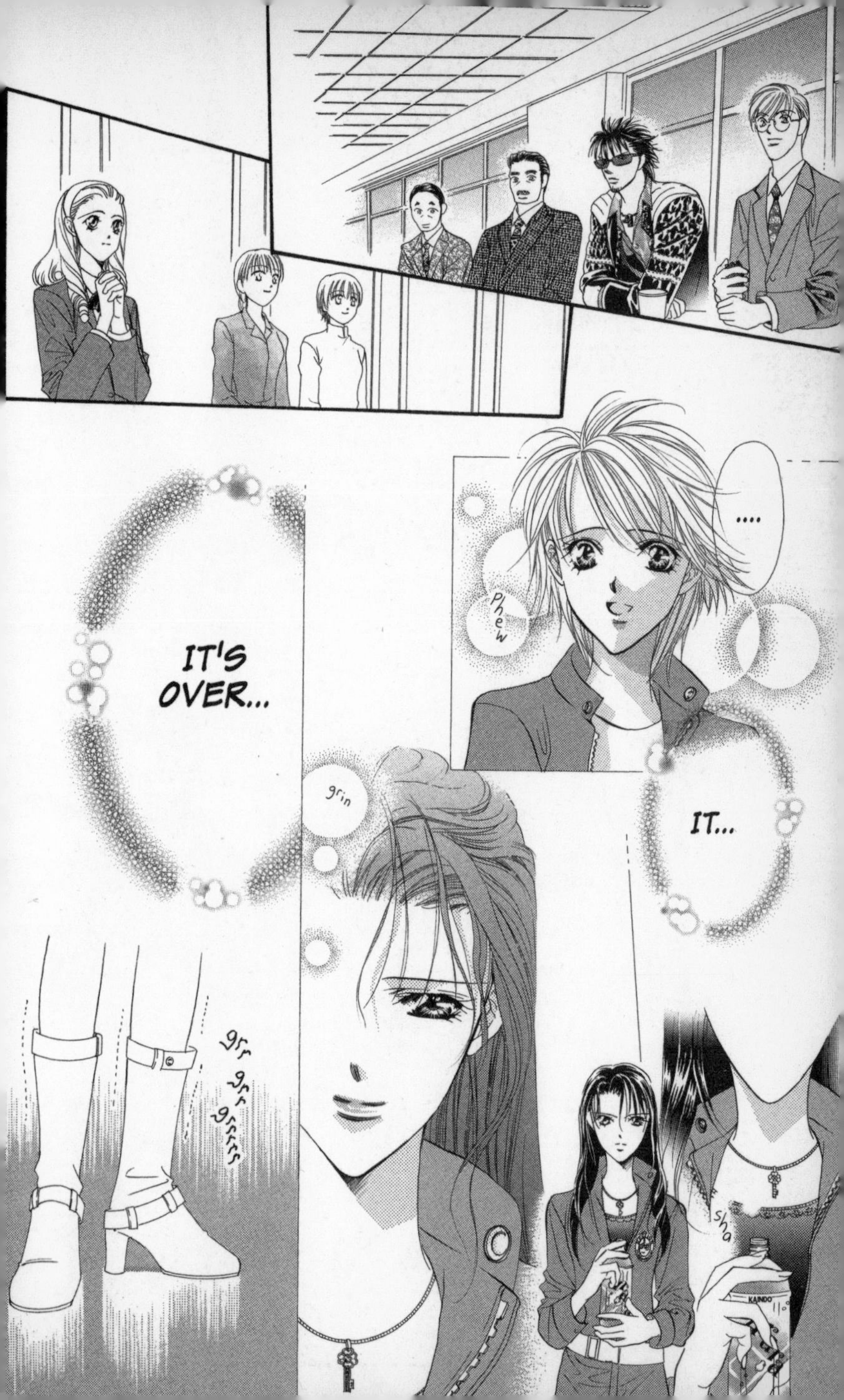
....
Phew
IT...
grin
IT'S OVER...
sha
KAINDO
grr grr grrrrr

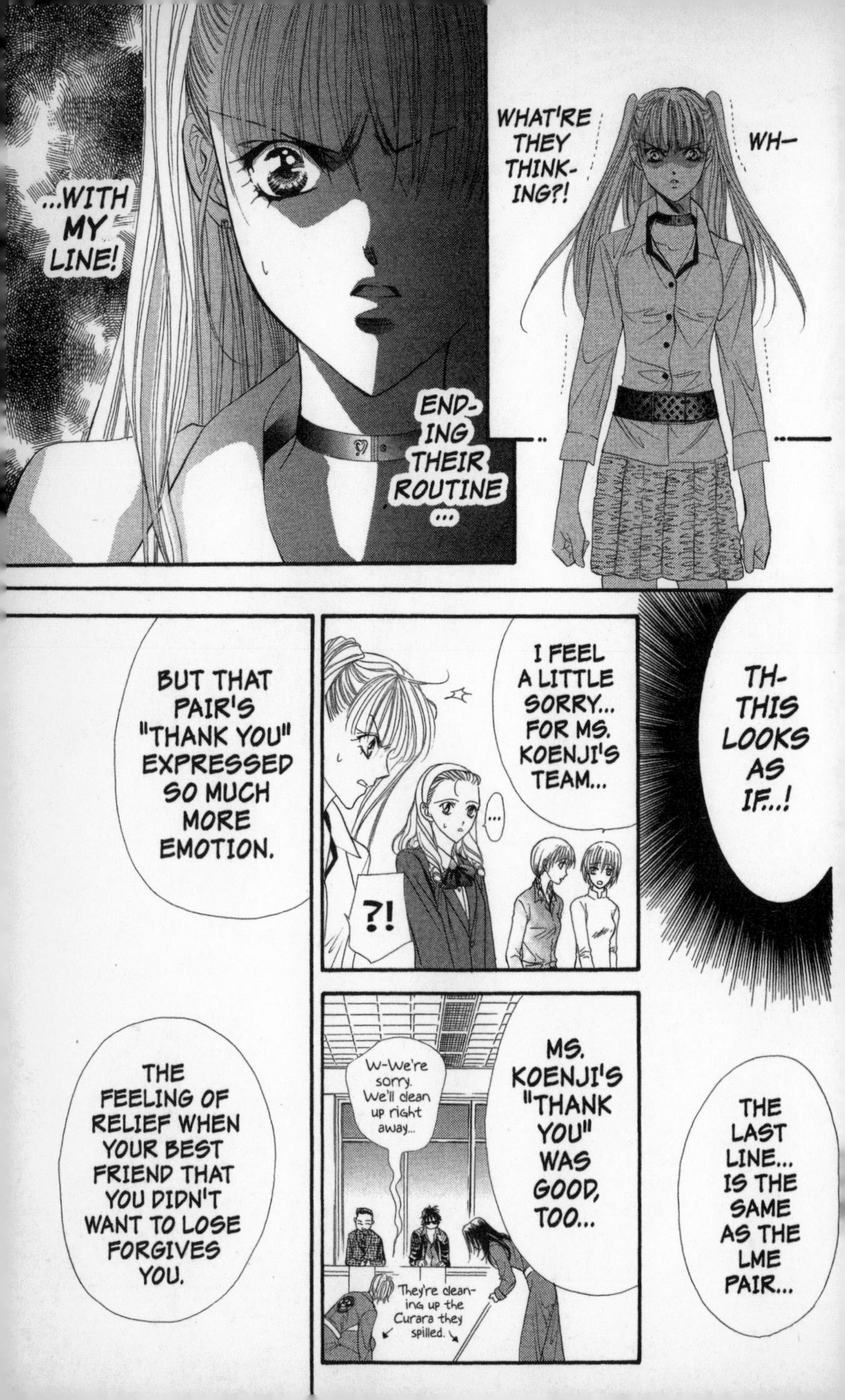
WH—
WHAT'RE THEY THINKING?!
ENDING THEIR ROUTINE...
...WITH MY LINE!
TH-THIS LOOKS AS IF...!
I FEEL A LITTLE SORRY... FOR MS. KOENJI'S TEAM...
...
?!
BUT THAT PAIR'S "THANK YOU" EXPRESSED SO MUCH MORE EMOTION.
THE LAST LINE... IS THE SAME AS THE LME PAIR...
MS. KOENJI'S "THANK YOU" WAS GOOD, TOO...
W-We're sorry. We'll clean up right away...
They're cleaning up the Curara they spilled.
THE FEELING OF RELIEF WHEN YOUR BEST FRIEND THAT YOU DIDN'T WANT TO LOSE FORGIVES YOU.

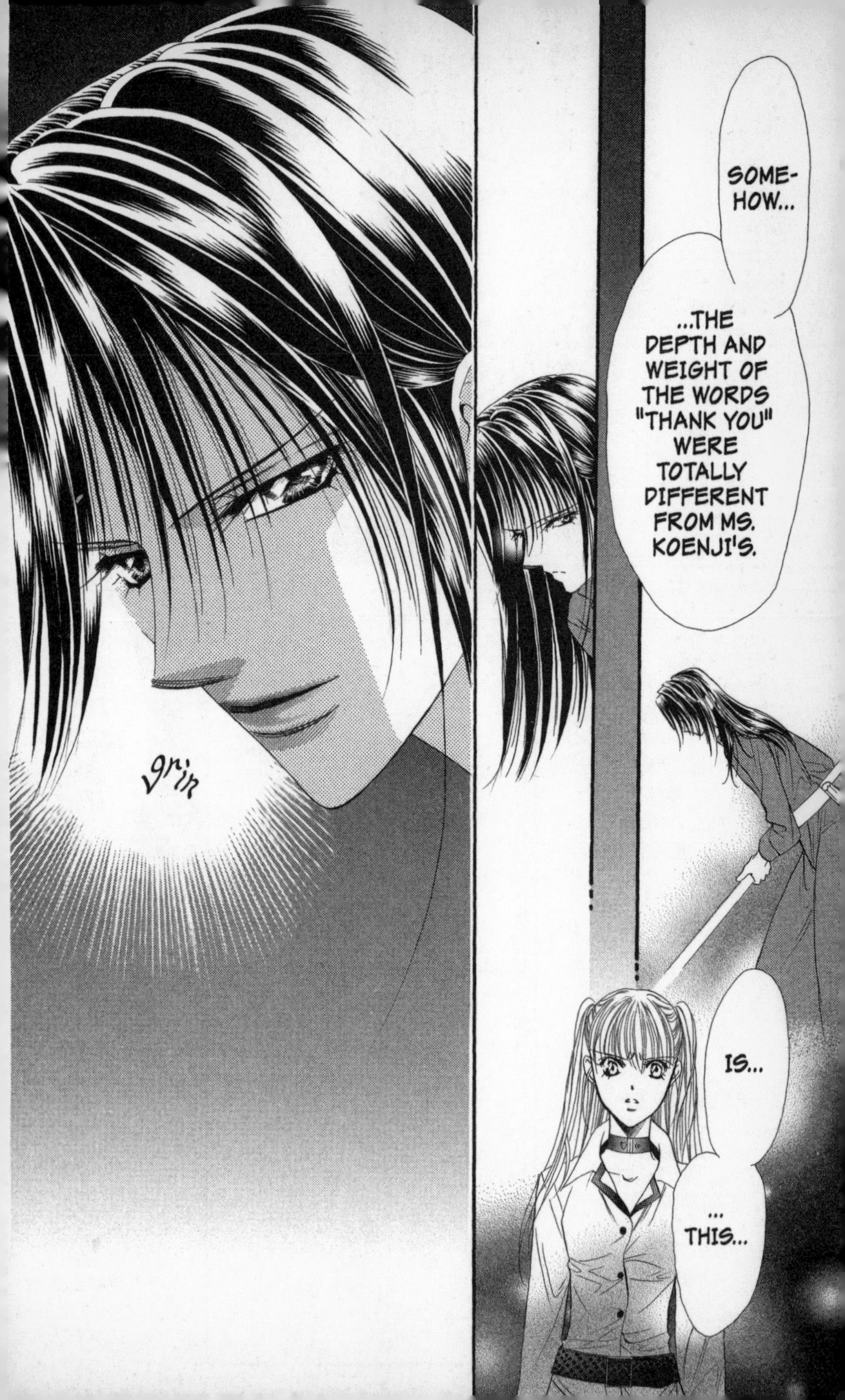
SOME-HOW...
...THE DEPTH AND WEIGHT OF THE WORDS "THANK YOU" WERE TOTALLY DIFFERENT FROM MS. KOENJI'S.
IS...
...THIS...
grin

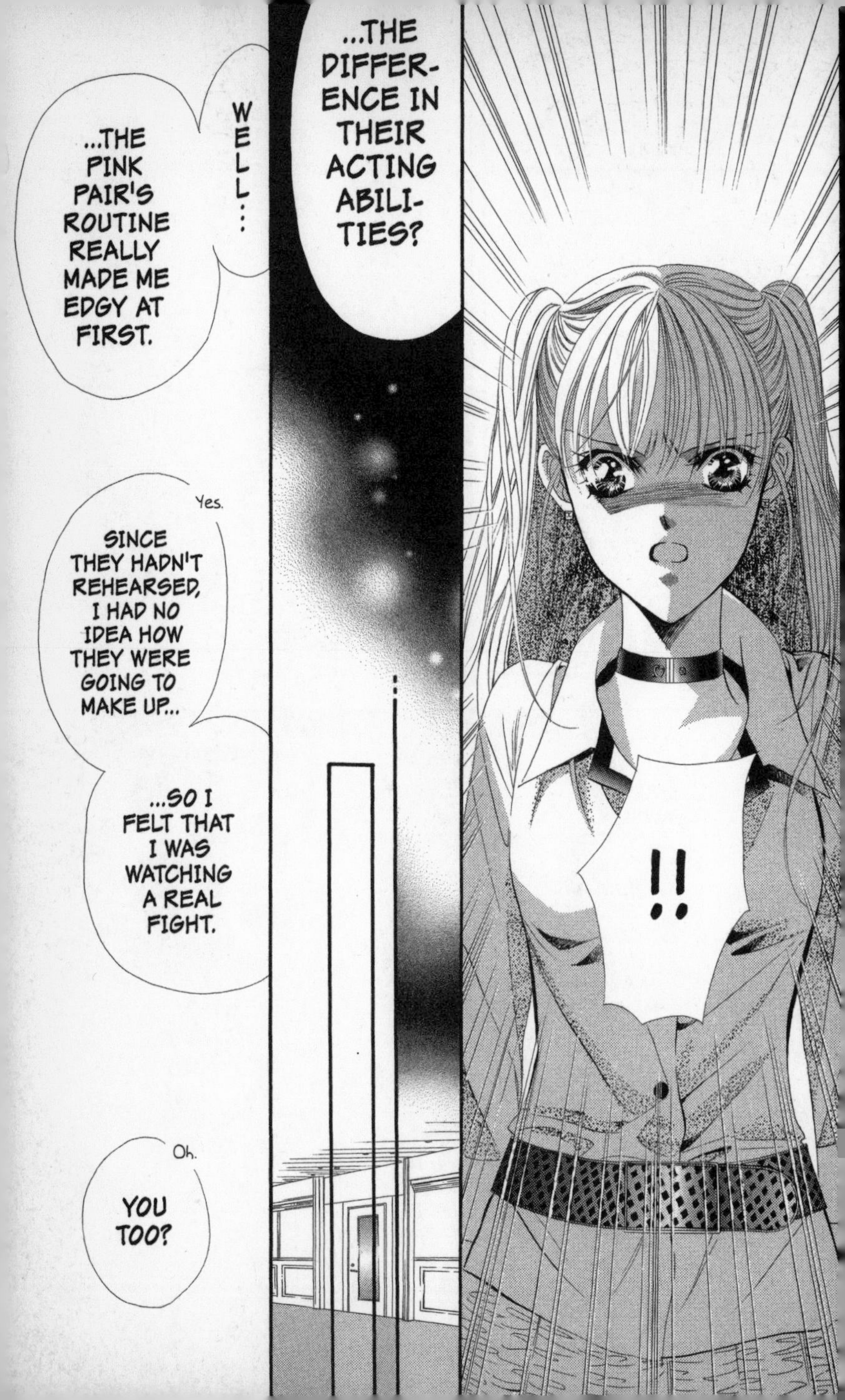
!!
...THE DIFFERENCE IN THEIR ACTING ABILITIES?
WELL...
...THE PINK PAIR'S ROUTINE REALLY MADE ME EDGY AT FIRST.
Yes.
SINCE THEY HADN'T REHEARSED, I HAD NO IDEA HOW THEY WERE GOING TO MAKE UP...
...SO I FELT THAT I WAS WATCHING A REAL FIGHT.
Oh.
YOU TOO?

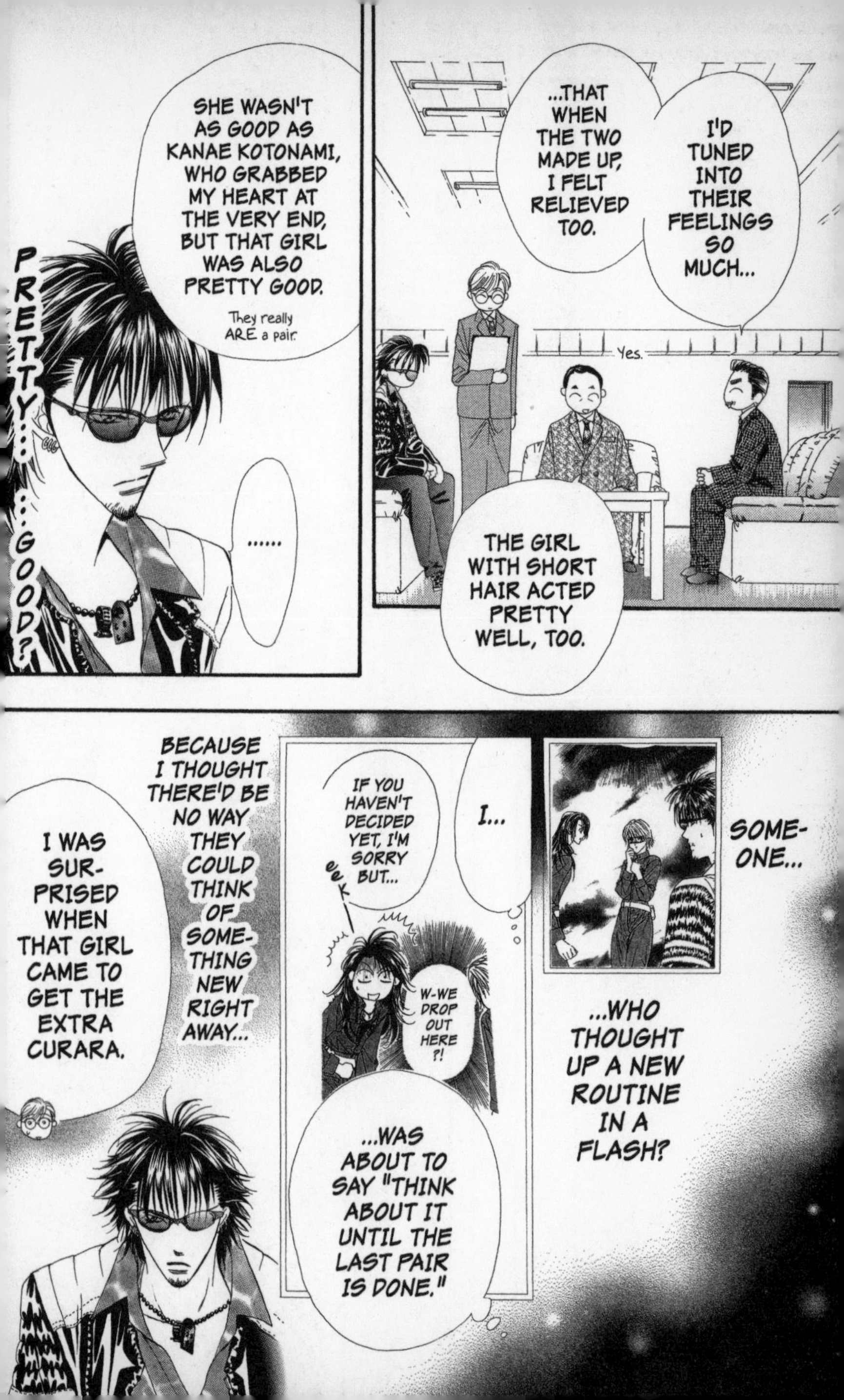
I'D TUNED INTO THEIR FEELINGS SO MUCH...
...THAT WHEN THE TWO MADE UP, I FELT RELIEVED TOO.
Yes.
THE GIRL WITH SHORT HAIR ACTED PRETTY WELL, TOO.
SHE WASN'T AS GOOD AS KANAE KOTONAMI, WHO GRABBED MY HEART AT THE VERY END, BUT THAT GIRL WAS ALSO PRETTY GOOD.
They really ARE a pair.
......
PRETTY... ...GOOD?
SOME-ONE...
...WHO THOUGHT UP A NEW ROUTINE IN A FLASH?
I...
IF YOU HAVEN'T DECIDED YET, I'M SORRY BUT...
eek
W-WE DROP OUT HERE?!
...WAS ABOUT TO SAY "THINK ABOUT IT UNTIL THE LAST PAIR IS DONE."
BECAUSE I THOUGHT THERE'D BE NO WAY THEY COULD THINK OF SOME-THING NEW RIGHT AWAY...
I WAS SUR-PRISED WHEN THAT GIRL CAME TO GET THE EXTRA CURARA.

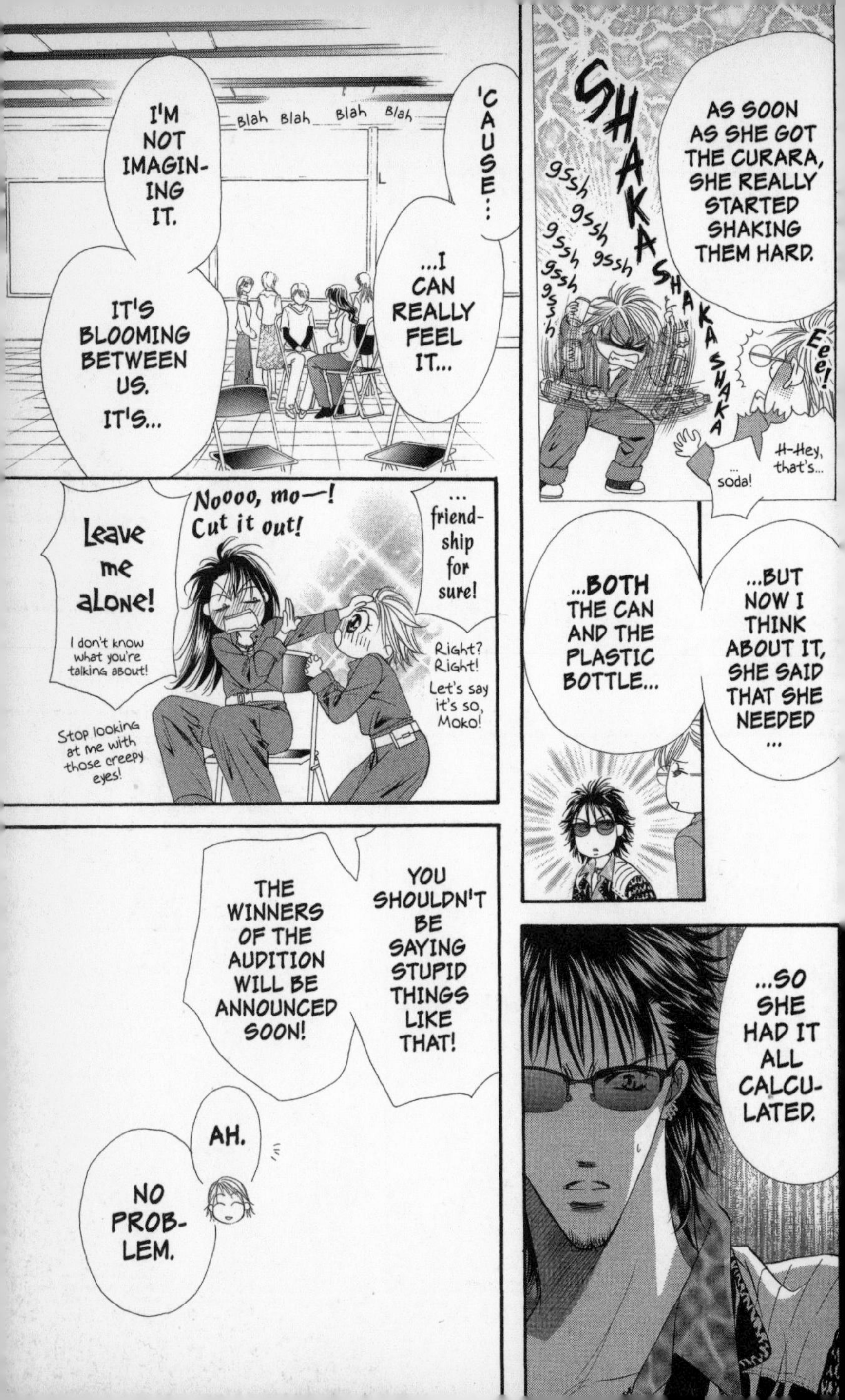
AS SOON AS SHE GOT THE CURARA, SHE REALLY STARTED SHAKING THEM HARD.
SHAKA SHAKA SHAKA SHAKA
gssh gssh gssh gssh gssh gssh
Eee!
H-Hey, that's...
... soda!
...BUT NOW I THINK ABOUT IT, SHE SAID THAT SHE NEEDED ...
...BOTH THE CAN AND THE PLASTIC BOTTLE...
...SO SHE HAD IT ALL CALCULATED.
'CAUSE...
...I CAN REALLY FEEL IT...
Blah Blah Blah Blah
I'M NOT IMAGINING IT.
IT'S BLOOMING BETWEEN US. IT'S...
... friendship for sure!
Right? Right! Let's say it's so, Moko!
Noooo, mo—! Cut it out!
Leave me alone!
I don't know what you're talking about!
Stop looking at me with those creepy eyes!
YOU SHOULDN'T BE SAYING STUPID THINGS LIKE THAT!
THE WINNERS OF THE AUDITION WILL BE ANNOUNCED SOON!
AH.
NO PROBLEM.

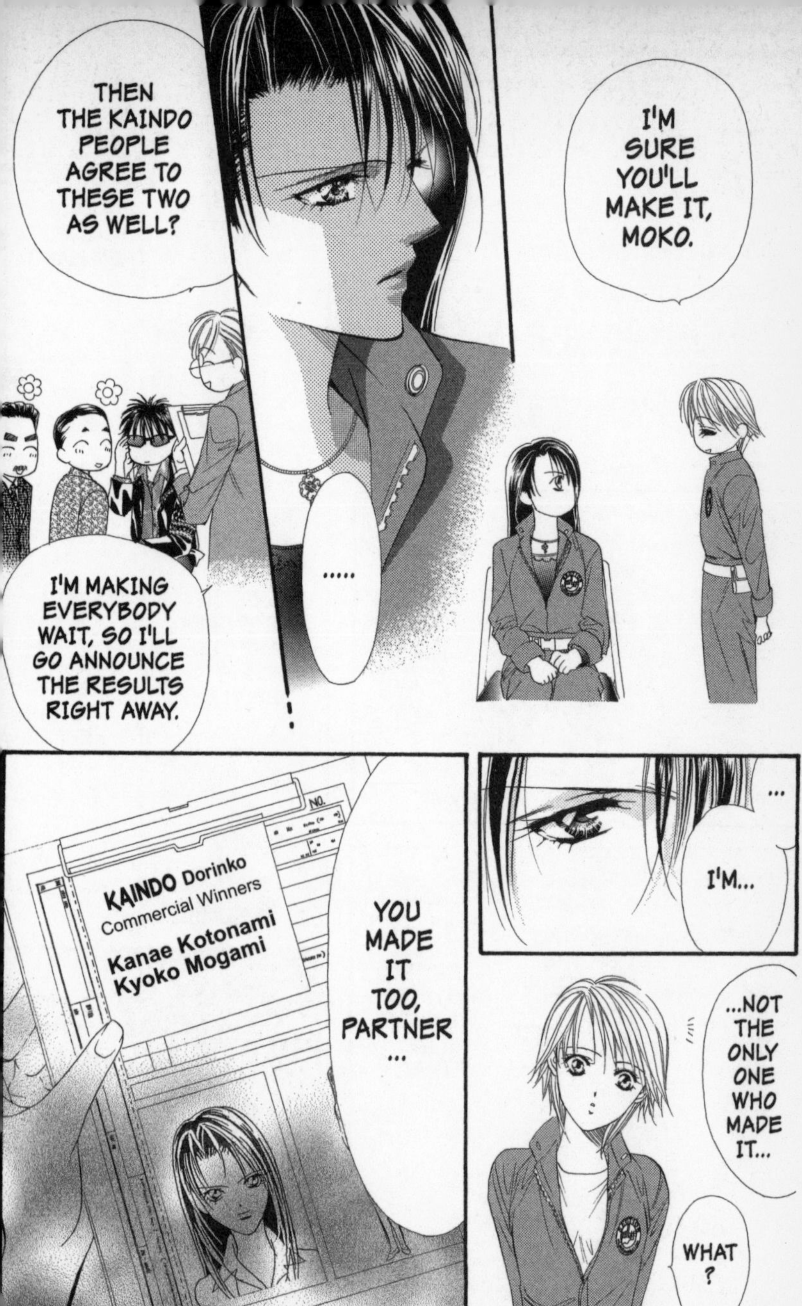
I'M SURE YOU'LL MAKE IT, MOKO.
THEN THE KAINDO PEOPLE AGREE TO THESE TWO AS WELL?
.....
I'M MAKING EVERYBODY WAIT, SO I'LL GO ANNOUNCE THE RESULTS RIGHT AWAY.
...
I'M...
...NOT THE ONLY ONE WHO MADE IT...
WHAT?
KAINDO Dorinko
Commercial Winners
Kanae Kotonami
Kyoko Mogami
YOU MADE IT TOO, PARTNER...

End of Act 29

Skip-Beat! End Notes
Everyone knows how to be a fan, but sometimes cool things
from other cultures need a little help crossing the language barrier.

Page 7, panel 5: Comedian and straight man
In the Kansai region of Japan, comedy teams are called *manzai*. The comedian is the *boke* and the straight man is the *tsukkomi*.

Page 10, panel 4: Amulet
Gokaku kigan, a type of amulet used for good luck in passing exams.

Page 81, panel 3: Kssssh
This is the sound of Ren's manager vomiting sand in reaction to Ren's sappy lines. In Japan, the saying goes, "That's so corny, I want to vomit sand."

Page 107, sidebar: Kuroshio
In Japan, nicknames are often formed by combining the first parts of the last and first name. Ushio Kurosaki's nickname is also the name of the Japanese Current, an ocean current similar to the Gulf Stream. Literally, it means "black stream."

Page 109, panel 5: A-ko and B-ko
Ko means "child", and is a common ending for girls' names. A-ko and B-ko are the same as Girl A and Girl B, but sound more like real names.

Page 150, panel 4: Toro?
A pun on the word *neta*, which can mean either "idea" or "the fish on sushi." *Toro* is fatty tuna, and a popular type of sushi.

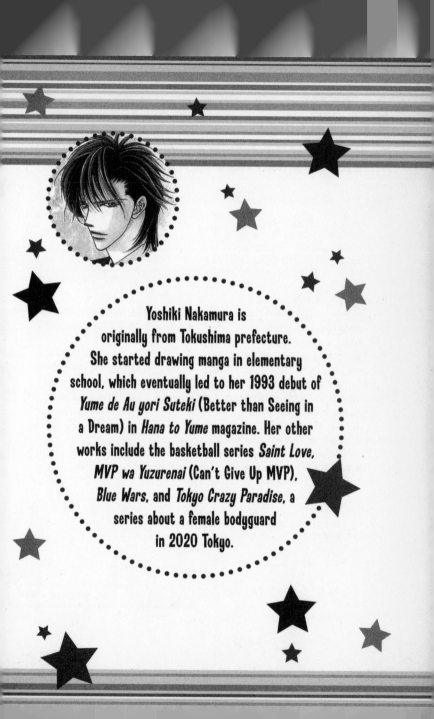

Yoshiki Nakamura is
originally from Tokushima prefecture.
She started drawing manga in elementary
school, which eventually led to her 1993 debut of
Yume de Au yori Suteki (Better than Seeing in
a Dream) in *Hana to Yume* magazine. Her other
works include the basketball series *Saint Love,*
MVP wa Yuzurenai (Can't Give Up MVP),
Blue Wars, and *Tokyo Crazy Paradise,* a
series about a female bodyguard
in 2020 Tokyo.

SKIP·BEAT!
Vol. 5
The Shojo Beat Manga Edition

STORY AND ART BY YOSHIKI NAKAMURA

English Translation & Adaptation/Tomo Kimura
Touch-up Art & Lettering/Sabrina Heep
Design/Yukiko Whitley
Editor/Pancha Diaz

Managing Editor/Megan Bates
Editorial Director/Elizabeth Kawasaki
VP & Editor in Chief/ Yumi Hoashi
Sr. Director of Acquisitions/Rika Inouye
Sr. VP of Marketing/Liza Coppola
Exec. VP of Sales & Marketing/John Easum
Publisher/Hyoe Narita

Printed in Canada

store.viz.com

Published by VIZ Media, LLC
P.O. Box 77010
San Francisco, CA 94107

PARENTAL ADVISORY
SKIP•BEAT! is rated T for Teen and is recommended for ages 13 and up. This volume contains suggestive themes.

Shojo Beat Manga Edition
10 9 8 7 6 5 4 3 2 1
First printing, March 2007

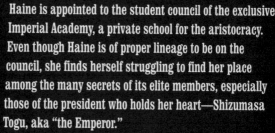

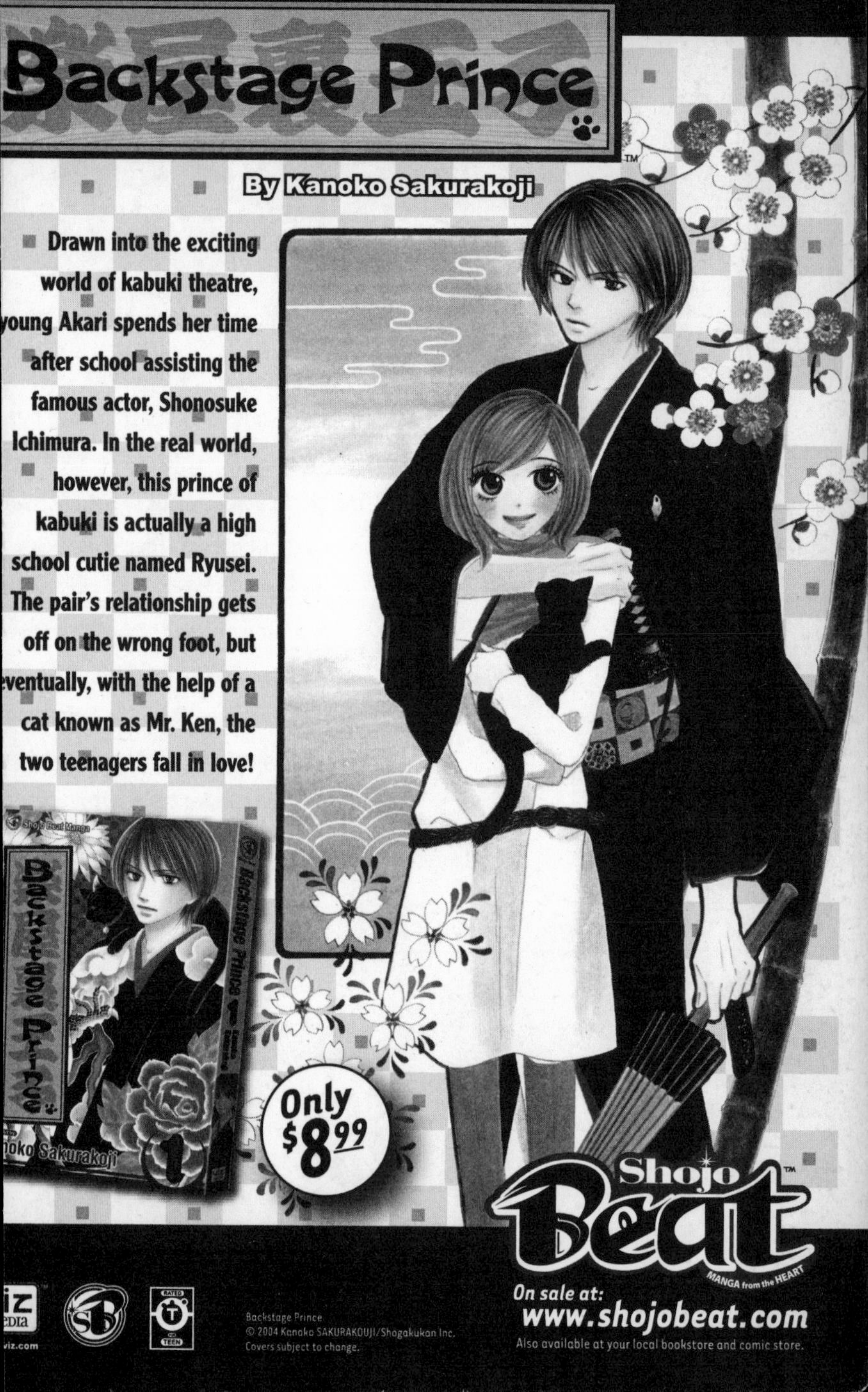

Backstage Prince
By Kanoko Sakurakoji
Drawn into the exciting world of kabuki theatre, young Akari spends her time after school assisting the famous actor, Shonosuke Ichimura. In the real world, however, this prince of kabuki is actually a high school cutie named Ryusei. The pair's relationship gets off on the wrong foot, but eventually, with the help of a cat known as Mr. Ken, the two teenagers fall in love!
Only $8.99
Shojo Beat
MANGA from the HEART
On sale at:
www.shojobeat.com
Also available at your local bookstore and comic store.
viz.com
Backstage Prince
© 2004 Kanoko SAKURAKOUJI/Shogakukan Inc.
Covers subject to change.

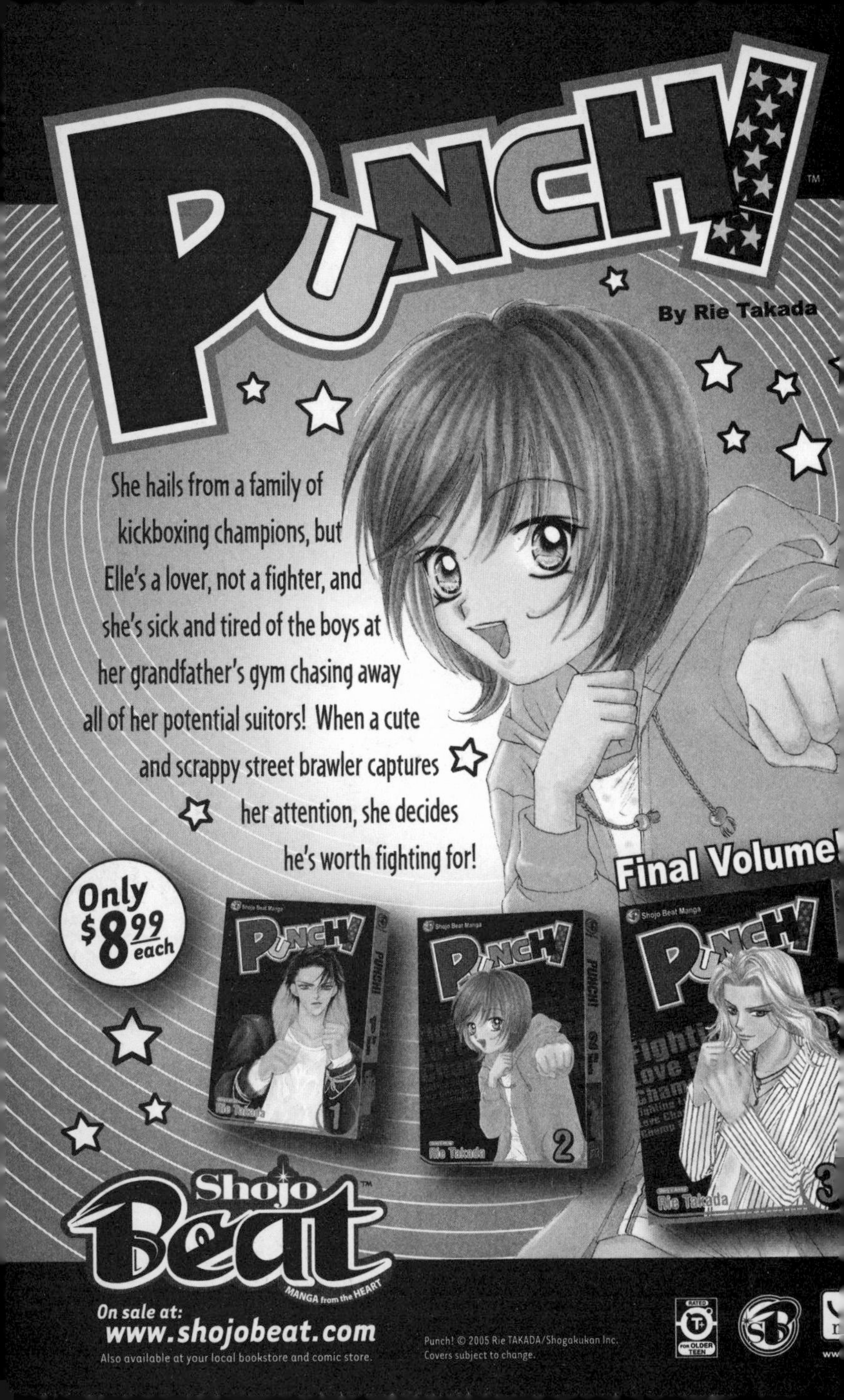
PUNCH!™
By Rie Takada
She hails from a family of kickboxing champions, but Elle's a lover, not a fighter, and she's sick and tired of the boys at her grandfather's gym chasing away all of her potential suitors! When a cute and scrappy street brawler captures her attention, she decides he's worth fighting for!
Final Volume!
Only $8.99 each
Shojo Beat™
MANGA from the HEART
On sale at:
www.shojobeat.com
Also available at your local bookstore and comic store.
Punch! © 2005 Rie TAKADA/Shogakukan Inc.
Covers subject to change.
RATED T+ FOR OLDER TEEN

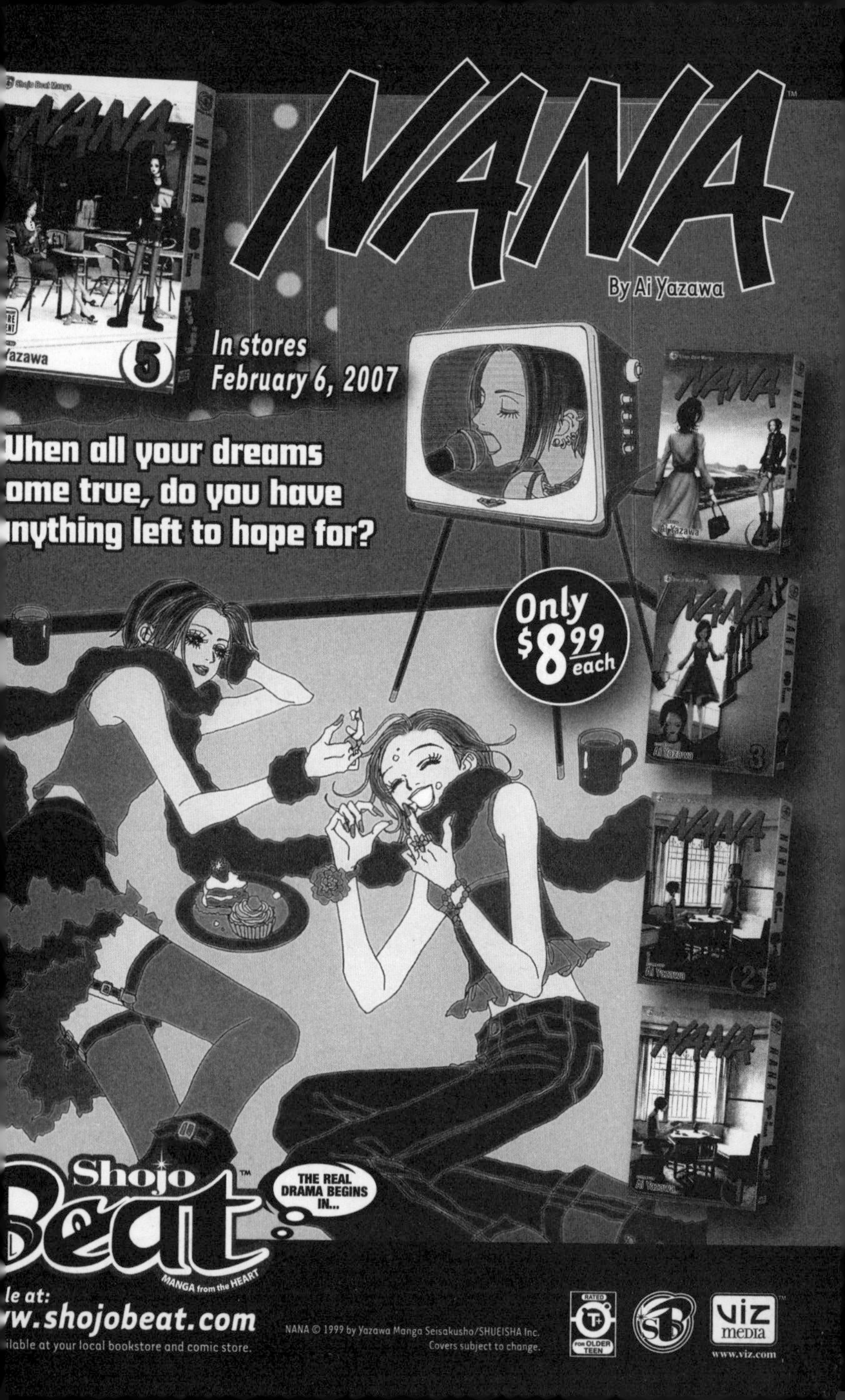

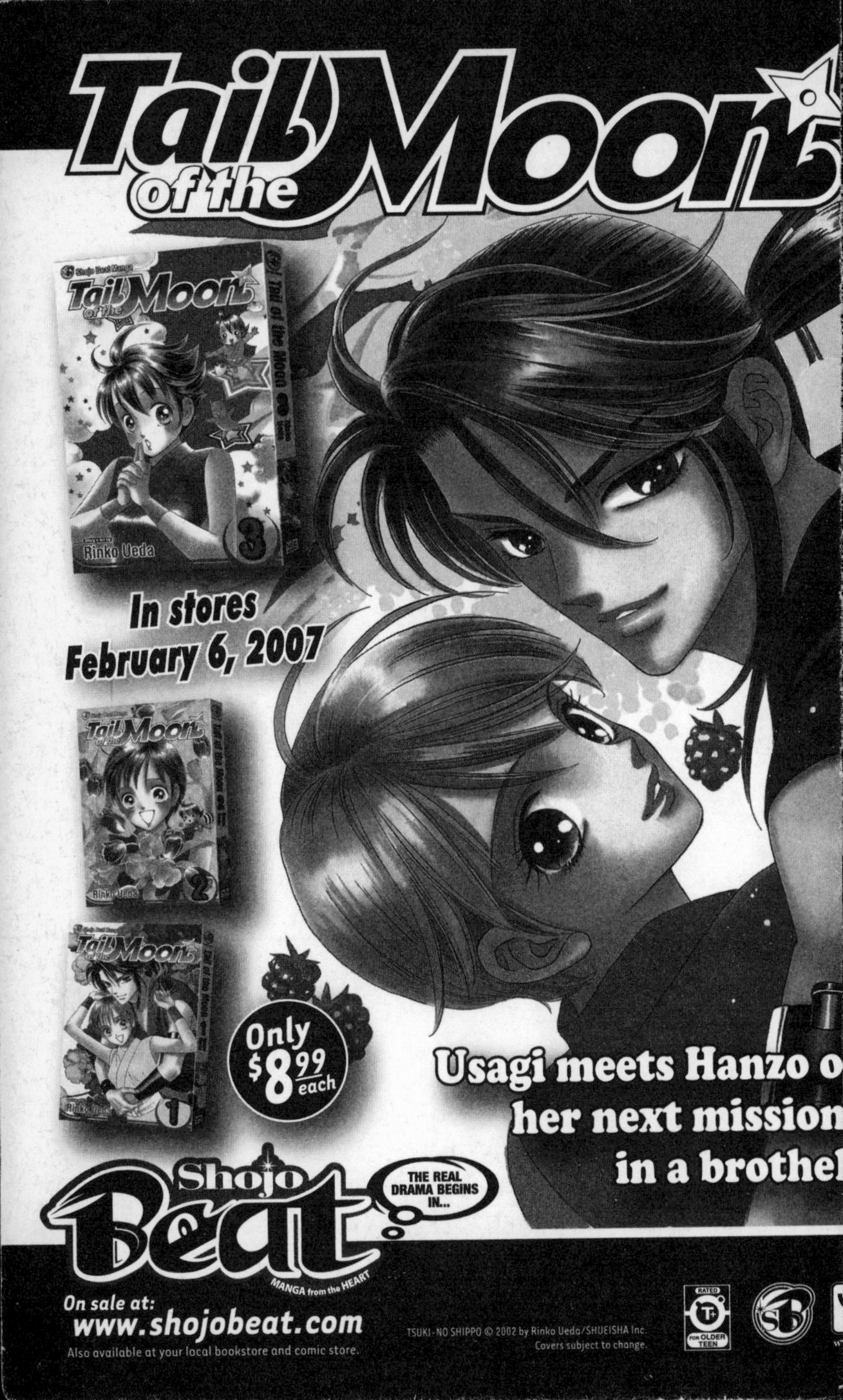

Tail of the Moon
Tail of the Moon 3
Rinko Ueda
In stores
February 6, 2007
Tail of the Moon 2
Rinko Ueda
Tail of the Moon 1
Rinko Ueda
Only $8.99 each
Usagi meets Hanzo o
her next mission
in a brothel
Shojo Beat
THE REAL DRAMA BEGINS IN...
MANGA from the HEART
On sale at:
www.shojobeat.com
Also available at your local bookstore and comic store.
TSUKI-NO SHIPPO © 2002 by Rinko Ueda/SHUEISHA Inc.
Covers subject to change.
RATED T+ FOR OLDER TEEN

Tell us what about Shojo Beat Manga!

Our survey is now available online. Go to:

shojobeat.com/mangasurvey

Help us make our product offerings better!

THE REAL DRAMA BEGINS IN...

Love. Laugh.

In addition to hundreds of pages of manga each month, *Shojo Beat* will bring you fashion, music, art, and culture—plus shopping, how-tos, industry updates, int

DON'T YOU WANT TO HAVE

$
12 G
51
the C

Subscribe Now!
Fill out the coupon
on the other side

Or go to:
www.shojobeat.com

Or call toll-f
800-541-78